Ius, Lex et Res Publica
Studies in Law, Philosophy and Political Cultures

Edited by Barbara Janusz-Pohl and Anna Jaron

Volume 32

Olga Sitarz / Anna Jaworska-Wieloch / Jakub Hanc

On the (Non)existence of the Right to Religious Freedom of Persons Deprived of Liberty

A Reconstruction of the Normative Standard Based on Polish and German Regulations in Comparison With Empirical Studies

PETER LANG
Berlin - Bruxelles - Chennai - Lausanne - New York - Oxford

Bibliographic Information published by the Deutsche Nationalbibliothek
The Deutsche Nationalbibliothek lists this publication in the Deutsche Nationalbibliografie; detailed bibliographic data is available in the internet at http://dnb.d-nb.de.

Library of Congress Cataloging-in-Publication Data
A CIP catalog record for this book has been applied for at the Library of Congress.

Publication co-financed by the University of Silesia in Katowice.

Książka wydawana ze środków projektu UMO-2018/31/B/HS5/02233 pt. „Standardy respektowania prawa do wolności religijnej osób osadzonych w zakładach karnych, aresztach śledczych oraz młodzieżowych ośrodkach wychowawczych i zakładach poprawczych.

Book published from the funds of the UMO-2018/31/B/HS5/02233 project titled "Standards for respecting the right to religious freedom of persons incarcerated in prisons, remand centers, youth educational centers and correctional facilities.

Cover illustration: Courtesy of Benjamin Ben Chaim.

UNIVERSITY OF SILESIA
IN KATOWICE

ISSN 2191-3250
ISBN 978-3-631-90371-1 (Print)
E-ISBN 978-3-631-91864-7 (E-Book)
E-ISBN 978-3-631-91865-4 (E-PUB)
DOI 10.3726/b21807

Published by Peter Lang GmbH, Berlin, Deutschland

info@peterlang.com - www.peterlang.com

This publication has been peer reviewed.

www.peterlang.com

Contents

Acknowledgements

This monograph is the end result of a research project: "The standards of respect the religious rights of persons detained in prisons, detention centres, educational and correctional centres for juveniles" (decision no. 2018/31/B/HS5/02233), funded by the National Science Centre (Poland).

Our joy at the publication of this study is all the greater because the road to its creation was extremely turbulent and difficult. The SARS-CoV-2 pandemic forced us to change the strategy of carrying out research and significantly lengthened the process of data acquisition and processing. Therefore, we wish, at this point, to thank the persons and institutions without whose help our efforts and enthusiasm could have been in vain.

First and foremost, we would like to thank the Ministry of Justice of the Republic of Poland and the Central Board of the Prison Service for giving consent to conducting our study on the premises of selected penitentiary facilities and detention centres.

Our sincere thanks for their support go to the directors and educators of penitentiary facilities, detention centres, youth educational centres and correctional facilities, where we were allowed to carry out our study. We are grateful for the enormity of your kindness and for your help in distributing and mailing our questionnaires.

Heartfelt thanks to our Mentor, beloved Chieftainess prof. zw. dr hab. Teresa Dukiet-Nagórska, for shaping our research workshop, without which it would be difficult for us to navigate the frontier of written law and its practical application. We also thank her for strengthening our special sensitivity to human rights violations, in particular, the rights of the vulnerable and the rejected.

We express great gratitude to the reviewer of this monograph – Head of the Department of Penal Enforcement Law at the Faculty of Law and Administration of the University of Łódź – dr hab. prof. UŁ Aldona Nawój-Śleszyński, for the insightful and critical comments that have made this monograph an even better work than it was at the outset.

Special thanks to Mr. Łukasz Gałecki, Peter Lang senior acquisitions editor for guiding us professionally through the entire publishing process.

Many thanks are due to dr Marta Byczek and all the staff of the Law Library of the University of Silesia in Katowice. Thank you not only for help in finding and obtaining the literature necessary for the work on the subject we have undertaken, but also for genuine kindness and selfless commitment.

And last but not least, thanks to mgr inż. Monika Łyczba from the Research Project Team of the Faculty of Law and Administration of the University of Silesia in Katowice, for the invaluable and unparalleled support at every stage of our project, without which the day we joyfully receive author copies of the monograph from Peter Lang would never come.

Olga Sitarz, Anna Jaworska-Wieloch & Jakub Hanc

Introduction

Researchers are keen to address the issues of human rights, including those of human beings deprived of their liberty as a result of a committed criminal offence. They are equally keen to address – on the level of sociology, psychology, religion studies or theology – the issues related to religion, religiosity and faith. Even when religious freedom in prisons is analysed, the focus is very rarely on prisoners' religious practices from the perspective of human rights. Undoubtedly, the leading Polish researchers in this field include Zbigniew Lasocik[1] and Jerzy Nikołajew.[2] This publication seeks to continue the trails laid down by the designated researchers, adding new issues.

The few studies to date indicate that faith and religion are of great significance for prisoners. A study carried out in the first half of March 2015 among prisoners incarcerated in the External Division in Zabłocie (Penitentiary facility in Biała Podlaska), which covered 95 % of prisoners (101 persons), showed that the religious attitudes were as follows: 6.9 % of respondents described themselves as strong believers, 74.2 % as believers, 12.9 % as undecided, 3.9 as indifferent and 3 % as non-believers.[3] Other studies revealed that faith and religion helped 14 % of long-term prisoners the most to serve their long sentence.[4] In other words, a huge number of prisoners attach special importance to religious rights and freedoms. The isolation conditions and prisoners' low efficiency mean that the extent to which these rights and freedoms are exercised must be evaluated directly at the prisoners' location. Ultimately, the religious reality in post-criminal

1 Z. Lasocik, *Praktyki religijne więźniów*, Warszawa 1993.

2 See: J. Nikołajew, "Specyfika duszpasterstwa więziennego w Polsce. Prezentacja badań własnych", *Teologia w Polsce*, vol. 3, no. 1, 2009, pp. 153 et seq.; J. Nikołajew, *Duszpasterstwo więzienne. Tradycje, teraźniejszość, perspektywy*, Lublin 2009; J. Nikołajew, "Reguły Minimalne i Europejskie Reguły Więzienne a prawo więźniów do wolności sumienia i religii w Polsce", *Studia z Prawa Wyznaniowego*, vol. 16, 2013, pp. 111 et seq.; J. Nikołajew, *Wolność sumienia i religii skazanych i tymczasowo aresztowanych*, Lublin 2012.

3 W. Romanowicz, D. Tomczyszyn, "Stosunek do religii osób odbywających karę pozbawienia wolności a miejsce religii we współczesnym świecie", *Rozprawy Społeczne*, vol. 9, no. 3, 2015, p. 96.

4 A. Polak-Kruisznik, "Doniesienia z badań nad wykonywaniem długoterminowych kar pozbawienia wolności", in K. Mrozek (ed.), *Z problematyki badań empirycznych w prawie karnym wykonawczym. Część 2*, Wrocław 2021, p. 141.

isolation units is co-shaped by the existing regulations of various levels, the involvement of individuals in the performance of their duties, the attitude of the penitentiary staff, prisoners themselves and their fellow prisoners.

This publication discusses the issue of the social and individual significance of religion. We believe that experiencing religious freedom by prisoners in isolation units teaches them respect for the law, the rights of others, difference and diversity and it may also, as Jeroen Temperman pointed out, minimize the radicalization of convicts and detainees.[5]

Isolation arising from the commission of a prohibited act, hereinafter referred to as criminal isolation, is accompanied by numerous limitations and deprivations, which, among other things, may relate to the sphere of performing religious practices. The question we sought to answer is mainly about **how much these practices are genuinely restricted, which practices are affected and to what extent these limitations are justifiable**. Such findings cannot be formulated in isolation from the adopted normative regulations and prisoners' opinions. The official prison statistics and those concerning the implementation of measures of education and reform involving juveniles do not have this information.[6]

The study was carried out on two levels – the first part covered the theoretical and normative issues, the second focused on questionnaires among prisoners in post-criminal isolation units and their educators in Poland.

The theoretical research was based on identifying the significance of religion both in social and individual terms.

The normative study consisted of identifying the international standards of religious freedom and determining how these principles are applied to the Polish and German national legal orders. A further step was to reconstruct the international and national rules relating to religious freedom in isolation facilities that incarcerate individuals in connection with the commission of a prohibited act. The scope of the normative study covered incarcerated adults and juveniles – children who committed a prohibited act. The selection of the Polish and German legal orders, within the previously discussed framework, is justified by the available research material (Poland) and the evident similarity between the two countries, both EU members, in which legal tradition derives from so-called continental law. Detailed and insightful comparative findings have

5 J. Temperman, "Freedom of Religion or Belief in Prison. A Critical Analysis of the European Court of Human Rights' Jurisprudence", *Oxford Journal of Law and Religion*, vol. 6, no. 1, 2017, pp. 48 et seq.

6 See: https://sw.gov.pl/dzial/statystyka (accessed 29.08.2023).

shown fundamental differences in the way prisoners' universal right to religious freedom is regulated.

The specificity of the study, its applicative value and its universal problems prompt us to present some key terms characteristic of the Polish criminal law system, which in their English translation may not always be understood by everyone.

The following terms are used below:

- **penal enforcement law** – a set of legal norms governing the enforcement of penalties and other related measures imposed in court proceedings and in cases involving minor offences;
- **Penal Enforcement Code (PEC)** – the law that most fully normalizes the enforcement of judgments in criminal proceedings, in cases involving fiscal crimes and minor offences, and in proceedings involving administrative penalties and coercive measures resulting in deprivation of liberty;
- **penitentiary facility (Polish: Zakład Karny, ZK)** – a penitentiary in which adults or juveniles that are held liable like an adult are incarcerated to serve a prison sentence. There are four types of penitentiary facilities: for young adults, individuals serving a first penalty, penitentiary recidivists and soldiers serving a sentence of military detention. Penitentiary facilities may be organized as closed, semi-open and open institutions.
- **detention centre (Polish: Areszt Śledczy, AŚ)** – a penitentiary in which adults or juveniles that are held liable like an adult are incarcerated to serve a prison sentence or to enforce a preventive measure in the form of pre-trial detention. Convicts serving a penalty of deprivation of liberty in detention centres serve it in conditions complying with the classification, that is, in accordance with a specified type and kind of penitentiary facility;
- **youth educational centre (Polish: Młodzieżowy Ośrodek Wychowawczy, MOW)** – the placement of a juvenile in a youth educational centre is an educational measure that may be applied to juveniles in response to demoralization or a criminal offence;
- **correctional facilities (Polish: Zakład Poprawczy, ZP)** – the placement of a juvenile in a correctional facility is a measure of reform that may be applied to juveniles who at the moment of the commission of the act have attained 13 years of age, but have not attained 17 years of age, committed a punishable act corresponding to a crime or a fiscal crime and, simultaneously, the application of such a measure is supported by the high degree of demoralization of the juvenile and the nature of the criminal act, the manner and circumstances of its commission;

- **post-criminal isolation units (PCIU)** – units in which the offender is placed in response to a committed criminal act (penitentiary facilities and detention centres in the case of individuals liable under the Criminal Code, youth educational centres and correctional facilities in the case of juveniles);
- **juvenile** – an individual who has not attained 17 years of age at the moment of the commission of a punishable act, and simultaneously has attained at least 10 years of age in the case of demoralization and 13 years of age in the case of a punishable act. Where they meet strict conditions, including the attainment of a minimum of 14 years of age, they may be liable under the rules provided for adults by the Polish Criminal Code;
- **adult within the understanding of the Criminal Code** – an individual who has attained 17 years of age at the moment of the commission of a prohibited act;
- **young adult** is an offender who has not attained 21 years of age at the moment of the commission of a prohibited act and 24 years of age at the time of first instance adjudication;
- **legal adult** – an individual who (as a rule) has attained 18 years of age.

Chapter I Social and individual significance of religion

It is a truism that the phenomenon referred to as "religion" has been studied for a long time, using various methods and perspectives. It is equally obvious that the concept of "religion" has not been uniformly defined. The history of the study of religion has seen many definitions of religion, some standing in opposition to each other, others being complementary. A very popular definition, which in the opinion of many researchers has the greatest potential for universality, was proposed by Max L. Stackhouse (1935–2016). He characterized religion as "a comprehensive worldview or metaphysical moral vision that is accepted as binding because it is held to be in itself basically true and just even if all dimensions of it cannot be either fully confirmed or refuted."[7] It is fair to say that no definition of "religion" has gained universal acceptance. Today, it is recognized it is impossible to construct a definition of religion that would include all the (intuitive and scientific) phenomena considered as "religious" and separate religious from non-religious phenomena completely. This is because the ambiguity of the term "religion" is due to the cultural richness of religious phenomena. Religion is an area of personal experiences of everyone and also a socio-cultural phenomenon. Both the existing religions and those that have disappeared have been determined by tradition and the place (geographic criterion) and time (temporal criterion) of their occurrence. The inability to develop universal definitional criteria generates different ways of capturing the essence and scope of religion and, consequently, leads to the existence of multiple definitions of the term.[8]

---

7 M. L. Stackhouse, *Globalization and Grace*, New York 2007, pp. 7 et seq.

8 A. Bronk, "Religia", in T. Gadacz, B. Milerski (eds.), *Religia. Encyklopedia PWN. Parys – Rut. Tom 8*, Warszawa, 2003, pp. 393 et seq. See also: F. Bowie, *The Anthropology of Religion: An Introduction*, Malden 2006, pp. 12 et seq.; J. Figl, "Religionsbegriff – zum Gegenstandsbereich der Religionswissenschaft", in J. Figl (ed.), *Handbuch Religionswissenschaft: Religionen und ihre zentralen Themen*, Göttingen 2003, pp. 62 et seq.; E. T. Lawson, "Defining Religion… Going the Theoretical Way", in T. A. Idinopulos, B. C. Wilson (eds.), *What is Religion? Origins, Definitions, and Explanations*, Leiden 1998, pp. 43 et seq.; M. Zarzecki, "Klasyczne i nieklasyczne definicje religii i religijności", in S. H. Zaręba (ed.), *Socjologia życia religijnego w Polsce*, Warszawa 2009, pp. 94 et seq.; Z. J. Zdybicka, *Religia i religioznawstwo*, Lublin 1992, pp. 353 et seq.

Constructing nominal definitions, a religious scholar will search for the meaning of the noun 'religion'. However, the etymology of the word is not unequivocal. The term 'religion' does not appear in all current and extinct cultures and it has no equivalent in many languages.[9] In the dispute over the origin of the term, reference is most frequently made to the reflections of the Roman philosopher Cicero (106–43 BCE), who derived the feminine noun *religio* from the verb *relegere/religere*, meaning "to re-read", "to go over again in thought". After Lactantius (250–330 CE) (*Divinae institutiones*, IV, 28), Christian tradition links the noun to the verb *religare*, meaning "to tie up, to bind" The trail was followed by Saint Augustine of Hippo (354–430 CE), who pointed out in his work *Retractationes* that: "To one God we aspire and with him we bind our souls (*animas nostras religantes*), from which the name of religion is derived" (*Retractationes* 13, 9). The word was written down for the first time in English in the 11th century.[10]

Notably, Christianity initially applied the term *religio* exclusively to itself (Christian centrism), setting itself against other beliefs and cults jointly referred to as 'pagan'. That opposition formed part of the European culture for many centuries. For a very long time, other forms of religiosity were viewed and evaluated through the prism of Christianity. The situation changed only after the contact with non-European cultures. Even during the Renaissance, when references were made to antiquity, ancient beliefs were more frequently called "mythology" than "religion". A range of factors contributed to the abandonment of the indicated dichotomy. Immense importance should be attributed to archaeological works, which discovered the religions of primitive, Chinese and ancient peoples, in particular, the ancient Egyptian, Assyrian-Babylonian and Sumerian beliefs. A significant contribution was also made by philosophy (questions about religious language and beliefs, the problem of evil and suffering, concepts of God, including the arguments for and against His existence and the phenomenon of miracles), sociology (religion is perceived as a social fact)

---

9 B. Nongbri, *Before Religion: A History of a Modern Concept*, New Haven – London 2013, *passim*.

10 F. Bowie, *The Anthropology…*, pp. 18 et seq.; A. Bronk, *Podstawy nauk o religii*, Lublin 2003, pp. 105 et seq.; J. Dobieszewski, *Filozofia religii. Wykład*, Warszawa 2022, p. 24; P. M. Kavros, "Religion", in D. A. Lemming (ed.), *Encyclopedia of Psychology and Religion*, New York 2010, pp. 1492 et seq.; M. Sieniatycki, *Apologetyka, czyli dogmatyka fundamentalna*, Kraków 1932, p. 2; Z. J. Zdybicka, "Czym jest religia i dlaczego istnieje religia", in H. Zimoń (ed.), *Religia w świecie współczesnym. Zarys problematyki religiologicznej*, Lublin 2003, p. 56; Z. J. Zdybicka, *Religia…*, p. 361.

and psychology (religion is a mental act, a form of human consciousness, encompassing various mental experiences, including cognitive and emotional ones).[11]

As is the case with the definition referring to the origin and significance of the word, no satisfactory results are produced by other reference definitions, including inductive (Socratic) and intuitive ones.[12] In turn, definitions derived from empirical sciences, which are real definitions, seek to characterize religion by its origins or structure. Thus, definitions with philosophical features emphasize faith-related aspects, psychological definitions focus on the significance of psychological factors, and sociological definitions point to institutional and ritual functions.[13]

The systemic and holistic approaches to religion comprehend it as a cultural system, consisting of symbols for communication and interpretation of cultural phenomena. What distinguishes lighting a candle on a restaurant table from lighting a candle on an altar in a Roman Catholic church is an attribute of the ritual act. It is not constituted by its content but by the symbolic significance by followers of a particular religion. A systemic and holistic approach to religion was presented, among others, by Clifford Geertz (1926–2006), who pointed out that religion is "a system of symbols which acts to establish powerful, pervasive, and long-lasting moods and motivations in men by formulating conceptions of a general order of existence and clothing these conceptions with such an aura of factuality that the moods and motivations seem uniquely realistic."[14] On a similar note, Antoine Vergote (1921–2013) emphasized the cultural reality of religion, defining it as "the entirety of the linguistic expressions, emotions and, actions and signs that refer to a supernatural being or supernatural beings."[15]

Genetic definitions are in turn obtained by an indication of the source and origins of religion (origin analysis).[16] The intellectual sphere may be one of such sources. Then religion becomes an imperfect and non-empirical attempt

11 A. Bronk, *Podstawy*..., pp. 108 et seq.; A. Bronk, "Religia"..., p. 394.
12 A. Bronk, *Podstawy*..., p. 116.
13 A. Bronk, "Religia"..., p. 395.
14 C. Geertz, *The interpretation of cultures. Selected essays*, London 1993, pp. 87 et seq. and H. Wienhold, "Clifford Geertz: Religion as a Cultural System (1966)", in Ch. Gärtner, G. Pickel (eds.), *Schlüsselwerke der Religionssoziologie*, Wiesbaden 2019, pp. 237 et seq.
15 A. Vergote, *Religion, Belief and Unbelief. A Psychological Study*, Amsterdam – Atlanta 1997, p. 16.
16 A. Bronk, "Religia"..., pp. 397 et seq.

to explain the incomprehensible phenomena occurring in the world around man. This approach is highly visible in the criticism of religion coming from Herbert Spencer (1820–1903).[17] He argued that the knowledge of phenomena requires only empirical proof. This is because we cannot know something that we have not learned. Since we cannot know the nature of reality, it is certain that there is something, in principle, unknowable. We do not know whether God exists or what his nature may be. Spencer believed that science forced religion to abandon its dogmas, that is, the fundamental beliefs that it could not justify. However, he concluded that religion and science were in agreement about one thing – the human mind is only capable of gaining "relative" knowledge. This is due to the limitations of the human mind, capable only of gaining knowledge of phenomena and but of the reality underlying the phenomena. Both science and religion must recognize that the force the universe reveals to us is completely unexamined. Adopting an agnostic attitude, he argued that theism cannot be recognized because we have no method of acquiring knowledge of the divine and cannot verify it. We do not know whether religious beliefs are true or false.[18]

The emotional sphere is another source of religion. Religion is, in this spectrum, an attempt to respond to the deepest and most crucial human needs. This approach is favoured among others, by Rudolph Otto (1869–1937), who introduced the term *numinous*, understood as "non-rational, non-sensory experience or feeling whose primary and immediate object is outside the self".[19] The theologian supported the argument that religious emotion is very specific and different in qualitative terms from other emotions. He based his argument precisely on the notion *numinous*, which is specific only to religion – it is its *sui generis* emotion. Although Otto adopted a more theological and less pragmatic and utilitarian approach to experience, he did not limit his research on religion

---

17 H. Spencer, *First Principles*, London 1867 – https://oll.libertyfund.org/title/spencer-first-principles-1867?html=true#Spencer_0624_97 (accessed 29.08.2023).

18 T. Fitzgerald, "Herbert Spencer's Agnosticism", *Religious Studies*, vol. 23, no. 4, 1987, pp. 477 et seq.; K. Kaczamrek, *Herbert Spencer a problemy socjologii religii*, Poznań 2007, pp. 15 et seq.; W. Sweet, "Herbert Spencer (1820–1903)", in J. Fieser, B. Dowden (eds.), *The Internet Encyclopedia of Philosophy*, https://iep.utm.edu/spencer/#H4 (accessed 29.08.2023); J. Waardenburg, *Classical Approaches to the Study of Religion. Aims, Methods, and Theories of Research. Introduction and Anthology*, Berlin – Boston 2017, pp. 193 et seq.

19 R. Otto, *Das Heilige. Über das Irrationale in der Idee des Göttlichen und sein Verhältnis zum Rationalen*, Gotha 1926, pp. 5 et seq. and R. Otto, *The Idea of the Holy*, London – Oxford – New York 1958, pp. 11 et seq.

solely to emotions and their social and individual impact. In his approach, rational elements (God within the theological meaning) and irrational elements (emotional and empirical part of divinity) make two complementary halves.[20] Similar views can be found in Friedrich Engels (1820–1895): "All religion, however, is nothing but the fantastic reflection in men's minds of those external forces which control their daily life, a reflection in which the terrestrial forces assume the form of supernatural forces."[21] Therefore, religion is a mechanism that worked in man who did not accept the fact that he or she is not infinite. Given that infinity – by virtue of mortality – is not their attribute, humans locate infinity through a projection mechanism in a personified and transcendental being. This procedure results, among other things, in alienation because in that case man cannot live to the fullness of his or her essence.

The objective definitions of religion define it in terms of its structure (beliefs, moral imperatives, forms of worship, modes of social organization), whereas functional definitions focus on fulfilled functions.[22]

By combining the two above methods, one can obtain object-function definitions that describe "religion" as a conceptual system, providing ways of interpreting the world, showing the place of man in the world, giving guidelines on how to live, adopting certain beliefs and fulfilling certain practices within a religious social structure.[23] The fundamentals of such approach can already be seen in the works of Edward Taylor (1832–1917),[24] who argued that humans

---

20 G. Klinkhammer, "Rudolf Otto: Das Heilige. Über das Irrationale und die Idee des Göttlichen und sein Verhältnis zum Rationalen (1917)", in Ch. Gärtner, G. Pickel (eds.), *Schlüsselwerke…*, pp. 151 et seq.; A. Locatelli, "Emotions and/in Religion. Reading Sigmund Freud, Rudolph Otto, and William James", in I. Jandl, S. Knaller, S. Schönfellner, G. Tockner (eds.), *Writing Emotions. Theoretical Concepts and Selected Case Studies in Literature*, Bielefeld 2017, pp. 80 et seq.; H. Nörenberg, "The Numinous, the Ethical, and the Body. Rudolf Otto's "The Idea of the Holy" Revisited", *Open Theology*, vol. 3, no. 1, 2017, pp. 546 et seq.; J. Waardenburg, *Classical…*, pp. 425 et seq.; G. D. Alles, "Rudolf Otto (1869–1937)", in A. Michaels (ed.), *Klassiker der Religionswissenschaft: Von Friedrich Schleiermacher bis Mircea Eliade*, München 2010, pp. 198 et seq.

21 F. Engels, "Herrn Eugen Dührings Umwälzung der Wissenschaften (Anti-Dühring)", in: *Marks-Engels Werke. Band 20*, Berlin 1962, p. 294.

22 A. Bronk, "Religia"…, p. 395 and M. Zarzecki, "Klasyczne…, pp. 101 et seq.

23 K. E. Yandell, *Philosophy of religion. A contemporary introduction*, New York – London 2016, pp. 10 et seq.

24 E. Taylor, *Primitive Culture: Research into the Development of Mythology, Philosophy, Religion, Art, and Custum*, New York 1871, *passim* and I. Strenski, *Thinking About Religion: A Reader*, Oxford 2006, pp. 65 et seq.

used religion to explain the phenomena occurring in the world, in particular, their origin. For example, God (Supreme Being/Divinity) created the sun to warm people and give them light. Taylor perceived animism (understood as the belief in spirits inhabiting and animating beings or souls existing in things) as the true natural religion, constituting the essence of religion. This is because it was the primitive and best answer to all the basic questions posed by man. The researcher pointed out that modern religious practitioners still believe in ghosts, thus, at least on that level, they do not seem to be more advanced than primitive peoples. He held the opinion that modern religious practitioners did not understand the ways of the universe and life because by excluding scientific explanation in their understanding of why and how things occur, he asserted modern religious practitioners were rudimentary. Taylor viewed faith in God as it was in his time as a form of retaining primitive ignorance. Interestingly, the anthropologist did not see atheism as a logical end of the cultural and religious development but rather as a reduced form of monotheistic deism.[25]

The European Judeo-Christian term of religion is mainly profiled by the monotheistic perspective.[26] The term is structurally profiled – it is a relationship between man and some transcendence (a being of a personal nature), whom man either seeks or who is revealed to him. This view is accurately reflected by Zofia Józefa Zdybicka, who believes that religion is a real, personal and dynamic relationship between man (a separate human being) and God (the transcendental and personal Absolute), on whom man is dependent in existence and action, and who, as the Supreme Good, is the ultimate goal of human life.[27]

Because God (the Absolute) is not available for empirical research, religious studies define religion, after Edward E. Evans-Pritchard (1902–1973), using data obtained in objective scientific studies on: human religious beliefs, religious

25 J. Josephson-Storm, *The Myth of Disenchantment: Magic, Modernity, and the Birth of Human Sciences*, Chicago 2017, pp. 98 et seq.; K. H. Kohl, "Edward Burnett Tylor (1832–1917)", in A. Michaels (ed.), *Klassiker…*, pp. 41 et seq.; R. A. Segal, "Animism for Tylor", in G. Harvey (ed.), *The Handbook fo Contemporary Animism*, London – New York 2013, pp. 53 et seq.; I. Strenski, *Thinking About Religion: An Historical Introduction to Theories of Religion*, Oxford 2006, pp. 93 et seq.; M. D. Stringer, "Building on belief: defining animism in Taylor and contemporary society" in G. Harvey (ed.), *The Handbook of Contemporary Animism*, London – New York 2013, pp. 63 et seq.; J. Waardenburg, *Classical…*, pp. 204 et seq.

26 J. Figl, "Gott – monotheistisch", in J. Figl (ed.), *Handbuch…*, pp. 545 et seq.

27 Z. J. Zdybicka, *Człowiek i religia. Zarys filozofii religii*, Lublin 1993, *passim*.

behaviour and institutions, symbolic means of religious expression juxtaposed with their impact on society, human feelings, ways of life and relations.[28]

The European understanding of religion also breaks down in cultures that do not distinguish religion as a distinctive set of phenomena, ideas, values, beliefs or behaviour.[29] Asian religions put greater emphasis on inner states than doctrine and religious practices.[30]

However, the monotheistic orientation is only one of many possibilities. Using the criterion of belief in transcendence, theistic (mono-, heno-, poli-, pan-, panen- theistic) and atheistic religions can be distinguished. Religions may be universal (major monotheistic religions) or ethnic (including tribal and national), but also inclusive and exclusive (the issue is the doctrinal attitude to other religions). As regards the sources of knowledge, they are divided into natural or revealed ones.[31]

The literature review shows another significant distinction of a theological-anthropological nature. Apart from 'religion', Paul Tillich (1886–1965) distinguishes two additional terms: pseudo-religion and *quasi*-religion. The former contains an intentional but deceptive (fraudulent) functional resemblance to religion, the latter bears a real but unintentional resemblance based on some specific identity points (such objects as a nation, knowledge, some particular form or stage of societal developmental are occasionally worshipped).[32] The researcher points to fascism and communism as the most striking examples of

---

28 E. E. Evans-Pritchard, *Theorien über primitive Religion*, Frankfurt am Main 1981, *passim* and B. Schnepel, "Edward Evan Evans-Pritchard (1902–1973)", in A. Michaels (ed.), *Klassiker…*, pp. 303 et seq.

29 G. Keher, *Einführung in die Religionssoziologie*, Darmstadt 1988, pp. 13 et seq.

30 A. Bronk, "Religia"…, p. 395.

31 A. Bronk, "Religia"…, p. 401.

32 The phenomenon of the so-called Smolensk monthly commemorations (that is, ceremonies organized every month by circles close to the "Law and Justice" party to commemorate the victims of the Smolensk catastrophe of 10 April 2010) came to be identified as "the Smolensk religion" in the Polish public discourse. However, it is difficult to classify that phenomenon under the typology proposed by Tillich, which supports the argument that it is either a hybrid phenomenon or an autonomous one in regard to that division. See: Z. Mikołejko, *Między zbawieniem a Smoleńskiem*, Warszawa 2017, *passim*; P. Sendyka, "Narodziny *mitu smoleńskiego*", *Zeszyty Naukowe Uniwersytetu Jagiellońskiego. Prace Etnograficzne*, vol. 41, no. 1, 2013, pp. 43 et seq.; Z. Pasek, "Czy miesięcznice smoleńskie były uroczystościami religijnymi? Prawo a polska kultura religijna", *Studia z Prawa Wyznaniowego*, vol. 24, 2021, pp. 68 et seq.

the phenomenon.[33] Based on this distinction, it is assumed that not only a certain type of ideologies but also so-called "philosophies of life", performing a function similar to religion, can be seen as substitute religions (parareligions). In analogy with "classic" religions, they give hope for a better life and promise salvation in the form of a future, ideal society built in this world, with its own authorities, writings, symbols, language, liturgy, rituals and secular public holidays. Fundamental or final matters can be expressed in purely secular terms.[34]

Many sociologists of religion accept the argument that there are no entirely secular societies. From the perspective of sociology, non-religious individuals are those who derive their view of the world and values from alternative secular cultural systems, and not revealed ones. Against this background, the concept of secular religion related to secular humanism, with elements of impact of religious doctrines, stands out in reference to the current social problems.[35]

In simplistic terms, it can be assumed that every religion is made up of two realities: non-empirical and empirical. The non-empirical (transcendental) reality is symbolic. It exists through a system of religious meanings, expressed in certain beliefs, behaviour and institutions. It is empirically elusive, but for a believer it is more real and it affects his or her existence more than the sensually perceived world. By contrast, the religion's empirical reality is objective and subjective. The former consists of religious beliefs, social and institutional structures and forms of worship. The latter is defined by the religious experience of a believer, manifested in beliefs, emotions, attitudes and practices.[36]

For William P. Alston, religion is wherever one can speak of: a belief in supernatural beings; a distinction between sacred and profane objects; ritual acts directed at sacred objects; a moral code sanctioned by the supreme being or gods; religious feelings connected with the presence of sacred objects; a prayer or other forms of communication with God/deities; a religious worldview, including the formation of a general picture of the world as a whole and the individual's place in it; a (more or less consistent) organization of life based on the worldview

33 P. Tillich, "Christianity and the Encounter of the World Religions", in R. P. Scharlemann (ed.), *Religious Writings. Hauptwerke. Volume 5/Band 5. Writings on Religion/Religiöse Schriften*, Berlin-Boston 1988 [reprint 2020], pp. 293 et seq. and M. Gonnerman, "Tillich Paul", in D. A. Lemming (ed.), *Encyclopedia of Psychology and Religion*, New York 2010, pp. 1799 et seq.

34 A. Bronk, "Religia"..., p. 396.

35 A. Bronk, "Religia"..., p. 396.

36 A. Bronk, "Religia"..., p. 398.

and a social group bound together by the above.[37] Following that author's classification, many researchers ultimately abandoned the attempt to provide one definition of religion in favour of an approach that avoids cultural biases and secular ideologies. Religion in that spirit is to include: doctrine (confession of faith), myth (historical, sacred narrative), ethic (moral code of sacred origin), ritual (use of sacred articles, participation in ceremonies, including the offering of sacrifices, also historical ones), religious experience (educational, social and pastoral). All the indicated elements are interconnected.[38]

It is nowadays accepted that 4 elements coexist with each other in every religion in different proportions. They are as follows: doctrinal, ethical, cultural and organizational.[39]

A religious doctrine is a coherent set of beliefs, assumptions, assertions about God(s) of the world and man, making a particular religious tradition unique. It explains the phenomena occurring in nature and the social world, including those concerning man, in a way that excludes randomness and gives them meaning. A religious doctrine consists of religious beliefs concerning the transcendental reality – supernatural forces and beings: God, deities, and the relationship between mortal life and the supernatural world, immortality of the soul, afterlife, possibility of deliverance from suffering, sin, salvation, etc. A doctrine is characterized by oneness and continuity, which makes it a source of knowledge about religion. The source of a doctrine most frequently lies in the revelation of God, deities or supernatural force and religious experience, justifying a believer's conviction and certifying the authenticity of his or her religion. Almost every doctrine is marked by the delimitation of the sacral (*sacrum*) and secular (*profanum*) spheres, that is, between the world of God/deities and the world of man. However, this aspect is not universal and characteristic of all religions – some of them, for example, see the entire cosmos as divine, or even being God. A doctrine is stored in (carried by) sacred writings of an inspired nature (Torah, Bible, Quran, Vedas), which are subjected to an authoritative

37 W. P. Alston, "Religion", in P. Edwards (ed.), *The Encyclopedia of Philosophy*, New York – London 1972, pp. 140 et seq.

38 P. M. Kavros, "Religion"..., pp. 1492 et seq.

39 This approach is sometimes called *polythetic*. In this case, the need to look for a common core for all religions is abandoned. However, it is noted that some mutually similar phenomena occur, although they do not always occur together. This approach allows us to establish phenomena that are "religious" beyond any doubt. See: T. J. Gunn, "The Complexity of Religion and the Definition of *Religion* in International Law", *Harvard Human Rights Journal*, vol. 16, 2003, pp. 194 et seq.

interpretation by selected individuals (priests, theologians) guided primarily by the desire to preserve the fidelity of the original text, and occasionally, to adapt the text to the needs of modern believers. To achieve that purpose, religions with no sacred books (Buddhism) use oral tradition, which is handed down, among other things, in the religious initiation process. In religions with a complex doctrine, the degree of identification with its findings is considered a measure of orthodoxy and religious affiliation. It is nurtured by priests and perpetuated by popular piety in oral and written tradition. It is primarily handed down by education, upbringing and initiation. Nowadays, in modern societies, the truths of faith forming part of the official religious doctrine are accepted selectively, leading in extreme cases to individual constructs of religious ideas.[40]

Religion offers its followers answers to fundamental questions regarding moral behaviour, and precise and numerous standards of conduct – often very detailed, regulating almost all areas of life. This takes place based on the authority of God himself and religious leaders and occasionally natural law. Some ethical principles seem to be universal (e.g., love God and thy neighbour as thyself), whereas others are specific to a given religion. Ethical standards of religious origin specify what behaviour is necessary to be a member of the community enjoying a good reputation. They may include ideals to which one should aspire. Religion becomes the guardian of moral values and moral order through ethical standards, sanctioning the behaviour of the individual and the entire community. The key place on the ethical level is occupied in many religions by the concept of sin.[41]

Religiosity is manifested by worship practiced individually or collectively, whose primary objective is to establish contact with God/deities, a supernatural force, and to show him/them due reverence. Depending on the degree of its development, every religion has its holy time (Lent, Ramadan, pilgrimages), holy places (worship centres – Rome, Mecca, Jerusalem, Varanasi, Lumbini), buildings (church, mosque, synagogue, mandir, stupa), objects (liturgical paraments, special garments excluded from secular use). Spontaneous and informal worship activities take the form of liturgy in doctrinally and organizationally developed religions.[42]

---

40 I. Borowik, "Doktryna religijna", in T. Gadacz, B. Milerski (eds.), *Religia. Encyklopedia PWN. Ciapinski – Fatima. Tom 3*, Warszawa, 2001, p. 247; A. Bronk, "Religia"..., pp. 398 et seq.; M. B. McGuire, *Religion. The Social Context*, Long Grove 2002, p. 99.

41 A. Bronk, "Religia"..., pp. 399 et seq.; M. B. McGuire, *Religion*..., p. 100; U. Tworuschka, M. Klöcker, "Ethik der Religion", in J. Figl (ed.), *Handbuch*..., pp. 718 et seq.

42 B. Bäumer, "Sakraler Raum und heilige Zeit", in J. Figl (ed.), *Handbuch*..., pp. 690 et seq.; M. B. McGuire, *Religion*..., p. 100; A. Bronk, "Religia"..., pp. 399 et seq.; H. G.

Most modern religions are public, social and institutional in nature. They function around tradition related to its founder and his teachings. They are hierarchically structured and assign different roles to individuals, determined especially by gender (separate for women and men)[43] or a performed function (priests/priestesses, monks/nuns).[44]

Referring to religion's communal and social nature, one cannot ignore the considerations of two prominent sociologists. For the first, Max Weber (1864–1920), religion was one of the fundamental forces in society.[45] Searching for elements characteristic of the western civilization, he concluded that the Calvinist religious ideas had a strong impact on social innovations and the development of the economic system of the broadly understood west, although they were not the only and exclusive factors of that development.[46] Weber left behind a socio-evolutionary model of religious changes (the transition from magic to polytheism, pantheism, monotheism, ethical monotheism and secularization). In his view, this model is a process of "disenchanting the world" strongly linked to rationality – the world is becoming more and more explainable and less and less mystical. At the heart of this evolution is growing economic stability, which institutionalizes and professionalizes religion. The deepening of social structures, encompassing new groups, and the centralization of power results in an orientation towards one universal God. Weber believed that research into an unspecified religion leads to absurd results. Socio-religious studies may examine only a specific religion.[47]

Hödl, "Ritual (Kult, Opfer, Ritus, Zeremonie)", in J. Figl (ed.), *Handbuch…*, pp. 664 et seq.

43 F. Bowie, *The Anthropology…*, pp. 82 et seq.; M. B. McGuire, *Religion…*, pp. 128 et seq.; B. Heller, "Gender und Religion", in J. Figl (ed.), *Handbuch…*, pp. 758 et seq.

44 A. Bronk, "Religia"…, pp. 400 et seq.

45 I. Strenski, *Thinking About Religion: A Reader…* pp. 135 et seq.

46 M. Weber, *Gesammelte Aufsätze zur Religionssoziologie I*, Tübingen 1963, pp. 10 et seq. and 83 et seq.

47 R. Bendix, *Max Weber: An Intellectual Portrait*, Berkley 1977, pp. 285 et seq.; I. Borowik, "Religia i społeczeństwo. Tropami klasyków w teoriach współczesnych socjologów religii", in S. H. Zaręba (ed.), *Socjologia…*, pp. 59 et seq.; G. Kehrer, "Max Weber (1864–1920)", in A. Michaels (ed.), *Klassiker…*, pp. 121 et seq.; H. G. Kippenberg, "(Welt-) Religionen", in H. P. Müller, S. Sigmund (eds.), *Max Weber-Handbuch. Leben – Werk – Wirkung*, Berlin 2020, pp. 150 et seq.; H. P. Müller, "Vorbemerkung (1920)", in H. P. Müller, S. Sigmund (eds.), *Max Weber-Handbuch…* pp. 305 et seq.; G. Neugebauer, "Max Weber: Die protestantische Ethik und der *Geist* des Kapitalismus (1904/1905)", in Ch. Gärtner, G. Pickel (eds.), *Schlüsselwerke…*, pp. 101 et seq.; J. Waardenburg, *Classical…*, pp. 346 et seq.; P. Ghosh, "Die protestantische Ethik und der Geist des

Émile Durkheim (1858–1917) was the second sociologist examining religion. He defined it as "a unified system of beliefs and practices relative to sacred things, i.e., things set apart and forbidden — beliefs and practices which unite in one single moral community called a Church, all those who adhere to them" (believers).[48] Religion is of fundamental importance for social morality. It performs a pro-social function, that is, it makes human society truly human, not just society in the natural sense (for example, a herd). Its integrating role makes it possible to resist the evil inclinations and weaknesses inherent in human nature. Durkheim sought to identify the social origin and function of religion because he believed it to be a source of love, solidarity, forgiveness, camaraderie, compassion, respect, trust, loyalty and fidelity. Moreover, he attempted to find a common denominator for all religions by identifying the connections between them. He also set out to identify the connections between certain religions in different cultures. His intention was to understand the empirical and social aspect of religions that is common to all of them and goes beyond the concepts of spirituality and God. Durkheim perceived religion as the most basic social institution of mankind, which, in his opinion, gave rise to other social forms ("Religion has given birth to all that is essential in society"). It is religion that has given mankind the strongest sense of collective consciousness, while constituting the heart and soul of every social group. In his opinion, religion unites people, in particular, in matters that elude empiricism and rationality.[49]

The argument that religion performs a function integrating the social system was called into question by, among others, Niklas Luhmann (1927–1998), who pointed out that there are religious movements capable of disintegrating the social system.[50]

---

87 Kapitalismus (1904–05; 1920)", in H. P. Müller, S. Sigmund (eds.), *Max Weber-Handbuch*... pp. 294 et seq.

48 E. Durkheim, *Les Formes élémentaires de la vie religieuse. Le système totémique en Australie*, Paris 2003, p. 65.

49 I. Borowik, "Religia..., pp. 56 et seq.; J. Dobieszewski, *Filozofia*..., pp. 64 et seq.; H. G. Kippenberg, "Emile Durkheim (1858–1917)", in A. Michaels (ed.), *Klassiker*..., pp. 103 et seq.; I. Strenski, *Thinking About Religion: A Reader*... pp. 195 et seq.; B. Olszewska-Dyoniziak, *Człowiek – kultura – osobowość. Wstęp do klasycznej antropologii kulturowej*, Wrocław 2001, pp. 39 et seq.; J. Terrier, "Emile Durkheim: *Les Formes élémentaires de la vie religieuse* [Die elementaren Formen des religiösen Lebens] (1912)", in Ch. Gärtner, G. Pickel (eds.), *Schlüsselwerke*..., pp. 121 et seq.; J. Waardenburg, *Classical*..., pp. 295 et seq.

50 N. Luhmann, *Funktion der Religion*, Frankfurt am Main 1982, pp. 10 et seq. and 246 et seq. and D. Pollack, "Niklas Luhmann: Funktion der Religion (1977)", in Ch. Gärtner, G. Pickel (eds.), *Schlüsselwerke*..., pp. 323 et seq.

Durkheim's views met with criticism also from Bronisław Malinowski (1884–1942). Among other things, he alleged that in the French sociologist's conception "society is admittedly the source of religion and the cause of holiness, but it is *the cause in a sense that the collective subject* (...) *invents and creates religious ideas*, recalling G. F. Hegel's Absolute, which *invents itself*". In his opinion, it is incorrect to see the origin of all religious phenomena in the manifestations of the crowd because it narrows the perception of the forms of social impact on religion and the sources from which man can draw his religious inspiration.[51] Moreover, he argued that the strongest religious experiences take place in solitude, concentration and focus, away from the world and the crowd. Consequently, religion does not have only a social dimension. It is no different from any other form of human activity – man takes it in a ready-made form from his or her surroundings.[52] Malinowski held that religious beliefs satisfy human needs, including psychological ones. Humans will place trust in religion when they have little control over the circumstances. They do not turn to supernatural forces in a situation where they can rely on they own skills or knowledge. Religion thus fills a gap in human life, creating a sense of control and comfort. It does not arise from speculation, reflection or illusion, but from the real tragedies of human life and the conflict between human plans and reality.[53]

Religious studies seek to identify the functions of religion. First, it is assigned a soteriological function – it is a means of achieving salvation.[54] This function is based on the assumption that religion is not limited to faith in the existence of transcendental reality, it enables a person to obtain life after death but through a relationship with supernatural forces.[55] Religion offers a release from sin, guilt, all evil and suffering. It gives man "existential certainty",[56] that is, a belief that there

51 B. Malinowski, "E. Durkheim, Les formes élementaires de la vie religiuse", *Folklore*, vol. 24, no. 4, 1913, pp. 525 et seq.; B. Malinowski, *Wierzenia pierwotne i formy ustroju społecznego. Pogląd na genezę religii ze szczególnem uwzględnieniem totemizmu*, Kraków 1915, pp. 311 et seq.

52 B. Malinowski, *Magic, Science and Religion and Other Essays. Selected and with an Introduction by Robert Redfield*, Boston – Glencoe 1948, pp. 37 et seq.

53 B. Malinowski, *Magic…*, pp. 8 et seq. See also: S. Gülker, "Bronisław Malinowski: Magic, Science and Religion (1925)", in Ch. Gärtner, G. Pickel (eds.), *Schlüsselwerke…*, pp. 159 et seq.; F. Stolz, "Bronislaw Kaspar Malinowski (1884–1942)", in A. Michaels (ed.), *Klassiker…*, pp. 247 et seq.; J. Waardenburg, *Classical…*, pp. 537 et seq.

54 M. J. Yinger, *Religion, Society and the Individual*, New York, 1957, pp. 60 et seq.

55 A. Bronk, "Religia"…, p. 400.

56 C. G. Ellison, "Religious involvement and subjective well-being", *Journal of Health and Social Behaviour*, vol. 32, no. 1, 1991, pp. 80 et seq. and M. J. Yinger, *Religion…*, pp. 60 et seq.

is "something" after death and it is worth striving for. In psychological terms, religion has a motivational function – it urges humans to undertake personal development, overcome existential fears, find the meaning of life.[57] This function tends to be called therapeutic in the sense of support in discovering the meaning of existence, especially in dramatic situations.[58] In sociological terms, religion performs the function of cultural and social identification. It satisfies a person's need to belong to a collective, including a community of followers, while through contact with other people, it quenches the desire for a sense of closeness.[59] There are studies confirming that a relationship with God provides humans with an analogous experience of support that exists in interpersonal relationships.[60] In the opinion of the American sociologist John Milton Yinger (1916–2011), religion can perform an integrative function (of a community, nation) depending on the satisfaction of the following minimum conditions: 1. presence of more than one religion in a community; 2. a situation where the expectations of members of a given religion have been thwarted; 3. the occurrence of social transformations that reduce the attraction of the system of religious beliefs and practices; 4. a situation where territorial mobility exceeding the limits of one community is high and a society consists of members accustomed to completely different patterns of behaviour; 5. a society is highly diversified in terms of class or hierarchy and its members perceive it as an oppressive fact; 6. outside influences divide a society.[61]

In sociological terms, religion also has a sanctioning function – it authorizes social standards and institutions and they do not necessarily have to be assessed as "good" today (slavery, caste-based division of society, human sacrifice).[62] In terms of political sciences, religion legitimizes and de/stabilizes the secular authorities. As regards the ethical level, it has a legalistic function because it defines the moral rules and principles of ethos.[63] The legalistic function is occasionally split into two: politically-ideological and educational. The former means that religion's key task is to defend and create a certain order and social order and model the behaviour of individuals in accordance with a religious

57 A. Bronk, "Religia"..., p. 401.

58 M. Wnuk, J. T. Marcinkowski, "Psychologiczne funkcje religii", *Problemy Higieny i Epidemiologii*, vol. 93, no. 1, 2012, pp. 239 et seq.

59 A. Bronk, "Religia"..., p. 401.

60 L. Kirkpatrick, "An attachment theory approach to the psychology of religion", *International Journal for the Psychology of Religion*, vol. 2, no. 1, 1992, pp. 3 et seq.

61 M. J. Yinger, *Religion*..., pp. 60 et seq.

62 M. J. Yinger, *Religion*..., pp. 60 et seq.

63 A. Bronk, "Religia"..., p. 401.

doctrine. The latter emphasizes the implementation of a system obligations and prohibitions, ethical and moral canons and the formation of the personality of an individual in accordance with a religious doctrine (according to an accepted pattern resulting from a specific vision of the world and the destiny of man).[64] Religion also has a culture-forming function – it motivates and inspires activity in the area of philosophy and broadly understood art and science.[65]

As William James (1842–1910) argued,[66] there are two aspects of religion: institutional and personal. The former has been described above, as it includes worship, theology and the church organization with its rituals. Personal religion reflects an inner disposition that prompts one to an individual prayer outside the ritual. James treated religious experiences as feelings, acts and experiences of particular persons in their solitude, as long as they understand they stand in relation to whatever they may consider divine.[67]

The reasons why an individual is or is not religious are very different. Most often, they are linked to one's life history and environmental conditions, including whether an individual was raised in a particular religious tradition, which one (consciously or not) accepted or rejected as a result of one's own experiences.[68]

A person's individual belief is one thing, a religious system is quite another. Everyone has some opinion on transcendence, which implicitly does not translate into any religious system. Whether it does will depend on self-identification with a given belief system.

Important answers on the individual aspects of religion were provided by two prominent physicians. Sigmunt Freud (1856–1939) was the first to propose a psychoanalytical interpretation of religion. In his work *The Future of an Illusion*,[69] among the moral values (protecting a civilization from destructive tendencies of individuals that form it), he included religious ideas, recognizing them (along with the psychological order and cultural ideals) as the most important values of

---

64 H. Swienko, "Źródła i funkcje religii", *Euhemer*, nos. 3–4, 1986, pp. 43 et seq.

65 A. Bronk, "Religia"..., p. 401.

66 W. James, *The varieties of religious experience: A study of human nature being the Gifford lectures on natural religion delivered at Edinburgh in 1901–1902*, New York 1958, p. 32.

67 S. Demmrich, U. Wolfradt, *William James: The Varieties of Religious Experience (1902)*, in Ch. Gärtner, G. Pickel (eds.), *Schlüsselwerke...*, pp. 83 et seq.; A. R. Fuller, *Psychology and Religion. Eight Points of View*, Lanham – London 1994, pp. 10 et seq.; J. Waardenburg, *Classical...*, pp. 181 et seq.; A. Locatelli, "Emotions..., pp. 77 et seq.

68 A. Bronk, "Religia"..., p. 396.

69 S. Freud, *Die Zukunft einer Illusion*, Wien – Zürich 1927.

their kind. He associated the concept of 'religion' exclusively with Christianity in its forms and practices found in Western Europe. He held the opinion that these ideas are based on unverifiable grounds and, despite their strong influence, are only illusions, though they are the fulfilment of humanity's deepest and most powerful wishes. He did not take a position on the veracity (or non-veracity) of religious doctrines. In the above-quoted work *The Future of an Illusion*, he showed that the idea of God is formed on a secular basis and is anchored in individual psychology. He referred to the notion of "the baby's helplessness" as a fear-causing factor. Human suffering, especially in the face of death, is identical to the physical and mental helplessness of a young child, fearing the loss of loved ones. Like a little child, an individual seeks help first from his mother and then from his father. Thus, the idea of God is patterned both on the state of helplessness of a little child and the relation with the father.[70] Religion stems from the feeling of guilt experienced by a son attempting to substitute his father. Moreover, in Freud's opinion, humans, as – on the whole – unhappy beings, try to escape their own misery by involvement in religious rituals. On a personal level, religion allows individuals to manifest religious precepts, simultaneously keeping their potentially incompatible internal intentions hidden.[71]

At the opposite extreme are the observations made by Carl Gustaw Jung (1875–1961).[72] Based on his own experiences and conducted analyses, he came to the conclusion that life must have some spiritual meaning that goes beyond the material realm. Thus, in his opinion, religion is a primal, archetypal manifestation of the collective unconsciousness. He also pointed out that religion facilitates personality development and individualization is the path to the self, and thus the path to divinity in man (the way to God).[73]

In the time of no spiritual stability, a human being needs a sense of heading in the right direction and spiritual experiences can contribute significantly to it, having a positive effect on the psyche.[74] In contrast to Freud, Jung accepted

---

70 J. M. Quinodoz, *Sigmund Freud. An Introduction*, London – New York 2018, pp. 89 et seq.

71 A. R. Fuller, *Psychology…*, pp. 35 et seq.; P. M. Kavros, "Religion"…, p. 1494; A. Locatelli, "Emotions…, pp. 77 et seq.; I. Strenski, *Thinking About Religion: A Reader…*, pp. 155 et seq.; J. Waardenburg, *Classical…*, pp. 354 et seq.; H. Zinser, "Sigmund Freud (1856–1939)", in A. Michaels (ed.), *Klassiker…*, pp. 90 et seq.

72 C. G. Jung, *Zur Psychologie westlicher und östlicher Religion*, Solothurn – Düsseldorf 1995.

73 E. Frick, B. Lautenschlager, *Auf Unendliches bezogen – Spirituelle Entdeckungen bei C. G. Jung*, München 2007, *passim*.

74 M. Stein, *Jung on Christianity*, Princeton 1999, pp. 277 et seq.

the transcendent, spiritual dimension in man, and this is what led him to the conviction that the spiritual experiences are necessary for a mental good state.[75] However, his analyses led him to believe that religious truths are sometimes empty and non-integrated. As a psychiatrist, he also concluded that the neurosis he studied was a state of war with oneself, which one can try to combat by using the Christian virtue of forgiveness.[76]

The above remarks clearly show that man is an indispensable part of every religion, regardless of its definition. Without a collective of individuals, religion becomes an empty set and loses all significance. There is no point in positioning God/deities in opposition to his/ their followers, because these two elements lose their meaning without each other, although they are located in different spheres (*sacrum – profanum*). Religion may have different meaning and importance for an individual depending, for example, on his or her stage of life and accidental events.

Meredith B. McGuire was correct in her view that there is no simple correlation between what a given group believes in and what an individual follower personally recognizes as crucial. An individual learns religious meanings and experiences a sense of personal and group identity through social interactions. However, one does not experience religion objectively but subjectively, being influenced by socially formed, learned meanings. Paradoxically, an individual's personal identity is profoundly social in nature because it is created based on continuous interactions with others, who – as is the case with parents, spouse or close friends – have a powerful, though partial, influence on the development of one's identity. At the same time, identity is not fixed – it changes when an individual takes on new roles or interacts with others. An individual is not born with religious beliefs, one's religious attitude develops, it is strengthened or weakened (ignored) in the course of the socialization process.[77]

It seems that the term 'religiosity' is a key concept in relation to individuals identifying themselves with a given religion because it includes their development or transformation. This term is understood as the arrangement of changes in the life of an individual, directed at building a higher quality relationship with God, which is expressed, among other things, by religious consciousness, feelings and

75 V. Crowley, *Jung: A Journey of Transformation: Exploring His Life and Experiencing His Ideas*, Wheaton 2000, *passim*; A. R. Fuller, *Psychology…*, pp. 71 et seq.; C. Morgenthaler, "Carl Gustav Jung (1875–1961)", in A. Michaels (ed.), *Klassiker…*, pp. 234 et seq.; J. Waardenburg, *Classical…*, pp. 519 et seq.

76 P. M. Kavros, "Religion"…, p. 1495.

77 M. B. McGuire, *Religion…*, pp. 51 et seq.

practices and a bond with the community of believers.[78] It is also defined as the manifestation of the full practical or spiritual effects of religion.[79]

Childhood is a fundamental period in the development of an individual's religion. At that time, a child is part of society, as it were, through the family, taking part in it only partially. The family home is also a religious or *quasi*-religious place, where religious practices (prayers before meals) or even paraliturgical practices (sharing a wafer on Christmas Eve in Poland) take place. It is assumed that every cohesive family expresses, but does not create, its unity through rituals and symbols, which in most cultures are frequently fundamentally religious. During childhood, the internalization of the moral norms and basic values of the group to which a child belongs occurs. Becoming a religious person is typically part of a broader process of becoming an adult, which is particularly strong in simple societies, which do not separate religious roles from other roles. By contrast, complex societies attach far greater importance to the intellectual sphere and mastering religious knowledge. At the same time, the distinction between religious knowledge and other important formal knowledge complicates a child's acquisition of religious knowledge.[80]

The family, neighbourhood, a religious or ethnic community provide the first sense of belonging and the basis for the emergence of identity. As Peter Berger (1929–2017) argued, the two aspects of religion, that is, providing meaning and a sense of belonging, are strictly interconnected. As they move out of their small communities, individuals encounter a diversity of other groups and social arrangements, including those that follow different belief systems and espouse a different way of life. In that case, pluralism means the co-existence of competing worldviews. Meanwhile, some individuals persist in the initial network that supported the credibility of their early beliefs and identities. Others break the bond and look for a social basis for their beliefs and who they are elsewhere. The possibility of breaking away from beliefs previously taken for granted and social

---

78 C. Walesa, "Religijności rozwój", in T. Gadacz, B. Milerski (eds.), *Religia. Encyklopedia PWN. Parys – Rut. Tom 8…*, pp. 423 et seq.

79 P. M. Kavros, "Religious", in D. A. Lemming (ed.), *Encyclopedia of Psychology…*, pp. 1509 et seq.

80 M. B. McGuire, *Religion…*, pp. 53 et seq. See also: M. M. Abo-Zena, A. Midgett, "Developmental Implications of Children's Early Religious and Spiritual Experiences in Context: A Sociocultural Perspective", *Religions*, vol. 10, no. 11, 2019, pp. 1 et seq.; L. D. Pearce, "The Influence of Early Life Course Religious Exposure on Young Adults' Dispositions Toward Childbearing", *Journal for the Scientific Study of Religion*, vol. 41, no. 2, 2002, pp. 352 et seq.

groups one was socialized into offers great freedom and, at the same time, makes beliefs and identity problematic for the individual.[81]

The periodization of religiosity tends to be divided into different stages. No consensus exists over their number and the precise age limits when they occur. The periods of religiosity of a child, an adolescent and an adult are most often discussed. The above division, proposed by Czesław Walesa (1934–2024) and developed by his co-workers, is largely based on the Roman Catholic perspective, the assumption of upbringing and remaining in a family that genuinely follows a given religion, and the exclusion of the negative social and psychological aspects that religion entails, including the phenomenon of converting to another denomination. Despite these reservations, the findings made by these researchers are referred to below because of their importance from the perspective of the survey we conducted. We are aware that this periodization formula may draw numerous objections, for example, that it describes an ideal state in which a person identifies with a particular religion and persists in it from birth until death. The description makes no mention of events inhibiting the development of that religiosity. It is understandable because if religion is abandoned, religiosity does not develop and the further stages do not occur.

The period of *quasi*-religious behaviour is chronologically the first distinguishable period of a child's religiosity (approximately between the ages of 8 and 15 months). It takes the form of incipient forms of capturing meanings and using typically religious words (*Amen*, *Hallelujah*), vocal and movement expression, including the adoption of a religious posture, or joining in the religious behaviour of adults, or becoming active in behaviour similar to play but tinged with religion. Behaviour of that type is an opportunity for a child to open up to religious reality. The period of first manifestations of appropriate religiosity runs between 2 and 3 years of age. At that time the child may already show the basic forms of religious understanding, knowledge and orientation and develop syncretic concepts for God, prayer, or objects for religious worship. On occasion, the child may gain an understanding of God's attributes (goodness, omnipotence). The child's religious awareness may manifest itself in simple questions, which, if formulated, indicate the need to receive answers adequate in content and form. The child's initiation of religious behaviour has complex causes, from self-serving (egoistic) to selfless (altruistic). At that time the child may show a basic understanding of evil and good deeds, and therefore may want to apologize to

81 P. L. Berger, *The Sacred Canopy: Elements of a Sociological Theory of Religion*, Garden City 1967, pp. 81 et seq. and 155 et seq.

God, thank him, or ask him for something. Moreover, a relationship being formed with God or a community of his followers may be evidenced by acting out or imitating liturgical or thematic scenes (e.g., building altars, church).[82] Between 3 and 6 years of age, the child enters a so-called period of magical religiosity.[83] The religious awareness of the child at the kindergarten age may manifest itself in deep religious feelings, such as, for example, compassion, love, trust, fear, sadness, grief, forgiveness. It is a time when the child's bond with co-believers is established through the family, especially by participating in family celebrations, including those of a religious nature, and performing religious practices at home (private worship) and in a community (public worship). Such practices tend to be purely imitative and ritualistic, but if they occur, they can reveal the child's great seriousness and commitment. The most frequent religious practices during that period include a prayer (especially for one's own health or that of others) – at that stage a child prays spontaneously, in his or her own words and adequately to the situation at hand. In the indicated age bracket, the child's religious morality takes shape, with its criteria for the rightness or wrongness of acts and the motives for committing them determined by the child's relationship to God. Between 5 and 6 years of age, the child acquires awareness of the fact that some transgressions qualify under the religious category of sin, which is a form of offending God and defying his expectations.[84] The so-called authoritarian-legal religiosity is the child's last religious periodization stage (between 7 and 11 years of age).[85] By then, the child's system of religious awareness may be formed and coherent. His or her religious feelings become increasingly diverse and, at the same time, integrated. This is also when the child begins to discern the contradictions and inconsistencies inherent in the system. The first conscious doubts of religious nature may also appear at the time, but religious decisions taken by the child still result from an attitude of trust and confidence in God. The child also gains independence in the area of undertaking religious practices, including practices performed in specific confessional groups (e.g., in the Roman Catholic Church, boys apply to the community of the liturgical altar service, intending to be an altar server). The child's religious practices from about 9 years of age very frequently arise from a belief in the formation of an authentic relationship with

82 C. Walesa, "Religijności…, pp. 423 et seq. and C. Walesa, *Rozwój religijności człowieka. Tom I. Dziecko*, Lublin 2005, pp. 137 et seq.

83 C. Walesa, *Rozwój religijności człowieka. Tom I…*, pp. 173 et seq.

84 C. Walesa, "Religijności…, p. 424.

85 C. Walesa, *Rozwój religijności człowieka. Tom I…*, pp. 221 et seq.

God and a sense of personal relationship with him. During that period religious commandments and the first contact with religious doctrine and dogma emerge as criteria for assessing one's own and other people's behaviour. The awareness of wrongdoing is anchored not so much in the intrinsic nature of an act itself, but in the authority of God and his religion.[86]

The adoption of one's own identity (different from that of the child, which is defined by family and community values) frequently takes the form of religious rebellion. A growing-up individual attempts to gain an adult identity by negating the aspects of life seen as symbolic of the childhood self and the bond with the parents or family. A clear example of such rebellion is joining a religious group totally opposed to the childhood religion or the adoption of a hyper-religious stance, while still adhering to the religion followed in childhood.[87]

Religiosity in adolescence is reduced to two periods. The first is autonomous religiosity – between 12 and 17 years of age. It is marked by the pursuit of full moral, intellectual and religious autonomy. A growing-up individual verifies and rejects some forms of personal authority (e.g., specific clergymen, theologians) or institutional authority, negating, for example, the need for religious community structures, but also the teaching authority (church) of the religious association in which he or she grew up. The religious life principles are accepted as one's own, re-formulated, or entirely rejected. Religion is no longer an end in itself. The instrumental and adaptive treatment of religion can be either reinforced or eliminated depending on various circumstances, including whether they are temporary or permanent. In the case of theistic religions, the picture of God is freed from sentimental and anthropomorphic elements. The ethical and doctrinal principles may be compared with the more intimate and personal aspects of an individual's life. Since approximately 16 year of age, idealism begins to take shape, especially generating the creation of models (such as the ideal marriage), but also expressed in the search for the meaning of life, suffering or death. The second religiosity period is the so-called authentic religiosity time (between 18 and 24 years of age). This is when a worldview and an ideological attitude towards religious practices are formed. During that period intransigence and radicalism of action, which in the case of proselytism is marked by openness and spontaneity, may emerge. Finding solutions to one's own (internal) religious conflicts of an intellectual, emotional and motivational nature during that period typically enhances religious authenticity. A failure to find a convincing

86 C. Walesa, "Religijności…, p. 425.
87 M. B. McGuire, *Religion…*, pp. 63 et seq.

answer to crucial questions leads to the weakening of religiosity or its complete disappearance.[88]

Inevitably, an adult's religiosity is determined by social institutions such as marriage and family and, consequently, procreation, sexual activity, and child-rearing and educational activities in relation to the offspring. While there is no clear event that confirms the acquisition of adult status in the case of a male (puberty only means the end of biological childhood, but it can be separated from social adulthood by many years), in the case of women, marriage represents entry into full adulthood. The impact of religion on marriage most frequently consists of 4 areas of social control: 1. the possibility of entering into marriage with a person from outside the religious group (exogamy) or not (endogamy); 2. regulation of sexual standards (e.g., prohibition on engaging in contacts before and during marriage with a person other than the spouse, prohibition on homosexual contacts, prohibition on engaging in unusual sexual practices); 3. regulation of the possibility or no possibility of dissolving marriage; 4. the reproduction issue (including the right to have biological and non-biological offspring; the number of offspring and the exclusion of the possibility of having offspring; there are proven correlations between religious affiliation and fertility).[89] Religion is no guarantee of happy marital and family life. It is connected, for example, with the toleration of violence in the family – against the spouse and children.[90] Some religious groups recommend the infliction of corporal punishment on children if it is aimed at breaking their will and making them conform to confessional

88 C. Walesa, "Religijności..., p. 426 and C. Walesa, M. Tatala, *Rozwój religijności człowieka. Tom II. Młodzież*, Lublin 2020, pp. 7 et seq.

89 M. B. McGuire, *Religion...*, pp. 64 et seq.

90 J. W. Black, "Sex, Abortion, Domestic Violence and Other Unmentionables: Orthodox Christian Youth in Kenya and Windows into Their Attitudes about Sex", *Religions*, vol. 8, no. 5, 2017, pp. 1 et seq.; C. G. Ellison, J. P. Bartkowski, K. L. Anderson, "Are There Religious Variations in Domestic Violence?", *Journal of Family Issue*, vol. 20, no. 1, 1999, pp. 87 et seq.; M. Pepper, R. Powell, "Domestic and Family Violence: Responses and Approaches across the Australian Churches", *Religions*, vol. 13, no. 3, 2022, pp. 1 et seq.; M. Truong, M. Sharif, A. Olsen, D. Pasalich, B. Calabria, N. Priest, "Attitudes and beliefs about family and domestic violence in faith-based communities: An exploratory qualitative study", *Australian Journal of Social Issues*, vol. 54, no. 4, 2022, pp. 880 et seq.

standards.[91] These phenomena are characteristic of religions that accept the idea of obedience in hierarchical relationships.[92]

Mass culture has perpetuated the perception that religion is more important in the lives of elderly than young people, which is not necessarily confirmed by empirical studies.[93] Religious involvement or developed spirituality[94] fits well with the concept of so-called positive ageing,[95] has a good effect on the health of the elderly, produces a protective effect against disability and allows seniors to cope with depression or prevent it.[96] Religious practices allow elderly persons to build an important resilience resource and encourage social interaction.[97] Although health problems may limit participation in public worship, the frequency of private forms of practicing religion does not decrease. Old age is a period in

---

91 G. Barton, I. Yilmaz, N. Morieson, "Religious and Pro-Violence Populism in Indonesia: The Rise and Fall of a Far-Right Islamist Civilisationist Movement", *Religions*, vol. 12, no. 6, 2021, pp. 1 et seq.

92 M. Pepper, R. Powell, T. McEwan, "The Impact of Marriage Norms and Gender on Anglican Clergy Actions in Response to Domestic Violence", *Religions*, vol. 14, no. 6, 2023, pp. 1 et seq.

93 G. Davie, J. Vincent, "Religion and old age", *Aging & Society*, vol. 18, no. 1, 1998, pp. 101 et seq. and M. B. McGuire, *Religion…*, pp. 69 et seq.

94 L. Lepherd, C. Rogers, R. Egan, H. Towler, C. Graham, A. Nagle, I. Hampton, "Exploring spirituality with older people: (1) rich experiences", *Journal of Religion, Spirituality & Aging*, vol. 32, no. 4, 2020, pp. 306 et seq. and L. Lepherd, C. Rogers, R. Egan, H. Towler, C. Graham, A. Nagle, I. Hampton, "Exploring Spirituality With Older People: (2) A rigorous process", *Journal of Religion, Spirituality & Aging*, vol. 32, no. 3, 2020, pp. 288 et seq.; D. O. Moberg, "Research in Spirituality, Religion, and Aging", *Journal of Gerontological Social Work*, vol. 45, no. 2, 2005, pp. 11 et seq.

95 J. Malone, A. Dadswell, "The Role of Religion, Spirituality and/or Belief in Positive Ageing for Older Adults", *Geriatrics (Basel)*, vol. 8, no. 3, 2018, pp. 1 et seq.

96 S.N Amir, N. Juliana, S. Azmani, et al., "Impact of Religious Activities on Quality of Life and Cognitive Function Among Elderly", *Journal of Religion and Health*, vol. 61, no. 2, 2022, pp. 1564 et seq.; E. L. Idler, S. V. Kasl, "Religion, Disability, Depression, and the Timing of Death", *American Journal of Sociology*, vol. 97, no. 4, 1992, pp. 1052 et seq.; K. J. Noronha, "Impact of Religion and Spirituality on Older Adulthood", *Journal of Religion, Spirituality & Aging*, vol. 27, no. 1, 2015, pp. 16 et seq.

97 D. E. Durón-Reyes, M. I. Mondragón-Cervantes, Y. C. Jiménez-Acosta, et al., "Religion, spirituality, and old age: A review of the literature", *The Journal of Latin America Geriatric Medicine*, vol. 5, no. 2, 2019, pp. 52 et seq. and M. Choczyński, "Religijność senioralna w kontekście dobrostanu społecznego", in I. Borowik, S. Grotowska, P. Stawiński (eds.), *Religia wobec wyzwań współczesności z perspektywy nauk społecznych*, Warszawa 2018, pp. 19 et seq.

which psychological, social and spiritual problems can come to the surface. These are associated with a sense of loss of meaning in life. The religiosity of elderly persons is largely a reflection of their social situation.[98] It may be affected by physical limitations, including, for example, the loss of ability to perform daily tasks, or financial issues.[99]

The religiosity of an adult consists of three periods. The period of realistic-stable religiosity (early adulthood from approximately 25 to 40 years of age) is a time of verification of earlier idealistic projections as they clash with the so-called 'reality of everyday life'. It grows in intensity when one takes up employment and starts a family. Raising one's own children combined with passing on the faith usually becomes a reason for revitalizing and solidifying personal religiosity, as is manifested by increased participation in religious practices.[100] The fulfilled religiosity period (mid-adulthood from approximately 40 to 60 years of age) is when the existing religious attitudes and practices are deepened, including, among other things, an everyday prayer, the adoption of radical doctrinal stances (love of one's enemies), full involvement in in the life of faith community. This attitude can be important for the transmission of religious beliefs among generations (between grandchildren and grandparents).[101] The religiosity of ageing man (late adulthood since approximately 60 years of age) is the final period. It is characterized by the use of the acquired wisdom of life, manifested in the attitudes of tolerance, understanding and kindness. Simultaneously, it is not without extraordinary events including, for example, changes in the current way of carrying out religious practices or making even more radical decisions than before (e.g., consent to the adoption of one of consecrated life forms – in the case of widow or widower). The religious individual is exposed to events normal to old age, such as severe or painful illness, terminal condition or, finally – death. The religious transcending processes offer a chance to overcome the occurring

---

98 A. B. Bakan, S. K. Arli, M. Yıldız, "Relationship Between Religious Orientation and Death Anxiety in Elderly Individuals", *Journal of Religion and Health*, vol. 58, no. 6, 2019, pp. 2241 et seq.

99 A. Abdi, A. Soufinia, M. Borji, A. Tarjoman, "The Effect of Religion Intervention on Life Satisfaction and Depression in Elderly with Heart Failure", *Journal of Religion and Health*, vol. 58, no. 3, 2019, pp. 823 et seq.

100 C. Walesa, "Psychologiczna problematyka człowieka dorosłego: struktura życia, droga życia i religijność", in C. Walesa, M. Tatala, E. Rydz, *Rozwój religijności człowieka. Tom III. Osoba dorosła*, Lublin 2023, pp. 13 et seq.

101 C. Walesa, "Psychologiczna…, pp. 17 et seq.

adversities and keep the faith, although it depends on an individual's earlier religious development and is highly individualized in nature.[102]

From the perspective of the conducted research, the psychological dimension of religion and religiosity assumes the greatest importance. After all, the importance of an individual approach to faith justifies religious rights and freedoms. This means that the focus here is on religion in a subjective sense, seen as man's subjective and individual response to the system of truths of faith, with the inclusion of his or her whole personality. The psychological analysis refers to the description and interpretation of religious experiences, a change in an individual's attitudes and convictions, not the supernatural reality.[103] The obtained results show that religiosity as *actus humanus* is a matter of choice. "The choice of sacred reality, as we know, proceeds in different ways: for some it is deep and connected with many layers of the psyche, while for others it touches only the margins of life. Parallel to one or another choice of God, a certain religious personality is formed. By religious personality we understand (...) a set of mental characteristics and behaviours characteristic of religious individuals."[104] It is important that a human religious act is affected by mental, social, cultural and even economic factors. The social environment, economic and cultural conditions shape the manifold forms of religious behaviour.[105]

Religion plays a specific role in the personality of the individual, performing a variety of (positive and negative) functions. In general terms, religion performs an integrative and guiding function in a believer's personality. Numerous detailed functions of religiosity are pointed out in the literature:

1. it gives meaning to life as a certain framework within which existence can be understood and interpreted; it explains the meaning of life, death and suffering; a religious point of view can allow one to find the hidden meaning of difficult situations or events often associated with suffering, which an individual cannot explain at a given moment. Religiosity uniquely 'puts in order' our relationship with the world, things, people, and our attitude to ourselves;

102 C. Walesa, "Psychologiczna…, pp. 26 et seq. and C. Walesa, "Religijności…, p. 427.

103 Z. Kulesz, "Religijność w perspektywie psychologicznej", *Studia Elbląskie*, vol. 14, 2013, p. 186.

104 J. Makselon, *Psychologia dla teologów*, Kraków 1990, p. 263 quoted after – Z. Kulesz, "Religijność…, p. 190.

105 Z. Kulesz, "Religijność…, p. 190.

2. it perpetuates the value system (in particular moral values), provides criteria for choosing particular behaviour, setting the direction of aspiration;
3. it satisfies the needs of security and trust by, among other things, providing belief in the indestructibility of human existence; it forms the basis for mental balance;
4. it allows for self-identification (self-determination), which leads to self-understanding and finding one's place in the universe;
5. it offers identification with a group, providing deep human ties often based on multi-generational traditions;
6. it performs an auto-psychotherapeutic function, removing sources of tension, giving meaning to human life; religion "restores mental equilibrium through penance practices and turns a person back from the path of deviating from the community"; thus a reference to a well-known sentence by C. G. Jung, who concluded based on his 30-year psychotherapeutic practice that "none of them has really been healed who did not regain his religious outlook."[106]

The literature mentions another key function of religion – service in the formation of hope, pointing out that hope is a multidimensional force of life, providing a guarantee for the achievement of the good that is obtainable and personally significant. Importantly, hope is reflected in the sphere of thoughts, feelings, behaviour and relations with other persons.[107]

Finally, a view is expressed that "a mature religious life brings great benefits to a person's normal functioning. Belief in a personal God gives ultimate meaning to life, answers the philosophical and theological questions we ask ourselves in life. Finding God and befriending Him ennobles a person and introduces the believer to deep mental and spiritual experiences. Very often, religious life motivates creative action, altruistic attitudes towards others, bringing peace and joy into a person's life."[108]

It is hardly surprising that Jan Dezyderiusz Pol asked whether religion is necessarily needed in prison. In response, that author himself acknowledged that religion fits naturally into the system of legal solutions and the practice

---

106 Z. Kulesz, "Religijność…, pp. 194 et seq. and the monograph he mentioned – C. G. Jung, *Modern Man In Research of a Soul*, New York 1993, p. 264.

107 W. Wnuk, J. T. Marcinkowski, "Psychologiczne funkcje religii", *Problemy Higieny i Epidemiologii*, vol. 93, no. 1, 2012, p. 242.

108 F. Głód, "Życie religijne jako pryncypialna wartość człowieka", *Perspectiva. Legnickie Studia Teologiczno-Historyczne*, vol. 10, no. 1, 2011, pp. 102 et seq.

of rehabilitation efforts,[109] although it should be clearly pointed out that the Polish enforcement provisions do not mention religious impacting as one of penitentiary impacting measures. The previously discussed mental functions of religion take on special significance under conditions of deprivation of liberty. Religion gives man hope in difficult moments, helps overcome life's setbacks, gives meaning to a person's life in moments of downfall. Incarceration is surely a difficult situation when one may feel threatened and which gives rise to anxiety. To a believer, religious practices can restore the inner balance.[110] Pol was correct in his view that "the incorporating of religion and religious practices into the social context of penitentiary facilities provides an opportunity to correct a specific hierarchy of values and initiate changes in the personalities of persons deprived of their liberty. The inmate social structure specific to penitentiaries and prisons, legal regulations, and the solutions adopted in practice, provide a starting point for further initiatives in relation to individuals deprived of their liberty. The process of rehabilitation influences the formation of desirable personality traits in convicts and fosters their search for moral norms consistent not only with the teaching of the Church, but also with social criteria."[111] Another rehabilitative context was emphasized by Kazimierz Pierzchała. He pointed out that an incarcerated person is under the strong influence of a stigmatizing penalty. Religion combined with rehabilitation may initiate the destigmatization process even in prison conditions, which is to result from the evolution of a prisoner into a state of socially acceptable functioning. The researcher believes that the criminal's downfall in human terms simultaneously becomes a chance for an inner change and a change of life path.[112]

---

109 J. D. Pol, "Czy religia jest w więzieniu koniecznie potrzebna?", https://jandezyderiuszpol.pl/publication/view/czy-religia-jest-w-wiezieniu-potrzebna/ (accessed 21.08.2023). Moreover, S. Meler noted that in many penitentiary systems, forms of educational influence include the possibility of using religious services and cooperation with churches and religious organizations. See: S. Meler, "Prawo więźniów do wolności religijnej", *Przegląd Więziennictwa Polskiego*, vols. 38–39, 2003, p. 61.

110 John Paul II, "9 July 2000, Jubilee in Prisons", http://www.opoka.org.pl/biblioteka/W/WP/jan_pawel_ii/przemowienia/wiezienia_09072000.html (accessed 30.06.2016).

111 J. D. Pol, *Więzienna szansa*, Warszawa 2008, pp. 132 et seq.

112 K. Pierzchała, *Destygmatyzacja przestępców w świetle Magisterium Kościoła oraz poglądów na resocjalizację*, Kraków 2016, pp. 167 et seq. The author makes a reference to the memorable words by J. Sikorski: "penitentiary pastoral care seeks to achieve in the convict a threefold reconciliation: with God, with society and with

It is indicated in the literature that a high frequency of religious practices coexists with an increase in pro-social behaviour. First, highly religious prisoners are more disciplined, are less likely to commit crimes while serving their sentences and have fewer interpersonal conflicts both with other prisoners and the prison staff. Second, in contrast to prisoners with external religious motivation and non-believers, prisoners with high religious sensitivity tend to have a higher sense of guilt for the committed crime and a more positive attitude towards moral norms. Individuals participating in religious programmes significantly less often experience negative emotions in the form of anger, bitterness and emotional coldness. Third, studies on the relationship between religiosity and cognitive functioning showed that high spiritual formation co-occurs with high levels of self-efficacy and objectives focused on putting into effect the values arising from the Decalogue.[113]

Specific data illustrating the beneficial impact of religious education during the execution of prison sentences have also been presented. According to an estimate, over 52 thousand individuals in 49 countries all over the world participated in *Alpha* courses[114] in 907 prisons in 2017. Unfortunately, these figures are under-reported because many organizers do not report their courses to the *Alpha* national offices. Studies show that 89 % of prisoners replied that the course had a positive impact on their life and 94 % recommended it to others. According to HM Prison Service statistics in Great Britain, among the prisoners that participated in an *Alpha* course (they are organized in more than half the

---

oneself" – J. Sikorski, "Duszpasterstwo więzienne", in M. Chmielewski (ed.), *Kościół w Polsce wobec potrzebujących*, Lublin 1994, p. 208.

113 I. Niewiadomska, "Polski model resocjalizacji więziennej", *Teka Komisji Prawniczej PAN Oddział w Lublinie*, vol. 9, 2016, pp. 115 et seq. The author indicates that an increasing trend to integrate prison ministry can be observed today. This can be exemplified by an American programme Inner Change Freedom Initiative, implemented in Texas penitentiaries. It aims to create an environment in prison for the spiritual transformation of prisoners and to rebuild their ties with society, in particular with their families. The programme's idea is implemented through Bible education, spiritual direction, organizing leisure activities, teaching conduct in accordance with Christian principles and forming skills to cope with life problems – see the study referred to by the author – C. McDaniel, D. Davis, S. Neff, "Charitable Choice and Prison Ministries: Constitutional and Institutional Challenges to Rehabilitating the American Penal System", *Criminal Justice Policy Review*, vol. 16, no. 2, 2005, p. 169.

114 See: https://alpha.org/ (accessed 20.09.2023).

prisons in GB) and got involved in Church life after release, the recidivism rate dropped from 70 % to 17 %.[115]

Regardless of the beneficial impact of religion on shaping the prisoner, religion and, more precisely, the right to profess and practice it, is the right of every human being and should therefore be respected and observed. It is not possible to accept uncritically the view expressed by Wiesław Romanowicz and Dorota Tomczyszyn that "The primary purpose of the functioning of religion in the entire penitentiary system is to stimulate convicted or detained persons to change their lifestyles and show a pro-social axiological system. This is an important task and, at the same time, one of the basic forms of exerting an impact on prisoners."[116]

In summary of the above preliminary remarks, as Janusz Dobieszewski correctly observes, the frequency of the occurrence of the "re" prefix to some extent suggests that the prior experience of exclusion, breakdown, loss of something primary, accompanied by a sense of loss or even sin, is the necessary prerequisite for religion. Subsequently, an attempt is made to rebuild the lost connectivity and order. This occurs by means of reference to the divine, which, in addition to bringing solace, carries mystery and never fully removes the fear of losing the connection with the 'ordinary', 'output' world. Religiosity results from man's struggle with himself and with the world and does not bring him complete solace. Religion is not a radical alternative excluding the world but an attempt to approach it in a new way, reinterpret and reintegrate it.[117]

The argument on the imminent end of religion advanced in one form or another in different historical times has not come true and is unlikely ever to become a reality. By contrast, the optimistic argument on the lack of radical secularization of the whole world[118] currently does not seem fully tenable. Even if one consciously removes it from the focus of analysis, the phenomenon of *fuzzy fidelity*, which refers to the concept of secularization examined and described by the American demographer and sociologist David Voas, cannot be ignored. The phenomenon relates to individuals who retain some fidelity to the denominational tradition, while showing marginal religious commitment. They do not go to church regularly, yet they are not consciously non-religious. They believe

115 See: https://www.gosc.pl/doc/8193214.Kursy-Alpha-za-kratami-Wchodzisz-do-wiezienia-o-zaostrzonym (accessed 20.08.20203).

116 W. Romanowicz, D. Tomczyszyn, "Stosunek..., p. 95.

117 J. Dobieszewski, *Filozofia*..., pp. 24 et seq.

118 A. Bronk, *Podstawy*..., p. 45.

"there is something out there" (God or life after death), they declare to embrace Christian values and may want to identify with this religion; they continue to take an interest in and attend church weddings and funerals, Christmas services, or local celebrations (for example, harvest festival).[119] Although Europeans can still specify their religious background, name their place of birth, secondary school or their parents' professions, this does not mean that these issues have any significant impact on how they perceive themselves or how they are perceived by others. Many people who are seemingly non-religious will routinely choose a religious affiliation if asked to do so, depending on the context and the wording of the question. Such "face value" Christians occasionally made up more than half the population of most European states.[120]

The argument that "the 21st century will be religious (spiritual) or it will not be", attributed to the French intellectual Andre Malraux (1901–1976), does not, of course, encourage exploration of this research area. His assessment was reflected in the new term "apatheism" coined by Jonathan Rauch at the beginning of the new century, which is a combination of two words "apathy" and "theism" Behind this neologism is the view that God and religion are irrelevant to human life.[121] Malraux's projection has also partially materialized in empirical research, which has seen the emergence of a new category of persons described as *nones*, that is, individuals with no religious affiliation. In a global study carried out by Pew Research Center in 2012, covering 230 countries worldwide, they represented as much as 16.3 % of the analysed world population.[122] However, Pew Research Center pointed out that their number will decline in the world population, whereas by the middle of this century, Muslims will almost match (projected growth from 1.6 billion in 2010 to 2.76 billion in 2050) the size of

---

119 D. Voas, "The Rise and Fall of Fuzzy Fidelity in Europe", *European Sociological Review*, vol. 25, no. 2, 2009, pp. 155 et seq. and I. Puga-Gonzalez, D. Voas, Ł. Kiszkiel et al., "Modeling Fuzzy Fidelity: Using Microsimulation to Explore Age, Period, and Cohort Effects in Secularization", *Journal of Religion and Demography*, vol. 9, nos. 1–2, 2022, pp. 111 et seq.

120 D. Voas, "The Rise..., p. 162 and an unpublished doctoral dissertation cited by him – A. Day, *Believing in Belonging in Contemporary Britain: A Case Study from Yorkshire*, Lancaster University 2006.

121 See: https://www.theatlantic.com/magazine/archive/2003/05/let-it-be/302726/ (accessed 29.08.2023).

122 See: https://www.pewresearch.org/religion/2012/12/18/global-religious-landscape-exec/ (accessed 29.08.2023) and https://www.pewresearch.org/religion/2012/10/09/nones-on-the-rise/ (accessed 29.08.2023).

Christians, who are currently the world's largest religious group.[123] Apart from the *nones* category, attention has recently been drawn to "Christians without religion", that is, individuals excluded from a religious community due to their strong identification with the LGBTQ+ community. They want to become equal members of this religion again, entitled to practice faith on their own terms and in accordance with their sexual orientation.[124]

The picture of religion and religiosity reconstructed above, though disappointing, incomplete and possibly, partially selective and exclusionary, gives one sufficient legitimacy to verify this phenomenon empirically, especially through the legal optics, which, contrary to appearances, is not often done.

123 See: M. Lipka, "7 key changes in the global religious landscape", 2.04.2015, https://www.pewresearch.org/short-reads/2015/04/02/7-key-changes-in-the-global-religious-landscape/ (accessed 29.08.2023).

124 See: https://www.designalive.pl/strachy-o-bezreligijnym-chrzescijanstwe/ (accessed 20.09.2023); http://rycharski.artmuseum.pl/en/wprowadzenie (accessed 20.09.2023).

Chapter II Religious freedom of adults and children: a reconstruction of international and Polish standards

2.1. Significance of religious freedom

As there is no single, universal definition of religion accurately capturing its essence and the elements that comprise it, so there is no general understanding of religious freedom. Given that there is no broad consensus on what religious freedom is, discrepancies arise as to what it consists of and what its limits are.[125] The lack of a legal definition of 'religion' in normative instruments is understandable due to the complex nature of the phenomenon of religiosity.[126] Moreover, the imposition of any definitional framework may negatively affect the legal status of beneficiaries of that freedom due to the risk of leaving certain beliefs outside the scope of the subject matter.[127] This does not release states from the obligation to ensure religious freedom and set its limits in conflicting situations.[128] This means that the term "religion" or its synonym (e.g., belief, religious practices, etc.) must appear in regulations that set out the rights of a person (including those deprived of liberty).

All the actors creating (national and international legislatures), applying (courts) or analysing (doctrine) law link the specific meaning of the term 'religion' with a particular legal standard, most often using the criterion of functionality. Lawyers' remarks on the concept of 'religion' are typically not in-depth. In most

---

125 P. Szymaniec, *Koncepcje wolności religijnej. Rozwój historyczny i współczesny stan debaty w zachodniej myśli polityczno-prawnej*, Wrocław 2017, *passim*.

126 However, the urgency (especially by legal authorities which are responsible for applying the law) of the need to find an adequate definition increases as religious faith becomes increasingly individualized and transformed. See: J. Kříž, "Judicial search for a legal definition of religion", *Studia z Prawa Wyznaniowego*, vol. 26, 2023, p. 30.

127 M. Ożóg, "Noszenie chusty islamskiej w miejscu pracy a prawa i wolności innych podmiotów prawa", *Studia z Prawa Wyznaniowego*, vol. 17, 2017, p. 314.

128 Jakub Kříž points out that the stricter the prohibition of contact between secular and religious authorities, the narrower the definition of religion must be for this purpose. Otherwise, an untenable situation would arise in which many moral claims about the content of the legal order could be rejected on the grounds that they establish an unacceptable connection with religion. See: J. Kříž, "Judicial search…, p. 28.

cases, the essence of 'religion' is reconstructed based on language dictionaries, findings of representatives of non-legal scientific disciplines, especially religious scholars, theologians, philosophers, historians, anthropologists or sociologists of religion.[129]

An eclectic definition of religion', seeking to incorporate all the elements reconstructed so far, may be exemplified by a proposal by Ewa Schwierskott-Matheson: religion is "a set of beliefs relating to the origin and purpose of the existence of man and humanity and the world. This faith is expressed in certain rituals, rules of conduct or moral principles. However, both these elements are institutionalized in the church appropriate to that faith."[130]

In the opinion of Grzegorz Maroń, the over-inclusiveness of the definition of 'religion' may cause it to lose its ability to determine the designators of the described concept, which is its basic function. Ultimately, an apparently utilitarian definition does not make it possible to distinguish religion from non-religious worldviews, philosophical trends or ethical doctrines. In terms of law, it is not admissible to declare that "everything is religion". Such an argument might well be approved by representatives of other fields of knowledge, but it is inapplicable to law. The sanctioning of religion in its unspecified (amorphous) form is as destabilizing to the legal system as impoverishing legal concepts in general.[131] Despite the indicated doubts, Grzegorz Maroń ultimately favours the 'traditional' understanding of 'religion'. In his opinion, the transcendent element – God(s), the supernatural or *sacrum* is its constituting element.[132] At the same time, he accepts Rafał Paprzycki's view that religion must "refer to God, deities, or a differently conceived higher power, which is beyond the human mind, the possibilities of sensory cognition and also often understanding. It is on a different level than the natural, real world, and is related to supernatural forces, more powerful than man and unbound by human limitations resulting from nature."[133]

Problems arising from the interpretation of the term 'religion' can also be seen in court rulings and conclusive decisions of public administration bodies.

---

129 J. Kříž, "Judicial search…, pp. 12 et seq. and G. Maroń, "O pojmowaniu religii w polskim porządku prawnym", *Forum Prawnicze*, vol. 65, no. 3, 2021, pp. 37 et seq.

130 E. Schwierskott-Matheson, *Wolność sumienia i wyznania w wybranych państwach demokratycznych*, Regensburg 2012, p. 151.

131 G. Maroń, "O pojmowaniu…, pp. 44–46.

132 G. Maroń, "O pojmowaniu…, p. 52.

133 R. Paprzycki, *Prawna ochrona wolności sumienia i wyznania*, Warszawa 2015, pp. 3–4.

In order to apply a specific legal standard, these bodies are forced to accept a definition of 'religion'. They repeatedly face a need to determine whether some specific behaviour may indeed be seen as part of religious practice within a given religion, particularly whenever a party to the proceedings, claiming to be able to bring them, invokes religious freedom. The most common situations are when some specific behaviour is a deviation from the generally applicable laws. The religious nature of behaviour does not *eo ipso* prejudge the guarantee of legal protection for that behaviour but is the first step in the court consideration of whether it is the fulfilment of religious freedom.[134] Bodies applying law should not be guided solely by the meaning of religion proposed by the parties to the proceedings. The idiosyncratic understanding of religion based on the very sincerity of the beliefs of an addressee of law, is dangerous and can be unreliable.[135]

In essence, the state is not entitled to question the fact of religious affiliation. Except for cases of clear abuse of the right, a declaration submitted by an individual is decisive in that regard.[136] A dispute does not arise when a given religion is registered in a given state (provided that a registration system of religious associations is in place). Otherwise, the court should verify whether an individual behaviour is a form of the manifestation of worldview. Such a need will arise in the event of a collision with another freedom or right. However, a lack of transcendent element in a citizen's behaviour may not by itself place his worldview at a disadvantage compared to the behaviour of other citizens with an unambiguous religious background.

The results of the interpretation of understanding 'religion' may raise serious objections, as exemplified by the ruling of the Polish Supreme Administrative Court of 23 January 1998 on a refusal to register a church. The Court held that an organization that "does not include the existence of God as holiness (*sacrum*) in its statutes" cannot be registered as a religious association because "religion is a link between man and God, in other words, a relationship between man and holiness (*sacrum*)."[137] The ruling met with criticism from, among others,

---

134 G. Maroń, "O pojmowaniu…, p. 41.

135 J. Falski, "Dyskryminacja ze względu na religię w miejscu pracy w kontekście orzecznictwa Trybunału Sprawiedliwości Unii Europejskiej", *Przegląd Sejmowy*, vol. 151, no. 2, 2019, pp. 62 et seq. and G. Maroń, "O pojmowaniu…, pp. 41–47.

136 O. Sitarz, A. Jaworska-Wieloch, J. Hanc, "Obowiązek zgolenia brody? (Nie) uzasadnione naruszenie wolności uzewnętrzniania religii przez osoby pozbawione wolności (rozważania na tle wyroku Sądu Apelacyjnego w Krakowie z dnia 24 kwietnia 2018 r., I ACa 1217/17)", *Forum Prawnicze*, vol. 69, no. 1, 2022, pp. 46 et seq.

137 Judgement of the Supreme Administrative Court of 23 January 1998 r., I SA 1065/97, LEX no. 34411. Similarly, U.S. Supreme Court, *Davis v. Beason*, 133 U.S. 342 (1890).

Wojciech Brzozowski, who pointed out that a refusal to grant the status of 'religion' because of a lack of "the personal supernatural being" in its doctrine is an unacceptable violation of the Polish constitutional and international regulations, as it introduces the criterion of "the resemblance to traditional religions", which is unknown to those instruments, in the form of the presence of God in them.[138] The restrictive position of the court,[139] prejudging the authoritative understanding of the concept of 'religion', is a simple consequence of the court's adoption of a particular (narrow) understanding of religion.

Despite the above shortcomings, the process of reconstructing the elements of religious freedom is feasible. Philosophers and lawyers agree that the issue is religious freedom, not the right to religion/religiosity. Freedom is primary in nature – one is permitted to do anything that is not forbidden or ordered.[140] Therefore, it is not necessary to indicate what is permitted. In the case of freedom, it is necessary to define orders, prohibitions and sanctions for their violation.[141] Man is not free if he cannot make a choice. The more man is allowed to choose, the freer he feels, and the greater the number of objects he can choose, the greater the extent of his freedom.[142] In the case of the right "to", it is necessary to define precisely and specifically – to whom, what and under what conditions is to be given or from whom taken away.[143]

Among researchers in different disciplines, different terms are used for the same freedom and distinctions between the particular phrases are only occasionally introduced. Namely, reference is made to: *freedom of religion*

---

138 W. Brzozowski, *Bezstronność światopoglądowa władz publicznych w Konstytucji RP*, Warszawa 2011, p. 108. See also: J. Kříž, "Judicial search…, pp. 13 et seq.

139 P. Borecki, "Status prawny osób bezwyznaniowych w Polsce", *Państwo i Prawo*, no. 4, 2007, p. 19.

140 J. Kříž, "Judicial search…, pp. 15 et seq.

141 M. Granat, "Granice wolności religijnej w społeczeństwie pluralistycznym", in J. Krukowski, O. Theisen (eds.), *Kultura i prawo. Materiały II Międzynarodowej Konferencji na temat „Religia i wolność religijna w Unii Europejskiej"*, Lublin 2003, pp. 175 et seq.; L. Wiśniewski, "Prawo a wolność człowieka – pojęcie i konstrukcja prawna", in L. Wiśniewski (ed.), *Podstawowe prawa jednostki i ich sądowa ochrona*, Warszawa 1997, pp. 53 and 58; L. Wiśniewski, "Zakres ochrony prawnej wolności człowieka i warunki jej dopuszczalnych ograniczeń w praktyce", in L. Wiśniewski (ed.), *Wolności i prawa jednostki oraz ich gwarancje w praktyce*, Warszawa 2006, pp. 22 et seq.

142 A. Sharma, *Problematizing Religious Freedom*, Dordrecht – Heidelberg – London – New York 2011, p. 75.

143 L. Wiśniewski, "Prawo…, pp. 58 et seq. and L. Wiśniewski, "Zakres…, pp. 22 et seq.

(FOR), *freedom of religion and belief* (FORB), *religious freedom* (RF) and *religious liberty* (RL).

It should be noted in advance that numerous normative instruments and scientific works refer to this freedom in a triad with freedom of thought (German *Glaubensfreiheit*, also understood as freedom of belief) and freedom of conscience (German *Gewissensfreiheit*, denoting the individual human capacity to distinguish between good and evil). A convincing distinction between the individual freedoms runs into difficulties and does not yield fully satisfactory results.[144] In the opinion of some researchers, this dissonance does not affect the scope of monitoring compliance with these freedoms.[145] At times freedom of thought and conscience 'is mentioned in the same breath,'[146] on other occasions it is argued that freedoms of thought, conscience and *Bekenntnisfreiheit* (understood as "confession", "belief") are jointly referred to as *Religionsfreiheit*.[147] Given the above and a lack of legal definitions of the indicated terms, it is postulated that these concepts are read holistically,[148] viewing freedom of thought, conscience and religion as a certain cluster of concepts, more understandable as a comprehensive phrase (idiom) than when each element is separated and subjected to a separate analysis.[149]

At times freedom of religion (German *Religionsfreiheit*) is opposed to freedom of worldview (German *Weltanschauungsfreiheit*). It is assumed that all these freedoms: *Glaubens-*, *Gewissens-* and *Bekenntnis-* oscillate between religion (*Religion*) and worldview (*Weltanschauung*). An attempt has been made to place freedom of religion and freedom of worldview against a certain

---

144 B. Hordecki, "Struktura semantyczna pojęć *wolność sumienia i religii*, *wolność sumienia i wyznania* (część I)", *Środkowoeuropejskie Studia Polityczne*, no. 2, 2014, pp. 105 et seq. and B. Hordecki, "Struktura semantyczna pojęć *wolność sumienia i religii*, *wolność sumienia i wyznania* (część II)", *Środkowoeuropejskie Studia Polityczne*, no. 2, 2015, pp. 99 et seq.

145 G. Neureither, "Grundfälle zu Art. 4 I, II GG", *Juristische Schulung*, vol. 46, no. 12, 2006, p. 1068.

146 U. Di Fabio, "Art. 4 GG", in T. Maunz, G. Dürig (eds.), *Grundgesetz. Kommentar. Band I. Art. 1–5*, München 2022 (98. EL März 2022), margin nos. 1 and 47.

147 U. Di Fabio, "Art. 4 GG…, margin no. 41.

148 M. Germann, "Art. 4 GG", in V. Epping, Ch. Hillgruber (eds.), *BeckOK Grundgesetz*, München 2022, margin no. 19.

149 W. Sobczak, "Art. 18", in R. Wieruszewski (ed.), *Międzynarodowy pakt praw obywatelskich (osobistych) i politycznych. Komentarz*, Warszawa 2012, p. 430 and J. Szymanek, "Wolność sumienia i wyznania w Konstytucji RP", *Przegląd Sejmowy*, vol. 73, no. 2, 2006, p. 44.

contrast – religious ideas are transcendent, while worldview ideas are immanent. The former concept is saturated with the *sacrum* sphere (spiritual, religious, sacral), while the latter is secular (worldly). Such a solution, however, has only heuristic value.[150]

It has been argued that one can only speak of 'religion' when man derives his or her picture of the world, their deepest conviction about good and evil from a higher authority that is not fully cognizable and attainable by human reason. It is a system exceeding the forms of purely rational reasoning. By contrast, a worldview explains the world and the final issues without references to the supernatural realm.[151] Occasionally, a more nuanced approach is taken by indicating that it is necessary to differentiate between religion and worldview, on the one hand, and "pure" religion, seemingly religious practices and behaviour and, on the other, protected and unprotected worldview.[152]

Finally, a fairly acceptable conclusion is that the feature distinguishing these two groups of beliefs from others (e.g., aesthetic, moral or political) is their totality – they interpret the sense of the world as a certain whole.[153]

It is accepted nearly unanimously in terms of human rights that *religious liberty* **is a fundamental subjective right of every human being (first-generation right), which allows humans to express freely and publicly their personal and individual beliefs related to their religion.** *Religious liberty* goes well beyond the area of "ordinary" religious tolerance, which has historically been a permission (concession) to practice religions other than the one officially imposed and in force as the only religion in a given area.

There is no common consensus in the literature on whether behaviour authorized in atheism is also subject to protection under freedom of religion. On the one hand, it seems that this freedom applies also to non-believers, atheists and agnostics because everyone has the right to decide freely whether they believe in transcendent forces or not and whether they follow a religion or not.[154] On the other hand, attempts to qualify atheism as a religion lead to conceptual

150 M. Germann, "Art. 4 GG…, margin no. 13.

151 U. Di Fabio, "Art. 4 GG…, margin nos. 18, 43, 45, 62, 63, 70.

152 A. Wróbel, "Art. 10", in D. Miąsik, N. Półtorak, A. Wróbel (eds.), *Traktat o funkcjonowaniu Unii Europejskiej. Komentarz, T. 1. (art. 1–89)*, Warszawa 2012, p. 238.

153 M. Germann, "Art. 4 GG…, margin no. 14. Similarly, U.S. Supreme Court, *United States v. Seeger*, 380 U.S. 163 (1965).

154 J. Woleński, "Sfera publiczna, sfera prywatna i wolność religijna", *Acta Universitatis Wratislaviensis. Przegląd Prawa i Administracji*, no. 110, 2017, p. 207.

chaos in law.[155] Further, it is difficult to accept the concept that freedom of religion includes an unprotected non-religious worldview.[156] Consequently, atheism cannot be recognized as religion but it enjoys protection stemming from freedom of speech,[157] and, more broadly, from the freedom of belief, the right to self-determination and the right to privacy.

Modern democratic states guarantee religious freedom to all their people. However, the choice of a specific religion often arises from social customs that bind a particular collective to a particular religion(s). Historically, the political power (the state) and religious power (the church) have imposed limitations on the freedom. Then and now, parental authority has been a limitation of the freedom.[158]

Today, the value obtained from providing an individual with religious freedom is indisputable. It is pointed out that religious freedom contributes to social stability[159] and economic prosperity (the freedom increases people's interaction between religions, which reduces cultural barriers to trade and increases economic activity).[160] It may improve state security[161] and reduce the violence rate.[162]

The above contemporary observations are confirmed by past events. The number of adopted documents shows that religious aggression and persecution have not been a marginal phenomenon. The rich European history has seen many events aimed at ensuring religious tolerance and bringing peace between religions. Putting aside the almost mythical importance of the edict of Milan issued by Emperor Constantine the Great in 313, the first guarantees of religious freedom (mainly in favour of the Jewish community) began to appear in the 13th century.[163] For example, in Poland, reference can be made to the Statute of Kalisz

---

155 W. Janyga, *Przestępstwo obrazy uczuć religijnych w polskim prawie karnym w świetle współczesnego pojmowania wolności sumienia i wyznania*, Warszawa 2010, p. 39.

156 P. Borecki, "Wolność sumienia…, pp. 29 et seq. and P. Borecki, "Status prawny osób bezwyznaniowych w Polsce", *Państwo i Prawo*, no. 4, 2007, pp. 19 et seq.

157 B. Banaszak, *Konstytucja Rzeczypospolitej Polskiej. Komentarz*, Warszawa 2012, p. 326.

158 A. Sharma, *Problematizing…*, p. 74.

159 M. Glendon, "Making the case for religious freedom in secular societies", *Journal of Law and Religion*, vol. 33, no. 3, 2018, pp. 329 et seq.

160 A. Gill, *The political origins of religious liberty*, New York 2008, *passim*.

161 T. F. Farr, "Diplomacy in an age of faith: Religious freedom and national security", *Foreign Affairs*, vol. 87, no. 2, 2008, pp. 122 et seq.

162 N. Saiya, *Weapons of peace: How religious liberty combats terrorism*, New York 2019, *passim*.

163 E. Schwierskott-Matheson, *Wolność*…pp. 46 et seq.

issued by Duke Bolesław the Pious on 16 August 1264,[164] which subsequently came to be the basic normative act regulating the situation of Jews throughout the Kingdom of Poland and contributed to the formation of a partially autonomous Jewish community. The statute guaranteed Jews personal freedom and security, freedom of religion, travel and trade. The issuance of the document may be all the more surprising given that it was drawn up only 49 years after the end of the Lateran IV Council (1215), which contained two directly anti-Semitic provisions (Jews were required to wear special clothing and were barred from holding public office – canons 68 and 69[165]). Documents regulating the issues of religious freedom were produced in great abundance in the 16th century, which was surely connected with the Reformation and the schism of Western Christianity. The Peace of Augsburg of 25 September 1555 concluded between Emperor Charles V and the Protestant German princes established the well-known principle *cuius regio, eius religio* (whose realm, their religion), which has long marked the relationship between the ruler and the ruled.[166] The principle underwent some change only on 24 October 1648 in the provisions of the Peace of Westphalia, ending the Thirty Years' War, where it was accepted that in the event of the conversion of a German prince, which occurred after 1624, the subjects of that ruler retained their old religion.[167] In turn, not until 26 years after the St. Bartholomew's Day Massacre (23/24 August 1572) did the Kingdom of France see King Henry IV of Bourbon issue the Edict of Nantes on 30 April 1598. The edict ended the bloody religious wars, regulated the situation of the Huguenots and introduced freedom of religion and equality of Protestants in relation to Catholics.[168] Drawing on the German and French experiences, the Polish-Lithuanian Commonwealth adopted the Act of Warsaw Confederacy as early as 28 January 1573. The Polish-Lithuanian nobility agreed not to wage wars among themselves over religious differences and forbade the use of violence in

---

164 W. Kościelniak, K. Walczak, *Kronika miasta Kalisza*, Kalisz 2002, pp. 25 and 30.

165 N. P. Tanner (ed.), *Decrees of the Ecumenical Councils, Volume 1. Nicaea I to Lateran V*, London – Washington 2016, pp. 266 et seq.

166 A. Kohnle, "Augsburger Religionsfrieden 1555", in I. Dingel, M. Rohrschneider, I. Schmidt-Voges, S. Westphal, J. Whaley (eds.), *Handbuch Frieden im Europa der Frühen Neuzeit/ Handbook of Peace in Early Modern Europe*, Berlin – Boston 2021, pp. 837 et seq.

167 S. Westphal, "Der Westfälische Frieden 1648", in I. Dingel, M. Rohrschneider, I. Schmidt-Voges, S. Westphal, J. Whaley (eds.), *Handbuch…*, pp. 929 et seq.

168 M. Greengrass, "The Edict of Nantes (1598)", in I. Dingel, M. Rohrschneider, I. Schmidt-Voges, S. Westphal, J. Whaley (eds.), *Handbuch…*, pp. 897 et seq.

matters of faith. The act prevented religious conflicts for years to come, ensuring religious pluralism and tolerance.[169] The modern understanding of religious freedom is essentially determined by the Enlightenment achievements. The programming document of the French Revolution, that is, the Declaration of the Rights of Man and of the Citizen of 26 August 1789, prescribed in point X that no man ought to be disquieted on account of his opinions, including his religious views, provided their manifestation does not disturb the public order established by law. Religious freedom cannot be understood apart from the content of the first amendment to the US Constitution of 15 December 1791, which prescribed that "Congress shall make no law respecting an establishment of religion, or prohibiting the free exercise thereof; or abridging the freedom of speech, or of the press; or the right of the people peaceably to assemble, and to petition the Government for a redress of grievances", and the copious case-law of the Supreme Court of the United States. Given that historical considerations are not the subject of detailed analysis here, we stop at the above arbitrary and laconic attempt to demonstrate the importance of religious freedom in the history of the Western world.[170]

Today specialists in human rights and constitutionalists alike point out that religious freedom, like any other freedom, has its positive and negative dimensions, which are defined differently.[171] The negative dimension may be understood as non-interference (so-called "freedom from") with the activities of an individual from anyone (another individual, the state).[172] In that case, it would mean the freedom not to be a member of a given religious community or to be able to leave it, and the freedom not to be forced to participate (actively or passively) in religious ceremonies, worship activities or other types of religious practices. In its second meaning, the negative dimension of religious freedom is to mean the imposition of an order on an individual to take a certain action only if it is prescribed by law.[173] The positive dimension may mean so-called "freedom

169 C. Voigt-Goy, "Warschauer Konföderation 1573", in I. Dingel, M. Rohrschneider, I. Schmidt-Voges, S. Westphal, J. Whaley (eds.), *Handbuch…*, pp. 877 et seq.

170 E. Schwierskott-Matheson, *Wolność…*pp. 55 et seq.

171 B. G. Scharffs, A. Maoz, A. Isaacson Wolley, "Introduction. Freedom of/form/within religion: conceptually inseparable rights", in B. G. Scharffs, A. Maoz, A. Isaacson Wolley (eds.), *Religious freedom and the law. Emerging contexts for freedom for and from religion*, London – New York 2019, pp. 1 et seq.

172 A. Michalak, "Wolności i prawa jednostki", in D. Górecki (ed.), *Polskie prawo konstytucyjne*, Warszawa 2015, p. 83 and L. Wiśniewski, "Prawo a wolność…, p. 52.

173 L. Garlicki, *Polskie prawo konstytucyjne. Zarys wykładu*, Warszawa 2015, p. 96.

to", allowing unfettered activity of the individual and expression of his or her autonomy in all decisions concerning him or her.[174] This means, for instance, freedom to form a religious community or joining it, participate in services, ceremonies or other religious practices. It also includes freedom to defend personal religious/worldview beliefs (e.g., taking the oath in a religiously neutral form or with a confessional element: "so help me God"). In its second meaning, the positive dimension means freedom to do all that is not prohibited by law.[175]

A distinction is made between the internal (*forum internum*) and external (*forum externum*) dimension of that freedom. The former includes so-called intellectual freedom of thoughts, ideas and beliefs (some identify it with freedom of thought – *Glaubensfreiheit*),[176]whereas the latter consists in influencing the surrounding reality.[177]

Liberal democracies have so far made two important assumptions. First, religious freedom is a fundamental value and, second, states respect religious freedom of all residents of their area – this was especially true for religious minorities. The second assumption was called into question in a study carried out by Jonathan Fox, thus casting doubt on the first one.[178] Nowadays doubts exist also as to the argument that the presence of Christianity increases religious tolerance.[179]

Religious freedom is not the one that does not come into conflict with the freedoms or rights of others. Therefore, the ongoing discussion on the limits of this freedom is an important part of the jurisprudence achievements. There is a need to develop a consistent approach to religious freedom. It is particularly important in view of the need to ensure the transparency, consistency and

174 A. Michalak, "Wolności…, p. 83 and L. Wiśniewski, "Prawo…, p. 52.

175 L. Garlicki, *Polskie…*, p. 96.

176 A. Ławniczak, "Zasada poszanowania wolności i jej ograniczenia", in M. Jabłoński (ed.), *Wolności i prawa jednostki w Konstytucji RP. Idee i zasady przewodnie konstytucyjnej regulacji wolności i praw jednostki w RP. Tom I*, Warszawa 2010, p. 369.

177 A. Ławniczak, "Zasada…p. 369.

178 J. Fox, "What is religious freedom and who has it?", *Social Compass*, vol. 68, no. 3, 2021, pp. 329 et seq.

179 J. Anderson, "The catholic contribution to democratization's third wave: Altruism, hegemony, or self-interest?", *Cambridge Review of International Affairs*, vol. 20, no. 3, 2007, pp. 383 et seq.; D. A. Martin, *A general theory of secularization*, Oxford 1978, pp. 25 et seq.; R. D. Woodbury, T. S. Shaw, "Christianity and democracy: The pioneering protestants", in D. R. Hoover, D. M. Johnston (eds.), *Religion and foreign affairs: Essential readings*, Waco TX 2012, pp. 47 et seq.

fairness of the legal system as a whole[180] and to resolve reasonably conflicts between various human freedoms and rights or conflicts between religious freedom of followers of different religions.

In the course of the work and discussions on this publication, we have repeatedly attempted to clarify what freedom is under analysis, whether it is *freedom of religion* (noun) or *religious freedom* (adjective). These two terms tend to be used interchangeably without indicating the criteria that distinguish one from the other. Given the assumptions of the empirical part of the study and limiting ourselves only to the linguistic layer of these phrases, we conclude that each contains a different aspect but each is essential to us, although not to the same degree. We are greatly interested in normative regulations governing an individual's religious rights (*religious freedom*), in particular, the right, or lack thereof, to adopt, reject or change a given religion, and to develop one's religiosity –thus the individual's personal freedom and its clash with the state. We are less interested in the issue of how institutional religion is regulated at the normative level (*freedom of religion*). The relationship between the state and religious associations is of interest to us insofar as the state restricts religion, for example, refusing to register a religion, and thus deny it its share in and access to the public (state) or private space of individuals. Where individuals can practice only one religion, they are not fully free, and the degree of their freedom increases with the number of religions they are allowed to practice.[181]

In advance of the further discussion, it should be noted that normative instruments tend to use the term *freedom of religion*, whereas scholarly texts prefer the term *religious freedom*. Given the above, hereinafter we use both terms interchangeably, unless we refer to the content of a normative act with the meaning contained in it.

2.2. Religious freedom of adults and children: international standards

Religious freedom is ensured by the international community in several legal instruments of varying rank, so our reconstruction of the standard is anchored both in the content of documents purely programmatic in nature and the content of legal instruments of global and regional (local) reach.[182] In the latter case, we

180 F. Raza, "Limitations to the Right to Religious Freedom: Rethinking Key Approaches", *Oxford Journal of Law and Religion*, vol. 9, no. 3, 2020, pp. 435 et seq.

181 A. Sharma, *Problematizing…*, p. 75.

182 F. Raday, "Freedom from religion in international human rights law", in B. G. Scharffs, A. Maoz, A. Isaacson Wolley (eds.), *Religious…*, pp. 56 et seq. and J. Krukowski,

are mainly interested in the standards developed on the European continent, especially within the framework of the European Union and the Council of Europe.

The Universal Declaration of Human Rights, which is a set of human rights and the principles of their application, is a programmatic document for all binding instruments of public international law. It was proclaimed by the United Nations General Assembly in Paris on 10 December 1948.[183] The Art. 18 prescribes that everyone has the right to freedom of thought, conscience and religion; this right includes freedom to change his religion or belief, and freedom, either alone or in community with others and in public or private, to manifest his religion or belief in teaching, practice, worship and observance. The Declaration provides in Art. 29 para. 2 that in the exercise of his rights and freedoms, everyone shall be subject only to such limitations as are determined by law solely for the purpose of securing due recognition and respect for the rights and freedoms of others and of meeting the just requirements of morality, public order and the general welfare in a democratic society. The above limitative clause is universal – it applies to all the rights and freedoms contained in the Declaration.[184] Given the merely aspirational nature of the document, one is not struck by some vague wording used in it, for instance, the fact that the limitations are imposed for "the general welfare in a democratic society".

The content of Art. 18 of the Declaration was applied to the International Covenant on Civil and Political Rights, an international agreement of global reach, of 16 December 1966,[185] being part of the family of UN regulations. Poland ratified the Covenant on 3 March 1977.[186]

"Ochrona wolności religijnej w umowach międzynarodowych", *Roczniki Nauk Prawnych KUL*, vol. 3, 1993, pp. 43 et seq.

183 See: http://www.un-documents.net/a3r217.htm (accessed 2.08.2023).

184 D. R. Hodge, "Advocating for the forgotten human right: Article 18 of the Universal Declaration of Human Rights – religious freedom", *International Social Work*, vol. 49, no. 4, 2006, pp. 431 et seq.; L. Lindkvist, "The Politics of Article 18: Religious Liberty in the Universal Declaration of Human Rights", *An International Journal of Human Rights, Humanitarianism, and Development*, vol. 4, no. 3, 2013, pp. 429 et seq.; L. Lindkvist, *Religious Freedom and the Universal Declaration of Human Rights*, Cambridge 2017, *passim*.

185 See: https://www.ohchr.org/en/instruments-mechanisms/instruments/international-covenant-civil-and-political-rights (accessed 2.08.2023).

186 Journal of Laws of 1977, No. 38, pos. 167.

The right to freedom of thought, conscience and religion was regulated, appropriately enough, also in Art. 18. It prescribes that everyone shall have the right to freedom of thought, conscience and religion. This right shall include freedom to have or to adopt a religion or belief of his choice, and freedom, either individually or in community with others and in public or private, to manifest his religion or belief in worship, observance, practice and teaching.[187] The content of the Declaration is repeated in that regard in the Covenant. Art. 18 para. 3 introduces a clause limiting freedom to manifest one's religion or belief. This freedom may be subject only to such limitations as are prescribed by law and are necessary to protect public safety, order, health, or morals or the fundamental rights and freedoms of others. The provision mentions a limitation on the freedom to manifest one's religion or beliefs on account of the fundamental rights and freedoms of others, but the Covenant does not define which rights and freedoms have such an attribute and which do not.[188]

The Declaration is creatively developed by the content of Art. 18 para. 2, which prescribes that no one shall be subject to coercion which would impair his freedom to have or to adopt a religion or belief of his choice. The Covenant establishes other guarantees. Under Art. 18 para. 4, the States Parties to the Covenant undertake to have respect for the liberty of parents and, when applicable, legal guardians to ensure the religious and moral education of their children in conformity with their own convictions.

Chronologically, freedom of religion was regulated earlier in an international agreement of regional scope, that is, The Convention for the Protection of Human Rights and Fundamental Freedoms of 4 November 1950,[189] being part of the normative output of the Council of Europe. Poland adopted the Convention provisions on 19 January 1993.[190]

Art. 9 para. 1 of the Convention guarantees everyone the right to freedom of thought, conscience and religion; this right includes freedom to change his religion or belief and freedom, either alone or in community with others and in public or private, to manifest his religion or belief, in worship, teaching,

---

187 S. Joseph, M. Castan, "The International Covenant on Civil and Political Rights. Cases, Materials, and Commentary", Oxford 2013, pp. 562 et seq.

188 M. T. Parker, "The Freedom to Manifest Religious Belief: An Analysis of the Necessity Clauses of the ICCPR and the ECHR", *Duke Journal of Comparative & International Law*, vol. 17, no. 1, 2006, pp. 91 et seq.

189 See: https://www.echr.coe.int/european-convention-on-human-rights (accessed 2.08.2023).

190 Journal of Laws of 1993, No. 61, pos. 284.

practice and observance.[191] Art. 9 para. 2 lays down that freedom to manifest one's religion or beliefs shall be subject only to such limitations as are prescribed by law and are necessary in a democratic society in the interests of public safety, for the protection of public order, health or morals, or for the protection of the rights and freedoms of others.[192]

In order to ensure compliance with the provisions of the European Convention, the State Parties established a judicial body to achieve that objective, that is, the European Court of Human Rights. The Strasbourg case-law is an example of an inclusive understanding of religion – many judicates show a broad and flexible understanding of religion based on the interpretation of Art. 9[193] However, the usefulness of the rulings is sometimes questioned because of the Court's holistic approach and comprehensive reading of freedom of thought, conscience and religion.[194]

The court rulings are based on the doctrine of margin of appreciation. It is used to assess whether a state party should be penalized for restricting the use of a given human right. The doctrine allows the Court to reconcile practical differences in the application of the Convention articles. The differences create a limited right for the contracting parties to waive partially the obligations defined in the Convention. When applying that doctrine, judges must take into consideration the differences between the national laws of the parties as regards content and procedure. The doctrine of margin of appreciation aims to balance individual rights with national interests and resolve any potential conflicts.[195]

---

191 W. A. Schabas, *The European Convention on Human Rights. A Commentary*. Oxford-New York 2015, pp. 423 et seq.

192 M. T. Parker, "The Freedom…, pp. 91 et seq.

193 M. Rozner, "Prawo do wolności religijnej w Europejskiej Konwencji Praw Człowieka z 1950 r.", *Studia z Prawa Wyznaniowego*, vol. 5, 2002, p. 114.

194 R. Paprzycki, *Prawna ochrona wolności sumienia i wyznania*, Warszawa 2015, pp. 5 et seq.

195 A. Jakuszewicz, "The doctrine of the margin of appreciation as a tool of relativisation of freedom of religion. Some reflections on the jurisprudence of the European Court of Human Rights", *Studia Prawnoustrojowe*, vol. 54, 2021, pp. 135 and seq.; J. A. Roffee, "No Consensus on Incest? Criminalisation and Compatibility with the European Convention on Human Rights", *Human Rights Law Review*, vol. 14, no. 3, 2014, pp. 541 et seq.; H. Wiczanowska, "Oddziaływanie doktryny marginesu uznania na rozstrzyganie konfliktu pomiędzy wolnością wypowiedzi a wolnością sumienia i wyznania w praktyce orzeczniczej Europejskiego Trybunału Praw Człowieka", *Przegląd Europejski*, no. 2, 2020, pp. 83 et seq.

Similar guarantees are prescribed by the Charter of Fundamental Rights of the European Union of 7 December 2000.[196] As the above documents, it ensures in Art. 10 para. 1 everyone's right to freedom of thought, conscience and religion. This right includes freedom to change religion or belief and freedom, either alone or in community with others and in public or in private, to manifest religion or belief, in worship, teaching, practice and observance. In turn, in Art. para. 2, it recognizes the right to conscientious objection, in accordance with the national laws governing the exercise of this right. Under Art. 14 para. 3, the freedom to found educational establishments with due respect for democratic principles and the right of parents to ensure the education and teaching of their children in conformity with their religious, philosophical and pedagogical convictions shall be respected, in accordance with the national laws governing the exercise of such freedom and right.

Rights recognized by the Charter which are based on the Community Treaties or the Treaty on European Union shall be exercised under the conditions and within the limits defined by those Treaties (Art. 52 para. 2). In so far as the Charter contains rights which correspond to rights guaranteed by the Convention for the Protection of Human Rights and Fundamental Freedoms, the meaning and scope of those rights shall be the same as those laid down by the said Convention. This provision shall not prevent Union law providing more extensive protection (Art. 52 para. 3).

Under Art. 52 para.1, any limitation on the exercise of the rights and freedoms recognized by the Charter must be provided for by law and respect the essence of those rights and freedoms. Subject to the principle of proportionality, limitations may be made only if they are necessary and genuinely meet objectives of general interest recognized by the Union or the need to protect the rights and freedoms of others.

The UN Declaration on the Elimination of All Forms of Intolerance and of Discrimination Based on Religion or Belief of 25 November 1981[197] is another important document, albeit of lesser impact. This document is based on the regulation of freedom of thought, conscience and religion of the previously discussed instruments. It also declares that no one shall be subject to discrimination by any State, institution, group of persons, or person on the

196 Official Journal of the European Communities of 18.12.2000, C 364/1 – https://www.europarl.europa.eu/charter/pdf/text_en.pdf (accessed 2.08.2023).

197 See: https://www.ohchr.org/en/instruments-mechanisms/instruments/declaration-elimination-all-forms-intolerance-and-discrimination (accessed 2.08.2023).

grounds of religion or belief (Art. 2 para. 1). The expression "intolerance and discrimination based on religion or belief" shall mean any distinction, exclusion, restriction or preference based on religion or belief and having as its purpose or as its effect nullification or impairment of the recognition, enjoyment or exercise of human rights and fundamental freedoms on an equal basis (Art. 2 para. 2).

All States shall take effective measures to prevent and eliminate discrimination on the grounds of religion or belief in the recognition, exercise and enjoyment of human rights and fundamental freedoms in all fields of civil, economic, political, social and cultural life. They shall make all efforts to enact or rescind legislation where necessary to prohibit any such discrimination, and to take all appropriate measures to combat intolerance on the grounds of religion or belief in this matter (Art. 4).

The Declaration contains separate provisions on the relationship between parents and children. The child shall be protected from any form of discrimination on the ground of religion or belief. He shall be brought up in a spirit of understanding, tolerance, friendship among peoples, peace and universal brotherhood, respect for freedom of religion or belief of others, and in full consciousness that his energy and talents should be devoted to the service of his fellow men (Art. 5 para. 3). Under (Art. 5 para. 5), practices of a religion or belief in which a child is brought up must not be injurious to his physical or mental health or to his full development. However, the limitative clause under Art. 1 para. 3 of the Declaration, which is identical to Art. 18 para. 3 of the International Covenant on Civil and Political Rights, is taken into account.

However, it is the parents or, as the case may be, the legal guardians of the child who have the right to organize the life within the family in accordance with their religion or belief and bearing in mind the moral education in which they believe the child should be brought up (Art. 5 para. 1). Every child shall enjoy the right to have access to education in the matter of religion or belief in accordance with the wishes of his parents or, as the case may be, legal guardians. The child shall not be compelled to receive teaching on religion or belief against the wishes of his parents or legal guardians, the best interests of the child being the guiding principle (Art. 5 para. 2). In the case of a child who is not under the care either of his parents or of legal guardians, due account shall be taken of their expressed wishes or of any other proof of their wishes in the matter of religion or belief, the best interests of the child being the guiding principle (Art. 5 para. 4).

The content of Art. 5 of the Declaration clearly shows the tension between the state and the child, the state and the parents and, the parents and the child. It appears that the position of parents/legal guardians in relation to their subordinate children is certainly stronger. The child's autonomy is not regulated at all in the Declaration, while the only standard for child protection is the concept of "the best interests of the child", which, however, has not been defined even in elementary form.

Art. 6 of the Declaration offers a list of indications of freedom of thought, conscience and religion, such as: to worship or assemble in connection with a religion or belief, and to establish and maintain places for these purposes; to establish and maintain appropriate charitable or humanitarian institutions; to make, acquire and use to an adequate extent the necessary articles and materials related to the rites or customs of a religion or belief; to write, issue and disseminate relevant publications in these areas; to teach a religion or belief in places suitable for these purposes; to solicit and receive voluntary financial and other contributions from individuals and institutions; to train, appoint, elect or designate by succession appropriate leaders called for by the requirements and standards of any religion or belief; to observe days of rest and to celebrate holidays and ceremonies in accordance with the precepts of one's religion or belief.

The Convention on the Rights of the Child of 20 November1989,[198] being part of the UN achievements, is a normative instrument of special rank and a milestone in the history of childhood.[199] Poland ratified this Convention on 7 June 1991.[200] In many areas it organizes and expands the *soft law* regulations contained in the previously discussed UN Declaration on the Elimination of All Forms of Intolerance and of Discrimination.

Under Art. 14 para. 1 of the Convention, States Parties shall respect the right of the child to freedom of thought, conscience and religion, a child meaning, for the purposes of the Convention, every human being below the age of eighteen years unless under the law applicable to the child, majority is attained earlier (Art. 1). At the same time, States Parties shall respect the rights and duties of the parents and, when applicable, legal guardians, to provide direction to the child in the exercise of his or her right in a manner consistent with the evolving capacities of the child (Art. 14 para. 2). Moreover, States Parties shall take all appropriate measures to ensure that the child is protected against all forms of discrimination

198 https://www.ohchr.org/en/instruments-mechanisms/instruments/convention-rights-child (accessed 2.08.2023).

199 F. Schweitzer, "Children's Right to Religion and Spirituality: Legal, Educational and Practical Perspectives", *British Journal of Religious Education*, vol. 27, no. 2, 2005, pp. 103 et seq.

200 Journal of Laws of 1991, No. 120, pos. 526.

or punishment on the basis of the status, activities, expressed opinions, or beliefs of the child's parents, legal guardians, or family members (Art. 2 para. 2).

The Convention prescribes that a child temporarily or permanently deprived of his or her family environment, or in whose own best interests cannot be allowed to remain in that environment, shall be entitled to special protection and assistance provided by the State (Art. 20 para. 1), which will ensure alternative care for such a child in accordance with its national laws (Art. 20 para. 2). The care is highly dependent on culture and religion, as is reflected in the content of Art. 20 para. 3, which lays down that such care could include, inter alia, foster placement, kafalah of Islamic law, adoption or if necessary placement in suitable institutions for the care of children. When considering solutions, due regard shall be paid to the desirability of continuity in a child's upbringing and to the child's ethnic, religious, cultural and linguistic background. This provision protects the child, making it necessary to take into account the continuity of his upbringing only if it is desirable. It is unfortunate that the Convention standard does not indicate a specific body (e.g., court or a special authority), which should take into account the previously mentioned prerequisites when deciding on care for a child.

Under Art. 30, in those States in which ethnic, religious or linguistic minorities or persons of indigenous origin exist, a child belonging to such a minority or who is indigenous shall not be denied the right, in community with other members of his or her group, to enjoy his or her own culture, to profess and practise his or her own religion, or to use his or her own language.

In terms of the shape of the limitative clause, the Convention bears a strong resemblance to Art. 18 para. 3 of the International Covenant on Civil and Political Rights because freedom to manifest one's religion or beliefs may be subject only to such limitations as are prescribed by law and are necessary to protect public safety, order, health, or morals or the fundamental rights and freedoms of others.

It is necessary to note that although the Convention on the Rights of the Child is a document of unquestionably special rank, many states parties have chosen to make reservations and declarations to it.[201] It was done primarily by religious

201 L. J. Leblanc, "Reservations to the Convention on the Rights of the Child: A macroscopic view of state practice", *The International Journal of Children's Rights*, vol. 4, no, 1996, pp. 357 et seq. and W.A. Schabas, "Reservations to the Convention on the Rights of the Child", *Human Rights Quarterly*, vol. 4, no. 4, 1996, pp. 472 et seq.

or *quasi*-religious states,[202] which viewed the provisions of the Convention as a threat to the patriarchal (traditional) family model. The activities of some of those countries have become the subject of reports by the Committee on the Rights of the Child in the aspect of limiting children's religious freedom.[203] Surprisingly, as a state that proposed the adoption of the document and submitted its preliminary draft, Poland submitted reservations (currently withdrawn) and declarations (still in force) to it. One of the declarations reads that the Republic of Poland considers that a child's rights as defined in the Convention, in particular the rights defined in articles 12 to 16, shall be exercised with respect for parental authority, in accordance with Polish customs and traditions regarding the place of the child within and outside the family. The second declaration lays down that family planning and education services for parents should be in keeping with the principles of morality.

At the same time, Polish lawyers argued that with ill will, the reservation made by a given state can lead to the annihilation of the essence of the values recognized by the Convention – although some traditions foster the child's freedoms, others show full disregard of his or her personality and freedom.[204] We reiterate the need for Poland to withdraw from the interpretative declarations submitted to the Convention on the Rights of the Child.[205]

2.3. Religious freedom of adults and children – Polish standards

Freedom of religion is located in the Constitution of the Republic of Poland[206] in the chapter titled "The Freedoms, rights and obligations of persons and citizens" – in Art. 53. The high rank of that freedom is evidenced by the fact that it is not subject to limitations in states of emergency (Art. 233 paras. 1 and 3 of the Polish Constitution). This freedom enjoys the status of constitutional

202 A. N. Schulz, "O Konwencji o prawach dziecka i jej wpływie na prawo polskie", in M. Andrzejewski (ed.), *Prawa dziecka. Konteksty prawne i pedagogiczne*, Poznań 2012, pp. 66 et seq.

203 UNICEF, *Implementation Handbook for the Convention on the Rights of the Child*, Geneva 2007, pp. 186 et seq.

204 A. Łopatka, "Konwencja Praw Dziecka w Polsce", in J. Bińczycka (ed.), *Prawa dziecka. Deklaracje i rzeczywistość*, Kraków 1999, p. 25.

205 O Sitarz, A Jaworska-Wieloch, J Hanc, "Wolność religijna w ośrodkach izolacji nieletnich w świetle polskich regulacji", *Prawo w Działaniu*, vol. 57, 2024, pp. 121 et seq.

206 Journal of Laws of 1997, No. 78, pos. 483 as amended.

principle,[207] is an individual's freedom of a personal nature and is directly related to the individual's mentality and desire to seek and experience transcendent values.[208]

Art. 53 para. 1 ensures freedom of conscience and religion to everyone who is on the territory of the Republic of Poland, though the Constitution does not define any of these terms. Some commentators argue that the Constitution offers no basis for deciding whether a particular set of beliefs and practices is or is not a religion. Important in this regard are the extra-constitutional findings or even extra-legal findings: philosophical, theological, ethnographic, or those made by cultural and religious studies.[209]

In contrast to freedom of conscience, the indications of freedom of religion are further clarified in Art. 53 para. 2. This freedom shall include the freedom to profess or to adopt a religion by personal choice as well as to manifest such religion, either individually or collectively, publicly or privately, by worshipping, praying, participating in ceremonies, performing rites or teaching. Freedom of religion shall also include possession of sanctuaries and other places of worship for the satisfaction of the needs of believers as well as the right of individuals, wherever they may be, to benefit from such religious services.

The constitutional list of indications of freedom of religion, although not preceded by the phrase "in particular" or "for example", does not seem enumerative. Paweł Sarnecki was right to argue that the list provided by the legislature in Art. 53 para. 2 performs primarily illustrative (communicative) and educational functions and it must not be inferred from it that it precludes the exercise of freedom of religion in ways not provided for by the Constitution. The freedom must be exercised within the limits of applicable law.[210] The Polish science of constitutional law quite unanimously accepts the open nature of that list, signalling the need for supplementing it with unmentioned behaviour, such as freedom to establish a new (previously non-existing) religion, spreading faith and converting to it (proselytism),[211] freedom to act in accordance with the dictates of religion, including in the area of morals (e.g., dressing in a certain

---

207 P. Sarnecki, "Art. 53", in L. Garlicki, M. Zubik (eds.), *Konstytucja Rzeczypospolitej Polskiej. Komentarz. Tom II. Art. 30–86*, Warszawa 2016, p. 278.

208 M. Florczak-Wątor, "Art. 53", in P. Tuleja (ed.), *Konstytucja Rzeczypospolitej Polskiej. Komentarz*, Warszawa 2019, p. 182.

209 P. Winczorek, *Komentarz do Konstytucji Rzeczypospolitej Polskiej z 2 kwietnia 1997 r.*, Warszawa 2000, p. 73.

210 P. Sarnecki, "Art. 53…, p. 280.

211 M. Florczak-Wątor, "Art. 53…, p. 183.

way, maintaining a certain body appearance, (not) eating certain foods, entering into confessional (endo- or exogamic) marriage, starting a family and bringing up children as required by religion),[212] or the possibility of pursuing a vocation to the clerical state (priesthood or religious order).[213]

Freedom to "adopt a religion" is to be understood within the meaning of the Constitution as the possibility of replacing atheistic attitudes[214] with religious ones, professing and extending an adopted religion, multiple changes of religion, founding a new religion, or finally, abandoning religion and adopting a neutral or hostile attitude toward a particular religion.[215]

The Polish Constitution ensures everyone the right to benefit from religious services, wherever they may be. The obvious places where such services are provided include detention institutions, which are of particular interest to us, including penitentiary facilities, detention centres, juvenile isolation facilities and health establishments (hospitals). The obligation assigned to prison authorities to provide prisoners with the opportunity to exercise their freedom of religion is unquestioned today. It is occasionally argued that this freedom is fulfilled to the maximum possible extent allowed by the organization of the penitentiary system and the purpose and nature of a sentence being served.[216] Setting the limits on that obligation was left to the common legislature. Notably, despite the list of the indications of manifesting freedom of religion, this freedom is not restricted only because its beneficiary is a person deprived of liberty by a final court ruling. The Polish Constitution explicitly ensures everyone the right to worship, either in public or in private, and practice a religion, which obviously entails the need to comply with religious customs, including, for example, confessional dietary regulations, wearing religious clothing (such as a headscarf or turban), but also modifications in terms of external appearance (wearing religious hair or beards).[217]

---

212 M. Olszówka, "Art. 53" in M. Safjan, L. Bosek (eds.), *Konstytucja RP. Tom I. Komentarz do art. 1–86*, Warszawa 2016, p. 1265.

213 P. Sarnecki, "Art. 53..., p. 280.

214 For some researchers, it means entry into the area of protection of freedom of belief and worldview. Otherwise, conceptual chaos is introduced – G. Maroń, "O pojmowaniu..., pp. 40 et seq.

215 B. Banaszak, *Konstytucja*..., pp. 325 et seq. and M. Olszówka, "Art. 53..., pp. 1265 et seq.

216 M. Olszówka, "Art. 53..., p. 1267.

217 O. Sitarz, A. Jaworska-Wieloch, J. Hanc, "Obowiązek..., pp. 29 et seq. and J. Hanc, "*My chickens would love this!*. Nutraloaf jako przykład naruszenia prawa skazanego

Further, the Polish Constitution prescribes that no one shall be compelled to participate or not participate in religious practices (Art. 53 para. 6) and that no one may be compelled by organs of public authority to disclose his or her worldview, religious convictions or beliefs (Art. 53 para. 7).

The freedom to manifest one's religion (*forum externum*) is subject to some normative limitations. The limitative clause under Art. 53 para. 5 of the Polish Constitution provides that the freedom to manifest one's religion may be limited only by means of statute and only where this is necessary for the defence of State security, public order, health, morals or the freedom and rights of others. Commentators, however, do not fully agree on whether this provision constitutes a special provision (*lex specialis*) in relation to Art. 31 para. 3 of the Polish Constitution, which contains a general clause limiting the exercise of constitutional freedoms and rights. These clauses are not identical. Under Art. 31 par. 3, "any limitations upon the exercise of constitutional freedoms and rights may be imposed only by statute, and only when necessary in a democratic state for the protection of its security or public order, or to protect the natural environment, health or public morals, or the freedom and rights of other persons. Such limitations shall not violate the essence of constitutional freedoms and rights." It is clear at a glance that Art. 53 para. 5 does not have a limitative prerequisite of "the protection of natural environment". Doubts may arise as to whether the adjective "public" also refers to the prerequisites "health" and "morals". In the opinion of the Polish Constitutional Tribunal, Art. 53 para. 5 does not exclude the proportionality principle under Art. 31 para. 3 to the extent that the normative content of these provisions does not overlap.[218]

The Polish Constitution treats the family in a unique way in the area of freedom of religion. Under Art. 53 para. 3, parents shall have the right to ensure their children a moral and religious upbringing and teaching in accordance with their convictions. This provision requires that Art. 48 para. 1 of the Polish Constitution, which ensures parents' fundamental right to raise their children according to their own convictions, shall apply as appropriate. The provision adds that such upbringing shall respect the degree of maturity of a child as well as his or her freedom of conscience and confession and also his or her convictions. It is hard to understand why the regulations relating to the child do not retain

---

do otrzymania przyzwoitego posiłku", *Archiwum Kryminologii*, vol. 44, no. 2, 2022, pp. 189 et seq.

218 Judgment of the Constitutional Tribunal of 16 February 1999, SK 11/98, LEX no. 36175.

the expression 'freedom of conscience and religion' instead of 'freedom of conscience and confession'. Despite semantic differences, these terms should be considered synonyms and no distinction should be made between them. Art. 72 is complementary with the above regulations. It prescribes that the Republic of Poland shall ensure protection of the rights of the child. Everyone shall have the right to demand of organs of public authority that they defend children against violence, cruelty, exploitation and demoralization (para. 1). In the course of establishing the rights of a child, organs of public authority and persons responsible for a child shall consider and, insofar as possible, give priority to the views of the child (para. 3).

Despite the lack of precision, commentators of the Constitution assume that pursuant to Art. 1 of the Convention on the Rights of the Child, a child means every human being below the age of eighteen, that is, until reaching the age of majority.[219] Thus construed "child" is a separate holder[220] of all human rights, although he or she cannot use all of them independently[221] because of his or her age and the limitations associated with it.[222] Ensuring and guaranteeing human rights, the Polish Constitution devotes a separate provision to the rights of the child, that is, the above-mentioned Art. 72 para. 1. During the time of child-raising, parents shall respect the degree of maturity of the child as well as his or her freedom of conscience and confession because such a separate concept is introduced by the Constitution (Art. 48 para. 1).

Despite this, the manner in which the situation of the child is regulated in the Polish Constitution is not fully satisfactory and his or her subjectivity is in fact incomplete. Recognizing the religious freedom of the child, the provisions of the Constitution do not indicate how and on what basis to assess whether a child is already capable of independently exercising this freedom in terms of spiritual or worldview choices. The lack of a consistent definition of the moment from which the child gains the full right to exercise that freedom has drawn criticism from some representatives of Polish confessional law.[223] The provisions of the

---

219 B. Banaszak, *Konstytucja…*, p. 299 and W. Borysiak, "Art. 72", in M. Safjan, L. Bosek (eds.), *Konstytucja RP. Tom I……*pp. 1659 et seq.

220 E. H. Morawska, "Ochrona praw dziecka w świetle art. 72 Konstytucji RP. Uwagi na tle orzecznictwa Trybunału Konstytucyjnego", *Kwartalnik Prawa Publicznego*, vol. 7, no. 4, 2007, pp. 126 et seq.

221 B. Banaszak, *Konstytucja…*, p. 429 and W. Borysiak, "Art. 72…, p. 1659.

222 M. Florczak-Wątor, "Art. 53…, p. 243.

223 M. Pietrzak, "Konstytucyjne podstawy prawa wyznaniowego", in M. Wyrzykowski (ed.), *Konstytucyjne podstawy systemu prawa*, Warszawa 2001, pp. 172 and 177.

Constitution are silent as to who is to monitor and enforce the decisions made by the child. For only the existence of such norms makes it possible to delineate realistically the limits of the child's religious freedom. Thus, the Constitution does not satisfactorily resolve the collision between parental authority and the child's religious freedom. This state of law leads one to accept that taking into consideration the degree of maturity of a child means that his or her will should be increasingly taken into account as he or she gets older when the parents make decisions concerning him or her. The child's degree of maturity increases with age, as long as there are no disorders that nullify this principle.[224] In other words, as the child grows older, the group of rights and freedoms that the child can exercise independently, without the intermediation of parents or guardians, increases.[225]

Under Art. 25, churches and religious organizations shall have equal rights (para. 1) and public authorities in the Republic of Poland shall be impartial in matters of personal conviction, whether religious, worldview and philosophical and shall ensure their freedom of expression within public life (para. 2). The relationship between the state and churches and other religious associations shall be based on the principle of respect for their autonomy and the mutual independence of each in its own sphere and on the principle of cooperation for the individual and common good (para. 3). The content of this constitutional standard corresponds to Art. 1 of the Concordat (international treaty) of 28 July 1993 between the Holy See and the Republic of Poland,[226] which lays down that the Republic of Poland and the Holy See reaffirm that the State and the Catholic Church are, each in its own domain, independent and autonomous, and that they are fully committed to respecting this principle in all their mutual relations and in cooperating for the individual and common good. The shape of these two standards determines the definition of the relationship between the Polish state and religious associations as an amicable separation of church and state,[227] in contrast to the complete "pure" separation existing in the United States or

---

224 W. Borysiak, "Art. 48", in M. Safjan, L. Bosek (eds.), *Konstytucja RP. Tom I…*, p. 1204 and M. Florczak-Wątor, "Art. 53…, p. 172.

225 L. Garlicki, M. Derlatka, "Art. 72", in L. Garlicki, M. Zubik (eds.), *Konstytucja Rzeczypospolitej Polskiej. Komentarz. II. Art. 30–86*, Warszawa 2016, p. 787.

226 Journal of Laws of 1998, No. 51, pos. 318.

227 K. Drewniowska, "Realizacja konstytucyjnej zasady rozdziału Kościoła od państwa – wybrane aspekty", in M. Stanulewicz, E. Plewa, C. Linowski (eds.), *Państwo wobec religii. Teraźniejszość i przeszłość*, Łódź 2021, pp. 193 et seq. and J. Krukowski, *Wstęp do nauki o państwie i prawie*, Lublin 2004, p. 53.

hostile (unfriendly) separation in force in France.[228] The relationship between the Republic of Poland and the Roman Catholic Church shall be determined by the international treaty concluded with the Holy See and by statute (Art. 25 para. 4), whereas the relationship between the Republic of Poland and other churches and religious associations shall be determined by statutes adopted pursuant to agreements concluded between their respective representatives and the Council of Ministers (Art. 25 para. 5).

Detailed regulations on freedom of religion can also be found in the Act of 17 May 1989 on the guarantees of freedom of conscience and confession.[229] The regulation was adopted before the current Constitution entered into life. Although it has not been repealed and has been subject to several amendments, one should keep in mind the date of its enactment and exercise common-sensical caution in the process of interpreting it.

This law uses terminology differing from that of the Constitution – it ensures freedom of conscience and confession. It also adopts a different legislative technique. In essence, Art. 1 para. 1 refers this freedom to a citizen, but Art. 7 extends it to foreigners (para. 1) and stateless persons (para. 2) residing in the territory of the Republic of Poland. These persons enjoy this freedom "on an equal footing with citizens".

Art. 1 para. 3 of the law prescribes that all believing citizens (regardless of confessional affiliation) and non-believers have equal rights in state, political, economic, social and cultural life. Given that the provision also refers to foreigners, it should be pointed out that the Polish normative regulations ensure freedom of conscience and confession fairly widely, including state and political life in that sphere.

The law specifies that this freedom includes the freedom to choose a religion or belief and to express it individually and collectively, privately and publicly (Art. 1 para. 2). It contains an exemplary and open list of forms of exercising it (Art. 3), which is heavily influenced by Art. 6 of the Declaration on the Elimination of All Forms of Intolerance and Discrimination Based on Religion or Belief. The list includes forms of manifesting one's conscience and confession of two types.

---

228 A. Romanko, "System państw świeckich na przykładzie wybranych państwa europejskich", *Biuletyn Stowarzyszenia Absolwentów i Przyjaciół Wydziału Prawa Katolickiego Uniwersytetu Lubelskiego*, vol. 15, no. 1, 2018, pp. 128 et seq. and S. Sowiński, "Modele stosunków państwo – Kościół w Unii Europejskiej", *Studia Europejskie. Centrum Europejskie Uniwersytetu Warszawskiego*, no. 3, 2008, pp. 43 et seq.

229 Journal of Laws of 2023, pos. 265.

Some are more strongly linked to the individual and his or her personal situation, while others show a strong affinity to the collective (community). The former category includes: participation, in accordance with the principles of one's religion, in religious activities and rituals and fulfilment of religious obligations and celebration of holidays of that nature (point 2); membership or lack thereof in churches and other religious associations (point 2a); professing one's religion or beliefs (point 3); child-rearing in accordance with one's religious convictions (point 4); remaining silent on matters of one's religion or beliefs (point 5); using sources of information on religion (point 7); choice of clerical or religious status (point 10); performing burial in accordance with religious principles or beliefs in matters of religion (point 12). The latter category includes: creation of religious communities (churches) and other religious associations established for the purpose of professing and spreading religious faith, having their own system, doctrine and worship rituals (point 1); maintaining contacts with co-believers, including participation in the work of religious organizations of an international reach (point 6); association in secular organizations in order to carry out objectives arising from one's religion or beliefs in matters of religion (point 11); manufacturing and acquiring objects needed for worship and religious practices and making use of them (point 8); manufacturing, acquiring and possession of articles needed for compliance with religious principles (point 9). Art. 5 regulates separately citizens' right to freely benefit churches, other religious associations and charitable and welfare institutions.

The above division and classification of behaviour is arbitrary, yet it allows for ordering the statutory matter.

It is assumed in the doctrine that the definition of the scope of freedom of confession contained in this law, by means of the list in Art. 3, is consistent with the understanding of "freedom" in democratic states under the rule of law.[230] However, this view should be considered doubtful. Since the legislature is unable to list all the protected indications of manifesting freedom of confession, it should not draw up an incomplete list. Moreover, one of the concepts of freedom discussed above assumes that the legislature should prescribe only orders, prohibitions and sanctions. What is not ordered / prohibited is permitted and this principle is no exception in the field of freedom of confession. In turn, the lack of ordering or prohibiting regulations may mean that the legislature refuses to resolve a conflict occurring between freedom of confession and another

230 A. Korzeniewska-Lasota, "Zakres wolności sumienia i wyznania", *Studia Warmińskie*, vol. 48, 2011, p. 216.

freedom or right, which, given the democratic legitimacy it possesses, is not desirable. Such refusal means that the decision on limiting (or not) freedom of confession is transferred to the judiciary.

Art. 4 of the said law ensures the right to benefit from religious assistance wherever one may be. In detail, the right to participate in religious activities and rites, fulfil religious duties and observe religious holidays (Art. 3 para. 2), and the right to possess and use articles necessary for worship and religious practices shall apply to individuals incarcerated in penitentiary facilities, correctional facilities, regional educational centres, youth educational centres, detention centres and juvenile shelters (Art. 4 para. 1 point 3). Apart from these individuals, the provision indicates two further categories, that is, persons performing military service or basic service in civil defence (point 1) and persons staying in medical institutions (hospitals), social welfare institutions, and children and young persons in camps organized on the territory of the country and camps organized by state institutions (point 2). The manner in which these rights are exercised is regulated in detail by separate laws – including the Penal Enforcement Code of 6 June 1997[231] and a new Act of 9 June 2022 on the support and rehabilitation of juveniles[232] and provisions issued on their basis.

The law regulates the restrictions on the exercise of freedom of conscience and confession in a somewhat unusual manner. The individual or collective manifestation of one's religion or beliefs may be subject only to statutory restrictions necessary to protect public safety, order, health or public morals or the fundamental rights and freedoms of others (Art. 3 para. 1). This clause corresponds more to the content of Art. 18 para. 3 of the Covenant than to the constitutional standards under Art. 31 para. 3 and Art. 53 para. 5. Moreover, the exercise of freedom of conscience and confession may not lead to evasion of public duties imposed by laws (Art. 3 para. 2). However, citizens may apply on the grounds of religious convictions or professed moral principles for assignment to alternative service on the terms and in the manner prescribed by the Law of 11 March 2022 on the Defence of the Homeland[233] (Art. 3 para. 3).

In summary, it should be concluded that freedom of religion, both on the national and international normative level, is regulated in a similar manner. None of the instruments defines the concept of "religion". They only declare the right to preserve freedom of thought, conscience and religion, and participate

231 Journal of Laws of 2023, pos. 127.
232 Journal of Laws of 2022, pos. 1700.
233 Journal of Laws of 2022, pos. 2305.

in religious practices, and provide similar grounds for restricting the sphere of religious freedom – this can only be done by law and after meeting additional conditions stemming from the principle of proportionality. The understandable generality of international regulations requires a clarification of the limitation of religious freedom by national law.[234]

The picture of this freedom seems to be fairly consistent. On the one hand, the large number and rank of legal instruments addressing this freedom are sufficient to conclude that this freedom is important for both the international community and the Polish legislature. On the other hand, the strength of adopted legal standards is not determined by their quantity, but, paradoxically, by the effective monitoring of their compliance (possible also at the international level, for example, under the jurisdiction of the European Court of Human Rights) or the comprehensive and precise national regulations of a lower rank. A reader of the above provisions may have a sense of echolalia. The standard of protection of religious freedom enshrined in laws of various ranks[235] does not necessarily have to be the standard of the real and effective protection of this freedom. Whether Poland has implemented the normative standard resulting from various legal acts for a special category of subjects (including broadly understood persons deprived of their liberty) will be verified below based on an analysis of regulations introduced by special laws and implementing acts issued to such laws. The final step in checking whether the postulated standard has been achieved will be to compare the law with prisoners' opinions given in questionnaires.

---

234 O. Sitarz, A. Jaworska-Wieloch, J. Hanc, "Public opinion on freedom of religion (and its limitations) in penitentiary establishments in the light of international regulations A Polish perspective", *Approaching Religion*, vol. 12, no. 1, 2022, p. 169.

235 O. Sitarz, A. Jaworska-Wieloch, J. Hanc, "A reconstruction of the international standards of religious education of juveniles in correctional institutions", *British Journal of Religious Education*, vol. 45, no. 4, 2023, pp. 370 et seq.

Chapter III Religious freedom of adults and children deprived of their liberty in post-criminal isolation units: international standards

The determination of international standards for the religious freedom of adults and children requires special attention to the situation of persons placed in post-criminal isolation units. This issue is very important because despite arguments about secularization of the world,[236] religion and the possibility of professing it are still one of the most important elements of human functioning. In the event of incarceration, or its equivalent in the case of juveniles, they fit naturally into the system of legal solutions and the practice of rehabilitative activities.

Over the years, recognizing the need for the empowerment of the prisoner, instruments of international law began to ensure prisoners' religious freedom, which is a special test of the state of democracy and respect for the rights of convicted persons and juveniles. It is the outcome of a long process of humanization of the execution of prison sentences, which is unfortunately not yet complete in some parts of the world. It is based on the idea that a prisoner retains his or her dignity and cannot be subjected to arbitrary conduct by the enforcement apparatus.[237]

A search for the international standard of protection of religious freedom of persons deprived of their liberty should start with the UN General Assembly Resolution 45/111 of 14 December 1990 titled "Basic Principles for the Treatment of Prisoners". Its principle no. 2 prescribes that there shall be no discrimination on the grounds of, among other things, religion, and principle no. 3 provides that it is desirable to respect the religious beliefs and cultural precepts of the group to which prisoners belong, whenever local conditions so require. It is hard to

---

236 See: for example: K. Bochenek, "Zjawisko laicyzacji w społeczeństwie ponowoczesnym (konteksty filozoficzne)", *Wschodni Rocznik Humanistyczny*, vol. 16, no. 1, 2019, pp. 77 et seq., but also: R. S. Czarnecki, "Meandry współczesnej laicyzacji", *Res Humana*, vol. 18, no. 3, 2009, pp. 46 et seq.

237 T. Przesławski, "Pozycja i funkcje polityki penitencjarnej w naukach o polityce publicznej", in J. Kwaśniewski (ed.), *Nauki o polityce publicznej. Monografia dyscypliny*, Warszawa 2018, p. 403.

imagine a more basic and minimal set of declarations respecting the rights of prisoners in the area of their religious freedom.

The standards of treating prisoners have been set for UN member states by legal instruments of a *soft law* nature. Attention should first be drawn to the Standard Minimum Rules for the Treatment of Prisoners adopted by the First UN Congress on the Prevention of Crime and the Treatment of Offenders held at Geneva in 1955, and approved by the Economic and Social Council by means of resolution 663 C (XXIV) of 31 July 1957 and 2076 (LXII) of 13 May 1977. It is unfortunate that many UN states treated them more like the target point than a starting point and the necessary minimum.[238] Due to changing realities and the need to modernize the minimum standards for the treatment of prisoners, the Mandela Rules were subsequently adopted at the United Nations,[239] which prescribe in rule no. 2 that there shall be no discrimination on the grounds of, among other things, religion. The religious beliefs and moral precepts of prisoners shall be respected. Under Rule 65, if the prison contains a sufficient number of prisoners of the same religion, a qualified representative of that religion shall be appointed or approved. If the number of prisoners justifies it and conditions permit, the arrangement should be on a full-time basis. A qualified representative appointed or approved under paragraph 1 of this rule shall be allowed to hold regular services and to pay pastoral visits in private to prisoners of his or her religion at proper times. Access to a qualified representative of any religion shall not be refused to any prisoner. On the other hand, if any prisoner should object to a visit of any religious representative, his or her attitude shall be fully respected. Under Rule 66, so far as practicable, every prisoner shall be allowed to satisfy the needs of his or her religious life by attending the services provided in the prison and having in his or her possession the books of religious observance and instruction of his or her denomination.

In terms of international law, the Mandela Rules create obligations only in the moral-political sphere, without the necessity to apply them to national

---

238 M. Płatek, "Zadania polskiej polityki penitencjarnej w świetle Europejskich Reguł Więziennych", *Czasopismo Prawa Karnego i Nauk Penalnych*, vol. 11, no. 1, 2007, p. 261.

239 UN General Assembly resolution the Standard Minimum Rules for the Treatment of Prisoners – https://bip.brpo.gov.pl/pl/content/reguly-nelsona-mandeli (accessed 15.07.2023). This resolution is an updated version of UN the Standard Minimum Rules for the Treatment of Prisoners prepared in 1955 and approved on 31 July 1957 by the UN Economic and Social Council – K. Mrozek, "Reguły Nelsona Mandeli", *Nowa kodyfikacja prawa karnego*, vol. 48, 2018, pp. 169 et seq.

orders.[240] However, they have been widely recognized as a minimum standard for the treatment of prisoners[241] and should therefore be taken into account in the enactment of national law by UN states in view of the need to consider their content during the formation of internal law and make efforts aimed at their actual implementation. Consequently, their use in the penitentiary practice plays a significant role in respecting the necessary minimum rights of persons serving a penalty of imprisonment.[242] As is the case with instruments of international law of a safeguarding nature, their content does not provide for specific minimum rights to which prisoners are entitled with regard to religious practices and services, limiting itself to the use of vague wording, such as "if the prison contains a sufficient number of prisoners of the same religion," or "so far as practicable, every prisoner shall be allowed to satisfy the needs of his or her religious life". This does not alter the general conclusion that, as a rule, the Mandela Rules ensure respect for prisoners' right to religious practices and services to the fullest extent possible, with attention given to the need to provide prisoners with access to representatives of different denominations, especially if the number of prisoners of a given denomination is significant.

Similar provisions in the area of so-called *soft law* are contained in the European Prison Rules (EPR),[243] dedicated to the member states of the Council of Europe. Their significance lies in recommending the observance in the penitentiary systems of states in our part of the world of principles and values that are important in the European circle of civilization and which were proclaimed in the Universal Declaration of Human Rights of 1948, then defined in the European Convention on Human Rights and the European Convention for the Prevention of Torture and Inhuman or Degrading Treatment or Punishment.[244] They are

---

240 D. Gajdus, B. Gronowska, "O potrzebie działań na rzecz poprawy sytuacji więźniów. Uwagi na tle standardów międzynarodowych", *Toruński Rocznik Praw Człowieka i Pokoju*, vol. 4, 1996, p. 71.

241 H. Puleng Motlalekgosi, "Religious Freedom and the Law: A Reality or Pipe Dream for Prisoners in South Africa?", *Journal for the Study of Religion*, vol. 32, no. 1, 2019, pp. 1 et seq.

242 K. Mrozek, "Reguły Nelsona…, pp. 173 and 183.

243 Recommendation of the Committee of Ministers to member states on the European Prison Rules adopted on 11 January 2006 at the 952nd meeting of the Ministers' Deputies – https://search.coe.int/cm/Pages/result_details.aspx?ObjectID=09000016805d8d25 (accessed 15.07.2023).

244 T. Szymanowski, J. Migdał, *Prawo karne wykonawcze i polityka penitencjarna*, Warszawa 2014, pp. 58 et seq.

not *hard law*, but a failure to comply with them entails specific consequences for a state, ranging from negative opinions from other states, NGOs, to a CPT report[245] and the ECHR case-law.[246] They aim to minimize the negative effects of serving a penalty of imprisonment by bringing the imprisonment conditions as close as possible to those at liberty.[247]

The EPR devote a separate place to religious freedom. Under Rule 29 para. 1, prisoners' freedom of thought, conscience and religion shall be respected. Under Rule 29 para. 2, the prison regime shall be organized so far as is practicable to allow prisoners to practise their religion and follow their beliefs, to attend services or meetings led by approved representatives of such religion or beliefs, to receive visits in private from such representatives of their religion or beliefs and to have in their possession books or literature relating to their religion or beliefs. Thus, the EPR emphasized the importance of respect for a prisoner in his or her religious rights,[248] with the scope of this safeguard being even more general than was the case with the Mandela Rules. In the latter case, all the rights relate to the possible scope of practicing a religion, with no indication of minimum rights to be made available to prisoners. Given that the formulation of prisoners' minimal rights regarding their access to religious practices and services is impractical insofar as some faiths, especially in certain regions, are not popular and providing prisoners with access to representatives of their faith could be difficult, if not impossible, it must be concluded that the EPR are only of a safeguarding nature, and do not set a minimum standard for religious freedom of persons deprived of their liberty.

It is extremely important that the manner in which the standards of international law are applied to national penitentiary law most often consists of the formulation of general observations that prisoners have the right to manifest their religion or beliefs to the fullest extent possible that is reconcilable with the special nature of the limitations they are subjected to,[249] or that it is the

245 European Committee for the Prevention of Torture and Inhuman or Degrading Treatment or Punishment.

246 Art. 46 of the Convention: The High Contracting Parties undertake to abide by the final judgment of the Court in any case to which they are parties. The final judgment of the Court shall be transmitted to the Committee of Ministers, which shall supervise its execution.

247 M. Płatek, "Wybrane zasady kodeksu karnego wykonawczego z 1997 r. w świetle Europejskich Reguł Więziennych z 11 stycznia 2006 r.", in S. Lelental, G. B. Szczygieł (eds.), *X lat obowiązywania kodeksu karnego wykonawczego*, Białystok 2009, p. 105.

248 J. Nikołajew, "Reguły Minimalne…, p. 123.

249 W. Sobczak, "Art. 18…, p. 442.

duty of national authorities to create opportunities for all prisoners, including detainees in detention centres, to attend services and contact their chaplains.[250] It is also recognized that the considerations of discipline and security inherent in the regime of penal enforcement law may justify the imposition of limitations leading to the impossibility of an adequate manifestation of one's own religion.[251]

Any limitations imposed by particular states on prisoners regarding their access to religious practices and services are largely dependent on the penitentiary systems of particular states and their approach to criminal law and the penalty of deprivation of liberty. In doing so, states parties have a wide margin of discretion in introducing possible limitations.[252] Although incarceration as a result of criminal act by its very nature involves many limitations, they should have their basis in law. It is clearly indicated in the Convention for the Protection of Human Rights and Fundamental Freedoms discussed above. It prescribes that freedom to manifest one's religion or beliefs shall be subject only to such limitations as are prescribed by law and are necessary in a democratic society in the interests of public safety, for the protection of public order, health or morals, or for the protection of the rights and freedoms of others. Restrictions on any rights are also subject to limitation in the already widely described International Covenant on Civil and Political Rights, which provides that freedom to manifest one's religion or beliefs may be subject only to such limitations as are prescribed by law and are necessary to protect public safety, order, health, or morals or the fundamental rights and freedoms of others.

As regards juveniles, the determination of the minimum standard of protection of their religious freedom is even more difficult given that, apart from a limitation on their access to religious practices and services, as is the case with adults, a specific conflict arises between the rights of juveniles and the rights of their parents to raise their child in accordance with their convictions. It is utterly incomprehensible to draw a demarcation line in this case. If a juvenile is placed in an isolation facility in response to the commission of prohibited act, then in

250 L. Garlicki, "Art. 9", in L. Garlicki (ed.), *Konwencja o ochronie praw człowieka i podstawowych wolności, Tom 1, Komentarz do art. 1–18*, Warszawa 2010, p. 570.

251 L. Garlicki, "Art. 9…, p. 570.

252 A. Gliszczyńska-Grabias, "Prawo do poszanowania wyznania i światopoglądu osadzonego", in *X Seminarium Warszawskie. Pozytywne i negatywne obowiązki państwa wobec osób pozbawionych wolności – aktualne wyzwania polskiego systemu penitencjarnego*, Warszawa 2017, pp. 120 et seq. and J. Meyer-Ladewig, S. Schuster, "Art. 9", in J. Meyer-Ladewig, M. Nettesheim, S. v. Raumer (eds.), *EMRK. Europäische Menschenrechtskonvention. Handkommentar*, Baden-Baden 2017, margin no. 14

the opinion of the state, he or she is mature enough to take responsibility for his or her actions. The question is whether he or she is simultaneously mature enough to make an independent decision on his or her religious education and practices, or whether his or her parents, who want to raise their child in accordance with their faith, should have the decisive opinion in this regard. At the same time, it is possible to consider whether giving primacy to the parents' right to raise their child in accordance with their own convictions should be affected by doubts about their parenting ability, because the child in their care committed a criminal act, which gave rise to taking him or her away from the family environment.

The provisions of international law do not prejudge this issue and are very sparing about the rights of juveniles and their parents to religious freedom and to raise their child in accordance with their faith. Although international law ensures simultaneously children's right to religious freedom and parents' right to child-rearing according to their convictions, it is often the case with international regulations that they do not specific which right should prevail in this regard.

One of the most important instruments of international law ensuring the rights of children is the Convention on the Rights of the Child. It does not contain specific regulations regarding the religious freedom of the detained child. Only Art. 37 indicates that every child deprived of liberty shall be treated with humanity and respect for the inherent dignity of the human person, and in a manner which takes into account the needs of persons of his or her age. Notably, a change of family environment shall be used only as a measure of last resort because every child deprived of liberty shall be separated from adults unless it is considered in the child's best interest not to do so and shall have the right to maintain contact with his or her family through correspondence and visits, save in exceptional circumstances. However, under Art. 20 paras. 1–3 of the Convention on the Rights of the Child, a child temporarily or permanently deprived of his or her family environment shall be entitled to special protection and assistance provided by the State, alternative care, and among other things, the right to retain his or her religious identity.

Religious freedom during the enforcement of an isolation measure in relation to the juvenile is also not mentioned by the United Nations Standard Minimum Rules for the Administration of Juvenile Justice ("The Beijing Rules"). The entire instrument refers to religion only once, declaring equal application of the Standard Minimum Rules, without distinction of any kind, for example as to religion.[253] Instead, emphasis is placed on the finality of the use of measures against

253 See: https://www.ohchr.org/fr/instruments-mechanisms/instruments/united-nations-standard-minimum-rules-administration-juvenile (accessed 15.07.2023).

juveniles as regards taking them out of the family environment, which shows that attention is paid to raising children in the family and, consequently, allowing parents to pass on their beliefs to their children. This issue is also emphasized in points 6, 7 and 11 of Recommendation No. R(87) 20 of the Committee of Ministers to member states on social reactions to juvenile delinquency.[254]

In turn, Recommendation CM/Rec(2008)11 of the Committee of Ministers to member states on the European Rules for juvenile offenders subject to sanctions or measures prescribes that juveniles' freedom of thought, conscience and religion shall be respected (Recommendation 87 para. 1). These recommendations further prescribe that the institutional regimen shall be organized so far as is practicable to allow juveniles to practise their religion and follow their beliefs, to attend services or meetings led by approved representatives of such religion or beliefs, to receive visits in private from such representatives of their religion or beliefs and to have in their possession books or literature relating to their religion or beliefs. Juveniles may not be compelled to practise a religion, follow a belief, attend religious services or meetings, take part in religious practices or to accept a visit from a representative of any religion or belief (recommendation 87 para. 3).[255] In turn, Rule 48 of the United Nations Rules for the Protection of Juveniles Deprived of their Liberty prescribes that every juvenile should be allowed to satisfy the needs of his or her religious and spiritual life, in particular by attending the services or meetings provided in the detention facility or by conducting his or her own services and having possession of the necessary books or items of religious observance and instruction of his or her denomination. If a detention facility contains a sufficient number of juveniles of a given religion, one or more qualified representatives of that religion should be appointed or approved and allowed to hold regular services and to pay pastoral visits in private to juveniles at their request. Every juvenile should have the right to receive visits from a qualified representative of any religion of his or her choice, as well as

254 See "Zalecenie Nr R (87) 20 Komitetu Ministrów dla państw członkowskich w sprawie reakcji społecznych na przestępczość nieletnich (przyjęte przez Komitet Ministrów w dniu 17 września 1987 r. na 410. zebraniu Zastępców Ministrów)", in P. J. Jaros (ed.), *Prawa dziecka. Dokumenty Rady Europy*, Warszawa 2012, pp. 463 et seq.

255 See: "Zalecenie CM/Rec (2008)11 Komitetu Ministrów dla państw członkowskich w sprawie zasad europejskich dotyczących kar i środków alternatywnych stosowanych wobec sprawców nieletnich (przyjęte przez Komitet Ministrów w dniu 5 listopada 2008 r. na 1040. zebraniu Zastępców Ministrów)", in P. J. Jaros (ed.), *Prawa dziecka. Dokumenty Rady Europy*, Warszawa 2012, pp. 555 et seq.

the right not to participate in religious services and freely to decline religious education, counselling or indoctrination.[256]

Finally, the Guidelines of the Committee of Ministers of the Council of Europe on child-friendly justice, adopted by the Committee of Ministers of the Council of Europe on 17 November 2010, indicate that children deprived of liberty in particular should have the right to enjoy freedom of thought, conscience and religion (guideline 21b). This is yet another example where, apart from ensuring the right to religious freedom, there is no specific declaration as to the permissible scope of limitation of this right due to the enforcement of isolation measures. Moreover, international law makes no attempt to resolve the issue of how the incarceration of a juvenile limits his or her parents or legal guardians' right to child-rearing in accordance with their convictions.

By contrast, the case-law of international courts recognizes the need to place limitations on certain powers of parents to pass on specific religious values on to children. For example, in a judgement of 22 June 1989 in the case of Eriksson v. Sweden,[257] the ECHR held that parents and legal guardians can lose the right conferred under Art. 2 of Protocol No. 1 if they have been deprived of their parental rights as a result of a court ruling or adoption dissolution. In turn, in a judgement of 24 March 1988 in the case of Olsson v. Sweden,[258] the Court held that in the case where parental rights are only limited, for example owing to an illness, the placement of a child in foster home or "taking the children into care" does not lead to a situation where children are not to be brought up in accordance with their parents' convictions or the religion followed by the parents. The above judgments lead to a conclusion that the placement of a juvenile in a post-criminal isolation centre may entail at least a limitation of the parents' rights to bring up the child in accordance with their religious convictions.

In extreme cases, parents' religious convictions may also form the basis for imposing limitations on parental authority. Case law has pointed to religious practices that may harm the child and require state intervention, such as a refusal to provide adequate medical care due to religious beliefs (e.g., no consent to a blood transfusion for a haemophiliac child based on the religious convictions

256 See: https://www.globaldetentionproject.org/wp-content/uploads/2016/06/UN-Resolution-45-113.pdf (accessed 16.09.2023).

257 ECHR, Judgment of 22 June 1989, case of Eriksson v. Sweden, application no. 11373/85.

258 ECHR, Judgment of 24 March 1988, case of Olsson v. Sweden, application no. 10465/83.

of a Jehovah's Witness parent[259]) or causing emotional suffering to a child whose parents have strong and conflicting religious beliefs (e.g., a fundamentalist Christian father trying to convert his orthodox Jewish son to his beliefs, among other things, by taking the son to religious services where he received the message that adults or children who do not accept Jesus Christ as their lord and saviour are destined to burn in hell).[260]

Religious freedom of both adults and children placed in post-criminal isolation centres is no longer questioned in the worldwide legal order. International laws ensure these rights very cautiously, with no mention of specific rights that may be exercised by interested parties. In the case of children, the standard of this freedom is further lowered by the reservations and declarations submitted to a concluded international treaty by states ratifying the conventions. Due to a conflict between the juvenile's right to religious freedom and the parents' right to child-rearing in accordance with their own convictions, which is significant in the case of children, it is desirable to define in relevant international documents the age from which a juvenile can decide independently about religious education and practice of religion. We believe that this issue should be resolved not only at the national level but also at the supra-state level – the child has the right, in the event of a conflict between his or her opinion and the parents' position on the subject of faith, to a judicial review of adult decisions relating to his or her education, including religious instruction, and to benefit from religious practices and services.[261]

259 See: *Levitsky v. Levitsky*, 231 Md. 388, 190 A.2d 621 (Md. 1963).

260 See: *Kendall v. Kendall*, 426 Mass. 238, 687 N.E.2d 1228 (Mass. 1997).

261 A different take on the issue is possible – the literature has pointed out, for example, the relevance of treating the child as a separate entity, with all the applicable rights, which makes it impossible to treat him or her as a measure used by the parents to fulfil their life goals and values – J. G. Dwyer, "Parents' Religion and Children's Welfare: Debunking the Doctrine of Parents' Rights", *California Law Review*, vol. 82, no. 6, 1994, pp. 1371 et seq.

Chapter IV Religious freedom of adults and children deprived of their liberty in post-criminal isolation units: Polish standards

4.1. Statutory grounds for religious freedom of persons deprived of their liberty in Poland

The issue of incarceration in an organized institution, such as a prison, requires the formulation of a statutory definition of prisoners' rights relating to their religious freedom and the rules on access to religious practices and services. Restrictions in this regard are natural – they stem from the essence of imprisonment and its depriving nature. On the other hand, the vulnerability of prisoners to violations of their rights and the fact that they are one of the most vulnerable groups in society requires far-reaching thoroughness in regulating their rights so that there is as little room as possible for any abuse. The right to exercise religious freedom includes primarily the possibility of an independent choice of confession,[262] its change,[263] and the abandonment of faith and adoption of an atheistic attitude.[264] In subjective terms, this freedom covers worship, teaching the principles of a professed religion, practice and ritual activities, including the manifestation of religious beliefs.[265] For the freedom of thought, conscience and belief to be a truly complete freedom that reflects the way an individual functions in society, protection is extended to the individual's inner autonomy and the manifestation of beliefs and confession – so-called *forum externum*.[266] Insofar as human

262 See: M. Pietrzak, *Prawo wyznaniowe*, Warszawa 2003, p. 33.

263 This right arises from, among others, Art 53 para. 3 of the Constitution of the Republic of Poland, and Art. 9 of the European Convention on Human Rights.

264 M. Pietrzak, *Prawo…*, p. 33 and ECHR, Judgment of 21 February 2008, case of Alexandridis v. Greece, application no. 19516/06 – M. A. Nowicki, *Europejski Trybunał Praw Człowieka, Wybór orzeczeń 2008*, Warszawa 2009, p. 199.

265 M. A. Abramowicz, "Przedmiotowy zakres wolności religijnej", *Studia z Prawa Wyznaniowego*, vol. 10, 2007, p. 331.

266 J. Bartoszewicz, "Wolność myśli, sumienia i wyznania w Polsce w świetle orzecznictwa strasburskiego", *Polski Rocznik Praw Człowieka i Prawa Humanitarnego*, vol. 3, 2012, p. 68.

independence in the spiritual sphere is absolute,[267] the freedom to manifest a religion may be subject to limitations.[268]

Prisoners are one of the groups affected by such limitations. The legal position of a prisoner is limited by provisions of law[269] that can limit or exclude the rights that citizens can freely exercise at liberty. The essence of modern imprisonment is not the deprivation of this freedom on all levels, but especially the freedom of locomotion. The penalty of imprisonment itself is a punishment, not a place where a penalty is served. Although prisoners have the right to benefit freely from religious practices and services and manifest their religious beliefs, it is necessary to take into consideration their situation.[270] The poor access to prison and the hierarchical and organized nature of every sphere of prisoners' life associated with that institution makes it inevitable that certain aspects of the manifestation of religious life are restricted. The question is whether the Polish legislature made efforts to ensure that any rationing is indeed justified and only to the extent that is technically or organizationally justified by placement in isolation.

Given the above, a review of laws was carried out in terms of guarantees of religious freedom, the right to practice it and the introduced limitations. The anchoring of any rights in a law is hugely important because the right to manifest faith and benefit from religious practices and services in prison may take only such forms as are permitted by law and by Prison Service officers.[271] On the one hand, law guarantees a strict definition of the conditions under which religious practices and services are held, on the other, it sets the rules on access for persons outside the prison who are to perform such ministries, limiting the possibility of infiltration of the prison environment by quasi-religious groups, which have a negative impact on its members – e.g., destructive sects.[272]

---

267 M. A. Nowicki, *Wokół Konwencji Europejskiej. Komentarz do Europejskiej Konwencji Praw Człowieka*, Warszawa 2017, p. 723.

268 M. A. Abramowicz, "Przedmiotowy…, p. 331.

269 L. Bogunia, "Kilka uwag dotyczących obowiązków skazanego na karę pozbawienia wolności w jego statusie prawnym", in K. Indecki (ed.), *Aktualne problemy prawa karnego, kryminologii i penitencjarystyki. Księga ofiarowana Profesorowi Stefanowi Lelentalowi w 45. Roku pracy naukowej i dydaktycznej*, Łódź 2004, p. 70.

270 K. Warchałowski, *Prawo do wolności myśli, sumienia i religii w Europejskiej Konwencji Praw Człowieka i Podstawowych Wolności*, Lublin 2004, pp. 130 et seq.

271 See: *Biuletyn RPO. Materiały. Stan i węzłowe problemy polskiego więziennictwa. Część I.*, Warszawa 1995, p. 74.

272 M. Kotowska, M. Romańczuk-Grącka, "*Wolność religijna w warunkach izolacji penitencjarnej*" in A. Nawój-Śleszyńska, J. Łuczak (eds.), *Wybrane problemy indywidualizacji wykonywania kary pozbawienia wolności i środków probacyjnych,*

Human rights, methods and extent of their limitation and exercise during the execution of prison sentences are governed by numerous legal instruments, including the provisions regulating the relationship of the Polish state to faith. Under Art. 32 para. 1 of the Act of 17 May 1989 on the relationship between the state and the Roman Catholic Church in the Republic of Poland, pre-trial detainees may perform religious practices and participate in Mass broadcast by the mass media and, with the consent of the authority at whose disposal they remain, benefit from individual religious services. Under para. 2, convicted persons shall be provided with the opportunity to perform religious practices, receive religious services and attend Mass celebrated on Sundays and feast days in a suitably adapted room in the facility where they are incarcerated. Persons who are unable to attend Mass celebrated on the premises of the facility should be given the opportunity to listen to Mass broadcast by the mass media. Under Art. 32 para. 2 of the cited law, juveniles staying in regional educational centres, correctional facilities and juvenile shelters are provided with the opportunity to perform religious practices, receive religious instruction and services, attend Mass on Sundays and feast days. The provisions governing the relationship between the state and the Roman Catholic Church ensure prisoners access to religious practices and services. These provisions do not fully correspond to the regulations governing the principles of imprisonment, the most important and extensive of which is the Penal Enforcement Code,[273] to be discussed below.

At the outset, it should be pointed out that the legislature is aware that incarceration entails numerous limitations and ensures prisoners' rights and freedoms in law, making a list of their rights and obligations. Art. 4 § 1 and 2 provide that penalties shall be carried out humanely, with respect for the human dignity of the convicted person. The convicted person retains civil rights and freedoms, while their limitation can only result from a law and from a final decision issued on its basis.[274] These provisions strongly emphasize the humanism

---

Łódź 2017, p. 150 and A. Kwieciński, "Podstawy prawne realizacji prawa do wolności religijnej w warunkach izolacji penitencjarnej. Rozważania na marginesie dyskusji o zjawisku multikulturowości populacji więziennej", in M. Jabłoński (ed.), *Księga jubileuszowa na siedemdziesięciolecie Wydziału Prawa, Administracji i Ekonomii Uniwersytetu Wrocławskiego. Część 2*, Wrocław 2015, p. 260.

273 Journal of Laws of 2023, pos. 127.

274 See more: B. Stańdo – Kawecka, "Execution of Prison Sentences in Poland – 20 Years of Application of the 1997 Code of the Execution of Penalties", in K. Drenkhahn, B. Geng, J. Grzywa-Holten, S. Harrendorf, C. Morgenstern, I. Puren (eds.), *Kriminologie und Kriminalpolitik im Dienste der Menschenwürde. Festschrift für Frieder Dünkel zum 70. Geburtstag*, Mönchengladbach 2020, pp. 941 et seq.

principle, placing a ban on limiting any rights of prisoners unless it results from a law or a final ruling.[275] Prisoners' rights are additionally ensured by Art. 5 § 1 PEC, enacting the principle of their subjective treatment.[276] It prescribes that the convicted person is the subject of the rights and obligations set forth in the Code. These norms are intended to be a general directive for penitentiary policy and practice,[277] constituting a criterion for specific solutions in the area of enforcing court rulings.[278] They should also serve as detailed "legislative guidelines" for the creation of (implementing) instruments of a lower rank.

It follows from the above provisions that the legal position of the convicted person is limited by provisions[279] that may limit or exclude rights that citizens freely enjoy at liberty. One such right subject to limitation is the right to profess religion freely. The literature emphasizes that this right takes on a special value in prison because this type of freedom cannot be excluded by any legal ruling.[280] Under no circumstances can a prisoner be deprived of the right to profess and worship his or her religion.[281] Although this view is true in the spiritual dimension, the external participation in various religious practices or the manifestation of one's belief may and, sometimes, must be limited. Consequently, a number of implementing provisions ensures fundamental religious rights and freedoms so as to establish a legal framework for prisoners' rights to manifest their religion in prison. It is necessary to analyse them briefly because they are the ultimate criterion for an assessment of the correctness of the regulations adopted by the Polish legislature.

First, mention should be made of Art. 102 para. 3 PEC, which lays down that the convict has the right to exercise religious freedom. It is a general rule that does not confer any specific entitlements on prisoners, but it plays a significant role in implementing the guarantees of the right to religious freedom defined in international law instruments and the Constitution into the Penal Enforcement

---

275 S. Pawela, *Prawo karne wykonawcze. Zarys wykładu*, Warszawa 2007, p. 66.

276 Z. Hołda, "Wstęp", in Z. Hołda, K. Postulski, *Kodeks karny wykonawczy. Komentarz*, Gdańsk 2006, pp. 22 et seq.

277 S. Pawela, *Prawo karne*..., p. 91.

278 T. Kalisz, "Zasady prawa karnego wykonawczego", *Nowa kodyfikacja prawa karnego*, vol. 17, 2005, p. 319.

279 L. Bogunia, "Kilka uwag..., p. 70.

280 J. Nikołajew, "Prawo do wolności religijnej więźniów według Jana Pawła II", in P. Marzec, J. Nikołajew (eds.), *Osoba i dzieło Ojca Świętego Jana Pawła II. Studium wybranych problemów*, Tomaszów Lubelski–Lublin 2009, p. 122.

281 Z. Lasocik, *Praktyki religijne*..., p. 169.

Code. The literature has associated this right with the freedom to profess or adopt a religion of one's own choice and to manifest one's religion individually or in community with others, publicly or privately, through worship, prayer, observance, practice and teaching.[282] The very general nature of the guarantee of this right does not make it possible to derive specific rights legitimizing the manifestation of adherence to a given religion. The legislature became aware of this circumstance, specifying prisoners' rights regarding freedom of religion in the subsequent provisions of the Penal Enforcement Code and the implementing instruments.

Under Art. 106 PEC, the convicted person has the right to perform religious practices and benefit from religious services, and to participate directly in services held in the prison on feast days and to listen to services broadcast by the mass media, and to possess the books, writings and objects necessary for this purpose.[283] Apart from a list of specific rights enjoyed by prisoners (e.g., right to participate in services held in the prison or possess necessary books), to be discussed in detail below, the legislature included a more general declaration, specifically, that the convicted person shall have the right to perform religious practices. The legislature did not choose to give a detailed list of prisoners' rights relating to the exercise of their religious beliefs, which would allow prisoners to make specific demands to the penitentiary facility (e.g., how many services per month the prisoner is entitled to), apart from the right to participate directly in services held in the prison on feast days. In essence, this means that the scope of other religious practices and services, in particular, their minimum availability to prisoners, has not been regulated at the statutory level. The specific issues involved will be discussed below.

4.2. Religious freedom of adults deprived of their liberty declared in legal instruments of a lower rank than a law

The provisions of the Penal Enforcement Code on the execution of prison sentences and temporary detention do not contain, save the above regulations, any more detailed standards specifying a method of fulfilment of the right to freedom of religion applicable to prisoners. Under Art. 106 § 4 PEC, this is to be achieved by the Regulation of the Justice Minister of 2 September 2003 on

282 S. Lelental, *Kodeks karny wykonawczy. Komentarz*, Warszawa 2001, p. 290.

283 See more: O. Sitarz, A. Jaworska-Wieloch, "Legitimacy of the limitation of freedom of religion during imprisonment (in the light of Polish and international regulations)", *Law Journal of New Bulgarian University*, vol. 17, no. 1, 2021, pp. 10 et seq.

detailed rules on performing religious practices and benefiting from religious services in penitentiary facilities and detention centres.[284] In § 5, this instrument grants the facility director the right to take the necessary measures to provide adequate conditions for religious practices and services and benefiting from these services and to hear a chaplain in the matter of the organization of religious services.

The above regulation is brief and scanty and it does not ensure and safeguard any specific rights for prisoners. It must be somewhat regretfully noted that the regulation on detailed rules for performing religious practices and benefiting from religious services does not introduce any specific rules in that regard. It only specifies that the facility director, as a body managing the prison, is responsible for the creation of conditions "adequate" for performing practices and benefiting from religious services on the premises of the facility.

Another provision of an extra-statutory rank is the Regulation of the Justice Minister of 23 December 2022 on the organizational-ordinal rules for serving a penalty of deprivation of liberty. It prescribes in § 10 item 1 point 6 letter B that a convicted person is entitled to possess up to 10 religious objects of no more than 250 × 150 mm in size. It also prescribes in § 11 item 2 point 12 that the prison director shall specify in the prison internal rules the days, hours and place of services, religious meetings and religious instruction. Further details on the access to religious practices and services of convicted persons have not been defined in the provisions of universally applicable law of a lower rank than a law.

4.3. Religious freedom of adults deprived of their liberty declared in prison internal rules

Incarceration in a total institution, such a prison, means that the true scope of prisoners' religious freedom, experienced by them directly, will depend on the way a given penitentiary institution is organized. The prisoners' daily rhythm and access to various activities, including those of a religious nature, are organized by the prison internal rules in force in a given facility, set by its director (Art. 73 § 2 PEC). Although the Regulation of the Justice Minister of 23 December 2022 on the organizational-ordinal rules for serving a penalty of deprivation of liberty[285] and the Regulation of the Justice Minister of 23 December 2022 on the organizational-ordinal rules for the execution of temporary detention[286]

---

284 Journal of Laws of 2003, No. 159, pos. 1546.

285 Journal of Laws of 2022, pos. 2847.

286 Journal of Laws of 2022, pos. 2848.

provide some minimum regulations to be included in such prison internal rules, many issues are ultimately determined in these instruments by prison directors, including the days, hours and place of services, religious meetings and religious instruction (§ 11 item 2 point 12 of the organizational-ordinal rules for serving a penalty of deprivation of liberty, § 8 item 2 point 12 of the organizational-ordinal rules for the execution of temporary detention).

The provisions do not regulate the specific rights that should be normalized in the prison internal rules regarding religious rights and freedoms, apart from a mention that convicted persons are entitled to possess up to 10 religious objects of no more than 250 × 150 mm in size. As indicated above, the legislature provides that the prison internal rules shall specify the days, hours and place of services, religious meetings and religious instruction. It does not impose an obligation to define other rules on practicing faith applicable in a particular denomination in the prison internal rules, although it would not be wrong to provide more detailed rules on practicing religion in the prison internal rules, as long as it does not violate generally applicable regulations. It is important to bear in mind Art. 106 § 3 PEC, which lays down that the exercise of religious freedom may not violate the principles of tolerance – the fulfilment of prisoners' religious needs may not interfere with the operation and achievement of the objectives of the institution and the rights of others.[287]

The introduction of detailed regulations on the exercise of religious freedom into prison internal rules may indeed provide details missing in the universally applicable law, however, it entails the risk of arbitrary decisions by directors of particular prisons in the area of religious freedom of prisoners. It is all the more dangerous because even though the established prison internal rules may be monitored by a penitentiary judge as part of supervision,[288] in the case where no specific right envisaged by the universally applicable law is violated, calling the prison internal rules of a given facility into question seems unlikely.

The final formation of prisoners' rights in terms of religious freedom based on technical-organizational provisions must raise serious doubts. The rights, freedoms and obligations of convicted persons or pre-trial detainees are directly shaped by prison internal rules – were the prison internal rules to be limited to indicating specific dates and places of religious practices and services (e.g.,

287 Z. Lasocik, *Praktyki religijne…*, p. 81.

288 See: § 2 of the Regulation of the Justice Minister of 26 August 2003 on the method, scope and mode of penitentiary supervision (Journal of Laws of 2003, No. 152, pos. 1496, as amended).

additional services are held in block I on Tuesdays, in block II on Thursdays), such a state of affairs would be fully acceptable. However, neither the Penal Enforcement Code nor prison internal rules define the minimum accessibility of religious practices and services and this area is left entirely to the discretion of prison directors setting prison internal rules. Given prisoners' particular vulnerability to the deprivation of rights, this phenomenon is undesirable and dangerous.

4.4. Significance of the registration of the church of a religious association for the scope of prisoners' religious freedom

The regulations do not indicate unequivocally whether prisoners' right to freedom of belief applies exclusively to registered religions – the importance of this issue was pointed out in previous chapters, which extensively described what can be considered a religion and whether it requires registration. The provisions relating to prisoners lack precision in this matter – on the one hand, the Penal Enforcement Code seems to advocate the necessity of legal recognition of prisoners' declared confessions, indicating in Art. 242 § 12 that "Church" and "other religious association" should be understood as a church or other religious association with a statutorily regulated legal situation.[289] In addition, in the case of Jakóbski v. Poland, justifying a prisoner's right to a meatless diet consistent with the precepts of his religion, the ECHR emphasized that Buddhism is one of major world religions officially recognized in many countries. The Court linked the prisoner's right to manifest his religious feelings to the recognition of his declared religion by the state. On the other hand, in a judgement of 26 June 2016 in the case of Izzettin Doğan et al. v. Turkey,[290] the ECHR emphasized that a refusal to recognize officially a particular religion means calling its religious nature into question, thus leading to an interference with freedom of belief ensured by Art. 9 of the European Convention. The Court also pointed out that pluralism is based on the honest recognition, respect, diversity and dynamism of cultural traditions, identities and religious beliefs – in a situation where the state denies the status of a religious denomination to one of its associations, doubts can be raised about the state's obligation to maintain true religious pluralism, which characterizes a democratic society.

289 A. Rogowska, "Wolność sumienia i wyznania w świetle przepisów polskiego Kodeksu karnego wykonawczego", *Acta Erasmiana*, vol. 1, 2011, p. 261.

290 ECHR, Judgment of 26 April 2016, case of Izzettin Doğan and Others v. Turkey, application no. 62649/10.

Then, the possibility to benefit from religious practices and services involving exclusively a state-recognized faith would excessively limit prisoners' freedom of religion in a situation where a state refused to register a given religion for specific and not always justified reasons. It would deprive prisoners of the right to manifest their faith and prevent participation in any form of spiritual encounter. Consequently, all religions should be included, not only the officially recognized ones, so as to ensure equality and pluralism in society. It is necessary, however, to examine whether the set of beliefs and the practices associated with them actually constitute a religion[291] to avoid the achievement of other objectives, for example, organization of illegal meetings of prisoners under the guise of religious contemplation. However, the last remark applies to all religions, both recognized and non-recognized by the state.

4.5. Scope of prisoners' religious freedom: should faith be manifested only in mandated forms in prison or also in forms recommended by a given denomination?

The question arises whether the scope of freedom to manifest a professed religion should include only elements mandated by a given religion, or whether a prisoner should retain the right to manifest faith in all forms "merely" recommended by a given religion.

This issue is not regulated by Polish legal provisions and the judicature broaches it only incidentally. In the case of Jakóbski v. Poland,[292] the European Court of Human Rights held that a refusal to provide a prisoner with a meatless diet that would be consistent with the precepts of his religion violated his right to manifest his religion by observing the tenets of the Buddhist religion, even though the Mahayana school of Buddhism, which by declaration the applicant followed, only recommends but does not mandate vegetarianism. This position seems to be right – since a prisoner retains all the rights to religious practices and services and to manifest his religion under freedom of religion, as long as they are not contrary to the provisions of law, it is difficult to make the form of manifesting one's feelings dependent on whether a particular practice is mandated or merely recommended by a particular denomination.[293]

---

291 M. A. Nowicki, *Wokół Konwencji...*, pp. 727 et seq.

292 ECHR, Judgment of 7 March 2011, case of Jakóbski v. Poland, application no. 18429/06.

293 ECHR, Judgment of 7 March 2011, case of Jakóbski v. Poland, application no. 18429/06. See also: M. Zawiślak, "The limitations of religious practices in polish prisons", *Review of European and Comparative Law*, vol. 30, no. 3, 2017, p. 118.

When determining whether a prisoner should have the right to manifest religion in a specified form, it should not be decisive whether it is a practice mandated or recommended by a given confession. Instead, it should be whether it is reconcilable with the essence of imprisonment, whether it does not violate universally applicable laws, and whether it is technically feasible to be performed in prison (in practical and financial terms).

4.6. Diversity of situations of convicted persons in different types of prisons, including dangerous convicts

The scope of convicted persons' religious freedom is largely dependent on the type of penitentiary facility in which they are incarcerated. Although there are many differences between the rights of convicts in closed, semi-open and open facilities (see Arts. 90–92 PEC), the much broader rights of convicted persons incarcerated in semi-open and open facilities as regards temporary release from penitentiary facilities come to the fore (Art. 91 point 7 PEC and Art. 92 point 9 PEC). Apart from special purpose licences, they can also get so-called system passes and passes to leave the penitentiary facility as a reward (Art. 138 § 1 points 7 and 8 PEC) or as preparation for life after release (Art. 165 § 2 PEC). This allows such prisoners to take part in pilgrimages, Corpus Christi processions, the sacraments of loved ones administered outside the penitentiary facility or a Christmas-time pastoral visit in their place of residence. The possibilities they may enjoy in that regard are much broader compared to convicted persons placed in closed facilities, as the latter may be temporarily released only in the case of a special purpose licence (Art. 141a PEC) or a break in serving a prison sentence. The prerequisite for the application of both these institutions is the so-called positive criminological prognosis, i.e., an opinion that a convicted person will abide by the law while at liberty and that the pass or break granted to him or her will be used as intended. Such a positive prognosis is typically much more difficult to obtain in the case of persons incarcerated in closed-type penitentiaries, thus their chances for participation in religious practices and services are much more limited.

Incarceration in closed-type prisons involves permanent residence in a cell (for almost 24 hours a day, except for a walk and classes), whereas cells are closed at night in semi-open prisons. Limited freedom of movement substantially reduces the possibilities of access to religious practices. Prisoners are not free to go to the chapel to pray, participate in prayer meetings or visit the library to borrow prayer books, or on the contrary, they cannot leave the cell when they do not wish to watch a cellmate listen to the Holy Mass, pray or talk in faith.

The type of penitentiary facility also affects the ability to wear one's own clothes (prisoners have such right in open and semi-open facilities, it depends on consent from the prison director in closed prison), which can be important where one wishes to wear clothing that conforms to a particular confession. The type of prison also determines the number of visits, which can be important for the allocation of time to meetings with representatives or followers of a particular religion. By contrast, it does not matter as regards the type of food issued to prisoners or the permission to have a TV set in the cell.

Much more far-reaching restrictions apply to dangerous convicts, who, under Art. 88b point 3 PEC, may participate directly in services, religious meetings and instruction only in the block in which they are incarcerated. Although the model for dealing with this group of prisoners is clearly dominated by the isolation-security function,[294] account must be taken of the fact that the number of dangerous prisoners has been on the decline in Poland.[295] The above raises the risk of solitary participation in a service or a religious meeting, being deprived of a sense of community in experiencing faith. After all, if only a portion of prisoners is interested in participating in religious practices, incarceration in a small and closely supervised ward for dangerous offenders can mean that no one other than a particular convict is interested in publicly manifesting religion, especially when the other prisoners follow a different confession. There is also a risk that small wards designed for such offenders will not have places for religious practices and services at all. Dangerous convicts cannot move on the prison premises independently, which affects their free access to the chapel and library and the need to participate in the religious practices performed by fellow prisoners. They are not allowed to wear their own clothing and footwear, which affects the ability to adapt their attire to the requirements of a particular religion.

The scope of religious freedom may also be subject to limitations in connection with an imposed disciplinary penalty of incarceration in an isolation cell (Art. 143 § 3 point 3 PEC). Such a penalty may be imposed on a convict who has committed a transgression that seriously violates the discipline and order in force in the prison, and it consists of incarcerating the convict individually in a cell and preventing him from having contact with other convicts. During its execution, the

---

294 T. Kalisz, "Osadzeni niebezpieczni. Procedura kwalifikacji, jej weryfikacja oraz zakres ograniczeń", *Nowa kodyfikacja prawa karnego*, vol. 43, 2017, pp. 177 et seq. and G. B. Szczygieł, *Społeczna readaptacja skazanych w polskim systemie penitencjarnym*, Białystok 2002, pp. 117 et seq.

295 See: https://www.ebos.pl/artykul/1741_niebezpiecznych_wiezniow_coraz_mniej.html (accessed 15.07.2023).

convict is deprived of the possibility of, among other things, direct participation, together with other convicts, in services, religious meetings and religious instruction. On the convict's request, he or she should be allowed to participate directly in a religious service in conditions that prevent him or her from having contact with other convicts. It is doubtful whether such a far-reaching limitation of the right to perform religious practices is justified. While one can understand restricting convicts' contacts of an entertainment nature with other prisoners during the execution of an isolation penalty, for example, by depriving them of the opportunity to participate in sports, cultural and educational activities, or at least conversations and activities in the cell, the application of such rules to the possibility of participating in services appears to be excessive. These are not activities consisting of interactions with fellow prisoners or choosing an activity of one's choice. Instead, they involve the celebration of service in a clearly defined order, with no possibility of free talk with other prisoners or engaging in other, freely chosen entertainment with them.

4.7. Diversity of situations of convicted persons and pre-trial detainees in terms of scope of religious freedom in prison

The scope of religious freedom of convicted persons and pre-trial detainees is not identical. Although Art. 214 PEC prescribes that the pre-trial detainee enjoys at least the same rights as a convicted person serving a penalty of imprisonment, the literature points out that the status of a person sentenced to a penalty of imprisonment is fundamentally different from the status of a pre-trial detainee. In theory, the principle of the presumption of innocence precludes the possibility of burdening a pre-trial detainee with obligations and applying to him or her a number of restrictions that would be incompatible with the objectives of temporary detention.[296] The content of the cited Art. 214 PEC (and in particular the expression "at least") and the opinions presented against its background[297]

296 P. Pałaszewski, "Status tymczasowo aresztowanego, wobec którego wykonywana jest kara pozbawienia wolności (art. 223a k.k.w.)", in A. Kwieciński (ed.), *Postępowanie z wybranymi grupami skazanych w polskim systemie penitencjarnym. Aspekty prawne*, Warszawa 2013, pp. 288 et seq.

297 For example: Art. 214 § 1 PEC sets a safeguarding standard; it sets the minimum in the sphere of rights and limitations of pre-trial detainees, ensuring that they enjoy at least such rights as are applicable to convicts serving a sentence of imprisonment – P. Pałaszewski, "Status tymczasowo..., p. 289. Besides, the substantiation to the Penal Enforcement Code reads that the rights applicable to a pre-trial detainee are at least the same as those applicable to a convicted person and were supplemented

may suggest a more favourable status of the pre-trial detainee compared to the person serving a penalty of imprisonment.

In reality, this is not the case – in large part because of the need to fulfil the objectives set for preventive measures, that is, the creation of adequate conditions for carrying out criminal proceedings and holding the perpetrator accountable. Art. 207 PEC prescribes that the execution of pre-trial detention serves the purposes for which this measure was applied, in particular, to secure the proper course of criminal proceedings. The procedure relating to pre-trial detainees is governed by Art. 209 PEC. It contains rules governing imprisonment, although they are to be applied accordingly, taking into account the objectives of pending criminal proceedings,[298] and every departure from the rules applicable to convicted persons requires the legislature to issue a specific and positive provision.

Art. 217 § 6 PEC has importance for the religious freedom of pre-trial detainees. The provision makes it possible to limit or define the manner in which the right of a pre-trial detainee to contact chaplains providing religious services or other persons is exercised if the need to ensure the proper course of criminal proceedings requires it. The provision substantially restricts the rights of pre-trial detainees compared to those applicable to convicted persons because Art. 106 PEC ensures convicts the use of religious services, direct participation in services on feast days, listening to services broadcast by mass media, participation in religious instruction conducted in the prison and individual meetings with a chaplain.[299]

The conformity of limiting the exercise of the right of a pre-trial detainee to contact a chaplain providing religious ministry with Art. 31 para. 3 of the Polish Constitution has been contested in the literature.[300] The rationality of the measure adopted by the legislature may raise doubts, as it is difficult to imagine a situation where contact with a chaplain could conflict with the objectives of an applied preventive measure. Consequently, the meaning of Art. 217 § 6 PEC should be read less like the possibility of restricting individual contacts with a

by the provisions of Art. 215 – *Nowe kodeksy karne z uzasadnieniami*, I. Fredrich-Michalska, B. Stachurska-Marcińczak (eds.), Warszawa 1997, p. 565.

298 K. Postulski, *Kodeks karny wykonawczy. Komentarz*, Warszawa 2012, p. 850.

299 On the significance of the right to perform religious practices, benefiting from prison ministry and participation in services held in penitentiary facilities and detention centres see more – J. Nikołajew, *Wolność sumienia i religii skazanych…*, pp. 137–183.

300 S. Lelental, *Kodeks karny wykonawczy. Komentarz*, Warszawa 2014, p. 722.

minister than staying in places of collective worship where a pre-trial detainee could contact other detainees.[301]

Notably, even if the disposing body sees the need to limit or define a prisoner's contact with a chaplain, it is not possible to exclude the possibility of contacting chaplains completely.

The significantly more difficult situation of pre-trial detainees, as compared to convicts, in terms of access to religious practices and services applies to a much broader area than just contact with chaplains. The issue is first and foremost the possibility of participating in services – under Art. 32 of the Act of 17 May 1989 on the relationship between the state and the Roman Catholic Church in the Republic of Poland, pre-trial detainees may attend Mass broadcast by mass media and, with the consent of the authority at whose disposal they remain, enjoy individual religious services. Thus, these provisions do not ensure the right of pre-trial detainees to participate directly in a service. Although the literature questioned the possibility of restricting the participation of a pre-trial detainee in the Holy Mass,[302] it seems that Art. 217 § 6 PEC admits such a possibility, as it is also a form of contact with a chaplain. This problem became one of the issues of contention in the case of Janusz Kawiecki v. Poland, being heard before the European Court of Human Rights, where one of the charges was a violation of Art. 9 of the European Convention by failing to allow a pre-trial detainee to attend Holy Mass. Although the ECHR did not finally consider the application, as it found that the time limit for bringing it had expired, it indicated in point 106 that the decision to isolate the applicant from other detainees and therefore, not to authorize him to participate in a group Sunday mass, was at all times lawful and was admissible under Polish law.[303]

Moreover, the Regulation of the Justice Minister of 2 September 2003 on detailed rules on performing religious practices and benefiting from religious

---

301 O. Sitarz, A. Jaworska-Wieloch, "Prawa osób tymczasowo aresztowanych na tle uprawnień przysługujących osobom odbywającym karę pozbawienia wolności", https://www.gov.pl/attachment/c57fff7b-2b4b-4b81-a75b-e7f7075b4a4c (accessed 22.09.2023) and O. Sitarz, A. Jaworska-Wieloch, "Prawo do praktyk religijnych osób osadzonych w areszcie śledczym i odbywających karę pozbawienia wolności w teorii i praktyce penitencjarnej", *Archiwum Kryminologii*, vol. 39, 2017, pp. 31 et seq.

302 In the opinion of J. Nikołajew, the disposing body may not refuse a pre-trial detainee to participate in the Holy Mass – see: J. Nikołajew, *Wolność sumienia i religii skazanych…*, p. 178.

303 ECHR, Judgment of 23 October 2012, case of Kawiecki v. Poland, application no. 15593/07.

services in penitentiary facilities and detention centres, which is applied to pre-trail detainees based on § 6, doubling the content of Art. 217 § 6 PEC, refers to the provisions of the Regulation without specifying only some of them. Consequently, it must be considered that all the standards contained in the above instrument, including those concerning participation in services and religious meetings, apply to pre-trial detainees, unless the disposing authority restricts such possibility or specifies how the contact is to take place.

As a rule, pre-trial detainees are excluded from participation in ceremonies that require leaving penitentiary institutions (pilgrimages, Corpus Christi processions, funerals of loved ones), which is a consequence of the significantly smaller number of institutions available to pre-trial detainees that make it possible to leave the prison temporarily. Pre-trial detainees can make use of one institution allowing temporary release from prison, that is, the special purpose licence defined in Art. 141a PEC. Importantly, under § 3 of the cited provision, the granting of such permission to a pre-trial detainee, who has the rights and duties of a convict serving a prison sentence, requires the issuance of a consent order by the authority at whose disposal the pre-trial detainee remains, i.e., the prosecutor or the court, depending on the stage of the proceedings.

4.8. Scope of informing prisoners about the rights relating to religious freedom and the possibility of collecting declarations of faith from prisoners

The right and duty of Prison Service officers to inform prisoners about religious practices held in a specific prison primarily depends on whether officers have knowledge of the religion a particular prisoner follows. In other words, the issue is whether officers can ask a prisoner about his or her attitude to religion. The right of an officer to question convicted persons about their religion does not derive from any provision and is even questionable in light of Arts. 47 and 51 of the Polish Constitution, mandating the legal protection of private life and prohibiting the disclosure of information about oneself on any basis other than a law. However, under § 4 and § 6 para. 2 and 3 of the Regulation of the Justice Minister on the organizational-ordinal rules on serving a penalty of deprivation of liberty, an informational interview and then a preliminary interview are carried out with a convict on admission. The provisions do not mention the right of the officer to ask a convict about religious issues. Instead, the provisions limit themselves to stating that the interviews are aimed at establishing the necessary information to ensure the proper execution of the sentence of imprisonment. Jerzy Nikołajew pointed out that the prison administration does not have data on the religious affiliation of particular prisoners and the information on the accessibility of the clergy of all faiths is given *in abstracto*.[304]

The lack of opportunity to ask convicts about their professed religion does not mean that they do not have to be informed by penitentiary administrations about their rights relating to religious freedom and the schedule of religious practices and services held in a given prison. As a rule, such information is included in the prison internal rules and they should be made available to convicts on admission.

This issue raises another problem – the significance of declaration of faith,[305] that is, whether and to what extent a convict's declaration of a professed confession is binding and is subject to proving, or relatively, whether a penitentiary facility can question that declaration. The issue has been raised on several occasions in the case-law because every now and then penitentiary institutions considered prisoners' demands for a religious diet to be instrumental, undertaken in order to get better quality food or to annoy prison authorities.[306] A prisoner's declaration of a desire to engage more deeply in his or her religion may arouse some suspicion among the prison administration. This is because a fear arises that the convict may seek to undertake a particular religious practice not for the declared purpose but in order to obtain some other kind of gratification, or simply to make life miserable for the prison administration. Ultimately, the Polish literature formulates a view that the Prison Service may not verify a professed religion or question the veracity of convicts' declarations even if they performed several acts of conversion.[307]

The European Court of Human Rights resolved these doubts unequivocally. In the case of Ivanova v. Bulgaria of 21 July 2016, it held that the right to freedom of thought, conscience and religion is of primary importance, and the state cannot dictate what a person should believe or take steps to force a change in

---

304 J. Nikołajew, *Wolność sumienia i religii skazanych…*, p. 167.

305 The Anglo-Saxon literature makes use of the concept of *religious sincerity*, which does not overlap with proving faith, but is nevertheless an important aspect of the issue. See: D. Golemboski, "Religious Sincerity and the Reasons for Religious Freedom", *Political Research Quarterly*, vol. 73, no. 4, 2020, pp. 866 et seq. and K. L. Brady, "Religious Sincerity and Imperfection: Can Lapsing Prisoners Recover Under RFRA and RLUIPA?", *The University of Chicago Law Review*, vol. 78, no. 4, 2011, pp. 1431 et seq.

306 J. Nikołajew, "Prawo osób pozbawionych wolności do wyżywienia przygotowywanego według wymogów religijnych. Regulacje normatywne a trudności praktyczne", *Kościół i Prawo*, vol. 4, no. 2, 2015, pp. 151 et seq.

307 M. Kotowska, M. Romańczuk-Grącka, "Wolność religijna…, p. 152.

his or her beliefs.[308] This view is based on a broader concept of determining the limits of freedom during the execution of a prison sentence. In a judgement of 5 January 2010 in the case of Jaremowicz v. Poland,[309] which concerned the issue of entering into marriage during incarceration, the ECHR drew attention to an important problem – if the law does not create obstacles to entering into marriage because a relationship was established during incarceration and it is a purely private matter, prison authorities have no right to assess the depth of feelings between the partners and fail to bestow respect on such a relationship. Religious issues should receive a similar treatment: the state is not entitled to question the fact of religious affiliation, because it is a prisoner's declaration that has, except in cases of clear abuse of the law, the decisive significance in this regard.[310] The state cannot assess the degree of a prisoner's faith or engagement in a declared religion, the veracity of his or her declarations or verify a declared confession in any other way, unless a declared confession simply does not exist.[311]

4.9. Representatives of religion in prisons

Representatives of various confessions[312] may provide religious ministry in penitentiary institutions based on an employment relationship or on a volunteer basis. A referral to serve in a prison is given by the diocesan ordinary, and the director of a given prison signs a contract with such a representative of a religion. The work of prison chaplains is coordinated by diocesan prison chaplains. The overwhelming number of prisoners in Poland declare their affiliation with the Roman Catholic Church, hence Catholic priests represent the largest number of chaplains employed in prisons and correctional facilities, where they also give

308 ECHR, Judgment of 21 July 2016, case of Ivanova v. Bulgaria, application no. 46577/15.

309 ECHR, Judgment of 10 January 2010, case of Jaremowicz v. Poland, application no. 24023/03.

310 See a judgement in the case of Kovalkovs v. Latvia, application no. 35021/05 and Vartic v. Romania, application no. 14150/08 – quoted after M. Hucał, "Wolność sumienia i wyznania osób pozbawienia wolności w orzecznictwie ETPCz", in J. Nikołajew, K. Walczuk (eds.), *Wolność sumienia i religii osób pozbawionych wolności. Aspekty prawne i praktyczne*, Warszawa 2016, p. 192. See also: O. Sitarz, A. Jaworska-Wieloch, J. Hanc, "Obowiązek zgolenia brody…, pp. 46 et seq.

311 See: a judgement of X. v. United Kingdom, application no. 7291/75 – quoted after M. Hucał, "Wolność sumienia…, p. 192.

312 See more: A. Mezglewski, "Pojęcie *duchownego* w przepisach prawa polskiego o zawieraniu małżeństwa", *Studia z Prawa Wyznaniowego*, vol. 2, 2001, pp. 3 et seq.

religious instruction. Religious practices and services may be provided in prisons by representatives of other confessions based on three rules: cooperation with the state, with representatives of other confessions and religious organizations, and providing pastoral care only for prisoners of their own confession so that the prison is not a place of religious proselytizing.[313]

Moreover, the Prison Ministry Council, which is an advisory and consultative body of the Director General and coordinates tasks in the field of pastoral activities in prisons and detention centres conducted for prisoners, is attached to the Central Board of the Prison Service. The Prison Ministry Council consists of supreme chaplains of the Roman Catholic Church, the Evangelical Church of the Augsburg Confession and the Eastern Orthodox Church, who coordinate, each in his own area, the pastoral activities of the priests of his church. A detailed number of representatives of the clergy cooperating with penitentiary institutions, broken down by confession and legal basis for the provision of services (employment contract, voluntary service) are presented below. Associations of a religious nature also operate in prisons.[314] The first group of lay volunteers holding faith-related meetings in prisons to organize themselves into an official association was the Prison Brotherhood, which was approved in 1993.[315]

4.10. Detailed elements of professing a religion and worship in the prison

The provisions of universally binding law, prison internal rules, the doctrine and case-law have selectively dealt with the specific scope of rights available to prisoners in terms of their professed religion, in particular, accessibility to religious practices and services. The particular rights in this area, normalized in the Polish legal order or raised in the doctrine or judicature, will be discussed below.

As regards the specific rights declared by the legislature, the right to participate directly in services held in prison on feast days comes to the fore. Under Art. 32 of the Act of 17 May 1989 on the relationship between the state and the Roman Catholic Church in the Republic of Poland, convicted persons

313 J. Sikorski, "Duszpasterstwo więzienne", in T. Szymanowski, J. Cegielska, J. Czołgoszewski, S. Lelental, J. Pomiankiewicz (eds.), *Księga jubileuszowa więziennictwa polskiego 1989–2009*, Warszawa 2009, pp. 214 et seq.

314 W. Woźniak, "Duszpasterstwo więzienne a resocjalizacja", *Studia Teologiczne*, vol. 20, 2002, pp. 225 et seq.

315 J. Sikorski, "Duszpasterstwo więzienne…, p. 212.

shall be provided with the opportunity to perform religious practices, receive religious services and attend Mass celebrated on Sundays and feast days in a suitably adapted room in the facility where they are incarcerated.[316] This provision corresponds to Art. 17 para. 1 of the Concordat, which lays down that persons in penitentiary, educational, rehabilitation and health and social care institutions, as well as in other institutions and facilities of this kind, shall be provided with the opportunity to attend Mass on Sundays and feast days. These provisions ensure prisoners the right to participate in services and prescribe that they are to be celebrated on Sundays and feats days.

Despite this, the Penal Enforcement Code, first, does not introduce a distinction between Sundays and feast days, ensuring the right to participate in services only on feast days, and second, it does not regulate the minimum number of Masses to be celebrated in a penitentiary institution during a given period. In formal terms, a failure to organize a service, even on a feast day, does not breach the laws because Art. 106 PEC ensures the right to participate directly only in such services that are held, that is, those that take place on the prison premises. The Polish provisions do not regulate the minimum number of Masses to be celebrated on the prison premises and do not address this issue in any other way, e.g., by making a reference to religious holidays. Thus, believers have no legal basis for alleging a violation of their rights if Mass is not celebrated on a feast day. This solution is not consistent with Art. 32 of the Act of 17 May 1989 on the relationship between the state and the Roman Catholic Church in the Republic of Poland, and Art. 17 para. 1 of the Concordat, and it violates prisoners' fundamental right to religious practices and services, in particular, in the event of a failure to organize a service on religious holidays in accordance with the rules applicable to their religion.[317] This problem has grown in importance especially since 1989, when the number of foreigners following various churches and religious associations, including those that are practically non-operational in Poland, increased in Polish penitentiary institutions.[318]

---

316 Given the dominant nature of the Roman Catholic confession in Poland, the discussion does not include laws regulating the relationship between the states and other confessions. It should be noted that, for example, the scope of religious freedom for juveniles of the Evangelical Church of the Augsburg Confession was similarly regulated – see Art. 23 para. 2 of the Act of 13 May 1994 on the relationship between the state and the Evangelical Church of the Augsburg Confession in the Republic of Poland (Journal of Laws of 1994, No. 73, pos. 323).

317 J. Nikołajew, *Wolność sumienia i religii skazanych…*, p. 146.

318 A. Kwieciński, "Podstawy prawne realizacji…, p. 263.

A failure to provide pastoral care in confessions declared by prisoners also means that the Polish penitentiary regulations do not ensure the minimum number of celebrated services, at least on feast days, which is most important from the point of view of a given confession. They also do not stipulate a minimum number of adherents of a particular religion obliging the prison to make efforts to establish cooperation with a particular chaplain. This violates Mandela Rule 66, which lays down that so far as practicable, every prisoner shall be allowed to satisfy the needs of his or her religious life by attending the services provided in the prison.

On the other hand, it is hard to deny that approach some pragmatism in a situation where a prisoner declares a very rare confession and it is extremely difficult to arrange a chaplain to hold a service, especially for a single prisoner. The application of prisoners' right to exercise freedom of religion to all religions does not mean that their right to perform religious practices and services is equally ensured. It is pointed out in the doctrine that, as a rule, the constitutional case-law rejects absolute egalitarianism, understanding it instead in a relative way:[319] even in the French system of relations between the state and religious associations, which is based on a strict equality of religions, it is concluded that equality is in fact not a strict parity.[320]

The further part of Art. 106 § 1 PEC gives prisoners the right to listen to services broadcast by the mass media. While it is a passive form of participation in Mass, it is at least available to everyone, regardless of organizational problems related to the number of chaplains of a given denomination or the need to separate a prisoner from others. A prison radio station system makes it possible to broadcast services also to cells where prisoners do not have their own television set or a radio receiver. Chaplains use the prison radio station system in many prisons, which allows them to reach the entire prison unit.[321] Notably, it is a prisoner's right not an obligation – thus, the compulsion to listen to loud religious programmes on the prison radio may be seen as an interference with

319 P. Borecki, "Państwo laickie w świetle dorobku współczesnego konstytucjonalizmu europejskiego", *Przegląd Prawniczy Uniwersytetu im. Adama Mickiewicza*, vol. 6, 2016, p. 184.

320 E. Cerexhe, H. Boel, "Orzecznictwo konstytucyjne w sprawach religijnych. Referat belgijski" [typescript copied], ATK, pp. 44–45 – quoted after P. Borecki, "Państwo laickie…, p. 184.

321 M. Paszkowski, J. Krzywkowska, "Prawo osadzonych do opieki duszpasterskiej i wykonywania praktyk religijnych na przykładzie zakładu karnego w Barczewie", in J. Nikołajew, K. Walczuk (eds.), *Wolność sumienia i religii osób pozbawionych wolności…*, p. 441.

the religious freedom of non-believing prisoners.[322] Moreover, respect for this right must not harm the rights of other prisoners in the same multi-bed cell. In a situation where one of the prisoners wishes to listen to a programme of that type and another does not, it would be desirable to air that content on the prison radio only during the absence of the latter (e.g., during his walk in the prison yard or during his recreation room time), alternatively, to air the service in the recreation room. One may wonder whether it is more beneficial to place prisoners of similar religious sensitivity in one cell to avoid potential conflicts, which is not envisaged by the PEC and implementing instruments. On the other hand, it would give rise to a dispute in the literature and judicature as to the questioning of prisoners by officers about their declared denomination.

Apart from the right to participate in a service, Art. 106 § 1 PEC ensures prisoners' right to perform religious practices and benefit from religious services. Prisoners can make use of the sacraments, and the literature emphasizes that Catholics enjoy the sacraments of marriage, baptism, confirmation and anointing of the sick without significant restrictions. There is no reason to restrict prisoners from praying during their free time.[323] Prison ministry may take non-traditional forms, such as meetings with persons of interest organized by chaplains, pilgrimages, evangelization retreats, religious competitions, assistance in establishing broken ties with loved ones or religious concerts.[324] Such non-standard forms of expression of faith, not provided by law, depend on the activity of chaplains in the institution and their cooperation with the prison administration. They primarily depend on whether a given penitentiary facility succeeded in establishing an ongoing relationship with a chaplain of a particular denomination, preferably involving an element of regularity, that is, based on an employment relationship established between a penitentiary institution and a chaplain.

Under Art. 106 § 2 PEC, the convicted person has the right to participate in religious instruction provided in the penitentiary facility, participating in the charitable and social work of a church or a religious association and individual meetings with clergymen of a church or a religious association he or she adheres to; the clergymen may visit convicted persons in the rooms where they stay. In this case too, the regulations do not guarantee participation in such religious

322 Z. Lasocik, "Funkcjonowanie oddziałów dla tzw. „więźniów niebezpiecznych", *Archiwum Kryminologii*, vol. 31, 2009, p. 337.

323 J. Nikołajew, *Wolność sumienia i religii skazanych…*, pp. 146 et seq.

324 M. Paszkowski, J. Krzywkowska, "Prawo osadzonych…, p. 441.

practices, making a prisoner's right to take part in them contingent on whether they are conducted at all in the prison. While the Code provides for the possibility of attending an individual meeting with a clergyman in the cell, it does not provide a minimum number of meetings with a specific chaplain. The right to such visits raises controversy in the doctrine due to potential breaches of the tolerance principle connected with the need for other prisoners occupying the same cell, who may not feel a similar need or even follow the same religion, to participate in the meeting as well.[325] In turn, were such meetings to take place outside the cell, it is necessary for prisons to set aside places for such meetings and possibly provide escorts by the Prison Service for those convicts who cannot move independently on the premises of the penitentiary institutions.

Under Art. 110a § 1 PEC, the convict has the right to have objects for religious worship in his or her cell. This provision is not clear, as the law does not specify what is meant by objects for religious worship. Other regulations (Art. 106 § 1 PEC) link this formulation to the right to possess books, writings and objects necessary for religious practice. This regulation is not consistent with Art. 110a § 1 PEC, which provides that the convict has to right to possess, among other things, objects for religious worship. In the same act, referring to the same category of things, the legislature used different terms, defined in different ways.[326]

In addition, the implementing provisions[327] limit the number of such objects only to 10 in sizes not larger than 250 x 150 mm. In this case, the regulation does not make use of the purpose for which an object is needed (presumably to perform religious practices), only replacing it with a completely different formulation: the object for religious worship, which, however, it does not define in any way. Meanwhile, attention has frequently been drawn to the concept of religious worship on the grounds of tax regulations, including the Law on Income Tax for Natural Persons, and in the case-law, where it has been indicated how vague and disputable the expression is.[328] It has been identified with

325 G. B. Szczygieł, *Społeczna readaptacja…*, p. 147.

326 O. Sitarz, A. Jaworska-Wieloch, J. Hanc, "Nowelizacja art. 106 § 1 k.k.w. i art. 110a § 1 Kodeksu karnego wykonawczego", *Prawo w Działaniu*, vol. 45, 2021, pp. 141 et seq.

327 § 10 para. 1 point 6 letter 6 of the Regulation of the Justice Minister of 23 December 2022 on the organizational-ordinal rules for serving a penalty of deprivation of liberty, Journal of Laws of 2022, pos. 2847.

328 B. Pahl, *Majątek kościołów i innych związków wyznaniowych. Zasady opodatkowania*, Olsztyn 2008, p. 124 and M. Tyrakowski, *Opodatkowanie dochodów Kościoła katolickiego w Polsce*, Warszawa 2005, pp. 92 et seq.

ritual practices through which religious followers manifest their reverence for the sacred in acts of worship, supplication and thanksgiving, emphasizing the external dimension of religion in contrast to the theoretical doctrine; the totality of religious rites and activities.[329]

Objects for religious worship are therefore not the same as objects possessed for the purposes of performing religious practices. Moreover, although the Regulation on the organizational-ordinal rules on serving a penalty of deprivation of liberty only implements the provisions of the Penal Enforcement Code, it uses a different definition of objects of a religious nature than Art. 106 § 1 PEC. This provision of the Penal Enforcement Code establishes the framework for prisoners' religious freedom and it should therefore describe the rights of convicts in this regard more specifically than Art. 110a § 1 PEC, which only specifies the objects that are allowed in the cell.

The Polish regulations on the possession of objects for religious worship in the cell and related limitations raise some doubts. Rule 29.1 of the EPR ensures prisoners' right to possess books or literature in that field, and Mandela Rule 66 prescribes that so far as practicable, every prisoner shall be allowed to satisfy the needs of his or her religious life by, among other things, having in his or her possession the books of religious observance and instruction of his or her denomination. J. Nikołajew pointed to the emphasis placed in this way on the significance of respect for a prisoner in terms of his or her religious rights and defining religious practices, which are to consist of, among other things, the possession of books and literature in their regard.[330] International law does not link the books and literature held by prisoners to the purpose of keeping them, referring only to the subject matter to which they are devoted.

It seems that prisoners' religious freedom would be preserved to a much greater degree if dimensional constraints were put in place on the items prisoners are allowed to have in the cell, while how much of these items would constitute religious objects should be left to their individual decision. The legislature should abandon the requirement that objects for religious worship are to serve a specific purpose, as this purpose was only selectively introduced in some provisions and was not specified, and it introduced an unnecessary element of evaluation as to which objects meet the requirements.

---

329 See: judgement of the Voivodeship Administrative Court in Łódź of 11 September 2012, I SA/Łd 781/1, LEX no. 1266487.

330 J. Nikołajew, "Reguły Minimalne…, p. 123.

One of the elements of practicing religion, in some religions, is eating a proper diet.[331] Polish penal enforcement law is aware of that fact, but it does not introduce a mandatory obligation to adapt the diet to the religious requirements formulated by a given confession. Under Art. 109 § PEC, the diet served to a prisoner incarcerated in a penitentiary facility or detention centre should, as far as possible, be adapted to his or her religious requirements. This implies no absolute necessity to adapt to the dietary conditions recommended by a given denomination. It may thus be that a prisoner whose religion sets specific requirements in terms of diet (for example, pork-free), has no possibility to observe that condition.

This standard is extended by the Regulation of the Justice Minister of 19 February 2016 on a diet served to prisoners in penitentiary facilities and detention centres.[332] It prescribes that a prisoner benefiting from meals prepared with regard to religious or cultural requirements shall receive the same meals after transportation to another penitentiary facility or detention centre, provided that it is possible to prepare them in that penitentiary facility or detention centre. The change of meals prepared taking into account religious or cultural requirements, which are served to a prisoner transported from another penitentiary facility or detention centre, to basic meals or to other meals available in a given penitentiary facility or detention centre may take place at the request of the prisoner or by decision of the prison director in the event that it is not possible to provide such a meal (§ 11 para. 2 of the cited Regulation).

Meanwhile, the European Prison Rules make no exception and age, health, physical form, religion, culture and type of work performed are seen as equivalent determinants of a meal to be served to a prisoner. Some dissatisfaction in terms of meeting international standards is caused by the regulation connected with taking into account religious requirements for meals served to prisoners. In this regards, the expression contained in the EPR (reg. 22.1), which prescribes that prisoners shall be provided with a nutritious diet that takes into account their religion, is far more safeguarding in nature than the Polish recommendation of considering it "as far as possible" (Art. 109 § 1 PEC). This solution appears incomprehensible especially from the point of view of the rights of those who remain in a situation of coercion, since the sensitivity of the matter of freedom of religion, including the choice of religious diet, is so great that it would be desirable to replace that clause with a specific solution limiting the unjustified margin of

331 See more: J. Hanc, "*My chickens*…, pp. 185 et seq.
332 Journal of Laws. 2016, pos. 302.

freedom not of the state but of the administration of a given penitentiary facility or detention centre.[333]

Although it has been argued that, in practice, complaints on this account are not filed,[334] in the case of Jakóbski v. Poland, the European Court of Human Rights held that a refusal to provide a prisoner with a meatless diet consistent with the demands of his confession violated his right to manifest his religion by following the tenets of Buddhism, even though the Mahayana school of Buddhism, which by declaration the applicant followed, only recommends but does not mandate vegetarianism. In the said judgement, the Court emphasized that adherence to dietary rules can be considered a direct expression of one's beliefs in practice within the meaning of Art. 9 of the European Convention, and a prisoner's request to be served meatless meals does not require a particular method of preparation, special products. In addition, the facility did not offer an alternative diet and did not consult the Buddhist mission, which led the Court to believe that Art. 9 of the European Convention had been violated.[335]

Another form of the exercise of freedom of conscience and religion is the right to manifest it individually[336] or in community with others and in public or private. Apart from persons providing ministry, the manifestation of one's religion by means of clothing is not common in the European civilizational circle. In religions and cultures other than European, clothing may be used as a means of manifestation of religious beliefs, for example, burqas and hijabs.[337]

The possibility of introduction by particular states of provisions restricting the right to wear clothes manifesting affiliation with a specific confession has been addressed on several occasions by the European Court of Human Rights. For example, in the case of Mann Singh v. France, the applicant, a practicing Sikh, claimed that the necessity of having his photograph taken for a driving licence without headwear interfered with his private life and his freedom of belief and conscience. The Court took the view that identity photographs for use on driving

333 J. Nikołajew, "Prawo osób pozbawionych…, pp. 164 et seq.

334 A. Kwieciński, "Podstawy prawne realizacji…, p. 263.

335 J. Bartosiewicz, "Glosa do wyroku ETPC z dnia 17 grudnia 2013 r., 14150/08", Lex/el 2014.

336 ECHR, Judgment of 25 May 1993, case of Kokkinakis v. Greece, application no. 14307/88.

337 A. Kuriata, "Źródła prawa muzułmańskiego wobec stroju kobiety muzułmanki", *Acta Erasmiana*, vol. 7, 2014, pp. 143 et seq. and E. Milczarek, "Symbole i stroje religijne w przestrzeni publicznej – uwagi na tle orzecznictwa Europejskiego Trybunału Praw Człowieka", *Kościół i Prawo*, vol. 11, no. 1, 2022, pp. 67 et seq.

licences which showed the subject bareheaded were needed by the authorities in charge of public safety and law and order, particularly in the context of checks carried out under the road traffic regulations, to enable them to identify the driver and verify that he or she was authorized to drive the vehicle concerned. It stressed that checks of that kind were necessary to ensure public safety.[338]

The Court also addressed the issue of provisions obliging a practicing Muslim to take off her scarf for an identity check – such an arrangement was deemed acceptable if it served a legitimate public safety purpose and was limited in time.[339] The case-law reiterates the admissibility of introduction of orders to remove religious symbols if they concern a person's security, for example, if helmets must be worn while riding a motorcycle[340] or if they apply only occasionally (e.g., a security check at the airport).[341]

In prisons, the issue of prisoners' clothing is regulated by the provisions of Polish law, although they do not make reference to the religious requirements formulated by other confessions. The Regulation of the Justice Minister of 19 December 2016 on the living conditions of individuals incarcerated in penitentiary facilities and detention centres[342] governs the issue of prison clothing issued to prisoners, making no reference to the possibility of issuing clothing or part thereof required by a given denomination. Prisoners incarcerated in open and semi-open facilities may wear their own clothes (Art. 91 point 6 and Art. 97 point 7 PEC), while in closed-type facilities, such possibility is subject to consent from the facility director (Art. 90 point 5 PEC). Pre-trial detainees may use their own clothing, underwear and footwear, unless this disrupts the order established in the detention centre or is opposed by security or sanitary considerations (Art. 216 § 1 PEC). That possibility is denied to convicts and pre-trial detainees deemed particularly dangerous (Art. 88 § 1 point 10 PEC, Art. 212b § 1 point 9 PEC). Moreover, under § 31 of the organizational-ordinal rules on serving a penalty of deprivation of liberty, using passes or permission to leave the prison, the convict shall use his or her own clothes, underwear and shoes, unless they

---

338 ECHR, Judgment of 27 November 2008, case of Mann Singh v. France, application no. 24479/07.

339 ECHR, Judgment of 4 March 2008, case of El Morsli v. France, application no. 15585/06.

340 ECHR, Judgment of 12 July 1978, case of X v. United Kingdom, application no. 7992/77.

341 ECHR, Judgment of 11 January 2005, case of Phull v. France, application no. 35753/03.

342 Journal of Laws of 2016, pos. 224.

are damaged or unsuitable due to the season. This means that, as a rule, the convict may use his or her own clothes only outside the prison, whereas inside the facility, the possibility depends on its type.

In a situation where prisoners can use their own clothes, the regulations do not set out specific types of clothing that can be worn by prisoners (e.g., a burqa or a hijab). Importantly, § 27 para. 1 of the Regulation on the organizational-ordinal rules on serving a penalty of deprivation of liberty provides only that the convict maintains proper personal cleanliness and takes care of neat appearance. There is no provision that bars prisoners from covering specific body parts. Only Art. 116a point 9 PEC prohibits a convict from altering his external appearance in a way that makes it difficult to identify him, in particular by shaving or growing his hair, beard or moustache, or changing its colour, unless he obtains consent from the prison director to do so. It is hard to argue that putting on a turban or a burqa alters external appearance, it is only part of clothing that may be taken off at any time to undergo an identification check.

The said provision (Art. 116a point 9 PEC) is relevant where a prisoner wishes to grow a beard, which is important in some religions.[343] It will surely change the external appearance of a prisoner, falling within the scope of application of the said provision. Introducing Art. 116a point 9 PEC, the legislature most likely sought to prohibit prisoners from making changes to their external appearance that could facilitate escape or mislead Prison officers about the prisoner's identity. The prohibition is not absolute because the prison director may consent to such a change in appearance.

Some have argued that a potential consent to a change in appearance may be given only if it does not hinder the identification of the convicted person,[344] which is hard to accept given that a change in appearance that does not impede identification is not included in the scope of Art. 116a point 9 PEC. It seems reasonable to accept that the legislature made the possibility of changing a prisoner's external appearance conditional on consent from the prison director to make him or her aware of the appearance modification the prisoner intends to make so that the possibility of prisoner identification is maintained.

---

343 O. Sitarz, A. Jaworska-Wieloch, J. Hanc, "Obowiązek zgolenia brody…, pp. 29 et seq.

344 S. Lelental – see: D. Gajos-Kaniewska, "Trybunał: Zakaz zapuszczenia brody w więzieniu naruszył Konwencję Praw Człowieka", 17.06.2016, https://www.rp.pl/Dobra-osobiste/306179950-Trybunal-Zakaz-zapuszczenia-brody-w-wiezieniu-naruszyl--Konwencje-Praw-Czlowieka.html (accessed 18.07.2023).

It may be assumed that the consent from the prison director or a lack thereof should be based on determining whether the information provided by the prisoner about his or her intention to change external appearance is sufficient for his or her subsequent identification or, on the contrary, the prison staff may have problems establishing his or her identity. Any refusals should be thoroughly considered, especially because the European Court of Human Rights in a judgement of 14 September 2016 in the case of Biržietis v. Lithuania[345] held that the ban on growing a beard cannot be justified by the need to identify prisoners. Consequently, a lack of consent to a change in external appearance solely due to the inability to identify the prisoner is highly debatable, especially since the facial image is not the only element identifying a prisoner.

The need to maintain hygiene in the prison may also be a reason for a refusal to permit a prisoner to grow a beard during incarceration. As a result, Art. 116 § 1 point 2 PEC imposes on the prisoner the duty to observe personal hygiene and maintain the cleanliness of the premises in which he or she resides. This provision corresponds to § 27 para. 1 of the Regulation on the organizational-ordinal rules on serving a penalty of deprivation of liberty, which lays down that the convict maintains proper personal cleanliness and takes care of neat appearance. The question thus arises whether growing a beard by a prisoner breaches hygiene. It is hard to accept that the increased risk of microbial transmission associated with facial hair means *in limine* a violation of the prisoner's duty of maintaining hygiene, given that the European Court of Human Rights indicated in the case of Biržietis v. Lithuania that the ban on growing a beard may not be justified by hygienic reasons and depriving the accused of the right to grow a beard, associated with the expression of his personality and identity, violates Article 8 of the European Convention by unduly interfering with his right to privacy. Consequently, a refusal to allow a prisoner to grow beard solely on hygienic grounds seems to be difficult to defend in the event of a complaint submitted to the ECHR.

Religious freedom in prisons may be affected by extraordinary situations. For example, the pandemic caused by the SARS-CoV-2 virus greatly affected the lives of people around the world, causing the curtailment of many civil rights and freedoms,[346]

---

345 ECHR, Judgment of 14 September 2016, case of Biržietis v. Lithuania, application no. 49304/09.

346 S. Trociuk, *Prawa i wolności w stanie epidemii*, Warszawa 2021, *passim*.

and it did not leave the broadly understood justice system untouched.[347]

Prisoners were one of the groups hardest hit by pandemic restrictions.[348] The penalty of deprivation of liberty involves by its very nature the deprivation of many human needs: biological, including the possibility of free movement, sensory-informational due to a significant reduction in sensations, emotional connected with a restriction or loss of contact with the loved ones, sexual[349] and religious and spiritual.[350] The crisis arising from incarceration is particularly painful on four levels: family relationships, interpersonal contacts (including with friends or acquaintances) and the possibility of self-growth (employment and the choice of its type and location). These areas, already vulnerable to deprivation by imprisonment itself, were heavily constrained by enforced social distancing.

The need to introduce a strict sanitary regime in prisons came as no surprise – the risk of spreading the virus in penitentiary institutions was extremely high due to the common confinement of prisoners in cells, small rooms and inadequate ventilation. The basic protective measures, such as social distancing and compliance with the hygiene standards, were more difficult to adopt than outside.[351] Consequently, in an effort to ensure the safety of prisoners and the staff, prison administrations went to great lengths to keep the number of visitors entering and leaving the prison premises as low as possible. The objective was achieved by imposing a ban on visits from the loved ones, therapists, teachers conducting training sessions and the exclusion of external employment. Chaplains providing pastoral care were also temporarily excluded from entering the prison premises, thus limiting the prisoners' access to religious practices and services.

---

347 B. Stańdo – Kawecka, "Poland", in F. Dünkel, S. Harrendorf, D. Zyl Smit (eds.), *The impact of COVID-19 on prison conditions and penal policy*, London – New York 2022, pp. 396 et seq.

348 P. Zieliński, "Izolacja penitencjarna w dobie COVID-19 w aksjologicznym wymiarze praw człowieka", in J. Jaskiernia, K. Spryszak (eds.), *Powszechny system ochrony praw człowieka w czasie wyzwań pandemicznych. Tom I*, Toruń 2022, pp. 640 et seq.

349 H. Machel, *Więzienie jako instytucja karna i resocjalizacyjna*, Gdańsk 2003, *passim*.

350 T. R. Clear, P. L. Hardyman, B. Stout, et al., "The Value of Religion in Prison: An Inmate Perspective", *Journal of Contemporary Criminal Justice*, vol. 16, no. 1, 2000, pp. 53 et seq.

351 See: https://www.coe.int/en/web/commissioner/-/covid-19-pandemic-urgentsteps-are-needed-to-protect-the-rights-of-prisoners-in-europe (accessed 15.07.2023).

The introduced restrictions were based on Art. 247 PEC, which prescribes that in cases justified by special sanitary or health reasons or a serious threat to security, the director of a penitentiary facility or a detention centre may, for a specified period of time, withhold or restrict, among other things, holding services and providing ministry. Thus, the restrictions on the above rights may apply only to holding services and providing ministry, whereas other forms of expression of religious freedom remain unaffected. If the said restriction or prohibition lasts up to seven days, the director of a penitentiary facility or a detention centre immediately informs a penitentiary judge about his or her decision. An extension of the duration of restrictions or prohibitions requires the consent of that judge, the absence of which does not suspend the implementation of the decision of the director of the penitentiary facility or detention centre. The director of a penitentiary facility or a detention centre may submit a complaint about a decision of the judge to the penitentiary court, applying respectively Art. 7 § 5 PEC (Art. 247 § 1 PEC).

The literature has rightly pointed out the exceptional nature of this norm and the applicability of the restrictions standardized in it only when the listed situations cannot be prevented using other measures foreseen in the Penal Enforcement Code and the remaining legal instruments governing the execution of prison sentences.[352] The COVID-19 pandemic led to the implementation of this provision, and drastic restrictions were placed on the ability of third parties to enter prisons.[353] This created a particularly difficult situation for prisoners, who did not have the opportunity to meet relatives at such a family time as Christmas or Easter and cherish a long-established tradition of sharing a wafer on Christmas Eve or an egg on Easter Sunday. Although many religious practices could be replaced by online religious and prayer meetings, remote talks with chaplains, a broader access to religious books and periodicals, these practices were not put in place, especially at the start of the pandemic. The activities of the Prison Service focused primarily on preventing the spread of the epidemic, either by preventing prisoners from using religious services or, at a later stage of the pandemic, allowing them to be used only on an individual basis.[354]

---

352 A. Kwieciński, "Podstawy prawne realizacji…, pp. 251 et seq.

353 See: https://wiadomosci.onet.pl/tylko-w-onecie/koronawirus-w-polsce-sluzba-wiezienna-przygotowuje-sie-na-radykalne-dzialania/qe8sb8t (accessed 17.07.2023) and https://www.sw.gov.pl/aktualnosc/centralny-zarzad-sluzby-wieziennej-ograniczenie-odwiedzin-we-wszystkich-zakladach-karnych (accessed 19.07.2023).

354 J. Krzywkowska, "Prawo osadzonych do korzystania z posług religijnych w dobie pandemii COVID-19", *Studia Prawnoustrojowe*, vol. 55, 2022, pp. 147 et seq.

In hindsight, it is important to develop a protocol for dealing with prisoners in the event of the need to reintroduce social distancing, envisaging tools intended to substitute prisoners' access to religious practices in the event of renewed inability to meet a representative of a specific confession directly.

4.11. Religious freedom of juveniles placed in post-criminal isolation units

The issue of religious freedom becomes all the more important for juveniles placed in an isolation unit. Incarceration in a youth educational centre or a correctional facility is not easy for any offender, and even more so for one who is still a child.[355] Juveniles placed in post-criminal isolation centres very frequently do not receive adequate support, especially emotional support, from parents or other well-wishers, some of them feel lonely, some are lost; all of them need more support and comfort. In such a situation, the opportunity to turn to religion or its teaching appears to be particularly important.

The problems connected with the restricted access to religious practices due to isolation, which were discussed with respect to adults incarcerated in penitentiary institutions, are compounded by another one – the question of who makes a decision in the area of the juvenile's religious freedom, including the issue of the parents' possible authority in relation to their child to make decisions in this area in the event that an educational or correctional measure is imposed.

The imposition of a correctional measure does not lead to a loss of parental rights by the parents. At the same time, the execution of an isolation measure genuinely deprives them of the possibility to decide on many important matters of the juvenile. The question is whether this also applies to the right to religious upbringing.

The Polish legal order regulates these issues quite precisely. Under the Art. 4 of the Act on the guarantees of freedom of conscience and confession cited above, the right to participate in religious acts and rites and to perform religious duties and celebrate religious festivals, as well as the right to possess and use objects needed for worship and religious practices are also enjoyed by, inter alia, persons placed in penitentiary facilities, correctional facilities, educational facilities, detention centres, social adaptation centres and juvenile shelters.

355 O. Sitarz, A. Jaworska-Wieloch, J. Hanc, "Religious freedom in the educational process conducted in isolation centers for juvenile perpetrators of criminal acts", in T. Huzarek, J. Wółkowski (eds.), *Educational Challenges of Religious Freedom*, Pelplin 2021, pp. 325 et seq.

Under Art. 107 para. 1 point 4 of the Act of 9 June 2022 on the support and rehabilitation of juveniles,[356] a juvenile placed in a youth educational centre, regional educational centre, correctional facility or a juvenile shelter has the right to exercise religious freedom.

Against the background of the previously applicable law, adding Art. 66a to the Act of 26 October 1982 on the procedure in cases of juveniles[357] on 15 September 2000, the proposer indicated in the explanatory memorandum that such provision "is the statutory expression of the possibility for a juvenile placed in a constant care facility to fully fulfil his or her freedom of conscience and religion, as guaranteed by Article 53 para. 1 of the Constitution."[358]

The law currently in force prescribes in Art. 113 that the juvenile's exercise of religious freedom must not infringe on the freedoms and rights of others or interfere with the internal order established in the youth educational centre, regional educational centre, treatment facility, correctional facility or juvenile shelter. The rights in terms of religious freedom are set out in Art. 114, which prescribes that a juvenile placed in a youth educational centre, regional educational centre, correctional facility or a youth shelter has the right perform religious practices and benefit from religious services, including to participate directly in the services held on feast days, listen to the services broadcast by the mass media and possess books, writings and objects for religious practice (para. 1). The juvenile has the right to participate in religious instruction taught in the centre, institution or shelter, charitable or social activity of a church or other religious association, and individual meetings with a chaplain from a church or other religious association which he or she follows. Those chaplains may visit juveniles in the premises where they stay (para. 2). The performance of religious practices and the use of religious services in the centre, institution or shelter take place in accordance with the will of the juvenile's parents, or at least the parent(s) in whose permanent custody the juvenile actually is, or the juvenile's guardian, or in accordance with the will of the juvenile if he or she is a legal adult (i.e. has reached the age of 18), expressed in a written declaration (para. 3). The place, manner and time of participation of juveniles in the performance of religious practices and the use of religious services shall be determined by the director of the regional educational centre, correctional facility or juvenile shelter in

356 Journal of Laws of 2022, pos. 1700.

357 Journal of Laws of 2018, pos. 969.

358 Journal of Laws of 2000, No. 91, pos. 1010. Explanatory memorandum: http://orka.sejm.gov.pl/Rejestrd.nsf/wgdruku/1214/$file/1214.pdf, (accessed 23.05.2022).

consultation with a chaplain of the church or other religious association which the juvenile follows (para. 4).

It is evident that the law currently in force allows for respecting religious beliefs of only those juveniles who are legal adults and have submitted a written declaration. In turn, the performance of religious practices and use of religious services by younger prisoners depends on a decision made by their parents, without the need to take the child's opinion into account, which is a regression in relation to the previous law – the Act of 26 October 1982 on the procedure in cases of juveniles. The 1982 Act ensured in Art. 66a the right to perform religious practices and benefit from religious services, participate directly in services held in correctional facilities and youth shelters on feast days, listen to services broadcast by the mass media, and possess books, writings and objects for religious practice. Moreover, this provisions formed the basis for Regulation of 14 September 2001 on the detailed principles of participation in religious instruction and practices, the use of religious services and the organization of pastoral work in correctional facilities and juvenile shelters. Under § 2 para. 1, participation of juveniles in religious instruction and practices, the use of religious services and the organization of pastoral work in the facility are carried out in accordance with the will of the parents (guardians) or taking into account the will of the juvenile, expressed in the simplest form of a declaration, within the framework of the organization of work in the facility, while ensuring the safety of the facility and respect for the rights of juveniles.[359] Currently there is no normative basis for taking into account the will of minor prisoners in the area of the exercise of religious freedom, in particular, because reaching the age of majority fits into Art. 12 para. 1 of the Act on the system of education,[360] which lays down that state kindergartens and primary schools organize religious instruction upon request of parents, state secondary schools upon request of either parents or students themselves; after reaching the age of majority, students decide whether they wish to receive religious instruction. Thus, in the view of the legislature, students acquire the right to decide independently on their participation in religious instruction only after reaching 18 years of age.

359 The alternative used in the above-mentioned legal acts makes the will of the juvenile only an optional complement when shaping the scope of the right of religious freedom and its manifestation. Thus, all the doubts raised earlier also materialize in this case.

360 Journal of Laws of 2022, pos. 2230.

Apart from the conflict over who is entitled to make a decision the juvenile's religious practice and instruction, the issue of accessibility of juveniles to religious practices and services was not resolved more effectively than in the case of convicted persons. The content of Art. 114 of the said Act bears resemblance to Art. 106 § 1 PEC, pointing to the right of a juvenile to engage in religious practice and to benefit from services, including the right to attend services directly on feast days, listen to services broadcast by the mass media and possess books, writings and objects for religious practice.

The right to participate directly in services held in correctional facilities on feast days comes to the fore. Under Art. 32 of the Act of 17 May 1989 on the relationship between the state and the Roman Catholic Church in the Republic of Poland, juveniles placed in regional educational centres, correctional facilities and juvenile shelters are provided with the opportunity to perform religious practices, receive religious instruction and religious services, attend Mass on Sundays and feast days. Juveniles who are unable to attend Mass should be given the opportunity to hear Mass broadcast by the mass media. In order to fulfil such entitlements, the administration of relevant establishments concludes agreements on the unpaid performance of chaplaincy duties with a clergyman delegated by the diocesan bishop. Thus, as is the case with adults, juveniles are not guaranteed the minimum number of services, including holding them on Sundays and feast days, but only participation in such Masses as are celebrated on feast days. The problems connected with the accessibility of transmission of services and ensuring the absence of the necessity to listen to them by juveniles who do not wish to do so still remain.

In terms of the juvenile's right to possess objects in the cell, in place of the unfortunate formulation "to possess the books, writings and objects necessary for this purpose" applicable to adults, the legislature indicated the right to possess books, writings and objects for religious practice. It did not choose to define how such religious practices are to be understood.

The above means that the juvenile's right to religious freedom in correctional facilities is not regulated in more detail than is the case with convicted persons, even though the issue, given prisoners' age, is more delicate and requires particularly strong safeguards. Moreover, the indicated problems affecting adults are compounded by a conflict of actors interested in the decision-making process regarding the juvenile's faith, which has not been resolved in any way by the legislature.

4.12. Summary of the Polish regulations on individuals incarcerated in post-criminal isolation units

An overview of the regulations relating to convicted adults incarcerated in prisons leads to several conclusions. First, many provisions ensure prisoners religious freedom. These assurances are not bolstered by specific rights that prisoners could enforce before judicial authorities. Second, many important issues regarding religious freedom remain unregulated: the possibility of taking a declaration of faith from prisoners, the frequency and minimum extent of religious practices and services to which a prisoner should have access while serving a penalty of imprisonment, types of confessions that should be respected by prison authorities, prerequisites for a refusal to serve a diet consistent with religious requirements to a prisoner. Consequently, there is a fairly high degree of discretion in meeting the requests of prisoners with regard to their religious needs and the authorities of particular prisons have leeway to make arbitrary decisions in this regard. Third, the considerable extent of unregulated access to religious practices and services by prisoners shifts the burden to prison administrations and prison internal rules formulated by them. As a result, it is possible to contest the view proposed by Marek Bielecki, who argued that the Polish legislature has sufficiently safeguarded the exercise of religious freedom by individuals sentenced to deprivation of liberty, it only depends on those applying the law to what extent these rules are applied.[361] In essence, the lack of boundary between law and freedom of religion makes this right largely illusory and, moreover, prevents or impedes the substantive monitoring of how convicts' rights are respected.

All the above comments also refer to juveniles placed in post-criminal isolation units. In their case, there are also new problems – the complete delegation of the decision on religious education and access to religious practices and services of minor children to their parents, a failure to regulate the decision-making procedures in the event of conflict between the wishes of the parent and the child and the manner in which respect for the right to religious freedom is monitored. This problem will remain unresolved without abandoning the order obliging juveniles to benefit from religious services in accordance with their parents' wishes until they reach the age of majority, which is provided by Act on the support and rehabilitation of juveniles. It would be desirable to introduce

361 M. Bielecki, "Instytucje polskiego prawa penitencjarnego na tle nauczania Jana Pawła II. Wybrane problemy", in P. Marzec, J. Nikołajew (eds.), *Osoba i dzieło Ojca Świętego Jana Pawła II…*, p. 81.

a qualification of, say, 13 years of age (in line with the Polish Civil Code) or, alternatively, 15 years of age, from which the child would decide independently on religion. This is reasonable insofar as we consider the juvenile in question to be mature enough to bear independently the consequences of commission of a prohibited act, we should also consider him or her mature enough to decide independently on his or her faith or its lack.

Chapter V Religious freedom of adults and children deprived of liberty in post-criminal isolation centres in the Federal Republic of Germany

5.1. Constitutional standard

In order to reconstruct the standard of religious freedom in force in the Federal Republic of Germany, it is necessary to refer to the content of the Basic Law of the FRG of 23 May 1949 (GG).[362] However, these considerations cannot be made without a reference to the concept of human dignity. Art. 1 (1) GG[363] provides that human dignity shall be inviolable. To respect and protect it shall be the duty of all state authority. The German people therefore acknowledges inviolable and inalienable human rights as the basis of every human community, of peace and justice in the world (Art. 1 (2) GG).[364] The fundamental rights listed in the Basic Law shall be bind the legislature, the executive and the judiciary as directly applicable law (Art. 1 (3) GG).[365]

As regards fundamental rights, the freedom principle is another important foundation on which the Basic Law rests. It is expressed (in the positive aspect) in Art. 2 (1) GG,[366] which lays down that every person shall have the right to free development of his personality insofar as he does not violate the rights of others or offend against the constitutional order or the moral code. Sect. 2[367] provides

---

362 *Grundgesetz für die Bundesrepublik Deutschland vom 23. Mai 1949*, Bundesgesetzblatt 1949, Teil I, no. 1, pp. 1 et seq.

363 "Die Würde des Menschen ist unantastbar. Sie zu achten und zu schützen ist Verpflichtung aller staatlichen Gewalt."

364 "Das Deutsche Volk bekennt sich darum zu unverletzlichen und unveräußerlichen Menschenrechten als Grundlage jeder menschlichen Gemeinschaft, des Friedens und der Gerechtigkeit in der Welt."

365 "Die nachfolgenden Grundrechte binden Gesetzgebung, vollziehende Gewalt und Rechtsprechung als unmittelbar geltendes Recht."

366 "Jeder hat das Recht auf die freie Entfaltung seiner Persönlichkeit, soweit er nicht die Rechte anderer verletzt und nicht gegen die verfassungsmäßige Ordnung oder das Sittengesetz verstößt."

367 "Jeder hat das Recht auf Leben und körperliche Unversehrtheit. Die Freiheit der Person ist unverletzlich. In diese Rechte darf nur auf Grund eines Gesetzes eingegriffen warden."

that every person shall have the right to life and physical integrity. Freedom of the person shall be inviolable, and these rights may be interfered with only pursuant to a law (negative aspect).

The relationship between human dignity and freedom was very aptly characterized by Klaus Stern (1932–2023), who indicated that these two values are complementary to each other – while dignity guarantees the individual's preservation of humanity, it is freedom that enables the individual's unhindered development. Without freedom – dignity is purely illusory, whereas dignity without freedom is merely a void declaration.[368]

The protection of human dignity is the foundation and axis of the entire constitutional and legal system of the Federal Republic of Germany. Dignity has been called the root of all fundamental rights[369] by the German Federal Constitutional Court (BVerfG).[370]

In the area of interest, the concept of dignity, along with the concept of freedom, means the recognition of human subjectivity, including in particular the individual's right to self-determination in a community of equals. The understanding of freedom stems from the circle of the original universalist utopia of the Christian vision of transcendence.[371] Dignity is not an idealized philosophical-normative category but is based on an ambivalent (realistic) image of the very man drawn from, among other things, the tradition of Renaissance humanism. Man is equally an independent and expansive being because "man is the measure of all things" (Protagoras), confident but also socially entangled and vulnerable, or in need of help. Thus, human dignity contains a peculiar tension between the individual right to self-determination and "the ethical minimum

---

368 K. Stern, *Das Staatsrecht der Bundesrepublik Deutschland. Band I: Grundlagen und Grundbegriffe des Staatsrechts, Strukturprinzipien der Verfassung*, München 1984, p. 790.

369 D. Hömig, "Menschenwürdeschutz in der Rechtsprechung des Bundesverfassungsgerichts", in W. Lembcke (ed.), *Das Dogma der Unantastbarkeit. Eine Auseinandersetzung mit dem Absolutheitsanspruch der Würde*, Tübingen 2009, pp. 25 et seq.

370 BVerfG, Beschluß vom 24.02.1971, 1 BvR 435/68, *Neue Juristische Wochenschrift*, vol. 37, 1971, pp. 1645 et seq.

371 H. Glaser, B. Makowicz, "Die Grundrechte in der Verfassungsordnung Polens und Deutschlands – Ein Grundlagenvergleich. Prawa podstawowe w porządkach konstytucyjnych Polski i Niemiec – porównanie zasadniczych zagadnień", in H. Glaser, B. Makowicz, M. Wyrzykowski (eds.), *Die Grundwerte- und Grundrechtsordnung in Polen und Deutschland. System podstawowych wartości i praw w Niemczech i w Polsce*, Baden-Baden 2019, pp. 163 and 328.

of species solidarity."[372] In anticipation of further considerations, note should be taken here of a judgement issued by BVerfG,[373] in which it is observed (in an attempt to balance the previously marked polarization) that in a state where human dignity is the highest value, and in which free self-determination of the individual is recognized as a community-building value, freedom of belief gives the individual legal space free from state interference, in which they can choose their path in life corresponding to their beliefs.

The fundamental rights mentioned in Art. 1 (3) GG are understood as a particular type of norms of secular modern law, distinctive from others, arising from the discourse on human rights that is ongoing in the western world.[374] They also show a specific correlation. From the point of view of an individual human being, these rights are a subjective entitlement to seek protection of the goods that they cover under the procedures envisaged by law. Fundamental rights are subjective rights that guarantee the individual the protection of a specific sphere of freedom in the form of demanding action defined by law from the state.[375] However, fundamental rights also play a role of objective values that set the standard for the entire legal system and are the most important directive of the process of establishing and applying law.

The above opinion was expressed in a judgement delivered by BVerfG,[376] which emphasized that fundamental rights aim primarily to protect the individual's freedom from violations by the state. However, the Basic Law is not a neutral value order. Its Chapter I, dedicated to fundamental rights, constitutes an objective value system (*objektive Wertordnung*). The system, with the human personality developing freely in the community at its centre, must serve as the touchstone in all areas of law. The judgment marked a shift of Germany's constitutional justice away from transcendental and legal-natural concepts of

---

372 U. Di Fabio, "Art. 4 GG…, margin nos. 28 and 29.

373 BVerfG, Beschluß vom 19.10.1971, 1 BvR 387/65, *Neue Juristische Wochenschrift*, vol. 8, 1972, p. 329.

374 H. Glaser, B. Makowicz, "Die Grundrechte…, pp. 27 and 194.

375 B. Banaszak, *System konstytucyjny Niemiec*, Warszawa 2005, p. 36 and M. Bożek, *System konstytucyjny Republiki Federalnej Niemiec*, Warszawa 2017, pp. 35, 38 and 46.

376 BVerfG, Urteil vom 15.01.1958, 1 BvR 400/57, *Neue Juristische Wochenschrift*, vol. 7, 1958, pp. 257 et seq.; F. Kübler, "Lüth: eine sanfte Revolution (BVerfGE 7, 198 ff.)", *Kritische Vierteljahresschrift für Gesetzgebung und Rechtswissenschaft*, vol. 83, nos. 3–4, 2000, pp. 313 et seq.

public law. Basing the constitutional control of a norm on the concept of natural law is now deemed unacceptable.[377]

The fundamental rights are, in principle, a coherent value system that legitimizes the entire constitutional order. This system is a regime, operating within the legal system, of rights defined in the case law and the doctrine with a certain degree of internal coherence.[378] In that aspect, the legislature has a distinctive role to play here. Not only should it refrain from enacting legislation that could violate the essence of fundamental rights, but it is also obliged to adopt such (institutional or procedural) solutions that promote the development of fundamental rights.[379]

Although the concept of an objective system of constitutional values met with an extremely enthusiastic response from most representatives of the science of German constitutional law and theory of law, it came in for considerable criticism. Many opponents see in it primarily the danger of the opportunistic actualization of the BVerfG value system[380] and refuse to accept the risk of a free choice of specific values from areas not only beyond (*praeter*) the Basic Law but also "outside it" (*de facto – contra*).[381] The opponents of that concept further point out that "objectivity" is only ostensible and verbalistic, and it serves purely to instruct the legislator authoritatively, thus limiting the possibility of the independent expression and fulfilment of people's will.[382]

This dispute seems to be resolved by Klaus Stern's assertion that in the case of fundamental rights – understood as a certain order – the point is not to establish the existence of an axiomatic or logical-deductive system of norms but for an adequately open and elastic system to offer the possibility of processing new

---

377 F. Günther, "Wer beeinflusst hier wen? Die westdeutsche Staatsrechtslehre und das Bundesverfassungsgericht während der 1950er und 1960er Jahre", in R. Chr. van Ooyen, M. H. W. Möllers (eds.), *Handbuch Bundesverfassungsgericht im politischen System*, Wiesbaden 2015, pp. 205 et seq.; H. Glaser, B. Makowicz, "Die Grundrechte…, pp. 67–73 and 100 and 230–236 and 263; O. Lepsius, "Die maßstabsetzende Gewalt", in *Das entgrenzte Gericht. Eine kritische Bilanz nach sechzig Jahren Bundesverfassungsgericht*, Berlin 2011, pp. 195 et seq.

378 H. Glaser, B. Makowicz, "Die Grundrechte…, pp. 25 and 192.

379 M. Bożek, *System…*, p. 38.

380 H. Glaser, B. Makowicz, "Die Grundrechte…, pp. 101–106 and 264–270.

381 G. Frankenberg, *Die Verfassung der Republik – Autorität und Solidarität in der Zivilgesellschaft*, Baden-Baden 1996, pp. 23 et seq.

382 G. Frankenberg, *Die Verfassung…*, pp. 110 et seq., 220, 233.

content.[383] The extra-normative value system is a more vague concept than the fundamental rights defined in the Basic Law.

5.2. Religious freedom in the Basic Law of the Federal Republic of Germany and selected statutory regulations

It is essential to refer to Art. 4 GG to reconstruct the standard of religious freedom. Under section 1, freedom of faith and of conscience and freedom to profess a religious or philosophical creed shall be inviolable.[384] In section 2, the law-maker guarantees the undisturbed practice of religion.[385] Under section 3, no person shall be compelled against his conscience to render military service involving the use of arms. Details shall be regulated by a federal law.[386]

Commentators consistently emphasize a strong anchoring of that provision in the international public law standards, including Art. 18 of the International Covenant on Civil and Political Rights, Art. 9 of the European Convention on the Protection of Human Rights and Fundamental Freedoms and Art. 10 of the Charter of Fundamental Rights of the European Union.[387] It is necessary to point out that the German Basic Law is, against the background of the above documents, chronologically the first (oldest) instrument. This can be seen in the semantic differences causing some interpretative perturbations. As indicated in Chapter II – Art. 4 (1) GG should be read as a whole, without separation of individual freedoms.

Arts. 4 (1) and (2) GG protect freedom to hold or not to hold beliefs, to accept or reject beliefs, to retain or abandon them, admit or not admit to a particular religion, and perform or refrain from performing a specified action due to religious reasons or maintain freedom from any religious motivation.[388] This

383 K. Stern, "Idee der Menschenrechte und Positivität der Grundrechte", in J. Isensee, P. Kirchhof (eds.), *Handbuch des Staatsrechts der Bundesrepublik Deutschland. Band IX. Allgemeine Grundrechtslehren*, Heidelberg 2011, margin no. 37.

384 "Die Freiheit des Glaubens, des Gewissens und die Freiheit des religiösen und weltanschaulichen Bekenntnisses sind unverletzlich."

385 "Die ungestörte Religionsausübung wird gewährleistet."

386 "Niemand darf gegen sein Gewissen zum Kriegsdienst mit der Waffe gezwungen werden. Das Nähere regelt ein Bundesgesetz".

387 U. Di Fabio, "Art. 4 GG…, margin no. 25 and M. Germann, "Art. 4 GG…, margin nos. 3 and 4.

388 U. Di Fabio, "Art. 4 GG…, margin no. 15 and M. Germann, "Art. 4 GG…, margin nos. 21 and 37.

conclusion is confirmed by a judgement issued by BVerfG,[389] where it was held that Art. 4 GG guarantees the individual a legal space in which one can determine one's way of life in accordance with one's beliefs, regardless of whether it is based on a religious belief or a non-religious worldview (including one that is hostile to religion). That freedom allows one not only to talk but also to be silent about what one believes or does not believe in. It also encompasses proselytism. BVerfG also shows that behaviour consisting in propagating (counter-propagating) specific religious or non-religious beliefs may be subject to restrictions (e.g. in the area of freedom of expression). However, not every behaviour will enjoy constitutional protection. A state that declares itself ideologically neutral cannot precisely define the content of the freedom of Art. 4 GG because it may not judge its citizens' faith or disbelief. It may, however, prevent the abuse of that freedom. Such a situation arises, in particular, when another person's dignity has been violated. As a rule, the permissible inducement of faith or dissuasion from it becomes an abuse where someone tries directly or indirectly, by dishonest methods or morally reprehensible means, including violence, to lead another person away from faith or persuade them to withdraw from a specific church. The above remarks are based on a factual situation during which a prisoner turned to agitation in the prison so that his fellow prisoners withdraw from a particular church, promising some of them cigarettes in return. The prisoner's behaviour resulted in a refusal to grant him consent for a conditional early release.

The interpretation of the scope of protection under Art. 4 GG entails the need for openness to a plurality of religious beliefs and worldviews.[390] This consequently implies a rejection of BVerfG's former view[391] that the Basic Law does not protect any specific view/belief but only those views which have developed among civilized nations, based on certain coherent, fundamental moral views shaped in the course of historical development. Today, the BVerfG case law[392] leaves no doubt that the Basic Law provides no indicator ("ethical standard") showing explicitly which belief is protected and which is not. It is open to a pluralism of religious beliefs and worldviews of the human, seen as a being endowed with

389 BVerfG, Beschluß vom 8.11.1960, 1 BvR 59/56, *Neue Juristische Wochenschrift*, vol. 5, 1961, p. 211.

390 U. Di Fabio, "Art. 4 GG…, margin no. 16 and M. Germann, "Art. 4 GG…, margin no. 16.

391 BVerfG, Beschluß vom 8.11.1960, 1 BvR 59/56, *Neue Juristische Wochenschrift*, vol. 5, 1961, p. 211.

392 BVerfG, Beschluß vom 17.12.1975, 1 BvR 63/68, *Neue Juristische Wochenschrift*, vols. 21–22, 1976, p. 948.

dignity, capable of self-determination, personal development, and having the ability to take responsibility for one's actions. This outlook enhances the religious and ideological neutrality of the Basic Law.

The protection of beliefs does not depend on statistical criteria, sociological significance or the number of followers. There are insufficient constitutional grounds to argue that beliefs held by dissidents enjoy less protection than the collective beliefs shared by a religious community.[393]

Therefore, the Basic Law protects internal, undisclosed beliefs (*forum internum*) and behaviour motivated by religion or worldview (*forum externum*). It is argued after BVerfG[394] that the Basic Law ensures the individual the right to adapt all one's behaviour to the teachings of one's professed faith and to act in accordance with one's inner conviction. By contrast, all forms of religious indoctrination are seen as an interference with *forum internum*. On the one hand, the state has the objective duty to protect the freedoms defined in Art. 4 GG from interference by third parties.[395] However, this duty does not go so far as to preclude intellectual polemics in religious and ideological disputes. Both religious communities and those that represent a specific worldview must accept the fact that they are subject to criticism from the public.[396]

It is frequently argued in the BVerfG case law[397] that the neutrality principle (*Neutralitätsprinzip*) presupposes that the state is "home for all citizens" (*Heimstatt aller Staatsbürger*), regardless of religious and ideological differences. The identification of the state with a particular religious position or worldview would have a disintegrating effect on citizens who do not share a given view.

At the same time, the neutrality principle does not entail that the state remains completely passive. It is undisputed that its legitimate activities will include taking action to protect the inalienable fundamental rights based on human dignity wherever religious beliefs or worldviews will pose a threat to them.[398] It implies the supremacy (monopoly) of the rule of law paradigm that arises from

---

393 M. Germann, "Art. 4 GG…, margin no. 17.

394 BVerfG, Beschluß vom 19.10.1971, 1 BvR 387/65, *Neue Juristische Wochenschrift*, vol. 8, 1972, p. 327.

395 M. Germann, "Art. 4 GG…, margin no. 69.

396 M. Germann, "Art. 4 GG…, margin no. 71.

397 BVerfG, Urteil vom 14.12.1965, 1 BvR 413/60, *Neue Juristische Wochenschrift*, vol. 4, 1966, p. 147, where this concept was first used and BVerfG, Beschluss vom 14.01.2020, 2 BvR 1333/17, *Neue Juristische Wochenschrift*, vol. 15, 2020, p. 1052 along with a list of judgments in which BVerfG refers to this concept.

398 M. Germann, "Art. 4 GG…, margin no. 82.

the basic liberal maxim – mutual respect and social peace – forming the core of the system of constitutional values and setting fundamental limits on every freedom.[399]

The requirement of neutrality cannot be understood as the state's prohibition on contacts with religious or ideological communities. The state protects ecclesiastical monuments to the same extent as secular monuments and includes such institutions as Caritas or Diaconia in the state protection system. Through support and cooperation, the state comes into contact with religious and ideological organizations without identifying with them.[400]

Religious and ideological neutrality and the state secularity (*Säkularität des Staates*) are nonetheless essential conditions that effectively guarantee the value system encoded in the Basic Law.[401] Despite the attempts at the rational separation of the state from a particular religion or worldview, based on the above considerations, one can see the so-called paradox of a constitutional state's neutrality (*Paradoxie der Neutralitätsposition des Verfassungsstaates*), which seeks to be neutral but cannot be so in the strict sense of the word.[402]

The freedoms under Art. 4 GG enjoy protection both on an individual and collective level. This means that although these rights are fundamental and personal, they are typically not exercised solely on a private basis. In most cases, religious identity is shaped in ritualized communities. Given the formation and shaping of religious communities in Judaism, Islam and Christianity, the right to religious freedom is inextricably intertwined with a community of like-minded people. The protection under Art. 4 GG was therefore not excluded in relation to specified communities, although it is clarified in other provisions.[403]

Against this background, religious freedom takes on particular importance. Religion becomes a collective good thanks to the unity with which a community of followers assiduously builds it. Consequently, the Basic Law and other normative instruments must provide it with an adequate protection standard.[404] The German literature points to a trap set for a tolerant society. Similarly to

399 U. Di Fabio, "Art. 4 GG…, margin nos. 17 and 24.
400 M. Germann, "Art. 4 GG…, margin no. 84.
401 U. Di Fabio, "Art. 4 GG…, margin no. 12.
402 U. Di Fabio, "Art. 4 GG…, margin nos. 16 and 44.
403 U. Di Fabio, "Art. 4 GG…, margin nos. 53 and 57.
404 Attention is occasionally drawn to the collective aspect of religion and its atypical status – a diversified social subsystem. I. Ausberg, K-H. Ladeur, *Toleranz – Religion – Recht. Die Herausforderung des »neutralen« Staates durch neue Formen der Religiosität in der postmodernen Gesellschaft*, Tübingen 2007, p. 51.

some political ideas, religion tends to gain omnipotence and worldview totality based on transcendental certainties. By contrast, the Basic Law puts man with his capacity for self-determination about matters that concern him in its sphere of decisions. Thus a discussion on threats to the constitutional order posed by religious freedom should not be treated as an anti-religious provocation. An approved view, which is an expression of affirmation of human dignity, is a statement that the Basic Law also protects isolated viewpoints that depart from the teaching of a given church or religious community, but the protection is given at the level of freedom of conscience.[405]

However, one does not have the constitutional right to renounce one's community by rejecting it and persistently violating its rules. A negative response from the community and the exclusion of a member based on internal regulations do not, in principle, give rise to the state's obligation to defend the individual.[406] However, a religious community may not prevent, unreasonably hinder or preclude (including the use of violence) its member – against his will – from withdrawing from it. Notably, ordinary courts may monitor the regulations on joining and withdrawing from a community in the case of reasonable suspicion that membership is based on coercion. A violation of an individual's right to self-determination by a community must not be ignored – in such a case, the right will prevail.[407]

The special status of the individual, including while serving a penalty of deprivation of liberty, does not exclude *eo ipso* the possibility of invoking the guarantees envisaged in Art. 4 GG.[408] In that case, however, interference with the individual's fundamental rights may be justified by security requirements and practical conditions for serving a penalty of deprivation of liberty.[409]

As indicated above, Art. 4 (1) GG also protects the individual's right to irreligiousness. The content of the provision complements the retained Art. 136 of the former Basic Law (so-called Weimar Constitution) dated 11 August 1919 (WRV),[410] which prescribes that civil and citizen rights and duties shall be neither conditioned upon, nor restricted by, the exercise of religious freedom (sect. 1). Moreover, the enjoyment of civil and citizen rights as well as eligibility to public office shall be independent of religious belief (sect. 2). In turn,

405 U. Di Fabio, "Art. 4 GG…, margin nos. 57 and 58.
406 U. Di Fabio, "Art. 4 GG…, margin no. 59.
407 U. Di Fabio, "Art. 4 GG…, margin nos. 89 and 96.
408 M. Germann, "Art. 4 GG…, margin no. 28.
409 M. Germann, "Art. 4 GG…, margin no. 58.
410 *Die Verfassung des Deutschen Reichs*, Reichsgesetzblatt 1919, no. 152, p. 1410.

pursuant to Art. 136 (3) WRV, no one shall be compelled to disclose his religious convictions. The authorities have the right to inquire into a person's membership in a religious association only in so far as certain rights and duties are dependent thereon, or in so far as may be required by legally instituted statistical studies. It is a significant difference when compared to Art. 53 (7) of the Constitution of the Republic of Poland, which strictly prescribes that no one shall be compelled by organs of public authority to disclose his worldview, religious convictions or belief. Notably, in the light of Art. 136 (4) WRV, no one shall be compelled to perform any religious act or to take part in religious acts or practices or to take oath in religious form.

Under Art. 137 WRV, freedom to form religious communities shall be guaranteed. The combination of religious communities shall be subject to no restrictions (sect. 2[411]). At the same time, there is no state church (sect. 1[412]). Every religious community shall regulate and administer its affairs independently within the limits of the law, applicable to all. It shall appoint its officers without the cooperation of the state or local authorities (sect. 3[413]). Religious communities shall become incorporated according to the general provisions of civil law (sect. 4[414]). Religious communities shall remain bodies of public law if this has been their status hitherto. The same rights may be accorded to other religious communities upon application if their constitution and the number of their members offer a guarantee of permanency. Where several such religious communities as are public bodies combine in a union, this union shall also be a public body (sect. 5[415]). Such communities shall be entitled to collect taxes based on civil tax lists in

411 "Die Freiheit der Vereinigung zu Religionsgesellschaften wird gewährleistet. Der Zusammenschluß von Religionsgesellschaften innerhalb des Reichsgebiets unterliegt keinen Beschränkungen."

412 "Es besteht keine Staatskirche."

413 "Jede Religionsgesellschaft ordnet und verwaltet ihre Angelegenheiten selbständig innerhalb der Schranken des für alle geltenden Gesetzes. Sie verleiht ihre Ämter ohne Mitwirkung des Staates oder der bürgerlichen Gemeinde."

414 "Religionsgesellschaften erwerben die Rechtsfähigkeit nach den allgemeinen Vorschriften des bürgerlichen Rechtes."

415 "Die Religionsgesellschaften bleiben Körperschaften des öffentlichen Rechtes, soweit sie solche bisher waren. Anderen Religionsgesellschaften sind auf ihren Antrag gleiche Rechte zu gewähren, wenn sie durch ihre Verfassung und die Zahl ihrer Mitglieder die Gewähr der Dauer bieten. Schließen sich mehrere derartige öffentlich-rechtliche Religionsgesellschaften zu einem Verbande zusammen, so ist auch dieser Verband eine öffentlich-rechtliche Körperschaft."

accordance with the provisions of state law (sect. 6[416]). Communities devoted to common cultivation of a philosophy of life shall be placed on the same footing as religious communities (sect. 7[417]). The execution of these regulations shall be within the competence of the federal legislator (sect. 8[418]).

An important guarantee of freedom of conscience and religion is provided by the retained Art. 141 WRV,[419] which prescribes that as far as there is a need for divine services and spiritual ministration in the army, hospitals, penal facilities and other public institutions, religious associations shall be admitted for the performance of religious acts without the exercise of any compulsion. The provision has remained in force under Art. 140 of the Basic Law currently in force.

Commentators emphasize that the standard under Art. 141 WRV is unique because it safeguards and fulfils the human right to religious freedom in state institutions, where human freedom is restricted. It is a form of compensation (*Kompensationsgedanke*), where an impediment to a person's enjoyment of his fundamental rights must be compensated for by state obligations. The provision gives religious communities, in the interest and for the protection of fundamental rights of a defined category of persons, a public subjective right that is functionally related to the collective aspect of religious freedom mentioned in Art. 4 (2) of the Basic Law.[420]

Art. 141 WRV foresees the state's objective obligation to create institutional frameworks that will enable the actual exercise of the fundamental rights of the individual, including religious (church) pastoral care. In that case, the state assumes custodian responsibility for meeting people's religious needs to the extent to which the institutional order prevents them from the free fulfilment of those

---

416 "Die Religionsgesellschaften, welche Körperschaften des öffentlichen Rechtes sind, sind berechtigt, auf Grund der bürgerlichen Steuerlisten nach Maßgabe der landesrechtlichen Bestimmungen Steuern zu erheben."

417 "Den Religionsgesellschaften werden die Vereinigungen gleichgestellt, die sich die gemeinschaftliche Pflege einer Weltanschauung zur Aufgabe machen."

418 "Soweit die Durchführung dieser Bestimmungen eine weitere Regelung erfordert, liegt diese der Landesgesetzgebung ob."

419 "Soweit das Bedürfnis nach Gottesdienst und Seelsorge im Heer, in Krankenhäusern, Strafanstalten oder sonstigen öffentlichen Anstalten besteht, sind die Religionsgesellschaften zur Vornahme religiöser Handlungen zuzulassen, wobei jeder Zwang fernzuhalten ist."

420 S. Korioth, "Art. 141 WRV", in T. Maunz, G. Dürig (eds.), *Grundgesetz. Kommentar. Band VII. Art. 107–146*, München 2022 (98. EL März 2022), margin nos. 1 and 2.

needs at their own will.[421] Art. 141 WRV refers solely to religious communities; a citizen, even if he is in a particular public institution, is subjectively and legally protected by the norm under Art. 4 GG.[422] This means, in practice, that the state must ensure organizational conditions for religious activity because it enjoys organizational sovereignty in those institutions. However, it must not organize pastoral care independently. The content of an activity and its organization falls under the responsibility of religious communities.[423] The right is realized once the users of a given institution have reported such a need, which they are entitled to at any time. Importantly, it is possible to ask the question about affiliation to a religious community during admission to a given institution, provided that it is simultaneously indicated that the answer is voluntary.[424] If organizational circumstances so require, a public institution must inform respective religious communities about the existing demand for their activity. Only if the prisoners show no need for pastoral care, a religious community does not have the right of access to a given public institution.[425]

The scope of the retained Art. 141 WRV includes the performance of "religious acts" (*religiöser Handlungen*). The scope of those acts falls under the also retained Art. 137 (3) WRV, pursuant to which every religious association shall regulate and administer its affairs independently within the limits of the law, applicable to all. The provision is an indispensable and legally independent guarantee of religious freedom, increasing the freedom of religious life and activity of churches and other religious communities. It provides the freedom of a given confessional organization in organizational matters, establishing norms and management necessary to carry out their functions.[426] An association's matters cover teaching and worship, which include, among other things, the manner and organization of community operation (also an organizational structure, which does not have to be democratic – most often it is hierarchical[427]) and ministries (divine

---

421 A. Hollerbach, "§ 140", in J. Isensee, P. Kirchhof (eds.), *Handbuch des Staatsrechts der Bundesrepublik Deutschland. Band VI. Bundesstaat*, Heidelberg 2009, margin no. 10.

422 S. Korioth, "Art. 141 WRV…, margin no. 3.

423 S. Korioth, "Art. 141 WRV…, margin nos. 3 and 5.

424 S. Korioth, "Art. 141 WRV…, margin no. 7.

425 S. Korioth, "Art. 141 WRV…, margin no. 7.

426 S. Korioth, "Art. 137 WRV", in T. Maunz, G. Dürig (eds.), *Grundgesetz. Kommentar. Band VII. Art. 107–146*, München 2022 (98. EL März 2022), margin no. 21.

427 BVerfG, Urteil vom 19.12.2000, 2 BvR 1500/97, *Juristische Schulung*, vol. 5, 2001, pp. 496 et seq.

services), administration of the sacraments, pastoral care,[428] as well as property management and economic activity, even if they are not directly connected with the performance of religious activity,[429] the establishment of canon standards and separate religious jurisdiction, and charity.[430]

There is also no objection to the fact that religious associations have the exclusive and autonomous right to determine who and on what terms may become a member of a given community. If the baptism (in the case of Christians) is a prerequisite and necessary condition for inclusion in the religious community, then in the case of an adult, a clear declaration of will on that matter is required (a so-called request for baptism). As regards child baptism, the declaration is submitted by his parents (legal guardians) acting as his representatives. This practice is historically well-established and is legally unchallengeable. It does not breach the child's fundamental rights, as infants cannot independently exercise the right to freedom of conscience and religion at the time of baptism because they do not have the capacity to evaluate religious dogmas. For baptism and the associated joining of a particular church, no consent from the family and guardianship court is required.[431]

The question of withdrawing from a given confessional community is slightly different. The fact of joining and withdrawing from a specified religious association leads to consequences in the area of levy law because the Federal Republic of Germany has the institution of so-called church tax (*Kirchensteur*). It is a pecuniary performance of a coercive and permanent nature, paid to a religious association, which is a body of public law, by its believers who have a habitual abode or domicile in the area of the tax law. Each state has its own separate regulation determining the type of tax, manner of payment, rates and forms of administration. The contribution is collected by tax authorities of individual states. A successful withdrawal from a religious association, giving rise to effects in the area of income law, is conditioned on the submission of an oral or written statement (subject to a fee) in person before a competent state authority (Registry Office or District Court), which contains an unambiguously expressed wish to withdraw from the association. It is not required to indicate the reason for the withdrawal. That solution takes into account the state religious

428 S. Korioth, "Art. 137 WRV…, margin no. 30 and 31.

429 BVerwG, Urteil vom 15.12.2005, BVerwG 7 C 20/04, *Neue Juristische Wochenschrift*, vol. 18, 2006, pp. 1303 et seq.

430 S. Korioth, "Art. 137 WRV…, margin nos. 38, 39, 41.

431 S. Korioth, "Art. 137 WRV…, margin no. 34.

neutrality principle and the resulting far-reaching restraint in religious matters. It is also the fulfilment of the postulate to consider a model statement submitted by parents (legal guardians) to school authorities on the non-participation of their children in religious instruction to be sufficient in this matter.[432]

In a judgment in the case of Wasmuth vs. The Federal Republic of Germany,[433] the European Court of Human Rights held that the obligation to reveal affiliation with churches or religious societies on a tax card constituted an interference with freedom of religion of the individual, who is protected by Art. 9 of the European Convention on the Protection of Human Rights and Fundamental Freedoms. However, the interference had a basis in German law, as it aimed to ensure the right of churches and religious societies to levy church tax. The Court found the interference proportionate because the reference on the tax card only indicated that the applicant did not belong to a church or religious society authorized to levy church tax. Besides, the German regulations fell within the doctrine of the margin of discretion that the European Convention grants in this regard to states that have ratified this international agreement. There is no European standard for funding churches and religious groups.

In turn, the Federal Administrative Court (BVerwG)[434] confirmed in one of its judgments the invalidity of so-called modified church exit (*modifizierten Kirchenaustritt*). That statement contained a declaration of will of withdrawing from a religious association, as a body of public law, with a simultaneous declaration of willingness to remain a follower of that religious community. BVerwG held that any person who wishes to leave a religious community, which has the status of a public law entity under state law, cannot limit his statement only to the relationship under public law, simultaneously remaining in the religious community.[435]

432 W. Góralski, "Problem wystąpienia z Kościoła katolickiego w Republice Federalnej Niemiec", *Prawo Kanoniczne*, vol. 1, 2015, pp. 7 et seq.; S. Korioth, "Art. 137 WRV…, margin no. 36; M. Kosek, *Podatek kościelny w niemieckim systemie prawnym*, Płock 2004, *passim*; M. Kosek, "Czy możliwa jest recepcja niemieckiego modelu podatku kościelnego w Polsce?", *Forum Teologiczne*, vol. 7, 2006, pp. 50–56.; J. Petersen, *Kirchensteuer kompakt. Strukturierte Darstellung mit Berechnungsbeispielen*, Wiesbaden 2020, *passim*.

433 ECHR, Judgment of 17 February 2011, case of Wasmuth v. Germany, application no. 12884/03.

434 BVerwG, Urteil vom 26.09.2012, BVerwG 6 C 7/12, *Neue Zeitschrift fur Verwaltungsrecht*, vols. 1–2, 2013, pp. 64 et seq.

435 "Wer aufgrund staatlicher Vorschriften aus einer Religionsgemeinschaft mit dem Status einer Körperschaft des öffentlichen Rechts austreten will, darf seine

The concept of religious acts referred to in Art. 141 WRV tends to be interpreted very broadly and is not reduced solely to divine services (*Gottesdienst*) or pastoral care (*Seelsorge*). The concept certainly encompasses: pastoral talks, activities connected with worship and liturgy, various forms of divine services, prayer groups or biblical circles. Thus, it is possible to provide religious assistance and support in all matters of human life.[436]

However, it is not possible to infer directly other state obligations from the provision of Art. 141 WRV, for example, funding pastoral care in a public establishment. The state or a public institution may take over such funding (in whole or in part), provided that the principle of neutrality and parity is respected. This solution is supported by, on the one hand, the idea of *Kompensationsgedanke* and, on the other, the general idea that the state advocates the fulfilment of freedom protected by guaranteed fundamental rights. There are no normative reasons why religion should be excluded from that area.[437]

Although it is argued that Art. 141 does not contain restrictions on the subjective public law of religious communities, commentators point to such limitations. They include other legal interests, also of a constitutional rank, and the joint obligation of the state and religious associations to take into account the goods of other actors. It follows that religious associations must respect the way a particular public institution operates. However, a person who manages a public institution cannot, by his behaviour, defeat the purpose of ministry, for example, by setting inadequate hours for providing religious services (e.g. only at night). Moreover, with regard to prisons, security needs are strongly emphasized because they may be the basis for precluding representatives of religious associations from having uncontrolled contact with persons under their pastoral care. It is ultimately concluded that the operation of religious associations in public institutions may not defeat the purpose of existence of a given institution and distort the conditions of its operation. The introduced restrictions must, of course, comply with the proportionality principle.[438]

The Basic Law of the Federal Republic of Germany declares in Art. 6 (2[439]) that the care and upbringing of children is the natural right of parents and it is

---

Erklärung nicht auf die Körperschaft des öffentlichen Rechts unter Verbleib in der Religionsgemeinschaft als Glaubensgemeinschaft beschränken."

436 S. Korioth, "Art. 141 WRV…, margin no. 8.

437 S. Korioth, "Art. 141 WRV…, margin no. 8.

438 S. Korioth, "Art. 141 WRV…, margin no. 9.

439 "Pflege und Erziehung der Kinder sind das natürliche Recht der Eltern und die zuvörderst ihnen obliegende Pflicht. Über ihre Betätigung wacht die staatliche Gemeinschaft."

primarily their responsibility to do so. However, the state community oversees parents' actions. The aspect of child upbringing is slightly extended in Art. 7 (2) GG,[440] which prescribes that persons with parental authority shall have the right to decide whether the child receives religious instruction.

Although it does not follow directly from the provisions of the Basic Law, parents should not do anything that prevents a child mature enough and capable enough to make his own decisions from making a free choice about their religion or worldview or renounce them. However, as a guardian of human rights, the state must secure the rights of the child, taking into account other fundamental rights. For example, parents may not use violence to force a child to participate in a religious (worldview) community if the child does not want to belong to such a community. They should not deprive their child of knowledge on religious and worldview pluralism, include him in religious communities that do not provide for leaving them at all, influence the child mentally (using manipulation or deceit) in such a way as to prevent him from changing his religion or worldview.[441]

The provisions of the Basic Law are connected with the regulations contained in the German Civil Code (*Bürgerliches Gesetzbuch*). Under § 1626 BGB, the parents have the duty and the right to care for the minor child. Their parental custody includes the care for the person and the assets of the child (sect. 1[442]). Exercising parental custody and raising a child, the parents take account of the growing ability and the growing need of the child for independent and responsible action. They discuss questions of parental custody with the child to the extent that, in accordance with the stage of development of the child, it is advisable and they seek agreement (sect. 2[443]). The best interest of the child, as a general rule, includes contact with both parents. The same applies to contact with other

---

440 "Die Erziehungsberechtigten haben das Recht, über die Teilnahme des Kindes am Religionsunterricht zu bestimmen."

441 W. Kellerwessel, "Das Recht der Kinder auf Religionsfreiheit – im Kontext der Rechte von Erziehungsberechtigten und staatlichen Pflichten", *Zeitschrift für Menschenrechte*, vol. 1, 2022, pp. 56 et seq.

442 "Die Eltern haben die Pflicht und das Recht, für das minderjährige Kind zu sorgen (elterliche Sorge). Die elterliche Sorge umfasst die Sorge für die Person des Kindes (Personensorge) und das Vermögen des Kindes (Vermögenssorge)."

443 "Bei der Pflege und Erziehung berücksichtigen die Eltern die wachsende Fähigkeit und das wachsende Bedürfnis des Kindes zu selbständigem verantwortungsbewusstem Handeln. Sie besprechen mit dem Kind, soweit es nach dessen Entwicklungsstand angezeigt ist, Fragen der elterlichen Sorge und streben Einvernehmen an."

persons with whom the child has ties if maintaining these ties is essential for its development (sect. 3[444]).

Although the care and upbringing right is defined in the Basic Law as the parents' "natural right", it seems that protection against interference from the state is a parents' fundamental right that can be inferred from the cited provisions.[445] Parents may pass on their personal views to their children and raise them with religious or worldview norms in mind.[446] This entitlement includes both the attitude of keeping the child away from the influence of any religion[447] and intense involvement in the life of a given community.[448] The parents have the full right to define the child's religious affiliation, including the performance of irrevocable religious initiation rites such as, for example, baptism.[449]

Any regulation by the legislature that affects parental rights requires substantiation based on the criterion of validity of the regulatory objective and is bound by the proportionality principle.[450] For instance, the parents may not consent to a sterilization of the child, nor can the child itself consent to the sterilization (§ 1631c BGB[451]). Moreover, the care for the person of the child includes the parents' right to give consent to the medically unnecessary circumcision of a male child who is incapable of reasoning and forming a judgment, provided that it is performed in accordance with the rules of medical practice (current medical knowledge). This does not apply if the circumcision, even considering its purpose,

444 "Zum Wohl des Kindes gehört in der Regel der Umgang mit beiden Elternteilen. Gleiches gilt für den Umgang mit anderen Personen, zu denen das Kind Bindungen besitzt, wenn ihre Aufrechterhaltung für seine Entwicklung förderlich ist."

445 P. Badura, "Art. 6 GG", in T. Maunz, G. Dürig (eds.), *Grundgesetz. Kommentar. Band II. Art. 6–16a*, München (100. EL Januar 2023), margin nos. 24, 97, 133; P. Badura, "Art. 7 GG", in T. Maunz, G. Dürig (eds.), *Grundgesetz. Kommentar. Band II. Art. 6–16a*, München (100. EL Januar 2023), margin no. 23.

446 BVerfG, Beschluß vom 17.12.1975, 1 BvR 63/68, *Neue Juristische Wochenschrift*, vols. 21–22, 1976, pp. 947 et seq.

447 BVerfG, Beschluß vom 16.05.1995, 1 BvR 1087/91, *Neue Juristische Wochenschrift*, vol. 38, 1995, pp. 2477 et seq.

448 K. A. Schwarz, "Kopftuchverbote für Minderjährige unter 14 Jahren in schulischen und vorschulischen Einrichtungen", *Neue Zeitschrift für Verwaltungsrecht*, vol. 5, 2020, pp. 265 et seq.

449 J. Kuntze, "Rechtsfragen zur religiösen Knabenbeschneidung", *Zeitschrift für evangelisches Kirchenrecht*, vol. 16, no. 1, 2013, pp. 44 et seq.

450 P. Badura, "Art. 6 GG…, margin no. 98.

451 "Die Eltern können nicht in eine Sterilisation des Kindes einwilligen. Auch das Kind selbst kann nicht in die Sterilisation einwilligen. § 1809 findet keine Anwendung."

jeopardizes the best interests of the child (§ 1631d sect. 1 BGB[452]). In the first six months after the child is born, circumcision may also be performed by persons designated by a religious group to perform this procedure if these persons are specially trained to do so and, without being a physician, are comparably qualified to perform circumcisions (§ 1631d sect. 2 BGB[453]). In turn, § 226a of the German Criminal Code (*Strafgesetzbuch* – StGB)[454] prohibits female genital mutilation under threat of a penalty of imprisonment for a term of at least one year (sect. 1[455]). In less serious cases, the penalty is imprisonment for a term of between 6 months and 5 years (sect. 2[456]). The two above restrictions, on the one hand, meet the religious needs of specific communities and, on the other, oppose cultural practices unacceptable in a pluralistic society. The German legislator left the way open for refusing to perform a circumcision of a male child if that procedure, taking into account its purpose, jeopardizes the interests of the child. It is not clear how that restriction is to be understood. Some commentators argue that it opens up the possibility of checking the parents' motivation – whether it is indeed religious, which is justified in the explanatory memorandum to the draft law introducing the indicated provisions, which provides two examples of motivation other than religious that may be qualified as an obstacle to the performance of circumcision. Namely, in the case where it is performed for purely aesthetic reasons or as a disincentive to render masturbation difficult. However, these examples are occasionally called into question.[457]

452 "Die Personensorge umfasst auch das Recht, in eine medizinisch nicht erforderliche Beschneidung des nicht einsichts- und urteilsfähigen männlichen Kindes einzuwilligen, wenn diese nach den Regeln der ärztlichen Kunst durchgeführt werden soll. Dies gilt nicht, wenn durch die Beschneidung auch unter Berücksichtigung ihres Zwecks das Kindeswohl gefährdet wird."

453 "In den ersten sechs Monaten nach der Geburt des Kindes dürfen auch von einer Religionsgesellschaft dazu vorgesehene Personen Beschneidungen gemäß Absatz 1 durchführen, wenn sie dafür besonders ausgebildet und, ohne Arzt zu sein, für die Durchführung der Beschneidung vergleichbar befähigt sind."

454 Reichsgesetzblatt of 15.05.1871, pp. 127 et seq.

455 "Wer die äußeren Genitalien einer weiblichen Person verstümmelt, wird mit Freiheitsstrafe nicht unter einem Jahr bestraft."

456 "In minder schweren Fällen ist auf Freiheitsstrafe von sechs Monaten bis zu fünf Jahren zu erkennen."

457 B. Veit, "§ 1631d", in W. Hau, R. Poseck (eds.), *BeckOK. Bürgerliches Gesetzbuch*, München 2023, margin no. 32 and P. Huber, "§ 1631d", in D. Schwab (ed.), *Münchener Kommentar zum Bürgerlichen Gesetzbuch. Band 10. Familienrecht II. §§ 1589–1921*, München 2020, margin no. 20.

Other initiation rituals interfering with the child's body are considered acceptable only when the child is already capable of making independent decisions and consents thereto. In general, practices causing harm to the child's body should be prevented even if they are motivated by religion or worldview. They include procedures adapting the body to ritual jewellery, tattoos, scars or other forms of stigma.[458]

The child should be treated as a subject and bearer of fundamental rights, as every human being,[459] and the parents are obliged to adjust their actions adequately to his good.[460] Parental rights find their justification only in the need to protect and help the child.[461] Thus, identically to Polish law, the interest of the child is the key guideline in assessing parental rights, including the right to raise a child. However, it is essentially the parents who decide, in accordance with their own religious and worldview convictions, what is in the best interest of the child,[462] and they have interpretative priority.[463] In the process of child-rearing, the state does not play the role of a teacher but an attentive guardian who intervenes in the case of neglect or a violation of the physical and mental integrity of the child. Such power dynamics between the state and parents does not imply a lack of conflict situations, especially in the case of a physical violation of the child's bodily integrity due to religious reasons (e.g. the above-mentioned practice of circumcisions) and violations involving irreversibility. State interference is justified in such cases, but the abstract collision criteria justifying interference proposed for application (in relevant situations) are not free from criticism and reservations.[464]

Religious education is a special point as regards religious freedom. Religious instruction shall form part of the regular curriculum state schools (with the exception of non-denominational schools). Without prejudice to the state's right of supervision, religious instruction shall be given in accordance with the tenets

---

458 W. Kellerwessel, "Das Recht…, pp. 59 et seq.

459 Although, in the opinion of some researchers, the content of Art. 6 (2) GG does not give grounds for inferring from it the fundamental right relating *expressis verbis* to the child. The child, of course, has his own human dignity and his own right to develop his personality – P. Badura, "Art. 6 GG…, margin no. 135.

460 T. Hörnle, S. Huster, "Wie weit reicht das Erziehungsrecht der Eltern? Am Beispiel der Beschneidung von Jungen", *Juristen Zeitung*, vol. 7, 2013, pp. 330 et seq.

461 P. Badura, "Art. 6 GG…, margin no. 133.

462 U. Di Fabio, "Art. 4 GG…, margin no. 129.

463 J. Kuntze, *Rechtsfragen…*, pp. 50 et seq.

464 U. Di Fabio, "Art. 4 GG…, margin no. 129.

of the religious community concerned. It is therefore a religious subject and teachers may not be obliged against their will to give religious instruction (Art. 7 (3) GG[465]).

The cited regulation of the Basic Law points to a strong mandate of the state. The parents' right includes the right to choose a school and an educational institution (so-called parental educational right) offered by the state, but it does not include the right to co-decide on the organization of schooling (setting the curriculum, subjects taught at school and the number of classes), the content given there and the significance of the child's achievements for his certificate and advancement to another class.[466] The state has the so-called educational independence.[467] Parents may not demand that a state school obey the commands and prohibitions appearing in life based on religious or worldview norms. This idea is reinforced by the assertion that the ability to make a direct educational impact is complete only in the out-of-school area[468] and is given to the parents. In the educational area, school plays a supplementary role to parental educational primacy.[469] Child-rearing is a joint task of the parents and school to be accomplished in interconnected cooperation.[470] In that case, the restriction of parental rights is balanced because the state remains neutral and tolerant when creating lessons, in particular, it refrains from exerting any influence in favour of a specific religious or worldview direction.[471] The function of school is to transmit values and promote constitutionally and legally defined attitudes.[472] Religious and worldview reasons do not justify the exemption of a child from universal compulsory education, and parents who withdraw their child from universal compulsory education for those reasons must expect their parental authority

465 "Der Religionsunterricht ist in den öffentlichen Schulen mit Ausnahme der bekenntnisfreien Schulen ordentliches Lehrfach. Unbeschadet des staatlichen Aufsichtsrechtes wird der Religionsunterricht in Übereinstimmung mit den Grundsätzen der Religionsgemeinschaften erteilt. Kein Lehrer darf gegen seinen Willen verpflichtet werden, Religionsunterricht zu erteilen".

466 D. Coester-Waltjen, "Art. 6 GG", in I. Münch, P. Kunig (eds.), *Grundgesetz-Kommentar. Band 1. Art. 1 bis 69*, München 2012, margin no. 102.

467 P. Badura, "Art. 6 GG…, margin no. 117.

468 BVerwG, Urteil vom 11.09.2013, 6 C 25/12 (VGH Kassel), *Neue Zeitschrift fur Verwaltungsrecht*, vol. 1, 2014, pp. 84 et seq.

469 P. Badura, "Art. 6 GG…, margin no. 130.

470 P. Badura, "Art. 7 GG…, margin no. 23.

471 U. Di Fabio, "Art. 4 GG…, margin no. 132.

472 P. Badura, "Art. 7 GG…, margin no. 17.

to be restricted.[473] The strong position of the state educational mandate must ensure the individual (child) freedom to develop his personality, so religious communities must accept that state education counteracts the isolation of a child from society.[474] The school must be a space for an objective examination of all religious views and every worldview, at the same time respecting the need for tolerance.[475]

The state has the duty of neutrality in religious and worldview matters, simultaneously ensuring institutional frameworks for religious education. As regards religious instruction, its subject is the beliefs of a particular community and the truths it communicates. A decision to allow students of another religion to participate in such lessons lies within the competence of a particular religious community (church).[476] However, religious instruction may not take place outside normal school hours and should be included in the lesson plan and general organization of the school.[477]

With age, the growth of the child's autonomy may come into conflict with the parents' rights and expectations. Their rights are reduced as the need to care for and educate the child decreases and his ability to bear responsibility increases.[478] Some conflicting situations were resolved in an Act of 15 July 1921[479] Law on the Religious Parenting (*Gesetz über die religiöse Kindererziehung*).[480] The right to religious upbringing is part of the right to child upbringing defined in § 1631 (2[481]) BGB. The law was constructed based on the paradigm of the free agreement of the parents on the religious upbringing of the child, insofar as they have the right and duty of care for the child (§ 1). In the opinion of Peter Huber, the German regulations from the previous century anticipated not only the parental equality principle and the modern concepts of exercising

---

473 U. Di Fabio, "Art. 4 GG…, margin no. 133.
474 U. Di Fabio, "Art. 4 GG…, margin no. 134.
475 P. Badura, "Art. 6 GG…, margin no. 121.
476 P. Badura, "Art. 7 GG…, margin no. 70.
477 P. Badura, "Art. 7 GG…, margin no. 75.
478 BVerfG, Urteil vom 9.02.1982, 1 BvR 845/79, *Neue Juristische Wochenschrift*, vol. 25,1982, pp. 1375 et seq.
479 Reichsgesetzblatt 1921, No. 78, pos. 8234, p. 939, as amended.
480 U. Di Fabio, "Art. 4 GG…, margin no. 126.
481 "Die Personensorge umfasst insbesondere die Pflicht und das Recht, das Kind zu pflegen, zu erziehen, zu beaufsichtigen und seinen Aufenthalt zu bestimmen" – The care for the person of the child shall include the right and duty to care (nurture), raise the child, supervise the child and determine the child's abode.

parental authority, but they also brought to reality the idea of a child's gradual maturation into self-determination.[482] This may be evidenced by the contents of § 5, pursuant to which (sentence 1), after reaching the age of fourteen, the child may decide which religion he wishes to adhere to. Neither his spiritual maturity nor his internal motives may be examined in that case.[483] His decision may be communicated orally or in writing, or it may be implied, to a statutory representative, religious community or, for example, the school principal.[484] In that case, the parents have the right to support such child in his religious efforts and in asserting rights arising from religious freedom.[485] In the case where a child engages in, for example, religiously motivated self-harm or does fasting that is dangerous to his health due to membership in a sect, the parents may rely on the provision of § 1666 BGB. It prescribes that where the physical, mental or psychological best interests of the child or the child's assets are endangered and the parents do not wish or are not able to avert the danger, the family and guardianship court is to take the measures necessary to avert the danger. In turn, under § 5 sentence 2 of the said Law, where the child has reached the age of twelve, he may not be raised against his will in a religion other than his existing one. Commentators assume that, thanks to ensuring the continuity of hitherto religious upbringing, this standard serves to prevent the child from falling into a conflict of conscience and spare him the necessity of resolving moral dilemmas arising from different worldviews.[486] Under § 6, the provisions of the Law shall apply accordingly to the education of children in a non-confessional worldview, meaning that if a child was raised according to such a worldview until reaching the age of 12, then he can demand its preservation, despite the parents' adoption of a given religion.[487] Importantly, under § 2 and 3 of the said Law, in the case of a

---

482 P. Huber, "Vor § 1 RelKErzG", in D. Schwab (ed.), *Münchener Kommentar zum Bürgerlichen Gesetzbuch. Band 10. Familienrecht II. §§ 1589–1921*, München 2020, margin no. 1.

483 L. Salgo, "Gesetz über die religiöse Kindererziehung", in H. Engler (ed.), *J. von Staudingers Kommentar zum Bürgerlichen Gesetzbuch mit Einführungsgesetz und Nebengesetzen. Band 4. Familienrecht. §§ 1626–1631. Anhang zu § 1631: RKEG. §§ 1631a-1633*, Berlin 2002, p. 469.

484 L. Salgo, "Gesetz über..., p. 470.

485 P. Badura, "Art. 6 GG…, margin no. 119.

486 P. Huber, "§ 5 RelKErzG", in D. Schwab (ed.), *Münchener Kommentar zum Bürgerlichen Gesetzbuch. Band 10. Familienrecht II. §§ 1589–1921*, München 2020, margin no. 4.

487 L. Salgo, "Gesetz über..., p. 471.

dispute between the parents or between them and a guardian or court-appointed guardian, the child shall be heard if he has reached the age of 10.

Although religious freedom, derived from the concept of dignity and a fundamental human right, is described as inviolable and inalienable, it is not non-conflicting. Otherwise, it would not be compared to other constitutional rights and freedoms, which is impossible. The right to religious freedom is not the right to do for religious reasons everything that an individual considers necessary or permitted by his religion.[488] The fundamental rights may therefore not be deemed absolute because otherwise they would be petrified.[489]

The conditions for permissible restrictions on fundamental rights are provided in Art. 19 GG. First, it follows from that provision that a law restricting a fundamental right must apply generally and it must specify the fundamental right affected (sect. 1[490]). In no way can the essence of the fundamental right be affected (sect. 2[491]).

An interference with a fundamental right does not mean its abolition but only a restriction on the possibility of exercising it. A restriction on a fundamental right must also comply with the proportionality principle (*Verhältnismäßigkeits prinzip*). This means that, first, a restriction on fundamental rights is admissible only by legal means by which the purpose justifying the restriction can be achieved. Second, if there are several possible ways to restrict a fundamental right, the least onerous one must be chosen. Third, it is necessary to weigh the conflicting rights and demonstrate which of them – in the given factual and legal circumstances – takes precedence.[492] Certainly, dignity is excluded from the above interference.[493]

The guarantee of fundamental rights resulting from human dignity is intended to strengthen the rank and importance of a particular right or to indicate its special protection. Despite their high status, freedom of thought, conscience and religion must fit in with the system of other fundamental constitutional

488 W. Kellerwessel, "*Das Recht*…, p. 52.
489 M. Germann, "Art. 4 GG…, margin no. 50.
490 "Soweit nach diesem Grundgesetz ein Grundrecht durch Gesetz oder auf Grund eines Gesetzes eingeschränkt werden kann, muß das Gesetz allgemein und nicht nur für den Einzelfall gelten. Außerdem muß das Gesetz das Grundrecht unter Angabe des Artikels nennen."
491 "In keinem Falle darf ein Grundrecht in seinem Wesensgehalt angetastet werden."
492 M. Wienbracke, "Der Verhältnismäßigkeitsgrundsatz", *Zeitschrift für das Juristische Studium*, vol. 2, 2013, pp. 148 et seq.
493 H. Glaser, B. Makowicz, "Die Grundrechte…, pp. 152 and 317.

rights, assuming the need for a comparison with the fundamental rights of other persons and the state's public interest.[494]

A conflicting situation may be exemplified by the facts of the ruling delivered by BVerfG,[495] in which the parents and their child (girl), being adherents of Islam, requested an exemption from coeducational swimming lessons. They did it even though the student wore an outfit that conformed to religious requirements (*Burkini/Haschema*). BVerfG held that compliance with the parents' request would prevent in that case the effective accomplishment of state functions in the educational-pedagogical area.

5.3. Federal system reform (*Föderalismusreform I*) and its criticism

On 16 October 2003, at the request of parliamentary groups: Social Democratic Party of Germany (SPD), Christian Democratic Union of Germany (CDU)/ Christian Social Union in Bavaria (CSU), the Greens (*Die Grünen*) and Free Democratic Party (FDP), the first legislative chamber of the Federal Republic of Germany (*Bundestag*) adopted a decision to set up a joint commission (for both houses of parliament) on the modernization of the federal system.[496] The main aim of the reform[497] was to reorganize legislative competences.[498] The commission was headed by Edmund Stoiber and Franz Müntefering and its main goal was to develop solutions to improve the ability of the federal and state (so-called Lands) governments to act and make decisions, sort out the political

494 U. Di Fabio, "Art. 4 GG…, margin nos. 36–38 and 85.

495 BVerfG, Beschluß vom 8.11.2016, 1 BvR 3237/13, *Neue Juristische Wochenschrift*, vol. 4, 2017, p. 228.

496 K. Laubenthal, *Strafvollzug*, Berlin 2019, pp. 94 et seq. It is believed to have been the biggest reform since the creation of the Basic Law – see: H. Schüler-Springorum, "Strafvollzug und Föderalismus", in H. Schöch, R. Helgerth, D. Dölling, P. König (eds.), *Recht gestalten – dem Recht dienen. Festschrift für Reinhard Böttcher zum 70. Geburtstag am 29. Juli 2007*, Berlin 2007, p. 405.

497 The following – second federal system reform (*Föderalismusreform II*), which entered into force on 1 August 2009, aimed to modernize the public finances system, including in particular to ensure sustained budget growth at the level of Lands and the Federation. See: F. Ekardt, D. Buscher, "Föderalismusreform II: Reform der Finanzbeziehungen von Bund, Ländern und Kommunen", *Die öffentliche Verwaltung*, vol. 3, 2007, pp. 89 et seq.

498 P. Selmer, "Die Föderalismusreform – Eine Modernisierung der bundesstaatlichen Ordnung?", *Juristische Schulung*, vol. 12, 2006, pp. 1052 et seq.

responsibility and increase the efficiency of task implementation.[499] The work of the Commission was halted by the 2005 German parliamentary elections. After the completion of the elections, the CDU/CSU coalition and SPD consented to an accelerated modernization of the federal system based on the existing findings of the Stoiber and Müntefering Commission. The coalition agreement[500] had an annex with detailed proposals of amendments to the Basic Law of the Federal Republic of Germany. Thanks to the agreement, on 10 March 2006, draft laws were simultaneously discussed in both parliament chambers.

On 30 June 2006, Bundestag passed a Law on Amending the Basic Law and Laws Accompanying Federal Reform with the following vote distribution: 428 – for, 162 – against and 3 – abstain. In turn, on 7 July 2006, the second German parliamentary chamber – Federal Council (*Bundesrat*) – approved the federal system reform, which finally put an end to disputes over the biggest systemic transformation in the history of the Federal Republic of Germany. In the vote, 14 out of 16 states were in favour of the amendment to the Basic Law. Only Mecklenburg-Vorpommern voted against it and Schleswig-Holstein abstained.[501] In the analysed case, out of 69 Federal Council members, a large majority (62 votes) voted in favour of the proposed amendments. The two-thirds majority (46 votes) needed to approve the amendments to the Basic Law was therefore achieved.

The amendments to the Basic law and other provisions of the reformatory laws came into force the day after their publication (1 September 2006), and the remaining regulations as of 1 January 2007.

The 2006 federal system reform did not meet with widespread approval, despite its broad support manifested by the vote results in Bundestag and Bundesrat.

---

499 P. Selmer, "Die Föderalismusreform..., p. 1054.

500 The motto of the agreement was as follows: "Together for Germany – with courage and humanity" (*Gemeinsam für Deutschland – mit Mut und Menschlichkeit*) – https://archiv.cdu.de/system/tdf/media/dokumente/05_11_11_Koalitionsvertrag_Langfassung_navigierbar_0.pdf?file=1&type=field_collection_item&id=543 (accessed 22.09.2023).

501 While the Bundestag is a representation of the entire German nation, being an identification of its unity, the Bundesrat is a representation of the Lands and reflects the diversity of the German people. Vote in the Federal Council is based on the principle of one vote, making the representatives of a given state vote uniformly. Members' votes are an expression of the will of the entire land, not of individuals, so state governments must agree on how to cast their votes before voting. See: M. Bożek, *System...*, pp. 99–101.

Critics of the amendments primarily pointed to a significant risk of restricting the principle of solidarity (*Solidaritätsprinzip*), the lack of which could lead to growing disparities between poor and rich states. The possibility of genuine crippling of the subsidiarity principle (*Subsidiarität*) was also suggested. Experts also pointed out that due to the complicated normative regulations regarding rules and exceptions, it would be impossible to fulfil the primary objective of the reform, according to which the citizen knows "who is responsible for what."[502] As compared with the past, the citizen would find it even more difficult to establish whether federal or state law applies to an issue in question.

Particularly strong objections to the amendment, as regards the transfer of legislative competence to the states to regulate issues related to penal enforcement law, were voiced by both the German public and the community of German social workers, psychologists, criminologists and lawyers (practitioners and academics alike).[503] When asked to comment on the proposed modifications, Claus Roxin, an icon of German criminal law studies, was genuinely surprised at "how anyone could come up with such a primitive idea."[504]

The modification was widely assessed as difficult to substantiate, outdated, causing the inevitable fragmentation of the law and putting an end to the "tried-and-tested unity and cohesion" between the penal procedure, the enforcement of law and the justice system in criminal cases.[505] It was pointed out that the execution of prison sentences was, until the implementation of the reform, an important area of the federation's activities, though some differences existed also in that area. A majority of states did not show legislative interest in the indicated area, viewing the introduced modifications as "an imposed enrichment".[506]

A great emphasis was also put on linking the functioning of the system of the execution of prison sentences with the budgetary situation of particular states. Numerous researchers argued that the new situation may lead to an unjustified differentiation in the conditions of the execution of prison sentences, depending

---

502 P. Selmer, "Die Föderalismusreform…, pp. 1056 and 1059.

503 H. Cornel, "Die Entwicklung des deutschen Strafvollzugs nach der Föderalismusreform des Jahres 2006 mit der Verlagerung der Gesetzgebungskompetenz auf die Bundesländer", *Neue Kriminalpolitik*, vol. 30, no. 1, 2018, pp. 16 et seq.; B. Maelicke, "Sinn und Unsinn der Föderalismusreform", *Neue Kriminalpolitik*, vol. 27, no. 3, 2015, p. 226; H. Schüler-Springorum, "Strafvollzug…, pp. 405–406.

504 H. Prantl, "Der Winnetou des Strafrechts – Der Forscher und Lehrer Claus Roxin wird 75", *Süddeutsche Zeitung* of 15.05.2006.

505 H. Schüler-Springorum, "Strafvollzug…, pp. 406 et seq.

506 B. Maelicke, "Sinn…, p. 226.

on the state of public finances of a particular state.[507] In addition to deepening the already existing differences, a risk of spending cuts on social rehabilitation may emerge and the stability of the penal policy may be undermined by its dependence on the changing balance of political power in the states.[508] Concerns were also expressed about the peculiar "shabbiness competition" (*Wettbewerb der Schäbigkeit*) between the particular states aiming to tighten the conditions of serving a penalty of imprisonment, which would attract immediate support from penal populists.[509] Even later opinions pointed out that under such a model, justice may become a matter of geography, which in no way satisfies the assumptions of a democratic state of law.[510]

The modification, according to many experts, will entail far-reaching interference with the area of rights of persons deprived of liberty, which may lead to the dismantling of the developed standards.[511] No rational reason can be seen why citizens sentenced on the basis of the uniform provisions of substantive criminal law should not have analogous rights and duties while serving a penalty of imprisonment.

So far, an independent impact assessment of delegating executive powers in the area of penal enforcement law-making to the states has not yet been conducted. Nevertheless, all the states enacted relevant laws on the execution of prison sentences. The Land of Berlin was the last one to adopt relevant regulations on 16 October 2016. Two trends emerged as regards the adopted regulatory technique.[512] Ten states (Berlin, Brandenburg, Bremen, Mecklenburg-Vorpommern, Rhineland-Palatinate, Saarland, Saxony, Saxony-Anhalt,

507 B. Maelicke, "Sinn…, p. 227.

508 F. Dünkel, "Die Europäischen Strafvollzugsgrundsätze von 2006 und die deutsche Strafvollzugsgesetzgebung", *Forum Strafvollzug*, vol. 3, 2012, p. 147; B. Maelicke, "Konsequenzen der Förderalismusreform für den Deutschen Strafvollzug. Auszug aus einem Vortrag auf dem 14. Bundeskongress der Psychologinnen und Psychologen im Strafvollzugam 19. September 2006, Rostock", *Neue Kriminalpolitik*, vol. 118, no. 3, 2006, p. 89.

509 H. Cornel, "Die Entwicklung…, p. 17; F. Dünkel, "Die Europäischen…, p. 146; F. Dünkel, H. Schüler-Springorum, "Strafvollzug als Ländersache? Der *Wettbewerb der Schäbigkeit* ist schon im Gange!", *Zeitschrift für Strafvollzug und Straffälligenhilfe*, vol. 5, 2006, p. 145 i n.; B. Maelicke, "Sinn…, p. 227.

510 H. Prantl, "Scharf, schärfer, am schärfsten", *Süddeutsche Zeitung* of 12.08.2016.

511 B. Maelicke, "Sinn…, p. 227.

512 F. Arloth, T. Geiger, "Der deutsche Strafvollzug nach der Föderalismusreform", in B. Mailcke, S. Schling (eds.), *Das Gefängnis auf dem Prüfstand. Zustand und Zukunft des Strafvollzugs*, Wiesbaden 2018, pp. 74 et seq.

Schleswig-Holstein and Thuringia) decided to prepare a joint model draft of the state penal code (*Landesstrafvollzugsgesetz*) released on 23 August 2011,[513] and then, their own state regulations were developed on its basis. In turn, six states (Baden-Württemberg, Bavaria, Hamburg, Hesse, Lower Saxony and North Rhine-Westphalia) prepared more or less independent draft laws based on the well-proven provisions of the Federal law on the execution of prison sentences and measures of reform and prevention involving deprivation of liberty of 16 March 1976[514] (*Strafvollzugsgesetz* – StVollzG).

5.4. Religious freedom of adults deprived of their liberty

Given the normative changes indicated above, it must be noted that a full reconstruction of the standard of religious freedom in penal facilities is partially hampered by the dispersion of regulatory matter among the individual states. On the one hand, the provisions regarding religious freedom bear a significant resemblance to each other. On the other, there are some differences in the overall enforcement matter, which, in the opinion of some researchers, are hard to justify by the specificity of a state.[515] Moreover, the differences in the normative regulations between the particular states may cause a similar normative standard to be implemented differently.

Consequently, this part refers to the model draft of the state penal code (*Landesstrafvollzugsgesetz*) and the StVollzG regulation, which served as the basis for a reconstruction of the written law standard. In the case where a particular state introduced a solution that differs from the old federal solutions, it was clearly indicated. Given the volume limit of this chapter, the analysis does not include issues relating to pre-trial detention, which are generally regulated by the German Code of Criminal Procedure (*Strafprozeßordnung* – StPO). As is the case with Polish law, religious freedom undergoes some necessary modification due to the specifics of that preventive measure.

---

513 *Musterentwurf zum Landesstrafvollzugsgesetz vom 23. August 2011* – https://www.justiz.bremen.de/sixcms/media.php/13/Musterentwurf%20LStVollzG%2006%2009%2011.pdf (accessed 14.11.2022).

514 *Gesetz über den Vollzug der Freiheitsstrafe und der freiheitsentziehenden Maßregeln der Besserung und Sicherung*, Bundesgesetzblatt 1976, Teil I, no. 28, pp. 581 et seq.

515 K. Laubenthal, *Strafvollzug…*, p. 32 and S. J. Jahn, "Germany: Inequality in Legal Practice – Managing Religion in Prisons", in J. Martínez-Ariño, A. L. Zwilling (eds.), *Religion and Prison: An Overview of Contemporary Europe*, Cham 2020, pp. 198 et seq.

The analysed enforcement provisions, including those on religious freedom, tend to be twofold in nature. On the one hand, they regulate the issues of relations between the state (represented by prison directors) and religious associations. This is especially true for the presence of chaplains and clergy of other religious communities. On the other, they relate directly to the prisoner's religious freedom.

The Federal law on the execution of prison sentences groups the key provisions in title VI entitled "Exercise of religion" (*Religionsausübung*). They contain regulations on: pastoral care (*Seelsorge*), religious activities (*religiöse Veranstaltungen*) and worldview communities (*Weltanschauungsgemeinschaf ten*).

Commentators are in agreement that those provisions directly implement the provisions of Art. 4 GG and Art. 141 WRV. In line with the federal legislator's assumption, fundamental rights apply without exception to the criminal system, but not without limitations necessary to maintain an orderly penal system. Such limitations include, for example, the purpose and meaning of imprisonment.[516]

It is also pointed out that this fundamental right was subject to serious, though justified, restrictions due to the pandemic.[517] That event showed the systemic importance of pastoral care, which has been recognized as an important, though often underestimated, part of the penal system.[518]

Section 53 (1) StVollzG[519] provides that the prisoner shall not be denied pastoral care by a chaplain of his religion. At his request, he shall receive assistance in establishing contact with a chaplain of his religion.

This provision does not give the prisoner a claim to provide him with pastoral care because it is not the function of a worldview-neutral state and its executive bodies. The prisoner has the right to be admitted to the religious community of his choice to receive pastoral care. However, the prisoner does not have the right to choose a specific chaplain outside the penal facility. Moreover, this provision does not give the prisoner the right to pastoral care from several religious

516 F. Arloth, "§ 53", in F. Arloth, H. Krä (eds.), *Strafvollzugsgesetze von Bund und Ländern*, München 2021, p. 298.

517 See more: F. Dünkel, C. Morgenstern, "Germany", in F. Dünkel, S. Harrendorf, D. Zyl Smit (eds.), *The impact of COVID-19 on prison conditions…*, pp. 224 et seq.

518 T. Müller-Monning, "Vor § 69 LandesR", in J. Fest, W. Lesting, M. Lindemann (eds.) *Strafvollzugsgesetze Bundes- und Landesrecht. Kommentar*, Hürth 2022, p. 613.

519 "Dem Gefangenen darf religiöse Betreuung durch einen Seelsorger seiner Religionsgemeinschaft nicht versagt werden. Auf seinen Wunsch ist ihm zu helfen, mit einem Seelsorger seiner Religionsgemeinschaft in Verbindung zu treten."

communities at the same time, without counting them as part of regular visiting hours.[520] It seems that the too-restrictive approach to pastoral care from a chaplain of a different religion than the one with which the prisoner identifies is not correct. As any other human being, the prisoner has the right to make a change of religion without any restrictions or reject it altogether. The process cannot take place without prior contact with other communities.[521]

The prisoner has the right to assistance in establishing contact with a representative of his religious community. The penal facility satisfies that requirement by providing him with a contact address. However, it should be ready to forward a request for contact to a respective chaplain. It is particularly important if a given facility does not have a chaplain of a religion with which the prisoner identifies.[522] Commentators argue that asking prisoners questions about their religious affiliation does not violate Art. 136 (3) WRV. It is a standard practice – prisoners are asked about their religious affiliation during a preliminary interview.[523] However, they are not obliged to give an answer.[524] The mere registration for a particular religious activity may, of course, be a voluntary disclosure of one's religious affiliation. However, at that point the prisoner may be at the stage of searching for faith and a specific religion, so his willingness to participate in a specific meeting does not have to identify his real religious affiliation. A penal facility must not inform chaplains against the will of prisoners of their admission to the facility.[525] The protection of personal data on the religious or philosophical confession of a prisoner is ensured in § 182 (1) StVollzG,[526] which provides that such particulars collected on the occasion of medical examinations may not be general knowledge within the facility. One

---

520 F. Arloth, "§ 53…, p. 299.

521 K. H. Schäfter, "§ 53", in H. D. Schwind, A. Böhm, J. M. Jehle, K. Laubenthal (eds.), *Strafvollzugsgesetz – Bund und Länder. Kommentar*, Berlin–Boston 2013, p. 554.

522 T. Müller-Monning, "§ 69 LandesR", in J. Fest, W. Lesting, M. Lindemann (eds.) *Strafvollzugsgesetze Bundes- und Landesrecht. Kommentar*, Hürth 2022, p. 622.

523 S. J. Jahn, "Germany…, p. 201.

524 T. Müller-Monning, "§ 69…, p. 619.

525 F. Arloth, "§ 53…, p. 300 and K. Laubenthal, *Strafvollzug…*, pp. 523 et seq.

526 "Das religiöse oder weltanschauliche Bekenntnis eines Gefangenen und personenbezogene Daten, die anläßlich ärztlicher Untersuchungen erhoben worden sind, dürfen in der Anstalt nicht allgemein kenntlich gemacht werden. Andere personenbezogene Daten über den Gefangenen dürfen innerhalb der Anstalt allgemein kenntlich gemacht werden, soweit dies für ein geordnetes Zusammenleben in der Anstalt erforderlich ist; § 180 Absatz 7 bis 9 bleibt unberührt".

may have doubts about the view[527] that the placement of a notice on the cell door that a prisoner is permitted to attend a specific divine service or other religious activity is permissible and organizationally required in order to ensure the proper and undisturbed functioning of the facility. This view seems to be anchored in § 182 (1) sentence 2 StVollzG, under which other personal data on the prisoner may be made general knowledge within the prison if this is necessary for ordered co-existence in the prison. Despite its compliance with § 182 (1) sentence 2 StVollzG, the above view is completely contrary to the right to privacy and non-disclosure of information about oneself.

Under that provision, a religious community has the right to take care of those who are sincerely interested in it, regardless of their formal affiliation to it. A community bears the burden of presenting and proving the pastoral skills of a person it delegates to provide pastoral care. This is important because, as a rule, there are no restrictions on the availability of religious communities. A penal facility may reject persons delegated to provide pastoral care only by citing security considerations that are supported by facts.[528]

Besides, a religious community must not engage in agitation in favour of its own confession, carry out actions involving the conversion of prisoners, and expect an opportunity to place brochures, leaflets or other materials relating to it on the premises of the facility.[529]

The concept of religious care (*religiöse Betreuung*) is broadly understood. Apart from acts such as worship, it encompasses personal talks, religious education, charity care (*Caritas*), and as part of diaconal work (*Diakonisches Werk*),[530] individual and group discussions, biblical groups, working with prisoners' loved ones, family visits and meetings, marriage seminars, and courses in restorative justice.[531] There is also no doubt that the religious community has the overriding authority to determine the religious nature of an act or activity. It is generally recognized that a chaplain should be allowed access to the facility in an emergency to provide his service (e.g. administration of the sacrament of extreme unction).[532]

527 F. Arloth, "§ 182", in F. Arloth, H. Krä (eds.), *Strafvollzugsgesetze von Bund und Ländern*, München 2021, pp. 653 et seq.

528 F. Arloth, "§ 53…, pp. 299 et seq.

529 T. Müller-Monning, "§ 69…, p. 621.

530 F. Arloth, "§ 53…, p. 300; K. Laubenthal, *Strafvollzug…*, p. 524; K. H. Schäfter, "§ 53…, pp. 550 et seq.

531 T. Müller-Monning, "Vor § 69…, p. 615.

532 T. Müller-Monning, "§ 69…, p. 618 and K. H. Schäfter, "§ 53…, p. 553.

The provision of § 53 (1) StVollzG corresponds to the content of § 157 (1) StVollzG,[533] under which chaplains shall be appointed on a full-time basis or engaged by contract on agreement with the respective religious community. It is accepted that the optimal solution is to leave chaplains in "the service of religion" and to qualify their legal relationship with the secular authority as a special type of legal relationship.[534]

The special status of chaplains working in penal facilities stems from the fact that they are holders of official secrets, pastoral secrets and secrets of confession and, at the same time, have the right to refuse to testify (§ 53 (1) (1) StPO[535]). They cannot be exempted from the last secret. By contrast, the issue of being exempted from pastoral secrecy remains unresolved.[536] In practice, a problem may also occur when distinguishing between pastoral secrecy and official secrecy.[537]

The chaplains' legal position depends on agreements concluded by states with religious associations based on federal agreements.[538] Moreover, their situation is generally based on the concept of *res mixtae* (*Doppelstellung*) – that is joint efforts made by the state and a recognized religious community for the common good.[539] In some states (e.g. Bavaria – Art. 176 (2)[540]), chaplains are a separate professional group, whereas in others not.

---

533 "Seelsorger werden im Einvernehmen mit der jeweiligen Religionsgemeinschaft im Hauptamt bestellt oder vertraglich verpflichtet."

534 K. H. Schäfter, "§ 157", in H. D. Schwind, A. Böhm, J. M. Jehle, K. Laubenthal (eds.), *Strafvollzugsgesetz – Bund und Länder. Kommentar*, Berlin–Boston 2013, pp. 552 et seq.

535 "Zur Verweigerung des Zeugnisses sind ferner berechtigt 1. Geistliche über das, was ihnen in ihrer Eigenschaft als Seelsorger anvertraut worden oder bekanntgeworden ist."

536 T. Müller-Monning, "§ 71 LandesR", in J. Fest, W. Lesting, M. Lindemann (eds.) *Strafvollzugsgesetze Bundes- und Landesrecht. Kommentar*, Hürth 2022, p. 843.

537 K. H. Schäfter, "§ 53…, pp. 552 et seq. and K. H. Schäfter, "§ 157…, p. 1135.

538 F. Arloth, "§ 157", in F. Arloth, H. Krä (eds.), *Strafvollzugsgesetze von Bund und Ländern*, München 2021, pp. 607 et seq.

539 S. J. Jahn, "Being Private in Public Space? The 'Administration' of' Religion' in German Prisons", *Journal of Religion in Europe*, vol. 9, no. 4, 2016, pp. 406 et seq.; T. Müller-Monning, "Vor § 69…, p. 616; K. H. Schäfter, "§ 157…, p. 1131.

540 "Für jede Anstalt ist entsprechend ihrer Aufgabe die erforderliche Anzahl von Bediensteten der verschiedenen Berufsgruppen, insbesondere des allgemeinen Vollzugsdienstes, des Werkdienstes, des Krankenpflegedienstes und des Verwaltungsdienstes, sowie von Seelsorgern, Ärzten, Pädagogen, Psychologen und Sozialarbeitern vorzusehen".

Regrettably, no satisfactory solutions in relation to Islam have been achieved in the indicated area.[541] On the one hand, this is due to the dispersion of the Muslim community and, on the other, the existence of such organizations as DITIB (*Diyanet Isleri Türk Islam Biriligi*) – Turkish-Islamic Union for Religious Affairs, whose imams are in fact Turkish civil servants who report to the Presidium for Religious Affairs (*Diyanet*) in Ankara and are therefore only partially subject to German legislation.[542] Cooperation with Islam pastoralists is needed and necessary, as it can prevent extremism. The rise of the Islamic State (ISIS), terrorist attacks and the promotion of religious fundamentalism, which is spreading in some prisons, have led to an increase in the demand for the employment of imams from different Muslim communities, who are to reduce the level of radicalization and to prevent extremism.[543] Ministry has by its very nature a liberating element, it aims to defy destructive processes inside and outside the individual. However, it may be misused, for example, to force self-restraint on individuals.[544] Importantly, apart from the performance of charitable functions and integration, Islamic religious communities teach the German language.[545]

A separate issue is whether the Muslim religious care corresponds to Christian-centrically oriented ministry.[546] In other words, is the imam indeed an equivalent to a Roman Catholic or Protestant chaplain? Vigor Fröhmcke argued that the imam is only the leader of the Friday prayer – the most important service of the week. He is merely a preacher, since he has knowledge about the strictly ritualized prayer rules. Moreover, he has knowledge of Arabic as the language of the worship service. He is, however, not a professional theologian; he has a civil profession in everyday life.[547] However, different views are being

541 S. J. Jahn, "Germany…, pp. 197 et seq.

542 S. J. Jahn, "Germany…, p. 206 and T. Müller-Monning, "Vor § 69…, p. 616.

543 S. Er, *Der Strafvollzug als Zwischenstation der Radikalisierung. Eine Studie zu Strafgefangenen und Haftentlassenen muslimischen Glaubens anhand biographisch-narrativer Gesprächsführung*, Wiesbaden, 2021, *passim*.

544 T. Müller-Monning, "Vor § 69…, pp. 613 et seq.

545 T. Müller-Monning, "§ 97 LandesR", in J. Fest, W. Lesting, M. Lindemann (eds.) *Strafvollzugsgesetze Bundes- und Landesrecht. Kommentar*, Hürth 2022, p. 838.

546 S. J. Jahn, "Being…, pp. 413 et seq.

547 V. Fröhmcke, *Muslime im Strafvollzug. Die Rechtsstellung von Strafgefangenen muslimischer Religionszugehörigkeit in Deutschland*, Berlin 2006, pp. 216 et seq.

formulated – Islam has ministry understood as religiously motivated and established support for the individual.[548]

A separate issue is the so-called institutional logic of penal facilities, that is, the way they perceive a particular religious organization. The German literature review shows cases of integration into the everyday life of imprisonment and the formal structures of the prison of religious organizations perceived as rehabilitation actors, regardless of their status in public law. By contrast, if a religious organization is perceived as a potential risk to order or safety, it is not considered part of prison and therefore is not integrated into it. This meant that, in practice, it was more important to view a religious organization through the lens of the goals of institutional logic and an organization's legal empowerment was less important.[549] The phenomenon may be well illustrated by the Jehovah's Witnesses community, perceived as "burdensome evil". Since 2017, it is publically recognized in all the states.[550]

Today, a discussion is taking place among German researchers about a common inter-religious standardization of prison pastoral care and the possibility of providing prisoners with spiritual care from all working chaplains.[551] This concept covers all religions and is not reduced solely to ecumenical movements.[552] Its aim is to develop training standards common to all chaplains. This initiative is related to the fact that religious care must respond to problems arising in prisons. Given a large fluctuation of prisoners, the multi-religious and multi-ethnic composition of the prison population and a growing number of elderly and

548 M. Arshad, "Schuld, Vergebung und Seelsorge im Islam", in B. Uçar, M. Blasberg-Kuhnke (eds.), *Islamische Seelsorge zwischen Herkunft und Zukunft. Von der theologischen Grundlegung zur Praxis in Deutschland*, Frankfurt am Main 2013, pp. 36 et seq.; M. Cimşit, "Islamische Seelsorge – Eine theologische Begriffsbestimmung", in B. Uçar, M. Blasberg-Kuhnke (eds.), *Islamische Seelsorge zwischen Herkunft und Zukunft. Von der theologischen Grundlegung zur Praxis in Deutschland*, Frankfurt am Main 2013, pp. 13 et seq.; A. Seyyar, "Die theoretischen Konzepte der Seelsorge aus islamischer Sicht", in B. Uçar, M. Blasberg-Kuhnke (eds.), *Islamische Seelsorge zwischen Herkunft und Zukunft. Von der theologischen Grundlegung zur Praxis in Deutschland*, Frankfurt am Main 2013, pp. 85 et seq.

549 S. J. Jahn, "Institutional Logic and Legal Practice: Modes of Regulation of Religious Organizations in German Prisons", in I, Becci, O. Roy (eds.), *Religious Diversity in European Prisons. Challenges and Implications for Rehabilitation*, Cham 2015, pp. 82 et seq.

550 S. J. Jahn, "Germany…, p. 210.

551 S. J. Jahn, "Germany…, p. 205 and T. Müller-Monning, "§ 97…, p. 838.

552 K. H. Schäfter, "§ 53…, pp. 551 et seq.

seriously ill prisoners, the use of a full-time chaplain seems reasonable,[553] even though one can dispute the argument that one chaplain can provide effective care for 250 prisoners.[554]

In the opinion of the Council of the Evangelical Church in Germany, prison ministry affirms the state's mandate to ensure law and social peace, and consequently, its *ius puniendi*. However, the penalty of deprivation of liberty should be the *ultima ratio*, and prison ministry cannot directly identify with criminal activities. Therefore, the chaplain can and must take care as far as possible of human problems and prisoners' interests, which also includes exposing irregularities in the penal system and calling for their elimination.[555]

Under § 154 (1) StVollzG,[556] all members of the prison services (including chaplains) shall cooperate and contribute towards fulfilling the functions of the prison. According to its function, each facility shall have the necessary number of staff of different categories, including medical staff, teachers, psychologists, social workers and chaplains (§ 155 (2) StVollzG[557]).

Despite increasing secularization, the chaplain is still the person with the highest chance of gaining the prisoners' trust and, at the same time, is not seen as part of the prison service. The prisoners' trust means that the chaplain must proceed in such a way as to build cooperation with the prisoners and maintain correct relations with educators.[558] Both the chaplain and the educators are obliged to seek ways of preventing constructively and combating such tensions.[559]

Where the small number of members belonging to a religious community does not justify religious care, religious care shall be permitted in some other way (§ 157 (2) StVollzG[560]). With the consent of the head of the facility, the prison chaplains may avail themselves of the services of free religious assistants

553 T. Müller-Monning, "§ 97…, p. 840.

554 K. H. Schäfter, "§ 157…, p. 1129.

555 T. Müller-Monning, "§ 97…, p. 840.

556 "Alle im Vollzug Tätigen arbeiten zusammen und wirken daran mit, die Aufgaben des Vollzuges zu erfüllen."

557 "Für jede Anstalt ist entsprechend ihrer Aufgabe die erforderliche Anzahl von Bediensteten der verschiedenen Berufsgruppen, namentlich des allgemeinen Vollzugsdienstes, des Verwaltungsdienstes und des Werkdienstes, sowie von Seelsorgern, Ärzten, Pädagogen, Psychologen und Sozialarbeitern vorzusehen."

558 T. Müller-Monning, "§ 97…, p. 846.

559 K. H. Schäfter, "§ 157…, p. 1134.

560 "Wenn die geringe Zahl der Angehörigen einer Religionsgemeinschaft eine Seelsorge nach Absatz 1 nicht rechtfertigt, ist die seelsorgerische Betreuung auf andere Weise zuzulassen."

and engage chaplains from outside the facility for divine services and for other religious activities (§ 157 (3) StVollzG[561]). Free religious assistants (*freier Seelsorgehelfer*) are pastoral assistants who do not have any legal relationship with the prison. They are representatives of a particular church, qualified to perform pastoral work, acting in consultation with the chaplain.[562]

Under § 53 (2) StVollzG,[563] the prisoner shall be permitted to have fundamental religious writings in his possession. He may be deprived of them only in the event of gross abuse. In terms of the analysed provision, it is fairly consensually accepted that the selection of writings does not have to be limited to materials of the prisoner's religious community. The prisoner may also have in his possession writings of a religion he does not adhere to.[564] The adjective "fundamental" (*grundlegend*) appears to be problematic in terms of interpretation. This is because it does not contribute to clarifying whether those writings include only the sources of a particular community's revelation (e.g. Torah, Quran, Bible, Vedas) or also materials used by a prisoner in everyday life (e.g. prayer book, songbook, catechism or other collection of truths of faith).[565] Some researchers point out that not every book (or magazine) related to the themes or objectives of a particular religious community falls within § 53 sect. 2 StVollzG. That standard is not fulfilled by items such as *Die Eroberung Persiens*, *Die Löwen des Islams*, *Das Buch des Universums*.[566] This position proves that some commentators put into question the nature of certain religious writings, thus leading to a restriction on the prisoner's right. Remarkably, all the quoted items relate to Islam. The issue of accessibility to religious literature depends on the library situation in a given facility. It is allowed to have German books that are new, originally packaged and from an official seller. A problem arises in the case of writings in a foreign language (e.g. Arabic) because there is no possibility of immediate verification of their content.[567]

561 "Mit Zustimmung des Anstaltsleiters dürfen die Anstaltsseelsorger sich freier Seelsorgehelfer bedienen und für Gottesdienste sowie für andere religiöse Veranstaltungen Seelsorger von außen zuziehen."

562 K. H. Schäfter, "§ 157…, pp. 1130 et seq.

563 "Der Gefangene darf grundlegende religiöse Schriften besitzen. Sie dürfen ihm nur bei grobem Mißbrauch entzogen werden."

564 K. H. Schäfter, "§ 53…, p. 555.

565 K. H. Schäfter, "§ 53…, pp. 554 et seq.

566 F. Arloth, "§ 53…, p. 301.

567 S. J. Jahn, "Germany…, pp. 211 et seq.

Similar problems arise from the use of the term "gross abuse" (*grobe Mißbrauch*). The literature makes no attempt to indicate abstract identification criteria. It is assumed, for example, that an abuse exists where religious writings are used to store illegal articles, the number of books and magazines in a cell is so large that it leads to disorder and confusion among the prison staff. The same applies to a situation where religious writings have handwritten comments (e.g. salafi). Simultaneously, the penal facility retains the right to check books and writings for the presence of such comments,[568] respecting the existing procedures and providing a substitute for such a publication (e.g. Quran without handwritten notes and comments).[569] Some researchers argue that regardless of the content of the provision, a chaplain shall be heard before depriving a prisoner of a particular writing (in analogy to § 54 (3) StVollzG).[570] That postulate was fulfilled in § 67 (2) of the Law on the execution of prison sentences in Schleswig-Holstein,[571] which explicitly provides that before depriving a prisoner of his religious writings, a chaplain of his denomination shall be heard.

Under § 53 (3) StVollzG,[572] the prisoner shall be permitted, to a reasonable extent, to retain articles for religious use. What constitutes such articles is again left to the internal regulations of a given religious association and cannot be arbitrarily determined by secular authorities. Articles for religious use include crosses, necklaces with crosses, rosaries, icons, Buddha figurines, holy images, a small prayer rug, benches/kneelers or cushions needed for meditation. They do not include joss sticks or Christmas trees.[573] In turn, the contentious issue is the status of prayer rugs[574] and occasionally also Tibetan singing bowls. Some experts do not question the prisoner's right to have phylacteries (tefillin) in his possession.[575] Others argue that for safety reasons (prevention of suicides), their use should not be allowed.[576]

568 F. Arloth, "§ 53..., p. 301.

569 T. Müller-Monning, "§ 69..., p. 623.

570 K. H. Schäfter, "§ 53..., p. 555.

571 "Die Gefangenen dürfen grundlegende religiöse Schriften sowie in angemessenem Umfang Gegen- stände des religiösen Gebrauchs besitzen. Diese dürfen den Gefangenen nur bei grobem Missbrauch entzogen werden. Die Seelsorgerin oder der Seelsorger soll vorher gehört werden."

572 „Dem Gefangenen sind Gegenstände des religiösen Gebrauchs in angemessenem Umfang zu belassen".

573 F. Arloth, "§ 53..., p. 301.

574 S. J. Jahn, "Being..., pp. 413 et seq.

575 K. H. Schäfter, "§ 53..., p. 555.

576 S. J. Jahn, "Germany..., p. 211.

§ 53 (3) StVollzG allow a restriction on the right to have articles of worship. Given that it is a fundamental right, restraint is recommended. Some conclude that this limit is set at the lack of transparency and order in the cell, whereas others argue that the point is a threat to the safety or violation of the fundamental rights of others. Consequently, due to fire risk, candles are forbidden,[577] though that position is not universally accepted.[578] Since prisoners are allowed to smoke and have lighters, it does not seem rational to restrict the possibility of using candles for religious purposes.[579]

§ 54 (1) StVollzG[580] gives the prisoner the right to attend divine services and other religious activities of his denomination. This right is a minimum guarantee of religious freedom, which should not be violated.[581] However, the chaplain may, on the basis of the internal regulations of the community in question, exclude a prisoner from participation in a particular activity; his decision is not subject to appeal before the state (lay) court.[582] This right cannot be restricted by the penal facility by organizing other important activities at the same time. It is also forbidden to put the prisoner in a situation of conflicting choices between the possibility of attending a religious meeting taking place at the same time as the minimum daily time spent outdoors.[583]

The concept of divine services (*Gottesdienst*) is defined by a specific community within its autonomy. It is a very sensitive area to determine what is meant by "other religious activities" (*anderen religiösen Veranstaltungen*).[584] On the one hand, the issue is the autonomy in religious matters attributable to religious communities. On the other hand, § 67 StVollzG[585] provides for forms

577 F. Arloth, "§ 53…, p. 301.

578 T. Müller-Monning, "§ 69…, pp. 623 et seq.

579 H. Ostendorf, "§ 6 Religionsausübung", in H. Ostendorf (ed.), *Jugendstrafvollzugsrecht*, Baden-Baden 2022, pp. 378 et seq.

580 "Der Gefangene hat das Recht, am Gottesdienst und an anderen religiösen Veranstaltungen seines Bekenntnisses teilzunehmen."

581 K. Laubenthal, *Strafvollzug…*, p. 525.

582 F. Arloth, "§ 53…, p. 303.

583 T. Müller-Monning, "§ 70 LandesR" in J. Fest, W. Lesting, M. Lindemann (eds.) *Strafvollzugsgesetze Bundes- und Landesrecht. Kommentar*, Hürth 2022, p. 625.

584 K. Laubenthal, *Strafvollzug…*, pp. 526 et seq.

585 "Der Gefangene erhält Gelegenheit, sich in seiner Freizeit zu beschäftigen. Er soll Gelegenheit erhalten, am Unterricht einschließlich Sport, an Fernunterricht, Lehrgängen und sonstigen Veranstaltungen der Weiterbildung, an Freizeitgruppen, Gruppengesprächen sowie an Sportveranstaltungen teilzunehmen und eine Bücherei zu benutzen".

of organization of prisoners' leisure time that may come into conflict with other religious activities. The provision lays down that the prisoner should be given an opportunity to attend classes, including sports, to watch television lessons, to attend courses and to take part in other training activities, in hobby groups, discussion groups, as well as sports activities, and to make use of a library. The limitation on taking part in divine services and other religious activities is subject to more restrictive conditions, as will be discussed below.

Participation in a discussion group turned out to be a contentious aspect of that right – a prisoner intended to participate in such a meeting organized by a chaplain in his facility. However, the head of the unit refused to allow him to participate for organizational reasons related to the facility. Called upon to interpret the concept of "other religious activities", the Higher Regional Court of Koblenz (*Oberlandesgericht Koblenz*) held that it is an activity that serves religious development, enables the believer to practice faith in traditional worship forms, opens a spiritual and emotional connection with God, teaches faith or strengthens it.[586] Today a broad understanding of "other religious activities" is accepted. Under Art. 137 (3) WRV, religious associations, within the scope of the autonomy granted to them, shall have the sole right to decide on religious matters, their competence prevails.[587] In the case of such activities, the chaplain is responsible for determining their content.[588] In cases of a suspected violation of law, the head of the prison should resolve this matter in dialogue with a specific chaplain who organizes a particular meeting. The prisoner should not be a hostage to an interpretation of two intersecting enforcement standards.

References have been made to certain limitations of the autonomy of religious communities. As regards Christian communities, the use of sacramental wine is prohibited during the Eucharist. This is explained by the harmful effect of even a small amount on wine on addicted persons and the security risk posed by such persons.[589] Regardless of the (ir)rationality of that position, it is rightly argued that, for example, in the Roman Catholic Church, Holy Communion can be received only in one form (the host). It is therefore rightly argued that

586 OGL Koblenz, 30.03.1987, 2 Vollz (Ws) 17/87, *Neue Zeitschrift für Strafrecht*, vol. 11, 1987, pp. 525 et seq.

587 K. H. Schäfter, "§ 54", H. D. Schwind, A. Böhm, J. M. Jehle, K. Laubenthal (eds.), *Strafvollzugsgesetz – Bund und Länder. Kommentar*, Berlin–Boston 2013, p. 558.

588 F. Arloth, "§ 53…, p. 303.

589 F. Arloth, "§ 53…, p. 305.

the chaplain should be given the possibility of using both wine and grape juice, depending on the prisoner group for which he celebrates the Eucharist.[590]

If the chaplain consents to it, the prisoner has the opportunity to talk to him individually after the religious service. This talk may take place in the chapel or in a separate cell and is generally not monitored, the presence of a correctional officer, within sight, is allowed.[591]

As regards the homily content, the chaplain essentially enjoys full independence. He may include not only purely theological reflection, but also current events and prisoners' everyday problems. This is important because, as Thobias Müller-Monning points out, the extra-religious aspect of prison life offers almost no opportunity to reflect on events (other than those in one's own life) that affect prisoners and the prison staff emotionally. A religious activity should relate to prisoners' life situation. As a result, its theological nature will be preserved, without attributing to it only the form of a "stepping-stone" from monotonous prison life.[592]

Both communal and individual religious practices must be achievable. For example, in a detention centre in Hesse, a prisoner refused to be transferred to the cell assigned to him due to its cramped living conditions – he could not spread his prayer rug there. Once the cell was inspected by an imam and a pastor, who confirmed his fears, he did not have to move to the assigned cell.[593]

Security concerns may justify the presence of correctional officers during religious services and activities. It may be necessary due to reliable information about attempts to use the meeting for illegal transactions or contacts posing a threat to security. Special care should be taken to avoid a violation of the *sacrum*.[594] A separate issue is the electronic monitoring of religious services using a video camera. It should not entirely replace the work of correctional officers. Attention is paid in the literature to the delicate nature of the indicated matter. Within the meaning of German law, a visual electronic record of worshipers is "personal data" belonging to the intimate sphere of the participant of the service, and as such, they are his personal rights and are subject to protection. Besides, participation in religious practices may cause very personal reactions, such as

590 T. Müller-Monning, "§ 70…, p. 625 and K. H. Schäfter, "§ 54…, p. 559.
591 F. Arloth, "§ 53…, p. 303.
592 T. Müller-Monning, "§ 70…, p. 626.
593 T. Müller-Monning, "§ 70…, p. 626.
594 F. Arloth, "§ 53…, pp. 304 et seq.

cry, contemplation, deep prayer, etc., therefore, the use of that tool should be limited.[595]

It is absolutely forbidden to draw any negative consequences from the fact that a prisoner refrains from attending any religious services.[596]

The prisoner shall be admitted to divine services and other religious activities of another religious community if the chaplain of that religion agrees (§ 54 (2) StVollzG[597]). The requirement of consent from the chaplain does not appear only in § 70 of the Law on the execution of prison sentences in Mecklenburg-Vorpommern.[598] Non-denominational prisoners who intend to establish contact with a given community retain the right to attend divine service or a religious activity, but a respective chaplain makes an independent decision on admitting such a person to a particular act.[599]

Under § 54 (3) StVollzG,[600] the prisoner may be excluded from attending divine services or other religious activities where this is required by overriding reasons of security or order, prior to this the chaplain shall be heard. The exclusion may concern only a specific person but not a whole group.[601] The application of that drastic measure is a last resort and should take place in obvious and serious situations. If possible, other measures milder than exclusion should be used, such as eye supervision or an appropriate seating arrangement. The examples of the admissibility of prisoner exclusion are as follows: serious disruption of past activities, serious-aggressive behaviour towards fellow prisoners and the staff, attempting to escape or preparing to escape, signs of intended hostage-taking, deep mental disorder, infection with a contagious disease and great danger from

595 T. Müller-Monning, "§ 70…, p. 627 and K. H. Schäfter, "§ 54…, pp. 562 et seq.

596 F. Arloth, "§ 53…, p. 305 and K. H. Schäfter, "§ 53…, p. 554.

597 "Zu dem Gottesdienst oder zu religiösen Veranstaltungen einer anderen Religionsgemeinschaft wird der Gefangene zugelassen, wenn deren Seelsorger zustimmt."

598 "(1) Die Gefangenen haben das Recht, am Gottesdienst und an anderen religiösen Veranstaltungen teilzunehmen. (2) Gefangene können von der Teilnahme am Gottesdienst oder anderen religiösen Veranstaltungen ausgeschlossen werden, wenn dies aus überwiegenden Gründen der Sicherheit oder Ordnung geboten ist; der Seelsorger oder die Seelsorgerin soll vorher gehört werden."

599 F. Arloth, "§ 53…, p. 305; T. Müller-Monning, "§ 70…, pp. 628 et seq.; K. H. Schäfter, "§ 53…, p. 554.

600 "Der Gefangene kann von der Teilnahme am Gottesdienst oder anderen religiösen Veranstaltungen ausgeschlossen werden, wenn dies aus überwiegenden Gründen der Sicherheit oder Ordnung geboten ist; der Seelsorger soll vorher gehört werden."

601 K. H. Schäfter, "§ 54…, p. 562.

other prisoners. By contrast, a simple insubordination or a minor infringement of the prison internal rules by a prisoner does not justify his exclusion from a religious activity.[602]

It is admissible not to hear the chaplain only in exceptionally justified cases. The general rule is to consult him, and a different practice is unacceptable. The chaplain should be informed about depriving the prisoner of his right in a situation where there was no opportunity to hear him.[603] This issue was otherwise specified in the state Law on the execution of prison sentences in the Land of Berlin. Under § 79 (3),[604] the chaplain must be heard beforehand (*ist dazu vorher anzuhören*), and in the event where the security of the facility is at risk, it may also be done later. In turn, under § 41 (3)[605] of the state Law on the execution of prison sentences in North Rhine-Westphalia, the chaplain must be heard (*ist zu hören*).

The provisions of § 53 and 54 StVollzG shall apply mutatis mutandis to worldview communities (§ 55[606] StVollzG). This standard is in turn an embodiment of the principle of equal treatment of religious and worldview communities (Art. 137 (7) WRV). Neither the Basic Law nor StVollzG specifies the defining features of such a community, so it is assumed that they are organizations based on systems of thought with coherence and structure similar to the commonly known religions.[607] It is a community that through its activity evaluates the entire world order and provides answers to questions about the origin, meaning and purpose of the world and man.[608] Such communities include the Humanist Association of Germany (*Humanistische Verband Deutschlands*). Their prime objective cannot be political or economic activity. Representatives of such a community, designated in accordance with its statutory rules, are to

---

602 F. Arloth, "§ 53…, pp. 305 et seq. and T. Müller-Monning, "§ 70…, p. 629.

603 T. Müller-Monning, "§ 70…, p. 630.

604 "Gefangene können von der Teilnahme am Gottesdienst oder anderen religiösen Veranstaltungen ausgeschlossen werden, wenn dies aus überwiegenden Gründen der Sicherheit oder Ordnung der Anstalt geboten ist. Die Seelsorgerin oder der Seelsorger ist dazu vorher anzuhören; bei einer Gefährdung der Sicherheit der Anstalt kann dies auch nachgeholt werden."

605 "Gefangene können von der Teilnahme am Gottesdienst oder anderen religiösen Veranstaltungen ausgeschlossen werden, wenn dies aus überwiegenden Gründen der Sicherheit oder Ordnung geboten ist. Die Anstaltsseelsorge ist zu hören."

606 "Für Angehörige weltanschaulicher Bekenntnisse gelten die §§ 53 und 54 entsprechend."

607 K. Laubenthal, *Strafvollzug…*, p. 528.

608 S. Korioth, "Art. 137 WRV…, margin no. 103.

be considered "chaplains" within the meaning of the enforcement regulations. This may be applied accordingly only in cases where a particular worldview community has something that may be interpreted as "pastoral ministry" and actively carries it out.[609]

If in doubt, in particular in the case of new religious movements, a consultation with lay representatives or clergymen dealing with sect issues is recommended (e.g. The Protestant Central Office for Worldview Issues – *Evangelische Zentralstelle für Weltanschauungsfragen*).[610] The Church of Scientology is considered to be an organization that is neither a religious nor worldview community. The Federal Labour Court (*Bundesarbeitsgericht*) expressly declined to recognize the organization as any of those communities.[611]

The prisoner's religious standing is also determined by § 21 (3) StVollzG,[612] which prescribes that the possibility is to be provided for a prisoner to obey religious instructions with regard to the consumption of food. The content of that provision is interpreted as the prisoner's right to the independent consumption of food according to the precepts of religion.[613] A penal facility must therefore enable him to buy foodstuffs consistent with his religious diet. This refers, for example, to *halal* meat for Muslims. It follows from a work by Sarah J. Jahn that nowadays every penal facility in the Federal Republic of Germany offers prisoners that type of product. Prisoners must make such a demand in the form of registration, similarly to prisoners with diabetes.[614] However, the prisoner has no right to a special diet.[615] It is not always possible for technical reasons to prepare, for example, kosher foods in the prison kitchen.[616] However, on a prisoner's request, food components that he is not allowed to consume should

---

609 F. Arloth, "§ 53…, p. 307.

610 T. Müller-Monning, "§ 71…p. 632.

611 BAG, Beschluß vom 22.03.1995, 5 AZB 21/94 (Hamburg), *Neue Juristische Wochenschrift*, vol. 2, 1996, pp. 143 et seq.

612 "Zusammensetzung und Nährwert der Anstaltsverpflegung werden ärztlich überwacht. Auf ärztliche Anordnung wird besondere Verpflegung gewährt. Dem Gefangenen ist zu ermöglichen, Speisevorschriften seiner Religionsgemeinschaft zu befolgen."

613 K. Laubenthal, *Strafvollzug*…, p. 530.

614 S. J. Jahn, "Germany…, p. 211 and S. J. Jahn, "Institutional…, p. 87.

615 F. Knauer, "§ 53 LandesR", in J. Fest, W. Lesting, M. Lindemann (eds.) *Strafvollzugsgesetze Bundes- und Landesrecht. Kommentar*, Hürth 2022, p. 474.

616 K. Keppler, N. Nestler, "§ 21", in H. D. Schwind, A. Böhm, J. M. Jehle, K. Laubenthal (eds.), *Strafvollzugsgesetz – Bund und Länder. Kommentar*, Berlin–Boston 2013, p. 336.

be replaced with others. The prison must also allow meals to be eaten at times that deviate from normal times if it is justified by religious reasons, for example, during Ramadan.[617] It should be pointed out that ensuring the possibility of complying with fasting during Ramadan significantly reorganizes the functioning of the prison.[618] It is also assumed that a prisoner's declaration is sufficient and a certificate from a representative of the religious association in question is not required in this regard.[619] Considering the case of a prisoner's change to a diet in accordance with Islamic requirements, The Higher Regional Court of Koblenz held that the sincerity of the religious conviction (*die Ernsthaftigkeit der Glaubensüberzeugung*) is the decisive factor.[620]

5.5. Religious freedom of children deprived of their liberty

German research works dedicated to juvenile criminal liability date back to the second half of the 19th century. Since approximately 1890, an increase in demands for the establishment of special courts for juveniles, consisting solely of judges with appropriate (educational and psychological) training, can be observed. Franz von Liszt (1851–1919) and his students from the sociological school also formulated proposals for separating adult and juvenile offenders and allocating them to separate facilities or special prison departments.[621]

The strongest foundations for the German system of juvenile criminal liability were laid by Berthold Freudenthal (1839–1929), who submitted a memorandum to the Prussian Ministry of Home Affairs in 1911, calling for the establishment of a correctional facility for juveniles, but only for those with the potential for improvement. The memorandum extended his idea of an educationally-oriented juvenile penal system. In his opinion, the achievement of the educational objective required a complete separation of juveniles from adults and a selection of only those individuals who show the potential for a change in behaviour and who are not deeply demoralized. The following measures were to be used

617 F. Arloth, "§ 21", in F. Arloth, H. Krä (eds.), *Strafvollzugsgesetze von Bund und Ländern*, München 2021, pp. 140 et seq.

618 S. J. Jahn, "Germany…, p. 211.

619 F. Knauer, "§ 53…, p. 474.

620 OGL Koblenz, 8.12.1993, 3 Ws 591/93, *Neue Zeitschrift für Strafrecht*, vol. 4, 1994, pp. 207 et seq.

621 J. Kühl, *Die gesetzliche Reform des Jugendstrafvollzugs in Deutschland im Licht der European Rules for Juvenile Offenders Subject to Sanctions or Measures (ERJOSSM)*, Mönchengladbach 2012, pp. 4 et seq.

to carry out the project: 1. broadly understood individualisation in terms of education (formation of prisoner groups along that line); 2. creation of a strong relationship of trust between the prison authorities and prisoners – the leader should have special educational qualifications and perform as few bureaucratic tasks as possible; 3. ministry and religious services in such a facility should be performed by chaplains with educational skills; 4. juveniles should be influenced by arousing healthy ambitions in them (e.g. an increase in freedoms should occur as the day of release comes nearer; the prospect of temporary release as a reward for good behaviour; non-application of disciplinary measures inappropriate for juveniles, including corporal punishment, being kept in the dark and limiting meals); the sanction in the form of withdrawal of concessions should be advocated instead of disciplinary sanctions – hope and not fear should motivate a juvenile to change into a good citizen; 5. regular physical education, military exercises, baths and similar activities, and providing enough food; 6. equipping prison libraries adequately, increasing the number of lessons, introduction of civic education and strengthening ties with the state.[622]

Freudenthal's proposals were implemented at the end of the German Empire on an experimental basis. On 1 August 1912, the first penal for juveniles was opened in Wittlich on the Moselle in a former penal facility for women. The facility could house 169 male prisoners from the then Prussian province of Rhine aged 18–21, sentenced to at least one year of imprisonment. The experimental stage was completed by an ordinance of the Prussian Minister of Home Affairs of 29 July 1913. Since then, the Wittlich facility operated as an independent special facility.[623]

The work on the first Juvenile Courts Act (*Jugendgerichtsgesetz*) was carried out by the then German Reich Justice Minister – Gustav Radburch (1878–1949). The Act was passed on 16 February 1923.[624] § 16 *in fine*[625] (in the version then in force) provided that further details on enforcement proceedings will be regulated

622 H. Ostendorf, "Vorbemerkungen", in H. Ostendorf (ed.), *Jugendstrafvollzugsrecht*, Baden-Baden 2022, pp. 71 et seq.

623 H. Ostendorf, "Vorbemerkungen…, p. 74.

624 Reichsgesetzblatt, Teil I, No. 14, pp. 135 et seq.

625 "Verbüßt ein Jugendlicher in einer besonderen Anstalt oder in einer befonderen Abteilung einer Anstalt eine Freiheitsstrafe, so kann er mit Genehmigung der Aufsichtsbehörde bis zur Vollendung des einundzwanzigsten Lebensjahrs in der Anstalt oder in der Abteilung verbleiben. Das Weitere über den Strafvollzug bestimmt die Reichsregierung mit Zustimmung des Reichsrats; dabei ist auf eine Mitwirkung des Jugendamts bei dem Straf vollzuge Bedacht zu nehmen."

by the Reich government with the approval of the Reichsrat and the involvement of the juvenile office.

Even after World War II, the German legislation did not see a single regulation devoted strictly to enforcement issues. There were only uniform federal administrative regulations for the system of the execution of prison sentences by the juvenile (*Bundeseinheitliche Verwaltungsvorschriften zum Jugendstrafvollzug*) dated 1 January 1977, which were largely based on the Federal law on the execution of prison sentences and measures of reform and prevention involving deprivation of liberty of 16 March 1976. However, they were intended to be temporary until comprehensive regulations were enacted.[626]

The law on the execution of prison sentences 1976 was enforced by a ruling of the Federal Constitutional Court dated 14 March 1972,[627] which abandoned the *besonderen Gewaltverhältnisses* concept (it is a special legal relationship between a citizen and the state that goes beyond the normal relations), which accepted an implied restriction on prisoners' fundamental rights. That statement could be exemplified by a judgment of Berlin's Superior Court of Justice (*Berliner Kammergerichts*) dated 9 December 1965,[628] which stated that as soon as a convict crosses the walls of a prison, he virtually loses all his fundamental rights; he enjoys only the unlimited right to life and physical integrity. By contrast, the Constitutional Court held that inferences with prisoners' fundamental rights that have no legal basis can only be temporary. In essence, this issue requires the adoption of standards at the statutory level. It is not without reason that this judgment is recognized as landmark and significant for the German penal law.[629]

On 29 September 1976, the Federal Justice Minister set up a special commission to develop a unified legal regulation regarding penal facilities for juveniles. The first working draft was presented on 30 June 1980 and it came in for heavy criticism. That resulted in the preparation of a new draft dated 1 June 1984, which was very strongly modelled on the Law on the execution of prison sentences. In 1988, "a practitioners' draft" was produced – (*Deutsche Vereinigung für Jugendgerichte und Jugendgerichtshilfen*), and in 1985, Jürgen Baumann's draft (1922–2003). Despite successive initiatives by the Federal Justice Ministry (1991,

---

626 J. Kühl, *Die gesetzliche…*, pp. 6 et seq. and H. Ostendorf, "Vorbemerkungen…, p. 77.

627 BVerfG, Beschluß vom 14.03.1972, 2 BvR 41/71, *Neue Juristische Wochenschrift*, vol. 18, 1972, pp. 811 et seq.

628 KG, Beschluß vom 9.12.1965, 3 VAs 34/65, *Neue Juristische Wochenschrift*, vol. 23, 1966, pp. 1089 et seq.

629 S. J. Jahn, "Germany…, p. 194.

1993, 2004, 2006), the central legislature was not able to pass an enforcement law on how to proceed in the case of criminal liability of the juvenile.[630]

The breakthrough in this matter came from a judgment delivered by the Federal Constitutional Court on 31 May 2006,[631] which concluded that the execution of prison sentences by the juvenile requires a separate legal basis. The Court held that copying the provisions of the Federal law on the execution of prison sentences and measures of reform and prevention involving deprivation of liberty was inadmissible. Penal facilities for adults and juveniles operate under such a variety of circumstances that the federal enforcement law applicable to adults would not comply with constitutional requirements were it to be copied in relation to juveniles, even if its application were expressly provided for the case of a prison sentence imposed on a juvenile. With regard to the purpose of enforcement proceedings, BVerfG defined it as making it possible for the juvenile to prepare for life free from penalty and isolation. This is because the state assumes special responsibility for the juvenile – including his further development.[632]

The adoption of the law on the execution of prison sentences by the juvenile was ultimately prevented at the central level due to the implementation of the above-mentioned federal system reform. The competence to issue enforcement regulations, as in the case of common penal enforcement law, was conferred on the states. The competence to organize juvenile courts was left to the federal level.

Today, all the (16) states have adequate but separate normative regulations.[633] Before introducing their own regulations, some of them (Brandenburg, Berlin, Bremen, Mecklenburg-Vorpommern, Rhineland-Palatinate, Saarland, Saxony-Anhalt, Schleswig-Holstein, Thuringia, and later also Saxony) prepared a so-called model project of enforcement proceedings for juveniles (*Musterentwurf – Neuner-Entwurf*), and then integrated it into their own regulations (not always consistently). The other states adopted their own regulations. Some of the regulations were issued in the form of a separate national law, while some were issued as part of the law on the execution of prison sentences by adults (!).[634] This state of affairs seriously calls into question the implementation of the judgement of the Federal Constitutional Court.

630 H. Ostendorf, "Vorbemerkungen…, p. 78.

631 BVerfG, Urteil vom 31.05.2006, 2 BvR 1673/04, 2 BvR 2402/04, *Neue Juristische Wochenschrift*, vol. 29, 2006, pp. 2093 et seq.

632 J. Kühl, *Die gesetzliche…*, pp. 21 et seq.

633 F. Arloth, T. Geiger, "Der deutsche…, p. 76.

634 J. Kühl, *Die gesetzliche…*, pp. 36 et seq.

The reform was carried out despite much criticism from theoreticians and practitioners dealing with the juveniles' support system and responding to manifestations of their demoralization. The existing division of the regulatory area between federal and state legislation is evaluated critically as legal chaos,[635] "a user-unfriendly" system leading to ambiguities.[636] A reconstruction of the standard of religious freedom of juveniles in institutions of a penal nature is therefore severely hampered because there has been (as in the case of adults) no federal normative act preceding the issuance of the states' regulations. Moreover, some enforcement regulations of the states have been subject to numerous amendments, whereas in some cases, a decision was made to create a completely new regulation. Thus, the risk of a faulty determination of the legal status still remains high.

An attempt to retrace the normative standard requires making a reference to the basic provisions of the Federal Youth Courts Act. This should contribute to a more consistent picture of criminal liability of juveniles in the Federal Republic of Germany.

Under § 19 StGB,[637] whoever is under 14 years of age at the time of the commission of the offence is deemed to act without guilt, unless the provisions of the Federal Youth Courts Act (*Jugendgerichtsgesetz* – JGG[638]) provide otherwise (§ 10 StGB[639]). Youth criminal law (*Jugendstrafrecht*) was therefore regulated separately and its scope includes (§ 4 JGG[640]) criminal liability for a criminal offence (be it a felony or a misdemeanour) within the meaning of the provisions of StGB.

The Federal Youth Courts Act provides for two categories of entities falling under its provisions (§ 1 (2)[641]). On the one hand, it defines the category of

635 H. Ostendorf, "Vorbemerkungen…, p. 78.

636 H. Ostendorf, "§ 1 Grundlagen", in H. Ostendorf (ed.), *Jugendstrafvollzugsrecht*, Baden-Baden 2022, pp. 123 et seq.

637 "Schuldunfähig ist, wer bei Begehung der Tat noch nicht vierzehn Jahre alt ist."

638 The current wording of the Act 1923 – Bundesgesetzblatt 1974, Teil I, no. 133, pp. 3427 et seq.

639 "Für Taten von Jugendlichen und Heranwachsenden gilt dieses Gesetz nur, soweit im Jugendgerichtsgesetz nichts anderes bestimmt ist."

640 "Ob die rechtswidrige Tat eines Jugendlichen als Verbrechen oder Vergehen anzusehen ist und wann sie verjährt, richtet sich nach den Vorschriften des allgemeinen Strafrechts."

641 "Jugendlicher ist, wer zur Zeit der Tat vierzehn, aber noch nicht achtzehn, Heranwachsender, wer zur Zeit der Tat achtzehn, aber noch nicht einundzwanzig Jahre alt ist."

juvenile (*Jugendlicher*), that is, a person who at the time of the commission of the offence reached the age of 14 but did not reach the age of 18. On the other, it introduces the concept of young adult (*Heranwachsender*), that is, a person who at the time of the commission of the offence reached the age of 18 but did not reach the age of 21.[642] The application of the regulations contained in JGG is above all to counter renewed criminal offences on the part of a juvenile and a young adult. The fulfilment of that aim requires proceedings based on the idea of educating young people, taking into account the parental right of upbringing (§ 2[643]).

Bearing criminal responsibility is possible if at the time of the commission of the offence the perpetrator was mature enough in terms of his moral and intellectual development to recognize the wrongfulness of the act and to act according to that discernment. The court may apply the same measures as the family and guardianship court in order to educate a juvenile who does not bear criminal liability due to his immaturity (§ 3[644]).

Youth penalty (*Jugendstrafe*) to be imposed on the juvenile shall mean deprivation of liberty in a special facility designated for its execution (*Jugendstrafanstalt*). The judge may impose a youth penalty if, as a result of harmful inclinations demonstrated by the juvenile during the act, educational measures (*Erziehungsmaßregeln*) or disciplinary measures (*Zuchtmittel*) are insufficient for the purposes of education or if such a penalty is necessary given the seriousness of the juvenile's guilt (§ 17[645]). *Jugendstrafe* shall be calculated so

642 The German criminal code uses the concept of the child (*Kind*) in its special part in connection with the standardization of the crime directed against sexual freedom. It is a person below 14 years of age (§ 176 (1) (1) StGB: "Mit Freiheitsstrafe nicht unter einem Jahr wird bestraft, wer 1. sexuelle Handlungen an einer Person unter vierzehn Jahren (Kind) vornimmt oder an sich von dem Kind vornehmen lässt."

643 "(1) Die Anwendung des Jugendstrafrechts soll vor allem erneuten Straftaten eines Jugendlichen oder Heranwachsenden entgegenwirken. Um dieses Ziel zu erreichen, sind die Rechtsfolgen und unter Beachtung des elterlichen Erziehungsrechts auch das Verfahren vorrangig am Erziehungsgedanken auszurichten. (2) Die allgemeinen Vorschriften gelten nur, soweit in diesem Gesetz nichts anderes bestimmt ist."

644 "Ein Jugendlicher ist strafrechtlich verantwortlich, wenn er zur Zeit der Tat nach seiner sittlichen und geistigen Entwicklung reif genug ist, das Unrecht der Tat einzusehen und nach dieser Einsicht zu handeln. Zur Erziehung eines Jugendlichen, der mangels Reife strafrechtlich nicht verantwortlich ist, kann der Richter dieselben Maßnahmen anordnen wie das Familiengericht."

645 "(1) Die Jugendstrafe ist Freiheitsentzug in einer für ihren Vollzug vorgesehenen Einrichtung. (2) Der Richter verhängt Jugendstrafe, wenn wegen der schädlichen Neigungen des Jugendlichen, die in der Tat hervorgetreten sind, Erziehungsmaßregeln

as to make it possible to achieve the desired educational purpose. The minimum duration of youth penalty shall be 6 months, the maximum duration shall be 5 years. If the act is a serious criminal offence for which general criminal law prescribes a maximum sentence of more than 10 years' deprivation of liberty, the maximum duration of youth penalty shall be 10 years (§ 18[646]). This directive also applies to young adults, however, § 105 (3) JGG[647] prescribes that if the offence is murder, and if the maximum sentence (10 years) is inadequate because of the particular grievousness of culpability, the maximum sentence shall be 15 years. The penalty of deprivation of liberty is obviously imposed as a last resort, so JGG foresees other means of influencing the juvenile.

As given above, ensuring religious freedom for a juvenile and a young adult convict has been assigned to the states. It appears that since a reduction of costs arising from the operation of penal facilities was reasonable to some extent, in the case of juveniles, due to the specific national and international guarantees, the lowering of enforcement standards seems rather unlikely.

The discussion below addresses selected guarantees of religious freedom of the juvenile, adopting a problem-focused approach rather than, as in the case of adults, the original federal normative act, because such an instrument has never been created for juveniles.

In the opinion of experts, by virtue of the above-mentioned normative provisions, the states take into account the high priority of freedom of conscience and religion guaranteed by Art. 4 GG. They are designed to regulate the practical exercise of the right to religious freedom under conditions of deprivation of liberty. They aim to reduce the side effects of isolation of the juvenile and reduce difficulties in the exercise of that fundamental right.[648]

---

oder Zuchtmittel zur Erziehung nicht ausreichen oder wenn wegen der Schwere der Schuld Strafe erforderlich ist."

646 "(1) Das Mindestmaß der Jugendstrafe beträgt sechs Monate, das Höchstmaß fünf Jahre. Handelt es sich bei der Tat um ein Verbrechen, für das nach dem allgemeinen Strafrecht eine Höchststrafe von mehr als zehn Jahren Freiheitsstrafe angedroht ist, so ist das Höchstmaß zehn Jahre. Die Strafrahmen des allgemeinen Strafrechts gelten nicht. (2) Die Jugendstrafe ist so zu bemessen, daß die erforderliche erzieherische Einwirkung möglich ist."

647 "Das Höchstmaß der Jugendstrafe für Heranwachsende beträgt zehn Jahre. Handelt es sich bei der Tat um Mord und reicht das Höchstmaß nach Satz 1 wegen der besonderen Schwere der Schuld nicht aus, so ist das Höchstmaß 15 Jahre."

648 H. Ostendorf, "§ 6 Religionsausübung…, p. 370.

The process of interpreting particular regulations is affected by the provisions of the international agreements to which the Federal Republic of Germany is a party, that is, Art. 9 of the European Convention for the Protection of Human Rights and Fundamental Freedoms, Art. 18 of the International Covenant on Civil and Political Rights, Art. 10 of the EU Charter of Fundamental Rights and Art. 14 of the Convention on the Rights of the Child.

Soft law regulations are also an adequate control pattern, including those discussed in Chapter III, point 29 of the European Prison Rules and, in particular, point 87 of the Recommendation of the Committee of Ministers to member states on the European Rules for juvenile offenders subject to sanctions or measures. It prescribes that the institutional regimen shall be organized so far as is practicable to allow juveniles to practise their religion and follow their beliefs, to attend services or meetings led by approved representatives of such religion or beliefs, to receive visits in private from such representatives of their religion or beliefs and to have in their possession books or literature relating to their religion or beliefs (point 87.2). Juveniles may not be compelled to practise a religion, follow a belief, attend religious services or meetings, take part in religious practices or to accept a visit from a representative of any religion or belief (87.3).[649]

Similar importance may be attached to the above-mentioned point 48 of the United Nations Rules for the Protection of Juveniles Deprived of their Liberty, under which every juvenile should be allowed to satisfy his or her religious and spiritual life, in particular by attending the services or meetings provided in the detention facility or by conducting his or her own services and having possession of the necessary books or articles of religious observance and instruction of his or her denomination. If a detention facility contains a sufficient number of juveniles of a given religion, one or more qualified representatives of that religion should be appointed or approved and allowed to hold regular services and to pay pastoral visits to juveniles at their request. Every juvenile should have the right to receive visits from a qualified representative of any religion of his or her choice, as well as the right to participate in religious services and freely to decline religious education, counselling or indoctrination.

Thus, identical to adult prisoners, juveniles cannot be deprived of pastoral care, and the facility may help them contact a clerical representative of their

649 J. Kühl, *Die gesetzliche…*, pp. 168 et seq.

religion.[650] Occasionally, the inviolability of confession and pastoral secrecy is also guaranteed.[651]

Juveniles can keep their faith intact in their conscience even in a closed prison. However, they cannot follow some religious practices independently without fellow brothers and sisters in the faith and without the presence of a chaplain. Consequently, the active role of the facility (on receiving a prior request) in facilitating a juvenile's contact with a representative of their religion is justified.[652] Organizations using the status of a religious association as a cover, achieving economic purposes and simultaneously using their members and those that promote the idea of total submission to their principles are not considered religious communities. Such organizations include: "Kinder Gottes", "Divine Light Mission" and, in the case of adult prisoners, the Church of Scientology.[653]

The state's religious and worldview neutrality means that a request for providing pastoral care may be directed to a specific religious community and not to the juvenile facility staff, who only acts as an intermediary in establishing a contact. Some religious association regulations prescribe that pastoral care over incarcerated juveniles is seen as sensitive activity and is therefore subject to verification under the security procedure by a specialized service.[654] A juvenile penal facility may refuse entry to a chaplain in the event of the possibility that he may violate the proper course of serving a penalty by a juvenile. Security reasons should at least be substantiated. Thus, the religious community carries the burden of showing the pastoral capacity of its representative. It is particularly important in the case of Muslim communities, whose status remains unregulated.[655]

Apart from holding religious services, pastoral responsibilities also include a personal talk with a juvenile. Juveniles seek such conversations not only for purely religious reasons, but also because of their anxiety, depressive states

---

650 § 80 JStVollzG Berlin, § 27 (1) JVollzGB Baden-Württemberg, § 81 JVollzG Brandenburg, § 79 LJVollzG Rheinland – Pfalz, § 80 JVollzGB Thüringen, § 90 JStVollzG Schleswig-Holstein, Art. 55 (1) JStVollzG Bayern, § 31 (1) JStVollzG Hessen, § 43 (1) JStVollzG Sachsen, § 53 (1) JVollzG Niedersachsen, § 70 JStVollzG Bremen, § 43 (1) JStVollzG Mecklenburg-Vorpommern, § 34 JStVollzG Nordrhein-Westfalen, § 43 (1) JStVollzG Saarland, § 80 (1) JStVollzG Sachsen-Anhalt, § 54 (1) JStVollzG Hamburg.

651 § 27 (1) JVollzGB Baden-Württemberg.

652 H. Ostendorf, "§ 6 Religionsausübung…, p. 374.

653 H. Ostendorf, "§ 6 Religionsausübung…, p. 376.

654 § 108 (4) LJVollzG Rheinland – Pfalz.

655 H. Ostendorf, "§ 6 Religionsausübung…, p. 377.

and suicidal thoughts. A comprehensive pastoral approach opens up many opportunities for action, a chaplain may, for example, arrange a contact with the prisoner's family, or as part of support after release, help to find a job or an apartment. Pastoral work is by no means easy because juveniles, especially during adolescence, feel the need to cross various boundaries, challenging both the authority of parents and teachers. The facility staff acts as a "compulsory" surrogate for them both. Applying his educational and theological skills, the chaplain has the opportunity to enter into a relationship with the juvenile and deactivate those negative tendencies.[656]

The juvenile may have religious literature in his possession. It can be taken away only in case of gross abuse.[657] Only in one state, at the request of the juvenile, it is required that his chaplain is informed about taking away such literature.[658] The issue of what "gross abuse" is and who has the power to determine that it has occurred remains unsaid. Not every culpable breach of duty is sufficient to assume that such abuse has occurred. It seems that an abuse occurs when security and order in the facility have been jeopardized or disrupted. This is the case when literature is used as a hiding place for dangerous items, escape plans or intoxicants. A similar situation arises in cases when, for example, the Bible or the Quran is used to spread hate speech and justify religious violence against followers of other religions, or for any other reason (sexual orientation).[659]

A slightly separate issue is the possession of articles of religious observance. All the states allow the juvenile to possess, to a reasonable extent, articles of religious worship. Some states foresee the possibility of taking them away (in the case of a gross abuse[660] or if it is justified by reasons of the security of the individual[661]), whereas others do

656 H. Ostendorf, "§ 6 Religionsausübung…, pp. 383 et seq.

657 § 57 JStVollzG Berlin, § 27 (2) JVollzGB Baden-Württemberg, § 59 JVollzG Brandenburg, § 58 LJVollzG Rheinland – Pfalz, § 59 JVollzGB Thüringen, § 68 (2) JStVollzG Schleswig-Holstein, Art. 55 (2) JStVollzG Bayern, § 31 (2) JStVollzG Hessen, § 43 (1) JStVollzG Sachsen, § 50 (2) JStVollzG Bremen, § 43 (2) JStVollzG Mecklenburg-Vorpommern, § 34 JStVollzG Nordrhein-Westfalen, § 43 (2) JStVollzG Saarland, § 80 (2) JStVollzG Sachsen-Anhalt, § 54 (2) JStVollzG Hamburg.

658 § 53 (2) JVollzG Niedersachsen.

659 H. Ostendorf, "§ 6 Religionsausübung…, p. 376.

660 § 57 JStVollzG Berlin, § 59 JVollzG Brandenburg,§ 58 LJVollzG Rheinland – Pfalz, § 59 JVollzGB Thüringen, § 68 (2) JStVollzG Schleswig-Holstein, § 50 (2) JStVollzG Bremen, § 80 (2) JStVollzG Sachsen-Anhalt,

661 § 53 (3) JVollzG Niedersachsen.

not.[662] Only in one case the necessity to hear the chaplain is decreed.[663] It is occasionally argued that in the case of taking away such an article it is necessary to indicate that its use violates the fundamental rights of others, which is a direct reference to the constitutional proportionality principle.[664]

Juveniles can attend religious services and other religious activities of their religion. They may be allowed to attend religious services and activities of other religion, with the consent of the chaplain of that religion. Juveniles may be excluded from attending religious services and other religious activities if it is necessary for overriding reasons of security or order. Before the exclusion, the chaplain should be heard,[665] or is heard (*ist zu hören*),[666] or has been heard (*ist dazu vorher anzuhören*).[667]

The interpretation of the concept of religious service is reserved for religious communities, although it is pointed out that it stems from the traditions and history of the religion in question. Similar disputes, regarding regulations covering adults, are taking place with regard to "other religious activities". There is no complete consensus on whether content criterion or the formal criterion matters for the interpretation of this concept. Problems arise in the case of, for example, operation of theatrical and musical groups led by chaplains. Ultimately, the broad interpretation of the phrase is accepted.[668]

The exclusion from the possibility of attending religious services and other religious activities is a discretionary decision, but it must be a last resort. It can be taken only in very serious and obvious cases. Their number is therefore limited. The reasons for the exclusion must be directly related to a juvenile or his individual situation. Organizational problems, including the increased

---

662 § 27 (3) JVollzGB Baden-Württemberg, Art. 55 (3) JStVollzG Bayern, § 31 (2) JStVollzG Hessen, § 43 (2) JStVollzG Sachsen, § 43 (3) JStVollzG Mecklenburg-Vorpommern, § 34 JStVollzG Nordrhein-Westfalen, § 43 (3) JStVollzG Saarland, § 54 (3) JStVollzG Hamburg.

663 § 68 (2) JStVollzG Schleswig-Holstein.

664 H. Ostendorf, "§ 6 Religionsausübung…, p. 379.

665 § 28 JVollzGB Baden-Württemberg, § 82 JVollzG Brandenburg, § 80 LJVollzG Rheinland – Pfalz, § 81 JVollzGB Thüringen, § 91 JStVollzG Schleswig-Holstein, Art. 56 JStVollzG Bayern, § 31 (3) JStVollzG Hessen, § 44 JStVollzG Sachsen, § 54 JVollzG Niedersachsen, § 71 JStVollzG Bremen, § 44 JStVollzG Mecklenburg-Vorpommern, § 44 JStVollzG Saarland, § 81 JStVollzG Sachsen-Anhalt, § 55 JStVollzG Hamburg.

666 § 34 JStVollzG Nordrhein-Westfalen.

667 § 81 JStVollzG Berlin.

668 H. Ostendorf, "§ 6 Religionsausübung…, p. 380.

supervision of juveniles, reduced staffing on Sundays and public holidays, are not a sufficient substantiation for a refusal to attend religious activities.[669] Heribert Ostendorf rightly points out that the exclusion from a religious activity may not be a hidden punishment or a disciplinary measure. Besides, even the application of a disciplinary sanction does not automatically deprive a juvenile of the right to participate in religious activities. As is the case with adult prisoners, juveniles must not be put in the position of choosing between attending a religious service and an outdoor leisure time.[670]

The above regulations apply accordingly to worldview communities.[671]

The juvenile should also have the possibility to observe religious dietary rules.[672] Occasionally, however, it is firmly declared that dietary rules will be observed.[673] In some cases, an alternative possibility is guaranteed – the consumption of meatless[674]/vegetarian[675] foods. It is also pointed out that during meal preparation in a facility, Muslim juveniles should be involved at work in the kitchen on dishes dedicated to them, as their testimony is the best guarantee to others that the dishes being prepared comply with Islamic requirements. Moreover, during Ramadan, Muslim juveniles should have the possibility of joint meals and should receive a hot meal after sunset.[676]

Different regulations also include the status of chaplains. This applies not only to wording – some states mention not only chaplains (*Seelsorger*) but also female chaplains (*Seelsorgerinnen*), which is justifiable because of the possibility

---

669 H. Ostendorf, "§ 6 Religionsausübung…, p. 381.

670 H. Ostendorf, "§ 6 Religionsausübung…, pp. 382 et seq.

671 § 82 JStVollzG Berlin, § 29 JVollzG Baden-Württemberg, § 83 JVollzG Brandenburg, § 81 LJVollzG Rheinland – Pfalz, § 82 JVollzGB Thüringen, § 92 JStVollzG Schleswig-Holstein, Art. 57 JStVollzG Bayern, § 31 (4) JStVollzG Hessen, § 45 JStVollzG Sachsen, § 55 JVollzG Niedersachsen, § 72 JStVollzG Bremen, § 45 JStVollzG Mecklenburg-Vorpommern, § 34 JStVollzG Nordrhein-Westfalen, § 45 JStVollzG Saarland, § 82 JStVollzG Sachsen-Anhalt, § 56 StVollzG Hamburg.

672 § 15 (2) JVollzG Baden-Württemberg, § 62 LJVollzG Rheinland – Pfalz, § 63 (1) JVollzGB Thüringen, § 71 (1) JStVollzG Schleswig-Holstein, Art. 143 JStVollzG Bayern, § 22 (1) JStVollzG Hessen, § 31 (1) JStVollzG Sachsen, § 23 JVollzG Niedersachsen, § 53 (1) JStVollzG Bremen, § 31 (2) Mecklenburg-Vorpommern, § 31 (1) JStVollzG Saarland, § 61 (1) JStVollzG Sachsen-Anhalt.

673 § 24 StVollzG Hamburg.

674 § 60 JStVollzG Berlin, § 63 (1) JVollzG Brandenburg,

675 § 20 (1) JStVollzG Nordrhein-Westfalen.

676 H. Ostendorf, "§ 3 Unterbringung und Versorgung", in H. Ostendorf (ed.), *Jugendstrafvollzugsrecht*, Baden-Baden 2022, p. 221.

of ordination (entrusting a clerical office, not sacramental in nature) of women as deaconesses and priestesses in some Protestant churches. As a rule, the status of chaplains reflects the StVollzG provisions. The states define the relations between a juvenile penal facility and chaplains (namely, an employment contract in agreement with a religious community) and also determine that where a negligible number of followers of a religious community does not justify pastoral care, it is permissible to provide such care differently. With consent obtained from the prison director, chaplains may avail themselves of the services of free religious assistants to conduct religious services and other forms of ministry.[677]

In rare instances, however, the enforcement standards become complex. In some cases, it is only declared that a juvenile penal facility should have an adequate number of chaplains needed to take pastoral care of juveniles.[678] Another standard prescribes that, for example, chaplains work closely with the juvenile penal facility staff to achieve the goals of enforcement proceedings, but they do so on their sole responsibility.[679] The Bavarian regulation is the most far-reaching one in that aspect. It prescribes that chaplains are involved in juveniles' medical examinations, the preparation, implementation and amendment of a rehabilitation plan, juveniles' leisure time, juvenile social assistance, and the training and further education of the prison staff.[680]

In some cases, it is explicitly prescribed that individual pastoral conversations, telephone calls to a chaplain and correspondence with him are not subject to supervision or monitoring.[681]

It is concluded in the comments on the above standards that the enforcement standards on religious freedom show more editorial deviations than substantive ones. No importance should be attached to semantic issues.[682] However, it is hard to agree entirely with this argument. Such a deviation may be exemplified by the possibility (or its lack) to take away articles of religious observance from

677 § 108 (1 and 3) JStVollzG Berlin, § 111 JVollzG Brandenburg, § 108 (1–3) LJVollzG Rheinland – Pfalz, § 109 JVollzGB Thüringen, § 133 JStVollzG Schleswig-Holstein, Art. 178 (1–3) JStVollzG Bayern, § 73 JStVollzG Hessen, § 94 JStVollzG Sachsen, § 179 JVollzG Niedersachsen, § 98 JStVollzG Bremen, § 103 JStVollzG Mecklenburg-Vorpommern, § 64 JStVollzG Nordrhein-Westfalen, § 103 JStVollzG Saarland, § 110 JStVollzG Sachsen-Anhalt, § 102 StVollzG Hamburg.

678 § 111 (1) JVollzG Brandenburg.

679 § 108 (2) JStVollzG Berlin and § 111 (1) JVollzG Brandenburg.

680 Art. 178 (4) JStVollzG Bayern.

681 § 108 (4) JStVollzG Berlin.

682 H. Ostendorf, "§ 6 Religionsausübung…, p. 370.

a juvenile. The same is true of the requirement to inform the chaplain about a specific incident or hearing his opinion.

Given the similarity of the state enforcement regulations for juveniles and the StVollzG provisions, it is proposed that the case-law and doctrinal notes formulated based on the execution of prison sentences by adults should be used, as long as the characteristics of proceeding with juveniles do not require a different assessment.[683] Despite its relevance, this proposal is difficult to apply in practice. On the one hand, there is a lack of literature and case-law devoted strictly to juvenile enforcement issues, on the other, the Federal Constitutional Court strongly emphasized in its 2006 judgement that the differences in the execution of prison sentences by adults and juveniles are so significant that the separation of the legislative layer and application practice between those groups should be clear and impenetrable. Consequently, references to notes formulated based on StVollzG should be made with great caution.

The objective of the federal system reform was, among other things, to reflect the socio-economic peculiarities of a given state in the normative layer. It seems that this objective has not been achieved. On the contrary, certain abuses can be observed in the area of enforcement proceedings involving juveniles in relation to whom a penalty of imprisonment has been pronounced. This may be illustrated by the provision of § 2 (2) JVollzG[684] of Baden-Württemberg, which regulates the rules of influence and upbringing of juveniles by prescribing that they are to be educated in reverence for God, in the spirit of Christian love, brotherhood among all people, love of peace, love for the homeland, moral and political responsibility, professional and social activity, and in the spirit of a free and democratic attitude. Education in reverence for God (*in der Ehrfurcht vor Gott*) may be wrongly understood as a form of conversion of juveniles and as a wrongly understood penal measure.[685] The guarantees under Art. 136, 140 and 141 WRV clearly show that the state cannot put any pressure on the individual to persuade him to attend religious services or other religious activities against his

683 H. Ostendorf, "§ 6 Religionsausübung…, p. 371.

684 "Die jungen Gefangenen sind in der Ehrfurcht vor Gott, im Geiste der christlichen Nächstenliebe, zur Brüderlichkeit aller Menschen und zur Friedensliebe, in der Liebe zu Volk und Heimat, zu sittlicher und politischer Verantwortlichkeit, zu beruflicher und sozialer Bewährung und zu freiheitlicher demokratischer Gesinnung zu erziehen."

685 H. Ostendorf, "§ 6 Religionsausübung…, pp. 372 et seq.

will. Thus, the provision of § 2 (2) JVollzG violates the principle of religious and worldview neutrality of Germany.[686]

Potential problems between juvenile – his parents – director of a juvenile penal facility are resolved in accordance with the provisions of the above-mentioned federal Law on the Religious Parenting dated 15 July 1921. Under § 5 sentence 1 – after reaching 14 years of age, the child is entitled to decide which religious denomination he wishes to adhere to. His decision may be communicated by any means to the facility director or a representative of the religious community. In turn, if the child has reached the age of 12, he cannot be brought up in a different denomination than before against his will (§ 5 sentence 2). Under § 6 of that law – its provisions shall apply accordingly to the education of children in a non-confessional worldview.

This does not solve all the problems. Juvenile penal facilities, as is the case with those for adults, have not so far developed a relationship with the Muslim community.[687] The percentage of Muslim juveniles in juvenile penal facilities located in metropolitan areas reaches even 40 %.[688] This generates the need to neutralize extremism, which is not possible without hiring and working with properly trained chaplains. The problem of the inadequate number of chaplains of that religious association is overlaid by a proposal that the chaplain of a juvenile penal facility should not provide pastoral care for more than 100 members of his denomination.[689]

---

686 J. Kühl, *Die gesetzliche*..., p. 169.
687 H. Ostendorf, "§ 6 Religionsausübung..., p. 373.
688 T. Müller-Monning, "§ 69..., p. 622.
689 K. H. Schäfter, "§ 157..., p. 1129.

Chapter VI Exercise of religious freedom in penitentiary facilities, correctional facilities and youth educational centres: results of a survey

6.1. Research objectives

The aim was to determine the extent to which religious freedom is respected in post-criminal isolation units (connected with the commission of prohibited act), including the right to practice a chosen religion or the right not to profess and practice any religion. Although the issue of religiosity of persons deprived of their liberty is an interesting research problem, it was relevant to us insofar as it served to reconstruct the standards of respect for religious freedom.[690]

We were interested in the situation of both incarcerated adults and juveniles, who, in legal terms, – remain in a different configuration with regard to the possibility of exercising their own will, among other things, in the area of practicing religion.

Apart from general questions about how prisoners perceive limitations in the area of religious freedom in connection with incarceration, we were also interested in specific practices and specific limitations. We studied the situation of Roman Catholics, but also individuals of different denominations and non-believers, before and during the pandemic.

The obtained results were complemented by comments from educators working with prisoners. We were presented with extremely interesting, if at times disturbing, material that gives much food for thought.

The methodology described below, the characteristics of the study groups, and the list of institutions under study allow us to conclude that the survey took into account a cross-section of the population of convicts, pre-trial detainees, juveniles placed in youth educational centres and correctional facilities and educators of those facilities. The adult prisoners were of different ages, came from localities of different status (rural and urban), had different levels of education, varied marital status. The convicted persons were serving longer and shorter

---

690 O. Sitarz, A. Jaworska-Wieloch, J. Hanc, "Prisoners' opinions about religious practices in Polish penitentiary facilities. An analysis of the results of a study", [Article submitted for review].

penalties of imprisonment. The multi-level diversity applied also to a study on juveniles.

6.2. Methodology

The survey was carried out from March to October 2022. It was largely based on anonymous questionnaires.

The choice of the questionnaire as a research method was influenced by two circumstances. First, it was difficult to enter prison facilities at the time of survey due to the ongoing COVID-19 pandemic. The second reason was more important. Being aware that the survey related to highly sensitive issues (religion and its practice) in uncomfortable circumstances (respondents being placed in penal, total institutions, which were to be examined in terms of the disadvantages of access to religious practices and services), we had concerns about the so-called interviewer effect (error), an inadequate picture of reality. The literature points out that "Interviewer effects appear to be most likely to occur when survey items query attitudes about sociodemographic characteristics or respondents' engagement in sensitive behaviours."[691]

The survey method was chosen despite our awareness that it is unreliable[692] and it requires the application of a specific methodological rigour that ensures relatively high relevance, reliability and objectivity of inference.[693] This method allowed us to achieve the research objectives to the fullest extent. Included in the group of empirical scientific methods, the survey focuses on solving the research problem relying on experiences, by capturing the conditions as close as possible to reality, allowing the researcher to explore the analysed issue from a scientific point of view.[694] The adopted method fits, by its nature, into the monothetic research approach aimed at seeking generalized judgements, laws and rules of the organization of the world. It is achieved using an inductive research avenue (mainly incomplete enumerative induction), allowing the truth of a phenomenon

---

691 R. E. Davis, M. P. Couper, N. K. Janz, C. H. Caldwell, K. Resnicow, "Interviewer effects in public health surveys", *Health Education Research*, vol. 25, no. 1, 2010, pp. 14 et seq.

692 K. R. Popper, *The Logic of Scientific Discovery*, London – New York 2005, pp. 21 et seq.

693 W. Czakon, "Rygor metodologiczny", in W. Czakon (ed.), *Podstawy metodologii badań w naukach o zarządzaniu*, Warszawa 2023, pp. 82 et seq.

694 H. Dźwigoł, "Założenia do budowy metodyki badawczej", *Zeszyty Naukowe Politechniki Śląskiej. Seria: Organizacja i Zarządzanie*, vol. 78, 2015, p. 102.

to be established on the basis of sentences which confirm its existence in certain cases only (out of all possible ones).[695]

The questionnaires included closed, open and semi-open questions, with a cafeteria option or a space for entering a different reply. The questionnaires were aimed at incarcerated adults and children – we sent them to penitentiary facilities, detention centres, youth educational centres and correctional facilities. Purposive (non-random) sampling was used – we sought to examine prisoners incarcerated in prisons of different kinds and types. We also sought a relatively wide territorial basis (which may have been significant due to religious heterogeneity – e.g., more Orthodox believers inhabit the eastern part of Poland). Given that we aimed to identify possible problems connected with respecting the right to religious freedom, the representativeness of the results and the implementation and use of a so-called "sampling frame" were less important. The classic statistical research is not so important for identifying violations of standards for respecting prisoners' rights. **The very identification of such violations – at the stage of making or applying enforcement law – is a signal that changes need to be made. Importantly, we did not examine religious beliefs, religiosity or religious maturity, but with the participation of prisoners and their educators, the state of observance (exercise) of the rights of prisoners in penitentiary institutions. In other words, the conducted survey served to determine the extent to which the standards for religious freedom are met in the selected facilities.**

Prior to the start of the study, we obtained approval from the Research Ethics Commission of the University of Silesia in Katowice (KEUS.7/03.2020). Relevant consents were also obtained from the Central Board of the Prison Service (BDG. 0184.16.2022.BA) and the Ministry of Justice of the Republic of Poland. The questionnaires were anonymous and participation in the research was completely voluntary, of which respondents were informed at the outset. First, they were also informed about the aims and principles of the study.

The questionnaires directed at adult prisoners consisted of 4 parts: introductory – addressed to all respondents, then consecutively: part addressed to Roman Catholics (printed on blue paper), part addressed to individuals of different confessions (printed on green paper), non-believers (printed on pink paper). The final part– metrics – was also addressed to all respondents (printed on white paper).

695 J. Niemczyk, "Metodologia nauk o zarządzaniu", in W. Czakon (ed.), *Podstawy metodologii badań w naukach o zarządzaniu…*, pp. 17 et seq.

The questionnaires addressed to juveniles placed in youth educational centres and correctional facilities also had separate parts for individuals of different confessions and non-believers (with no division by colour). In that case, however, there were no separate questions relating to the time before and during the pandemic due to the shorter, in principle, stay of juveniles in isolation centres.

The questionnaires for educators were very similar in the groups of adults and juveniles. The questions took into account the possibly different situation of prisoners of different religions and non-believers. The questions also included questions about pandemic-related limitations and their reception by the prisoners.

The questionnaire questions were consulted with a professor of theology (Roman Catholic clergyman), whose tasks, within the framework of its scientific and pastoral activity, included religious issues, including ecumenical ones. It should be conceded that the respondent replies contain theological inaccuracies because even believers are not always well versed in the Catechism of the Catholic Church, the particular law of the local church, the provisions of canon law, and even the basic theological elements of faith. A doctor of sociology was the second consultant.

6.3. Characteristics of the study group

6.3.1. Convicted persons and pre-trial detainees

The survey included 556 prisoners, including 34 females and 444 males (68 persons gave no reply as to their gender).

The declared age of the respondents was as follows:

- up to 24 years of age: 27
- 25–30: 78
- 31–40: 189
- 41–50: 124
- 51–60: 57
- 61 and more: 20
- no reply: 51.

The declared civil status of the respondents was as follows:

- single: 269
- married: 98
- widowed: 16

- divorced: 104
- no reply: 59

Declared educational background:

- primary (including incomplete): 56
- lower secondary school: 79
- vocational: 160
- secondary school: 150
- university education: 45
- no reply: 57

Declared place of residence at liberty:

- rural: 95
- town with a population of up to 100,000 inhabitants: 158
- town with a population of over 100,000 inhabitants: 213
- no place of permanent residence or stay: 24
- no reply: 56

Status of penitentiary isolation during the survey:

- convicts: 451
- pre-trial detainees: 19
- convicted and simultaneously detained in another case: 19
- no reply: 56

Length of imposed penalty (or total penalties) of imprisonment:

- up to 1 year: 66
- between 1 year and 3 years: 99
- between 3 and 5 years: 83
- between 5 and 15 years: 169
- over 15 years: 65
- pre-trial detention: 10
- no reply: 54

Remaining period of imprisonment:

- up to 1 year: 185
- between 1 year and 3 years: 150
- between 3 and 5 years: 48
- between 5 and 15 years: 56

- over 15 years: 33
- not applicable: 15
- no reply: 60

Place of incarceration during the study:

- penitentiary facility: 412
- detention centre: 75
- no reply: 60

Subgroup:

- young adults: 7
- serving a first penalty: 232
- penitentiary recidivists: 229
- pre-trial detainees: 17
- no reply: 62

Type of institution:

- closed: 279
- semi-open: 182
- open: 26
- not applicable: 4
- no reply: 56

System of serving a penalty:

- programmed impacting: 261
- standard: 176
- therapeutic: 37
- not applicable: 14
- no reply: 59

The status of a particularly dangerous convict or detainee was given to 24 respondents (463 respondents did not have that status, 59 respondents did not reply).

The full picture requires the following data:[696]

- 71,228 individuals were incarcerated in Poland on 31 December 2022;

696 See: https://www.sw.gov.pl/strona/Statystyka (accessed 12.07.2023).

- including: 8,149 pre-trial detainees, 62,339 convicts (plus 740 individuals punished for a petty crime);
- including: 3,442 females,
- including: 175 incarcerated individuals did not reach 18 years of age (one even 16 years of age), and 3,395 were over 61 years of age.

6.3.2. Educators in penitentiary facilities and detention centres

In total, 164 educators took part in the study. The survey group was diverse in terms of where they performed their duties; they worked in the following departments (with the numbers not adding up to the number of educators surveyed, as some indicated more than one division):

- penitentiary facility for recidivists – 114;
- penitentiary facility for prisoners serving a first sentence – 104;
- penitentiary facility for young adults – 42;
- detention centre – 43;

including:

- closed penitentiary facility (1) – 100;
- semi-open penitentiary facility (2) – 66;
- open penitentiary facility (3) – 20.

The shortest length of service of the surveyed teachers and educators in the prison system at the time of the survey was 2 weeks, the longest 26 years.

6.3.3. Juveniles in youth educational centres and correctional facilities

In total, 209 juveniles took part in the survey. They included 71 girls and 122 boys (16 respondents did not indicate their gender).

The age distribution of the juvenile respondents was as follows:

- up to 14 years of age: 17;
- 15–16 years of age: 76;
- 17–18 years if age: 80;
- 19 years of age: 16;
- no reply: 20.

Their declared educational background was as follows:

- elementary (including incomplete): 132 juveniles;

- lower secondary school: 11;
- vocational: 40,
- secondary school: 7,
- no reply: 17.

The declared place of residence at liberty:

- rural: 30 juveniles;
- town with a population of up to 100,000 inhabitants: 88;
- town with a population of over 100,000 inhabitants: 66;
- no permanent place of residence or stay: 6;
- no reply: 19.

The length of stay in the facility:

- up to 6 months: 48 juveniles;
- between 6 months and 1 year: 46;
- between 1 year and 3 years: 63;
- between 3 and 5 years: 19;
- over 5 years: 12;
- no reply: 21.

6.3.4. Educators in youth educational centres and correctional facilities

In total, 108 teachers working in juvenile institutions participated in the survey, 51 from youth educational centres and 57 from correctional facilities. A vast majority of them were pedagogues, educators, teachers, psychologists. The questionnaires were also completed by a guard, a resident hall director, chaplain – religious instructor, catechist, director, deputy director. The longest service period was 42 years, the shortest 2 months.

6.4. Description of the institutions surveyed

It total, the survey covered 35 penitentiary institutions, and in them – 556 adult convicts and pre-trial detainees and 164 educators, and 209 juveniles placed in youth educational centres and correctional facilities and 108 educators.

	Institution	Number of prisoners surveyed	Number of educators surveyed
1.	Penitentiary facility in Nowogard	28	4
2.	Penitentiary facility in Wrocław no. 1	38	6
3.	Penitentiary facility in Bydgoszcz Fordon	8	4
4.	Penitentiary facility in Gorzów Wielkopolski	7	6
5.	Penitentiary facility in Tarnów	35	10
6.	Penitentiary facility in Rzeszów	25	5
7.	Penitentiary facility in Lubliniec division Herby	46	13
8.	Penitentiary facility in Racibórz	38	16
9.	Penitentiary facility in Pińczów	44	10
10.	Penitentiary facility in Jastrzębie Zdrój	47	4
11.	Penitentiary facility in Brzeg	28	9
12.	Penitentiary facility in Krzywaniec	5	5
13.	Penitentiary facility in Kwidzyn	15	5
14.	Penitentiary facility in Hrubieszów	15	4
15.	Penitentiary facility in Gdańsk	47	37
16.	Detention centre in Warszawa-Służewiec	22	4
17.	Detention centre in Białystok	16	4
18.	Detention centre in Poznań	25	4
19.	Detention centre in Warszawa Białołęka	68	13
20.	Racibórz – Correctional Facility and Juvenile Shelter	10	8
21.	Warszawa Falenica – Correctional Facility and Juvenile Shelter	8	9

	Institution	Number of prisoners surveyed	Number of educators surveyed
22.	Białystok – Correctional Facility	1	4
23.	Nowe nad Wisłą – Correctional Facility	8	4
24.	Grodzisk Wielkopolski – Correctional Facility	7	13
25.	Mrozy – Correctional Facility and Juvenile Shelter	6	9
26.	Świecie nad Wisłą – Correctional Facility	10	5
27.	Trzemeszno – Correctional Facility	5	4
28.	Szubin – Correctional Facility – Youth Educational Centre	5	0
29.	Youth Educational Centre – Wrocław	16	10
30.	Youth Educational Centre – Kuźnia Raciborska	10	2
31.	Youth Educational Centre – Lubaczów	24	7
32.	Youth Educational Centre – Łódź	30	5
33.	Youth Educational Centre – Jaworze	35	5
34.	Youth Educational Centre – Sobótka	21	11
35.	Youth Educational Centre – Krupski Młyn	13	11

The selected penitentiary facilities included all types and kinds: facilities for recidivists, individuals serving a first penalty of imprisonment, for young adults, of a closed, semi-open and open type. The survey covered convicted persons serving a penalty in the therapeutic system, programmed impacting and standard system.

The selected post-criminal isolation units are located throughout Poland.

6.5. Survey results

6.5.1. Prisoners in penitentiary institutions: penitentiary facilities and detention centres

The questionnaires (in a way that allows interpretation of the results) were completed by a total of 556 prisoners, including 451 (81.1 %) convicts, 19 (3.4 %) pre-trial detainees, 19 (3.4 %) individuals having simultaneously a status of convict and pre-trial detainee, 56 (10.1 %) individuals gave no reply.

The first question related to the attitude to belief, the replies were as follows:

- 193 respondents identified themselves as practicing believers (which is 34.71 % of the study population);
- 245 – as non-practicing believers (44.06 %);
- 67 – as non-believers (12 %);
- 21 – as searching for faith (3.78 %),
- 5 respondents indicated the answer "other" (0.9 %); adding: "at the beginning of practicing," "questioning," "believes in Satan," "ready for a change of belief after getting to know it";
- 19 respondents did not reply to that question (3.41 %).

When asked about their religion, 368 respondents declared Christianity in the Roman Catholic variant (which is 66.19 % of the study population); 9 (1.62 %) – Eastern Orthodox; 10 (1.8 %) – Protestant; 6 – Islam; 4 – Jehovah's Witnesses; 2 – Buddhism and 1 – Judaism. In turn, 88 (15.83 %) respondents indicated "other" (most frequently by stating that he or she does not believe in any religion or by generally stating – "Christianity"), and 49 (8.81 %) respondents gave no reply.

The right image of prisoner religiosity requires the respondents' own assessment as to any changes in their religiosity during penitentiary isolation:

- for 86 respondents (15.5 %), religion and belief **became more important** during incarceration;
- for 28 respondents (5 %) – religion **took on importance only in prison**;
- for 254 inmates (45.7 %) – religion **has the same importance**;
- simultaneously for 62 inmates (11.2 %), it **is less important** during incarceration;
- and for 56 inmates (10.1 %), it **lost importance completely**;
- 31 respondents (5.6 %) indicated an answer "other," most often without explaining their position. Exceptionally, there were annotations "meaningless," "no change";
- 30 respondents (5.4 %) did not reply to that question.

The follow-up questions related to a change of confession before and during incarceration. As regards the situation before incarceration, 508 (91.4 %) respondents replied that **they had not changed confession before incarceration**, 24 (4.3 %) gave no reply, and only 22 (3.9 %) respondents changed confession, where 6 Roman Catholics indicated another confession and 3 respondents a specific change, declaring faith in Satan, Hitler, Jesus. Two respondents converted to Roman Catholicism before incarceration.

During incarceration, 14 (2.5 %) respondents changed confession. Some explained that they were in search of confession, others converted from Roman Catholicism to Islam, Jehovah's Witnesses, Buddhism. Three respondents converted to Roman Catholicism.

The overall picture of prisoners' religiosity also consists of information about religious feasts and rituals particularly important to them. Not surprisingly, a vast majority point to Christmas (sometimes called "Christmas Eve") and Easter (respectively, 353 – 63.5 % and 241 – 43.3 % indications). Moreover, mention was also made of the Assumption of the Blessed Virgin Mary, Corpus Christi, All Saints' Day. Less frequent mentions included Ash Wednesday, Palm Sunday, Epiphany, Pentecost, the feast of Christ the King, Divine Mercy and the Stations of the Cross. Some stated that all church holidays were important, while others took the opposite view – no religious holidays matter during incarceration. Notably, one comment included all the following: "Rosz Haszana, Jom Kipur, Sukot, Szmini Aceret, Simchat Tora, Chanuka, Purim, Pesach, Jom Ha Szoa, Jom Ha Zikkaron, Jom Ha Acmaut, Lag Ba Omer, Jom Jeruszalim, Szawuot, Tisza Be Aw, Tu Be Aw". Its author was the only respondent who indicated Judaism as the professed religion. Others indicated Ramadan (2), Pentecostal holidays (1) and Nirvana Day (1). An Orthodox respondent pointed to "Christmas, Easter, Spas, Wołosieka", similarly to his fellow believer. It is hard to take seriously a statement about the 11th November holiday or Hitler and Goebbels' birthdays, New Year's Eve, name days and birthdays. It should be noted that, when choosing Christmas (and sometimes Easter) as the important feasts, many prisoners added that the family aspect pointed towards their choice.

As regards religious rituals and practices that prisoners deem to be important, references were most frequently made to baptism, Holy Communion, Mass attendance, Christmas Eve. Less frequently, the prisoners indicated: prayer, praying the rosary, fasting, sharing the wafer, confession, Midnight Mass, Christmas-time pastoral visit, reading the Bible. The prisoners occasionally pointed to the Stations of the Cross, going to church, sacrament of marriage, Confirmation, Rorate Mass, days of recollection, blessing of food, funerals and even dressing the Christmas tree. The exceptional mentions included

Zen meditation, Ramadan fast, chasing away evil spirits. One prisoner stated that rituals divide people. Some comments could be considered provocative, such as "burning pyres, kabbalah, human sacrifice", others bordered on the mysterious: "National and International Congress". Simultaneously, a significant number of respondents (47 – 8.5 %) claimed that no rituals were important to them or were important in prison.

The general part of the questionnaire concluded with questions about procedures related to religious freedom in penitentiary facilities and detention centres.

Responding to whether they were questioned about their confession or religion during incarceration, as many as 117 (21 %) respondents replied **yes**, 34 respondents **notified the administration about it**, and 383 (68.88 %) respondents indicated that **no such questions were asked**.

Responding to whether during the so-called informational interview they were informed about the possibility of performing religious practices, only 194 (34.89 %) respondents replied **yes**. As many as 328 (59 %) respondents indicated that they were **not informed** about the possibilities of performing religious practices (25 respondents gave no reply, 2 others could not recall). Importantly, one prisoner indicated that none of the penitentiary institutions in which he was incarcerated (he enumerated 6 detention centres and a penitentiary facility) informed him about that possibility.

6.5.2. Roman Catholic prisoners

Another part of the questionnaire was devoted to the religious practices of Roman Catholic believers. The questions focuses on three distinct periods – incarceration in a penitentiary institution before the pandemic, during the pandemic and the time outside. That part was completed by 421 prisoners (75.7 %), who can be considered prisoners of the Roman Catholic denomination (not all of them replied to all the questions).

6.5.2.1. Catholics before the pandemic while serving a sentence or in detention

	Every day		**Once per week**		**Once per month**		**Several times per year**		**Never**		**Don't know**	
Attending Holy Mass	**1**	0.2 %	**76**	18.1 %	**46**	10.9 %	90	21.4 %	**119**	28.3 %	**42**	10 %
Listening to Holy Mass on the radio or other source	**9**	2.1 %	**72**	17.1 %	**22**	5.2 %	69	16.4 %	**148**	35.2 %	**55**	13.1 %
Listening to or watching religious programmes	**11**	2.6 %	**42**	10 %	**31**	7.4 %	72	17.1 %	**182**	43.2 %	**39**	9.3 %
Taking Holy Communion	**1**	0.2 %	**29**	6.9 %	**27**	6.4 %	66	15.7 %	**183**	43.5 %	**61**	14.5 %
Confession	**0**	0	**10**	2.4 %	**33**	7.8 %	80	19 %	**182**	43.2 %	**61**	14.5 %
Morning / evening prayer	**162**	38.5 %	**30**	7.1 %	**11**	2.6 %	52	12.5 %	**81**	19.2 %	**40**	9..5 %
Prayer before/after a meal	**32**	7.6 %	**10**	2.4 %	**5**	1.2 %	18	4.3 %	**243**	57.7 %	**47**	11.2 %
Reading the Bible independently or in a group	**26**	6.2 %	**27**	6.4 %	**26**	6.2 %	69	16.4 %	**158**	37.5 %	**60**	14.3 %
Reading religious press and books	**17**	4 %	**21**	5 %	**28**	6.7 %	**95**	22.6 %	**157**	37.3 %	**58**	13.8 %
Talk to a chaplain	**7**	1.7 %	**29**	6.9 %	**30**	7.1 %	**93**	22.1 %	**148**	35.2 %	**65**	15.4 %

On the question of wearing **a cross, a medallion or any other faith symbol**, the prisoners replied as follows:

- 206 (48.3 %) – yes;
- 165 (39.2 %) – no;
- 7 (1.7 %) – don't know;
- 43 (20.2 %) – no reply.

On the question of the **possession of a cross, a medallion or any other faith symbol in the cell**, the prisoners replied as follows:

- 296 (70.3 %) – yes;
- 83 (19.7 %) – no;
- 41 (9.7 %) – no reply.

On the question of **observing the recommended or imposed fasting**, the prisoners replied as follows:

- 107 (25.4 %) – yes;
- 141 (33.5 %) – no;
- 75 (17.8 %) – don't know;
- 29 (6.9 %) – no reply.

On the question of **accepting a Christmas-time pastoral visit**, the prisoners replied as follows:

- 101 (24 %) – yes;
- 261 (62 %) – no;
- 27 (6.4 %) – don't know;
- 31 (7.4 %) – no reply.

The question whether **the practicing of any of the above activities was impossible or difficult** was answered as follows:

- 142 (33.7 %) – yes;
- 180 (42.8 %) – no;
- 64 (15.2 %) – don't know;
- 35 (8.3 %) – no reply.

When asked to indicate **which practices the respondents had specifically in mind**, they most frequently pointed to the following: Holy Mass, Christmas-time pastoral visit, talk to a chaplain, confession and fasting. They also occasionally mentioned: Christmas Eve, Midnight Mass, group meetings, the Light-Life Movement, the Corpus Christi procession, the Stations of the Cross, watching/listening to the service on TV/the radio, lack of access to the free Catholic press, the blessing of food, and even prayer. One prisoner indicated a pilgrimage to the Jasna Góra Monastery.

In the opinion of the prisoners, **the difficulties were due to**:

- legal regulations – which was indicated by 38 prisoners (9 %);
- lack of individual consent from the prison director – 43 prisoners (10.2 %);
- technical and organizational obstacles – 104 prisoners (24.7 %);
- dislike from fellow prisoners – 29 prisoners (6.9 %);
- lack of time – 15 prisoners (3.6 %);
- lack of persistence – 15 prisoners (3.6 %);
- others – 30 prisoners (7.1 %), indicating: the priest failed to appear, difficulties in getting a prisoner to the chapel, prisoners talking in the chapel, "they don't

take prisoners using prison slang to the Mass," frequent transportations, "holding services at times that interfere with work." One prisoner noted that "On the premises of the Detention Centre in Warszawa Białołęka, in connection with an unlawful ordinance, the Director forces prisoners to wear camp uniforms (euphemistically called prison clothing) outside the premises of the penitentiary facility, as a result, convicts who refuse to unlawfully wear these uniforms are denied access to services." It should be added that, at various points in the questionnaire, prisoners also indicated little involvement of chaplains and, relatively often, a reluctant attitude of Prison Service officers and other staff members.

Another question was about other practices that the prisoners missed. They primarily indicated: the wafer, a Christmas-time pastoral visit, a meeting with a priest.

The questionnaire contained a question about their reason for attending Mass on the prison premises. The prisoners wrote about the need, faith, tradition or habit, a desire to receive Holy Communion, prayer, a need to have contact with God, a substitute for freedom (as the prisoner attended Mass at liberty), a need for quiet, a promise made to a loved one, curiosity, 'to kill time', an opportunity to get out of the cell. One prisoner wrote: "The purpose of screening Jewish cells, recording them for later implementation".

The last set of questions concerned practices typically performed at liberty (and on the prison premises only in exceptional circumstances).

The share of prisoners in religious practices performed **at that time at liberty** (having obtained a temporary release):

- Baptism – 21 (5 %) respondents took part, 241 (57.2 %) – did not as there was no such occasion, 7 (1.7 %) – did not take part because a prisoner did not want to, 96 (22.9 %) – did not take part because a prisoner did not obtain consent to leave the prison;
- First Communion – 25 (5.9 %) respondents took part, 233 (55.3 %) – did not as there was no such occasion, 16 (3.8 %) – did not take part because a prisoner did not want to, 87 (20.7 %) – did not take part because a prisoner did not obtain consent to leave the prison;
- Confirmation – 22 (5.2 %) respondents took part, 263 (62.5 %) – did not as there was no such occasion, 11 (2.6 %) – did not take part because a prisoner did not want to, 65 (15.4 %) – did not take part because a prisoner did not obtain consent to leave the prison;
- Church wedding – 17 (4 %) respondents took part, 251 (59.6 %) – did not as there was no such occasion, 17 (4 %) – did not take part because a prisoner did not want to, 78 (18.5 %) – did not take part because a prisoner did not obtain consent to leave the prison;

- Catholic funeral – 48 (11.4 %) respondents took part, 218 (51.8 %) – did not as there was no such occasion, 16 (3.8 %) – did not because a prisoner did not want to, 88 (20.9 %) – did not take part because a prisoner did not obtain consent to leave the prison.

The share of prisoners in religious practices performed on **the prison premises**:

- Baptism – 13 (3.1 %) respondents took part, 358 (85 %) – did not as there was no such occasion, 1 (0.2 %) – did not because a prisoner did not want to, no one ticked the answer that a prisoner did not take part because of a lack of consent to leave the prison;
- First Communion – 21 (5 %) respondents took part, 344 (81.7 %) – did not as there was no such occasion, 0 – did not because a prisoner did not want to, 0 – did not take part because a prisoner did not obtain consent to leave the prison;
- Confirmation – 29 (6.9 %) respondents took part, 344 (81.7 %) – did not as there was no such occasion, 0 – did not because a prisoner did not want to, 0 – did not take part because a prisoner did not obtain consent to leave the prison;
- Church wedding – 9 (2.1 %) respondents took part, 354 (84.1 %) – did not as there was no such occasion, 0 – did not because a prisoner did not want to, 0 – did not take part because a prisoner did not obtain consent to leave the prison;
- Catholic funeral – 18 (4.3 %) respondents took part, 344 (81.7 %) – did not as there was no such occasion, 0 – did not because a prisoner did not want to, 0 – did not take part because a prisoner did not obtain consent to leave the prison.

A perusal of the data on attendance at religious ceremonies on the prison premises may give rise to doubts as to whether the respondents understood the questions correctly (in particular, looking at the declared participation in a Catholic funeral – 18 individuals!). It must be admitted that the Polish reality is that baptisms of prisoners, their First Communion, Confirmation and – exceptionally – marriage ceremonies do take place in prisons.

Prisoners were also requested to **evaluate the change in the frequency of religious practices.** The following replies were obtained:

- the option "practice more frequently outside" was indicated by 175 Catholic prisoners (41.6 %);
- the option "practice more frequently in a penitentiary facility" – 52 Catholic prisoners (12.4 %);
- "don't know" – indicated by 122 Catholic prisoners (29 %).

The explanations given by the respondents are worth quoting:

- in the first group, the comments included organizational limitations in penitentiary facilities and detention centres, the need to sign up for the Mass in advance, limited accessibility of chaplains, dislike from fellow prisoners, no need to participate in practices in a penitentiary institution, a lack of hope, the family and tradition were the main reasons for the participation in religious practices outside;
- more frequent religious practice during incarceration was explained by having more time, a stronger need for God, trust that God will grant the wishes, getting closer to God or belief, reflection over one's own life.

6.5.2.2. *Catholics during the pandemic while serving a sentence or in detention*

	Every day		**Once per week**		**Once per month**		**Several times per year**		**Never**		**Don't know**	
Attending Holy Mass	**1**	0.2 %	**53**	26.6 %	**36**	8.6 %	**68**	16.2 %	**180**	42.8 %	**46**	10.9 %
Listening to Holy Mass on the radio or other source	**9**	2.1 %	**77**	18.3 %	**24**	5.7 %	**64**	15.2 %	**168**	39.9 %	**47**	11.2 %
Listening to or watching religious programmes	**11**	2.6 %	**46**	10.9 %	**32**	7.6 %	**62**	14.7 %	**201**	47.7 %	**36**	8.6 %
Taking Holy Communion	**1**	0.2 %	**23**	5.5 %	**18**	4.3 %	**57**	13.5 %	**229**	54.4 %	**49**	11.6 %
Confession	**0**	0	**9**	2.1 %	**22**	5.2 %	**70**	16.6 %	**220**	52.3 %	**51**	12.1 %
Morning / evening prayer	**172**	40.9 %	**24**	5.7 %	**13**	3.1 %	**36**	8.6 %	**105**	24.9 %	**36**	8.6 %
Prayer before/after a meal	**36**	8.6 %	**11**	2.6 %	**4**	1 %	**25**	2.9 %	**252**	59.9 %	**45**	10.7 %
Reading the Bible	**34**	8.1 %	**28**	6.7 %	**29**	6.9 %	**63**	15 %	**174**	41.3 %	**55**	13.1 %
Reading religious press and books	**21**	5 %	**36**	8.6 %	**34**	8.1 %	**80**	19 %	**167**	39.7 %	**48**	11.4 %
Talk to a chaplain	**6**	1.4 %	**27**	6.4 %	**21**	5 %	**71**	16.9 %	**196**	46.6 %	**58**	13.8 %

When asked to what extent pandemic-related restrictions impeded religious life in the penitentiary facility or the detention centre, the prisoners replied that they did not experience such impediments (most often it was the case with non-practicing ones) or replied that such impediments did not apply to them because one can always pray or read the Bible and God is everywhere. Others pointed to specific practices that were made more difficult – most frequently, the Holy Mass, meetings and contact with a priest, and going to confession. Importantly, without being asked to make any comments in that regards, the respondents eagerly added that they understood the pandemic situation and knew that also religious practices became more limited outside. Moreover, some indicated that although Holy Masses were not held, they were aired on the prison radio. One prisoner's statement is distinctive: "The accessibility to religious meetings, religious press, sacraments, Holy Mass, talks to a priest vary depending on a specific penitentiary facility. Surely, the pandemic made access to the above much more difficult, but I know from experience that the reason why prisoners cannot be brought to Mass and others is often staff shortages in the Prison Service. The access is regular in this facility, but I haven't had a chance to get hold of, for example, *Good Thief* yet."

6.5.2.3. Participation in practices at liberty

	Everyday		**Once per week**		**Once per month**		**Several times per year**		**Never**		**Don't know**	
Attending Holy Mass	**8**	1.9 %	**100**	23.8 %	**42**	10 %	**98**	23.3 %	**68**	16.2 %	**27**	6.4 %
Listening to Holy Mass on the radio or other source	**8**	1.9 %	**47**	11.2 %	**21**	5 %	**63**	15 %	**181**	43 %	**45**	10.7 %
Listening to or watching religious programmes	**8**	1.9 %	**41**	9.7 %	**22**	5.2 %	**70**	16.6 %	**179**	42.5 %	**49**	11.6 %
Taking Holy Communion	**1**	0.2 %	**49**	11.6 %	**48**	11.4 %	**97**	23 %	**109**	25.9 %	**64**	15.2 %
Confession	**2**	0.5 %	**17**	4 %	**48**	11.4 %	**121**	28.7 %	**109**	25.9 %	**69**	16.4 %
Morning / evening prayer	**141**	33.5 %	**34**	8.1 %	**12**	2.9 %	**53**	12.6 %	**99**	23.5 %	**34**	8.1 %
Prayer before/after a meal	**34**	8.1 %	**10**	2.4 %	**8**	1.9 %	**31**	7.4 %	**231**	54.9 %	**46**	11 %
Reading the Bible	**24**	5.7 %	**26**	6.2 %	**23**	5.5 %	**76**	18.1 %	**167**	39.7 %	**51**	12.1 %
Reading religious press and books	**16**	3.8 %	**25**	5.9 %	**20**	4.8 %	**90**	21.4 %	**175**	41.6 %	**45**	10.7 %
Talk to a chaplain	**3**	0.7 %	**24**	5.7 %	**32**	7.6 %	**113**	26.8 %	**137**	32.5 %	**62**	14.7 %

When asked if and to what extent, in the opinion of a respondent, his or her practiced religion put him or her at a disadvantage during incarceration as compared to prisoners of other denominations, the replies were as follows:

- no – 319 (75.8 %);
- yes – 45 (10.7 %), pointing to ridiculing, disrespect, and being made fun of by officers and fellow prisoners – several prisoners provided the above explanation, moreover, an indication was also made of the lack of consent from fellow prisoners to watch Mass on television and an opinion was expressed that "The Government of the Republic of Poland discriminates against and delegalizes my religious practices, my denomination and prophets."

6.5.3. Prisoners of other confessions

In essence, 51 respondents (9.2 %) showed interest in Part III of the questionnaire, which was addressed to persons of other confessions and religions.

When asked about celebrating the religious holidays of their confession, some prisoners replied that they did not celebrate them at all, others did it in the cell or on their own. Occasional responses included: "fasting during Ramadan", praying in the chapel, eating meals together, meeting with co-followers, meetings, writing icons, talking to a clergyman (Pop), reading Scripture. One respondent wrote: "I got baptized by Protestant rites in the Penitentiary Facility in Lublin."

When asked to identify **practices or rituals that were not possible**, but which were important to the prisoner, a mention was made of: "pork-free" diet, "liturgies", meetings with persons of the same belief, prayer with an Imam, Memorial of Jesus Christ's death, Protestant services, pilgrimage. A relatively large proportion wrote that no ritual or practice was missing in the prison. When asked to identify the reason for the absence of the indicated practices, the respondents cited a failure to hold such practices on the premises of a penitentiary facility or a detention centre, a lack of chaplain, organizational obstacles, a lack of tolerance, a lack of consent from prison authorities, or wrote "don't know".

On the question of the **possession of symbols of their confession or religion in the cell**, the prisoners responded as follows:

- 22 (43.1 %) – **yes**;
- 24 (47 %) – **no**.

On the question of **contact with a representative of their confession or religion** while serving a penalty of imprisonment or being in detention, the prisoners responded as follows:

- 32 (62.7 %) – **yes**;
- 14 (27.5 %) – **no**.

Responding to whether, in their opinion, they were forced to participate in the practices or rituals of another religion or denomination, 7 prisoners (out of 39 prisoners who replied to that question, which is 18 % of the responding persons and out of 51 identifying themselves as having a different belief/religion, which is 13.7 %) replied yes, citing, among others, "When I didn't have the radio and television equipment, I had to listen to the Catholic Mass on the prison radio. The meals served on Catholic feasts are subordinated to their belief", "No one forced me directly, but in multi-person cells, I was an observer of practices that irritated me greatly", "When I went to a micro AA therapy, I had to pray to Jesus, although I am an Islamist."

Responding to whether, **in their opinion, their own religion put them at a disadvantage during incarceration as compared to followers of other confessions or religions**:

- 14 (27.5 %) prisoners said yes, indicating harassment, a failure to understand Islam, "Islamophobia", or formulated a belief that "Catholic priests are the only clergymen who come here";
- 32 (62.7 %) prisoners said no.

The prisoners were unable or unwilling to indicate which regulations, related to penitentiary isolation, were particularly burdensome as regards their practiced religion or confession. Only the regulations on fasting and access to chaplains were indicated. At the same time, according to the prisoners of that group, the restrictions related to the pandemic did not in principle (additionally) hinder religious life in the penitentiary facility/detention centre, but there were no more meetings during that period.

When asked about practices and rituals they observed at liberty, the prisoners from that group indicated: "all", Easter, Christmas, Days of Recollection, meetings with co-followers, services in the Orthodox church, baptism, pilgrimages, fasting, "Commemoration of the death of Jesus Christ", National Congress, International Congress, congregation meetings.

6.5.4. Non-believing prisoners

As regards non-believers, the applicable part of the questionnaire was completed by 83 persons (although they did not reply to all the questions).

Responding to whether, in their opinion, they were forced to take part in any religious practices or rituals, a vast majority replied – no; there were only

5 positive replies. The following statement by one of the prisoners may serve as a specific diagnosis: "Yes. The diets are suited to Catholics and on Catholic feasts the meals are served according to the Catholic tradition. Sharing the wafer at Christmas, etc. If there is no TV-set in the cell, then I am forced to listen to the prison radio, and on Sunday, Roman Catholic Mass takes half of the programme." The following comment may be cause for concern: "In a semi-open unit for recidivists, to have a family visit (wife, children, treat), you had to attend religious meetings in an open-type prison for recidivists, that's why I had no chance for a third visit, despite endless willingness."

Responding to whether, in their opinion, **their lack of denomination put them at a disadvantage during incarceration as compared to believers**:

- 70 respondents of that group (84.3 %) said **no**;
- 7 respondents (8.4 %) said **yes**.

One prisoner made the following comment: "Believers have meetings on their holy days, they create themselves as humble, honest, innocent persons who have learned from their mistakes and rigidly follow the Catholic religious canon. They try to create a contrast to others in behaviour. Non-believers are not as bad as the rest, unfortunately, they can't hold meetings on Sunday to have a talk." Another one made the following comment: "At first I wanted to indicate no, but yes, there is one thing. Believers can leave their cell for a while and change the surroundings (the chapel). I don't have that additional possibility." Another prisoner noted that "A large number of newspapers and books in the library explore Catholic religious themes." By contrast, note should be taken of the following view: "Year by year, attitudes towards belief are changing and non-believers are treated just like believers."

In the opinion of non-believing prisoners, the pandemic did not change much in their situation as non-believers.

6.5.5. Educators in penitentiary institutions: penitentiary facilities and detention centres

Educators completed 164 questionnaires. Responding to whether prisoners were willing to "admit" their religion, the educators replied as follows:

- **yes** –123 (75 %);
- **no** – 33 (20.1 %);
- 8 (4.9 %) – no reply.

In their comments on this question, the educators most frequently indicated that it is an individual matter for prisoners and that some prisoners are willing to talk about their religion (most freely in one-to-one conversations or when declaring their willingness to participate in a particular event), while others are not. One educator noted that religious issues are often treated merely as tools, e.g., in connection with a diet, leaving the cell on the occasion of meetings of religious groups.

Responding to whether prisoners wear religious symbols or place them in "their" part of the cell, the educators replied as follows:

- 132 (80.5 %) – **yes** (these are most frequently medallions worn by prisoners, some hang crosses or holy pictures in their part of the cell, moreover, one survey stated that some convicts make icons of saints);
- 24 (14.6 %) – **no**;
- 8 (4.9 %) – no reply.

It is worth quoting some disturbing comments: "The convicts accept the ban on hanging pictures on the residential cell walls", "They often write requests to be able to hold religious symbols (chains)" or "upon consent from the director".

Responding to whether, in their opinion, prisoners **could freely practice their religion before the pandemic**, the educators replied as follows:

- **yes** – 151 (92.1 %) respondents, highlighting that there were no difficulties, two questionnaires had a clarification that freely under conditions of isolation. An important opinion was also given: "Rather yes, but the predominance of Catholic practices marginalizes other religious movements";
- **no** – 7 (4.3 %) respondents: "Definitely not. The priest is here only once a week during Mass";
- 6 (3.7 %) no reply.

The following questions concerned the needs and difficulties related to the practice of different religions.

On the question of difficulties in the case of Roman Catholic confession, positive replies were given by only 10 (7 %) respondents, whereas 149 (90.9 %) thought there were none, 4 (2.4 %) respondents failed to give a reply. Two comments in justification of negative reply are worth citing: "The weekly mass cannot be attended by everyone (because of groups, associates [conflicts]); it would be advisable to increase the number Masses for prisoners", "Priests rarely initiate meetings on ordinary Sundays. On feast days there is no such problem." The surveyed educators indicated that prisoners declare a wish to attend Mass or go to confession and they have that opportunity. They did not receive any information about other ('additional', 'extraordinary') religious needs of Roman Catholic prisoners.

Another question concerned possible difficulties in practicing other religions or confessions. On that question, 18 (11 %) respondents **confirmed** the existence of such difficulties, 140 (85.4 %) – **denied** it, and 6 – 3.7 % failed to give a reply. This comment is given as a clarification to the answer about the difficulties: "Problems with the availability of representatives of other confessions". Rather briefly (and somewhat unprofessionally), the respondents also made the following comments: "prayer at a specific time for an hour", "It's not a hotel", "Usually it's Muslims", "Islam ban from CZSW [Central Board of the Prison Service]". When asked to indicate which religion or practice caused the mentioned difficulties, the surveyed penitentiary staff pointed to: Islam, "pentecostalists", "jehovah's" [Polish: jehowi], Eastern Orthodoxy and Hinduism. For these confessions, it was difficult to make contact with a religious/spiritual representative. There was also a statement: "Muslims. They need so many objects for religious rituals, which may be a nuisance to their cellmates."

One educator raised another issue: "Muslim representatives [illegible] verify the apparent affiliation of prisoners very quickly by asking a few simple questions about Islam. It turns out that the prisoners' affiliation remains only in the realm of (illegible)."

The next questions assessed the situation of non-believers – whether they were forced to take part in specific religious practices. 14 (8.5 %) surveyed educators responded **yes**, 143 (87.2 %) – **no**; 7 respondents gave no answer. In particular, listening to broadcasts of Mass (e.g. "Mass on Sunday morning on the prison radio (with a red card) – change of work organization in the facility") was mentioned as an example of a forced situation. Attention should also be devoted to a comment: "They are not forced, religious practices take place in separate rooms", which may be compared with a comment by another educator: "Some convicts, depending on a selected diet, fast on Fridays, even if they do not identify with the Catholic confession. On Sundays, a mass is broadcast via the prison radio, which is some form of (illegible) dominant religion in this latitude."

The educators were divided in their views on the assessment of limitations introduced in connection with the pandemic. Some believed that those limitations did not affect the possibility of practicing religion. This may illustrated by such comments as "nothing is missing and has not been missing" or "each inmate has had the opportunity to benefit from religious practices according to their needs". Others pointed out that the possibility of attending Mass was limited, but it was broadcast on the prison radio, while later it was celebrated under a sanitary regime. Contact with a chaplain and community meetings involved more difficulty. As one respondent pointed out, "Quantitative restrictions during the celebration of Mass. Representatives of other religions not allowed on prison premises. Only the Catholic chaplain was allowed to perform practices." Another educator pointed out that Jehovah's Witnesses meetings took place on Skype. One questionnaire drew attention to "negative dimension" for many prisoners of restrictions in the sphere of religious practice. Many surveyed educators additionally noted that prisoners did not complain about restrictions in this area, some of them showed full understanding.

Given the experience of that study group, educators were asked for suggestions for changes to existing legislation (including – organizational) that would facilitate the full respect of religious freedom in penitentiary facilities and detention centres. **A vast majority (130 educators) replied that no changes were necessary** – "everything works fine", all the more so as one respondent pointed out: "religious life is connected with spirituality and may be practiced on an individual basis." The only comments with a sharper edge were as follows: "Cooperation, contact with other religions should be established", "More frequent opportunities to attend Mass", "Priests should be more accessible to prisoners. One Mass per week is not enough."

The problem of incarceration of juveniles (under the age of 18), being under parental authority, has made it necessary to establish a practice in penitentiary centres and detention centres regarding the participation of young persons in religious rituals and the consent to such participation. As many as 42 (25.6 %) respondents failed to answer the question regarding this issue. As for those who did, a vast majority indicated that their institution incarcerated only legal adults. A large proportion indicated that the prisoner (even a minor) decides independently on the practiced religion. In two questionnaires, the prison director was indicated as the decision-maker, in one – the cultural-educational officer, another one pointed to "the disposing organ", others to a priest, chaplain or a representative of another confession (sic!). Two questionnaires had the answer that the decision was up to the minor's legal guardian. One may be well surprised by the ignorance of law shown by such comment: "No minors – there are young adults."

6.5.6. Juveniles in post-criminal isolation centres: youth educational centres and correctional facilities

The questionnaires were completed in total by 209 juveniles placed in youth educational centres and correctional facilities.

On the question of their attitude to belief, the juveniles replied as follows:

- **practicing believer**: 62 respondents, which was 29.66 % of the study population;
- **non-practicing believer**: 79, which was 37.8 % of the study population;
- **non-believer**: 48, which was 22.96 % of the study population;
- **searching for faith**: 5, which was 2.39 % of the study population;
- **other**: 7, which was 3.35 % of the study population; the respondents indicated: belief in myself, atheist, belief in the universe, satanist, "I believe that there is nothing out there, and even if there is something, I don't care";
- no reply was given in 8 questionnaires.

The juveniles declared the following confessions:

- Catholicism: 105 (50.7 %) surveyed juveniles;
- Eastern Orthodoxy: none;
- Protestantism: 2 juveniles;
- Jehovah's Witness: 1 juvenile;
- Islam: 3 juveniles;
- Judaism: none;
- Buddhism: 2 juveniles;
- other: 59 (28.2 %) juveniles, indicating most frequently in general terms "Christianity", much less frequently – "none", "none of the above", exceptionally: Satanism, pastafarianism, belief in oneself;
- 37 (17.7 %) juveniles gave no answer.

On the question of thc dynamics of faith during incarceration, the juveniles replied that, compared to the period before their incarceration, their faith and religion:

- had become more important for them – 28 (13.4 %);
- had become less important for them – 27 (12.9 %);
- had lost its importance completely – 34 (16.3 %);
- had taken on importance only in that place – 7 (3.3 %);
- was equally important – 89 (42.6 %);
- other – 16 (7.7 %);
- 7 (3.3 %) respondents gave no reply.

A clear downward trend could be observed for juveniles. Overall, **there were more juveniles for whom faith lost its meaning (partially or completely) than those for whom it took on importance (greater or any at all), respectively, 61 (29.2 %) and 35 (16.7 %).**

The juveniles were also asked about any change of confession before incarceration. This fact was confirmed by 19 (9.1 %) juveniles (Satanism was indicated twice, Buddhism once), 180 (86.1 %) provided a negative answer.

Another question concerned a change of confession during incarceration. 11 (5.3 %) juveniles confirmed the change (to Satanism, from Satanism to Christianity, to Buddhism), with 183 (87.6 %) negations and 15 (7.2 %) no-replies. As regards the acceptance of confession, 17 (8.1 %) confirmed the fact (pointing to Satanism, Catholicism and "Confirmation") while 162 (77.5 %) respondents negated it. In turn, 30 (14.4 %) respondents gave no reply.

The juveniles were asked to name religious feasts and rituals they deemed important. The most frequent mentions included Christmas (or Christmas Eve) – 126 (60.3 %), Easter – 52 (24.9 %); some also mentioned Corpus Christi and All Saints' Day. New Year's Eve was also named several times. Some indicated that no feasts were important, very few respondents said that they all were important. Rituals that are important to juveniles included Mass (30 indications – 14 %), prayer (35 – 16.7 %), the Stations of the Cross, confession, confirmation, Holy Communion, sacraments in general and the blessing of food. Baptism and marriage were occasionally mentioned. In a similar vein, some respondents (47 – 22.5 %) stated that no sacraments and rituals were important. One made a comment: "None. I am forced to go to church. I live with the nuns."

Another question concerned participation in religious instruction during incarceration. The replies were as follows:

- 91 (43.5 %) – yes, it was my own choice;
- 27 (12.9 %) – yes, because my parents/guardians decided so;
- 31 (14.8 %) – yes, for other reasons (saying: because I want to, I've always attended religious instruction, because I have to – the nuns, "such is the compulsion", "not going does harm", "you cannot opt out", "compulsory lesson", "because we have to", "we have no choice", "no way out");
- 16 (7.7 %) – no, because it was my own choice;
- 1 – no, because my parents decided so;
- 2 – no, for other reasons (finished school, no religious instruction is provided);
- 41 (19.6 %) – no reply.

A few questions concerned formal issues. The first one was: Were you asked about your confession by the institution staff during your stay? The replies were as follows:

- yes – 85 (40.6 %) respondents;
- I told them myself – 11 (5.3 %);

- no – 58 (27.8 %);
- don't know – 48 (23 %);
- 7 respondents provided no reply.

Another question was: Were your parents or legal guardians asked about your confession by the institution staff during your stay? The replies were as follows:

- yes – 49 (23.4 %) respondents;
- they told them themselves – 3 respondents;
- no – 77 (36.8 %);
- don't know – 73 (34.9 %);
- 7 (3.3 %) respondents provided no reply.

Responding to whether during the informational interview (on admission) they were informed about the possibilities of participating in religious practices, the juveniles gave the following replies:

- yes – 118 (56.5 %);
- no – 44 (21.1 %);
- don't know – 35 (16.7 %);
- 11 (5.3 %) – no reply.

The next questions were addressed to individual groups, distinguished on the basis of confession: Roman Catholics, juveniles of different confessions and non-believers.

As regards Roman Catholics, the applicable part of the questionnaire was completed by 155 juveniles (although they did not reply to all the questions).

The Roman Catholic juveniles were asked about the following practices:

- **during their stay in an institution**:

	Every day		**Once per week**		**Once per month**		**Several times per year**		**Never**	
Attending Holy Mass	**1**	0.6 %	**51**	32.9 %	**8**	5.2 %	**49**	31.6 %	**35**	22.6 %
Listening to Holy Mass on the radio or other source	**1**	06 %	**6**	3.9 %	**10**	6.5 %	**10**	6.5 %	**116**	74.8 %
Listening to or watching religious programmes	**0**	0	**8**	5.2 %	**9**	5.8 %	**20**	12.9 %	**105**	67.7 %
Taking Holy Communion	**0**	0	**6**	3.9 %	**26**	16.8 %	**60**	38.7 %	**51**	32.9 %
Confession	**3**	1.9 %	**15**	9.7 %	**17**	11 %	**52**	33.5 %	**56**	36.1 %

	Every day		Once per week		Once per month		Several times per year		Never	
Morning / evening prayer	**19**	12.3 %	**14**	9 %	**13**	8.4 %	**15**	9.7 %	**81**	52.3 %
Prayer before/after a meal	**6**	3.9 %	**5**	3.2 %	**5**	3.2 %	**13**	8.4 %	**113**	72.9 %
Reading the Bible independently or in a group	**2**	1.3 %	**11**	7.1 %	**11**	7.1 %	**22**	14.2 %	**98**	63.2 %
Reading religious press and books independently or in a group	**5**	3.2 %	**7**	4.5 %	**8**	5.2 %	**11**	7.1 %	**113**	72.9 %
Talk to a chaplain	**14**	9 %	**30**	19.4 %	**12**	7.7 %	**30**	19.4 %	**58**	37.4 %

– **outside the institution** (e.g., on furlough, on leave):

	Every day		Once per week		Once per month		Several times per year		Never	
Attending Holy Mass	**8**	5.2 %	**35**	22.6 %	**9**	5.8 %	**38**	24.5 %	**46**	29.7 %
Listening to Holy Mass on the radio or other source	**6**	3.9 %	**7**	4.5 %	**2**	1.3 %	**10**	6.5 %	**110**	71 %
Listening to or watching religious programmes	**4**	2.6 %	**9**	5.8 %	**4**	2.6 %	**10**	6.5 %	**108**	69.7 %
Taking Holy Communion	**7**	4.5 %	**7**	4.5 %	**18**	11.6 %	**40**	25.8 %	**64**	41.3 %
Confession	**7**	4.5 %	**15**	9.7 %	**14**	9 %	**38**	24.5 %	**62**	40 %
Morning / evening prayer	**19**	12.6 %	**7**	4.5 %	**12**	7.7 %	**14**	9 %	**83**	53.5 %
Prayer before/after a meal	**9**	5.8 %	**6**	3.9 %	**7**	4.5 %	**5**	3.2 %	**106**	68.4 %
Reading the Bible independently or in a group	**4**	2.6 %	**6**	3.9 %	**8**	5.2 %	**8**	5.2 %	**108**	69.7 %
Reading religious press and books independently or in a group	**8**	5.2 %	**1**	0.6 %	**7**	4.5 %	**8**	5.2 %	**112**	72.3 %
Talk to a chaplain	**10**	6.5 %	**10**	6.5 %	**10**	6.5 %	**21**	13.5 %	**83**	53.5 %

On the question of the reason for attending Mass on the premises of an institution, the juveniles pointed to the need to attend Mass, to pray, faith, tradition, a possibility to solve problems. However, they also stated it was because "everyone/colleagues do it", because "they have to" or "they tell you to", because "it pays off", "it won't hurt", "out of boredom".

Responding to whether **they wore a cross, medallion or any other faith symbol permanently during their stay in the institution**, 51 (32.9 %) juveniles responded **positively**, 98 (63.2 %) **negatively**, while 7 (4.5 %) provided no answer.

On the question of **the possession of a cross, picture or any other faith symbol in the room**, 68 (43.9 %) respondents said **yes**, 83 (53.5 %) said **no**, 5 (3.2 %) gave no answer.

On the question of **the observance of fasts** recommended by the Church, the following responses were obtained:

- yes – 53 (34.2 %) Catholic juveniles;
- no – I don't know what they are or when they take place: 27 (17.4 %);
- no – I don't feel the need: 54 (34.8 %);
- no – I don't have that option: 16 (10.3 %);
- no reply – 6 (3.9 %).

On the question of accepting a **Christmas-time pastoral visit** during their stay in the institution, the following responses were obtained:

- yes because I want to: 47 (30.3 %) Catholic juveniles;
- yes because I have to: 17 (11 %);
- no because I don't want to: 35 (22.6 %);
- no because I don't have that option: 46 (29.7 %);
- no reply: 11 (7.1 %) juveniles.

On the question of **difficulties** in practicing any of the above practices: 19 (12.3 %) juveniles responded **positively** and 128 (82.6 %) **negatively**. When asked about the nature of the difficulties, the respondents indicated (among the possible options):

- legal regulations: 15 (9.7 %);
- lack of individual consent from the prison director: 10 (6.5 %);
- technical and organizational obstacles: 17 (11 %);
- dislike from fellow prisoners: 8 (5.2 %);
- lack of time: 35 (22.6 %);
- lack of persistence: 14 (9 %);
- other: 9 (5.8 %), that is, one person cited personal reasons, another pointed to a lack of possibility of going to church on one's own, and the rest stated the issue was a lack of limitations in general.

The juveniles were asked to what element of religious life they were missing on the premises of an institution. Three respondents indicated medallion, two respondents indicated going to church.

The next questions concerned participation in the sacraments of Christian initiation in the institution and after obtaining consent to leave it.

<table>
<tr><th></th><th colspan="2">Baptism</th><th colspan="2">First Communion</th><th colspan="2">Confirmation</th></tr>
<tr><td></td><td>On the premises</td><td>Having obtained consent to leave the institution</td><td>On the premises</td><td>Having obtained consent to leave the institution</td><td>On the premises</td><td>Having obtained consent to leave the institution</td></tr>
<tr><td>Yes</td><td>22 (14.2 %)</td><td>37 (23.9 %)</td><td>17 (11 %)</td><td>40 (25.8 %)</td><td>46 (29.7 %)</td><td>36 (23.2 %)</td></tr>
<tr><td rowspan="4">No</td><td rowspan="4">114 (73.5 %)</td><td>105 (67.7 %), including:</td><td rowspan="4">118 (76.1 %)</td><td>100 (64.5 %), Including:</td><td rowspan="4">100 (64.5 %)</td><td>106 (68.4 %), including:</td></tr>
<tr><td>86 (55.5 %) – there was no such occasion</td><td>83 – there was no such occasion</td><td>92 (59.4 %) – there was no such occasion</td></tr>
<tr><td>9 (5.8 %) – I did not want to</td><td>8 (5.2 %) – I did not want to</td><td>10 (6.5 %) – I did not want to</td></tr>
<tr><td>10 (6.5 %) – I did not obtain consent to leave the institution</td><td>9 (5.8 %) – I did not obtain consent to leave the institution</td><td>4 (2.6 %) – I did not obtain consent to leave the institution</td></tr>
</table>

When asked to compare the frequency of participation in religious practices before and after placement in an institution, 92 (59.4 %) juveniles stated that it **was not greater before placement**, whereas 42 (27.1 %) juveniles stated that it **was greater before placement**, 22 (14.2 %) respondents gave no reply. As the reasons for becoming more active in this area, juveniles cited increased free time, more opportunities in the institution, stronger faith during their time there, and greater motivation. Moreover, they go to church more often because they have to, they have to fit in, there is no other activity. Others, however, noted that they practiced religion more frequently at liberty because of family, more freedom, and at present, because of indolence and influence exerted on them by fellow juveniles in the institution.

When asked for a justification and an example of whether, in the juvenile's opinion, the Roman Catholic denomination he or she practices puts him or her in a better or worse position than persons of other denominations, 27 (17.4 %) Catholic juveniles stated they were in a **worse** position and 67 (43.2 %) Catholic juveniles stated they were in a **better** situation. Longer opinions were very scarce.

One respondent noted that the better situation is due to the fact that: "Only the Catholic denomination can be practiced". The rest either wrote explicitly that they could not provide a justification, or indicated that the better situation was due to the fact that the Catholic faith was practiced.

The questions addressed to juveniles of other denominations were answered by 9 individuals, which is 4.3 % of all juvenile respondents. One of them is trying to mediate, the second spends time in a group, the third one spends religious holidays as his parents do. They do not participate in any religious practices in the institution, one of them would like to participate in confirmation. When asked if they had symbols of their faith in their room, 5 of them confirmed this (with only one person specifying it was a cross), one denied it and three refused to give an answer.

Five individuals from that group declared that during their stay in the institution they had contact with a representative of their religion or confession, one did not have aby, and three persons gave no reply. When asked about the need to take part in the practices of another religion, two respondents replied positively without indicating which practices they were referring to. Ultimately, two respondents thought they were in a worse situation than followers of other religions (providing no extra information), one deemed the situation to be better, six respondents gave no answer.

The last part was addressed to non-believers – it was completed by 44 individuals (21.1 % of all surveyed juveniles). 26 (59.1 %) surveyed juveniles **did not feel compelled to participate** in any religious practices or rituals during their stay in the institution, whereas 11 (25 %) individuals **thought otherwise**. When asked about burdensome regulations relating to these issues, they did not know any. However, several respondents indicated that the inability to opt out of religious instruction and the lack of ethics classes as a substitute for religious instruction could be seen as burdensome regulation.

11 (25 %) respondents believed they were in a worse situation as non-believers, 6 individuals thought otherwise, 27 (61.4 %) respondents provided no reply. Only one person chose to give a justification: "I think the teacher looks at me differently (treats me differently from believers), the religion teacher."

6.5.7. Educators in juvenile institutions: youth educational centres and correctional facilities

Educators completed 108 questionnaires.

Responding to whether juveniles are "open" about their religion, 79 (73.1 %) educators replied **positively** and 26 (24.1 %) **negatively** (4 respondents gave no reply). The comments to that question drew attention to the fact that some are very open about their religion and want to talk about it, others, on the contrary, talk about their negative attitude towards their faith. Some juveniles do not want to talk about their confession at all. In this regard, the following comment made by a female catechist is worth quoting: "Juveniles placed in an institution frequently declare themselves non-believers, thus, they do not acknowledge their religion. During their stay in the institution, the attitude of juveniles changes towards faith. This is evidenced by an upward trend in the practice of faith, that is, attending Mass, services, going to confession, prayers before religious instruction (at times, boys pray the rosary in the evening), going on a pilgrimage to St. Anne's Mountain, taking part in weekend spiritual retreats organized by the Young on the Threshold Foundation, preparatory meetings for the sacrament of Confirmation, biblical circle, trips to Licheń."

On the question of whether juveniles wear religious symbols or place them in their room, the respondents replied: **yes** – 56 (51.9 %) educators, **no** – 49 (45.4 %) educators; 4 respondents gave no reply. The educators pointed out that some wear such symbols and others do not. They emphasized that the cross is occasionally a piece of jewellery and not a sign of faith. In bedrooms there are occasionally holy pictures, crosses, the Bible, a rosary.

Another question was whether juveniles could freely practice their religion or confession fully before the pandemic. An many as 104 (96.3 %) respondents replied **positively**. The opposite opinion was held by 3 educators, 2 educators did not answer the question. The comments pointed to the possibility of attending Mass, religious instruction, organized ceremonies of Confirmation and even Baptism. In the opinion of a vast majority of respondents (101 educators – 93.5 %), before the pandemic, a Roman Catholic juvenile had no difficulty in performing of some practices in the institution. The opposite view was held by 5 educators, with 3 more providing no reply. It was indicated that it was occasionally the case that going to church was not possible (e.g., lack of a carer). The juveniles most frequently reported a wish to undergo Confirmation and go to confession.

In the opinion of the surveyed educators, juvenile followers of other confessions had no difficulty in performing the practices and rituals of their religions – 101 (93.5 %) respondents. Only 1 respondent held the opposite view, 7 respondents provided no reply. The educators most frequently indicated that juveniles of other confessions were simply not present in their institution or they did not report any religious needs. The juveniles of other confessions included Protestants, Jehovah's Witnesses, Pentecostalists, Baptists, followers of Eastern Orthodoxy and Islam.

On the question of whether non-believers had to participate – for organizational reasons – in specific religious practices, 18 (16.7 %) educators replied **yes**, 83 (76.9 %) – **no**, 8 (7.4 %) educators gave no reply. The comments provided to that question indicated that attending Mass was voluntary, so was participation in other sacraments, and the communal Christmas Eve was treated as part of tradition rather than a religious practice. However, others saw other aspects, writing: "The organization of the institution takes into account Catholic feasts, e.g., fasts. Because there is one kitchen, juveniles declaring themselves as non-believers had to eat fish", or "Participation in spiritual retreats as school classes". Another educator made the following comment: "The juveniles have to be looked after at all times, so they had to be together with everyone else at Mass or religious holidays." Finally, the following comments hint at the positive dimension of compulsory participation: "For non-believers – a lesson on how to behave in a place of worship" or "Attending (presence at) Mass as a behavioural skills training in an open environment".

We also sought the opinion of the educators on the COVID-19 pandemic restrictions, so another question concerned the extent to which the restrictions changed the possibility of practicing religion and how it was perceived by the juveniles. Some educators explained that the pandemic did not affect religious practices in any way, some added that the chapel was on the premises of an institution, so services could be held there. By contrast, educators from other institutions pointed out that there were "fewer or no opportunities to go on pilgrimages and Mass outside the facility". The attitudes of the juveniles also varied – some seemed unaffected by the restrictions, while others showed full understanding and did not demand the implementation of certain practices. The educators believed that some juveniles greatly missed attending Mass.

The educators were unanimous in their positive assessment of the current provisions relating to religious issues during a juvenile's stay in isolation institutions and the internal organization of the institution. This may be well illustrated by the following comment: "I think the provisions do not run contrary to the possibility of exercising one's faith. We seek to enable everyone to practice their faith to the best of their ability and we do not force anyone to take part in any specific religious practices."

The last question was to determine who, in the case of underage charges, in practice makes the decision on practicing religion (to whom the question is addressed). In response, educators most frequently pointed to parents or legal guardians, sometimes adding that "Declarations on attending Mass are signed by parents/legal guardians." There is also such a statement: "In the case of underage individuals, a question is addressed to the parents. However, the final decision is made by a chargé." The following words of another educator may complement and visualize the situation: "We send a question to the parent/guardian and ask a charge to make a declaration; in practice, however, this is primarily decided by the charge. It should be noted that the majority of them are legal adults or almost legal adults (typically 17 years of age)." The other comments are on a similar note, for example: "In the case of underage individuals, a question is sent to the parents. The final decision is made by the charge" or "The decision is made by the charge, upon consent from the legal guardian. I have never experienced any problems of that sort." Finally, a different approach: "The will of the charge is always taken into account and they decide on the matter. I have never encountered difficulties." The educators rarely made comments on the participation of their charges in religious instruction. However, they were unanimous in indicating that "Parents or legal guardians sign consents to attend religion lessons" or more precisely: "Legal guardian – decision to attend religious instruction. Charges – a decision to participate in religious rituals." The following comment is also of interest: "On consent from the parent, the charge attended Sunday Mass. The boy's mother believed it was a lesson of tolerance. The boy had no objection to this, nor did he wish to remain in another educational group during the time."

6.6. Discussion

Before the particular results are discussed, a few remarks of a general nature should be made.

The questionnaires completed by adult prisoners showed their impatience – some answers were missing (in particular, to detailed questions). The comments were occasionally illegible, some were inserted into wrong boxes. There were mocking or sarcastic responses. By contrast, the surveyed juveniles showed much more 'discipline', their answers were sometimes even surprisingly critical. The answers given by educators struck us as rather poor in content. Almost every question offered the opportunity to make a detailed comment, but few of the surveyed educators took advantage of it. The given comments were brief, although at times extremely accurate.

It must be admitted that the objections raised by adults and juveniles occurred in practically every surveyed institution, the negative comments were not "cumulated" only in a few biggest groups under analysis.

6.6.1. Religion and how it is practiced: a point of view of adult prisoners

To recall, in the study population of adult prisoners, 193 respondents identified themselves as practicing believers (which is 34.71 %), 245 – as non-practicing believers (44.06 %), 67 – as non-believers (12 %), 21 – as searching for faith (3.78 %), 5 indicated "other" (0.9 %); adding: "at the beginning of practicing," "questioning," "believes in Satan," "ready for a change of belief after getting to know it".

When asked about their professed religion, the prisoners declared themselves as follows: 368 Christians in the Catholic variant (66.19 % of the study population), 9 (1.62 %) – Orthodox variant, 10 (1.8 %) – Protestant variant. 4 respondents identified themselves as Jehovah's Witnesses, 6 as followers of Islam, 1 as a follower of Judaism and 2 as Buddhists. In turn, (15.83 %) respondents indicated "other" (most frequently explaining that they do not believe in any religion or pointing generally to Christianity), and 49 (8.81 %) respondents gave no reply.

The obtained results are broadly in line with the nationwide data. As Sławomir Cebula rightly argued, the multitude of sources regarding Poles' faith may vary slightly from one to another, yet they agree on the basic information: more than 90 % of Poles are believers of the Roman Catholic confession.[697] According to the Public Opinion Research Centre (CBOS), a vast majority of Poles declare themselves believers. The share of individuals identifying themselves as believers (including deeply religious) has invariably exceeded 90 % since the end of the 1990s. It remained at 96 % until 2005 and has been declining very slowly but steadily for the last ten years. In 2020, it reached its lowest level since the issue was monitored.[698] Although 87.6 % of Poles declared their affiliation with the Roman Catholic Church in the 2011 census, which translated into 33.7 million followers, the first data on confession from the subsequent census released in 2023 revealed the number of 27.1 million believers, that is, only 71.3 % of the inhabitants of Poland.[699]

The study population of prisoners had 78.77 % of believers in total and less than 4 % of individuals declaring themselves as "searching". There were more

697 S. Cebula, *Prawa i wolności religijne we współczesnej Polsce. Ustawodawstwo a realia społeczno-kulturowe*, Kraków 2011, pp. 52–59.

698 See: Public Opinion Research Centre, *Religiosity of Poles in the last 20 years. Research communication no. 63/2020*, https://cbos.pl/SPISKOM.POL/2020/K_063_20.PDF (accessed: 20.08.2023).

699 Statistics Poland, *Tables with final data on national-ethnic affiliation, language spoken at home and religious affiliation*, https://stat.gov.pl/spisy-powszechne/nsp-2021/nsp-2021-wyniki-ostateczne/tablice-z-ostatecznymi-danymi-w-zakresie-przynaleznosci-narodowo-etnicznej-jezyka-uzywanego-w-domu-oraz-przynaleznosci-do-wyznania-religijnego,10,1.html?fbclid=IwAR3nB6bh6bQij8apHTrNJ_wkWLpVR-eVnyl7zdL_hxInYPkb5jeHVJxe-OU (accessed 1.10.2023).

individuals declaring themselves to be non-believers than the CBOS data indicate – 12 %. It cannot be ruled out that the data from the penitentiary institutions do not fully correspond to the reality. Apparently, some prisoners decided not to take part in the survey, considering that since they are non-believers, "the matter does not concern them". This may mean that the percentage of non-believers in today's penitentiary facilities and detention centres is even higher.

Account should be taken of other studies on religiosity in penitentiary facilities cited in the literature. The majority of convicts declare a positive attitude towards faith in God (66.3 %), an ambivalent attitude – 19.3 %, and a negative attitude – 13.2 %. At the same time, commitment to the practical dimension of performing religious practices characterizes only 20.3 % of prisoners. The highest number of negative and ambivalent attitudes towards pastoral services is found among penitentiary recidivists. It is indicated that the reluctant attitude towards religious engagement in that group may have various reasons, among others, it may be the effect of reduced moral sensitivity as a result of repeated incarcerations, the use of strong defence mechanisms, the difficulty of admitting one's own mistakes or the fear of exclusion from the prison subculture.[700]

The general denominational structure in the surveyed institutions closely resembles the denominational structure of the Polish society. According to a study by Statistics Poland (GUS), the community of believers in the Roman Catholic Church amounts to 33,729,000 individuals, which is 87.6 % of the overall population. All the other types of denominational identification, including declarations by believers of non-Latin rites of the Catholic Church, totalling 493,000 believers, are of a distinctly minority nature in Poland. The data show that the Orthodox Church, which is the largest community of believers in that group, has over 156,000 members, which is 0.41 % of the Polish population. A Statistics Poland census shows that Poland's population of Jehovah's Witnesses' followers and sympathizers amounts to more than 137,000, or 0.36 % of the total population. Other than Roman Catholics, the Lutherans are the third-largest denomination in Poland. They are believers of the Evangelical Church of the Augsburg Confession of the Republic of Poland, numbering almost 71,000 individuals, which is 0.18 % of Poland's total population. Half as large as the Lutherans are members of the Catholic Church practicing a non-Latin rite, which is the most widespread in the Catholic Church, i.e. the Byzantine-Ukrainian rite, also known as the Greek Catholic Church. The community of Greek Catholics in Poland has 33,000 (0.09 %) followers. In the Polish realities,

700 I. Niewiadomska, "Polski model..., p. 115.

the largest non-Catholic denominations include the Pentecostal Church with, according to the declarations of the census takers, 26,000 followers (0.07 % of the total population), the community of the Old Catholic Mariavite Church with less than 10,000 followers (approx. 0.03 %), the Polish-Catholic Church with 8,800 followers and the Baptist Christian Church with 6,000 followers. Members of more than 150 other churches, religious associations and movements, as well as adherents of various types of religious currents and trends, constitute a collective comprising a total of 44,400 inhabitants of Poland, which is 0.12 % of the Polish population.[701]

According to the obtained data, 66 % of the study population declared the Roman Catholic confession. To recall, as many as 88 (15.83 %) respondents indicated "other" (in most cases adding that they do not believe in any religion or generally marking "Christianity"), and 49 (8.81 %) respondents refused to give a reply, which is a large proportion of those surveyed.

It should be pointed out that the changes in adult inmate religiosity in fact cancel each other out – in total, religion took on importance (or greater importance) for 114 (20.5 %) prisoners during incarceration, whereas for 118 (21.22 %) prisoners – conversely, it lost importance (partially or completely). There is a substantial group (over 45 %) of inmates for whom religion is equally important. Therefore, from the perspective of belief, there is no basis for attributing special importance to prisons or detention centres as places where one "loses God" or "finds God."

Feasts and rituals are a hugely important part of religious identity in the individual sphere, especially at the level of practising religion. For convicts and detainees, it is primarily Christmas and Easter. In Poland, dominated by the Roman Catholic denomination, these feasts are very family-oriented. There are no state, national or historical holidays in the Polish culture that would have such extensive rituals and, at the same time, contain such a strong emotional and family element (the only non-religious holiday that is willingly and pompously celebrated, often with friends and less often with family, is New Year's Eve). A large number of non-believing Poles celebrate these feasts as an expression of national identity and family bond. It was often emphasized by the prisoners themselves. They believe Christmas Eve (the festive dinner preceding Christmas) and the Easter breakfast are the most important religious feasts. In many cases it is more

701 Statistics Poland, *Religious confessions in Poland in 2019–2021*, Warszawa 2022 (https://stat.gov.pl/obszary-tematyczne/inne-opracowania/wyznania-religijne/wyznania-religijne-w-polsce-2019-2021,5,3.html (accessed 20.08.2023).

about tradition, longing for family, uniqueness of the moment, than experiencing the birth and resurrection of Jesus. Notably, the more ritualism is involved in a given liturgical feast, the more important it seemed for the prisoners and was thus more frequently mentioned in the questionnaires. Out of the religious practices most important to them, prisoners most frequently mentioned Mass, which is a weekly obligation for every Christian. Other sacraments and sacramentals were also mentioned, and even rituals traditionally associated with the most important feasts but not deriving from religious doctrine – such as sharing a wafer or decorating a Christmas tree.

The respondents of other denominations shared little of their opinions in this regard, most often pointing to practices in the form of Zen meditation and fasts.

It came as no surprise that religious practices were most intensely presented in the Catholic group. The widespread presence of this religion in the history of Poland and in the present day means that its rites are widely known and traditionally performed, and numerous organizational solutions (e.g., the calendar of public holidays and days off, cuisine in communal feeding, availability of different artefacts and objects of worship) make the practice of that religion immeasurably easier in daily life.

Here are the most important findings of the study carried out in the different groups of prisoners, categorised by denomination and lack of denomination.

6.6.1.1. *Opinions of incarcerated Catholics*

The primary duty of a Catholic, the omission of which is a grave sin, is weekly attendance at Mass. In the group of believing Catholics taking part in the survey, 76 prisoners (18 % of Catholic) attended Mass once a week and 46 (10.9 %) prisoners once a month. It seems that these indications can be combined, as it is not always possible for prisoners to attend Mass every week for organizational reasons. This means that almost 30 % of Catholics regularly attend Mass, which is close to the values revealed in church statistics. Interestingly, the combined figures relating to the study population (data on Mass attendance once per week and once per month) differ only to a certain extent from the number of those individuals attending Mass on the premises of an institution during the pandemic and at liberty. These are, respectively:

- Mass was attended regularly during the pandemic by: 53+36=89 (21.1 % of incarcerated adult Catholics);
- at liberty: 100+42=142 (33.7 %),
- before the pandemic – the aforementioned 76+46=122 (29 %).

Holy communion was taken once a week or once a month by, respectively, 29 and 27 prisoners, in total 13.3 % of Catholics in the surveyed institutions (56 prisoners). These figures are almost identical to those for persons practicing religion outside.

The practices of believers outside follow a similar pattern. In 2021, in Poland, the *dominicantes* rate (it determines the percentage of those who attend Sunday Mass in relation to the total number of followers) was 28.3 %. The highest *dominicantes* rate was recorded traditionally in the dioceses of Tarnów (59.1 %), Rzeszów (49.7 %) and Przemyśl (46.9 %).The *communicantes* rate (persons taking Holy Communion during Mass) was 12.9 % of the followers.[702]

The pandemic restrictions caused some decline in the number of individuals participating in the said religious practices, in the same way as the deprivation of liberty led to a decline compared to practices at liberty. The declines are not radical and dramatic and are understandable in the light of the circumstances. This also allows for a cautious conclusion that the Polish legal and organizational standards on participation in this sacrament do not seem to be inadequate. Admittedly, as the educators pointed out, more Masses could indeed be held, but it is hard to speak of fundamental violations of religious freedom in this respect.

The prisoners were asked about the reason for attending Mass on the premises of the institution. They pointed to the existence of such a need, faith, tradition or habit, desire to receive Holy Communion, prayer, need for contact with God, substitute for freedom (as the prisoner attended Mass at liberty), need for clear one's head, promise made to a loved one, curiosity, 'to kill time', opportunity to leave the cell. Participation in liturgy is not always religiously motivated. Notably, the isolation unit authorities do not have the right to examine whether a declaration to attend Mass is religiously justified (and complies with the canons of a given religion). The faithful outside are not verified before attending Mass as to the real reason for participating in such activity (whether it is religious reasons or, for example, social reasons, fear of gossip, a desire to kill time).

Studies show that prisoners are also keen to practice religion in other ways, participating in other sacraments, sacramentals or practices recommended by the Church (also known as popular devotional practices).[703] The detailed data

702 See: Statistical Portal, *Catholic Church – how many Poles attend Sunday Mass?*, 24.03.2023, https://portalstatystyczny.pl/kosciol-katolicki-ilu-polakow-bierze-udzial-niedzielnych-w-mszach/ (accessed 20.08.2023).

703 United State Conference of Catholic Bishops, "*Popular* devotional *practices: basic questions & answers*", *Salvatoris Mater*, vol. 5, no. 4, 2003, pp. 341 et seq.

are given above. For example, nearly half of the incarcerated Roman Catholics surveyed (48.9 %) wear a cross, medallion or other faith symbol and 24 % of them accept a Christian-time pastoral visit in prison. **It is important to note these high rates, as the practices certainly do not bring any immediate benefit to the adult prisoners and in principle are free – one can assume – from manipulation and extra-religious intentions.**

A hugely important point is that 142 (33.7 %) prisoners admitted that practicing certain activities was impossible or difficult, with only 30 (7.1 %) of them putting the blame on themselves (lack of time or lack of persistence). The others saw the reasons for the impediments in the regulations or in the organization of an institution. It is also significant that 29 (6.9 %) prisoners "complained" about dislike shown to them by fellow prisoners for practicing their religion. Some concern is also raised by a statement by the director of an institution who, according to a prisoner, gave an order that prisoners attending Mass must wear prison clothing and, consequently, denied access to services to those who are unwilling to wear such "uniforms".

The study also shows that inmates lack primarily the wafer, a Christmas-time pastoral visit, a meeting with a priest. This is important for two reasons. **First, the nature of the above pious practices is almost free from manipulation or abuse. Second, they are after all extremely easy to bring into the reality of penitentiary facilities to a fuller extent. They do not require great financial or organizational outlays – what is in fact needed is chaplains' good will and involvement.**

The last group of questions concerned practices that are generally attended at liberty (and only exceptionally carried out within the prison institution). These seem to be defined as the ceremonies of passage – Baptism, the First Communion, Confirmation, marriage, funerals. The detailed data are presented above. Close attention should be given to the refusal of the director of an institution to allow a prisoner to leave the institution to participate in a sacrament. Notably, these figures (no consent) outnumber the consents given to participate in the said ceremonies. For example, 21 prisoners took part in baptism outside and 96 prisoners did not because of a lack of consent, the figures for funeral were, respectively, 48 and 88. This is understandable insofar as it is the area that can most easily be abused by prisoners who may attempt to gain certain privileges (in the form of additional time out of prison) in a fraudulent manner or in circumstances that give rise to some concern (e.g., no-return). In this regard, it should be added that none of the respondents report the fact that he or she was unable to take part in such ceremonies held on the premises of an institution because of a lack of consent from the director.

When asked about the pandemic-related restrictions, the prisoners replied that they did not experience such impediments (most often it was the case with non-practicing ones) or replied that such impediments did not apply to them because one can always pray or read the Bible and God is everywhere. Others confirmed the existence of difficulties, pointing to specific practices (most often Mass, meetings and contact with a chaplain, going to confession). Importantly, without being asked to make any comments in that regards, the respondents eagerly added that they understood the pandemic situation and knew that also religious practices became more limited outside. Moreover, some indicated that although Holy Masses were not held, they were aired on the prison radio. Ultimately, it must be concluded that the pandemic period did not cause religious unrest among the prisoners.

In general, incarcerated Catholics do not feel at a disadvantage compared to individuals of other confessions or non-believers; as many as 319 (75.8 %) agree with this sentence. Prisoners feeling at a disadvantage saw the reason for it in ridiculing, disrespect, and being made fun of by officers and fellow prisoners. These circumstances are unrelated to the nature of the place in which they found themselves and the constraints imposed by the deprivation of liberty. The rule *homo homini lupus* came into play in a benign form.

6.6.1.2. Opinions of prisoners of other denominations

51 surveyed prisoners declared following other denominations. They provided few details on their religious life. Occasional responses on feasts and rituals important for them were simply limited to "fasting during Ramadan", praying in the chapel, eating meals together, meeting with co-followers, meetings, writing icons, talking to a clergyman (Pop), reading Scripture. Some respondents replied that they did not celebrate feasts at all, others did it in the cell or on their own. The data on the manifestation of faith may also be of interest. Nearly a half (43.1 %) of the respondents indicated in the questionnaire that they had symbols of faith or confession in their cell.

To recall, when asked to identify practices or rituals that were not possible, but which were important to the prisoner, a mention was made of: a "pork-free" diet, "liturgies", meetings with persons of the same belief, a prayer with an Imam, Memorial of Jesus Christ's death, Protestant services, a pilgrimage. A relatively large proportion wrote that no ritual or practice was missing in the prison. When asked to identify the reason for the absence of the indicated practices, the respondents cited a failure to hold such practices on the premises of a penitentiary facility or a detention centre, lack of chaplain, organizational obstacles, lack of tolerance, lack of consent from prison authorities. At the same time, as many as 32 (62.7 %) respondents admitted that they had contact with a representative of their confession or religion while serving a penalty of imprisonment or in detention.

Equally important was a prisoner's assessment of his or her situation in terms of religious freedom. Responding to whether they were forced to participate in the practices or rites of another religion or denomination, 7 prisoners (out of 39 prisoners who replied to that question, which is 18 % of the responding persons and out of 51 identifying themselves as having a different belief/religion, which is 13.7 %) replied positively, citing, among others, "When I didn't have the radio and television equipment, I had to listen to the Catholic Mass on the prison radio. The meals served on Catholic holidays are subordinated to their belief", "No one forced me directly, but in multi-person cells, I was an observer of practices that irritated me greatly", "When I went to a micro AA therapy, I had to pray to Jesus, although I am an Islamist."

Comparing their situation to the situation of followers of other confessions or religions, 14 (27.5 %) prisoners concluded that they were at a disadvantage, indicating harassment, a failure to understand Islam, "Islamophobia", or formulated a belief that "Catholic priests are the only clergymen who come here." At the same time, 32 (62.7 %) prisoners said they did not feel at a disadvantage.

As the reason why the practice of their religion is hindered, the prisoners pointed to the provisions impeding the observance of fasts and contact with chaplains. At the same time, according to the prisoners of that group, the restrictions related to the pandemic did not in principle (additionally) hinder religious life in the penitentiary facility/detention centre, but there were no more meetings during that period.

6.6.1.3. Opinions of incarcerated non-believers

83 individuals (14.9 % of the study population) declared themselves non-believers. A vast majority of the non-believers did not feel forced to participate in religious practices. Only 5 individuals thought otherwise. One of them gave the following justification: "The diets are suited to Catholics and on Catholic holidays the meals are served according to the Catholic tradition. Sharing the wafer at Christmas, etc. If there is no TV set in the cell, then I am forced to listen to the prison radio, and On Sunday, Roman Catholic Mass takes half of the programme." Although coercion to participate in practices does not occur in the active form, passive coercion does take place. The organization of the functioning of a large number of people in a relatively small space and certain

organizational deficiencies mean that non-believers are "passive" participants in the rites and even the sacraments of the dominant religion. This situation can certainly be improved, although it requires a lot of effort and resources.

The situation described by another prisoner, which takes the form of some sort of blackmail, is unacceptable: The following comment may be cause for concern: "In a semi-open unit for recidivists, to have a family visit (wife, children, treat), you had to attend religious meetings in an open-type prison for recidivists, that's why I had no chance for a third visit, despite endless willingness."

On a similar note, a vast majority of non-believers (70–84 %) concluded that non-denominationalism does not put them at a disadvantage compared to other prisoners. However, the statements to the contrary have been very well argued, so it is worth recalling them again in full. One prisoner pointed out that: "Believers have meetings on their holy days, they create themselves as humble, honest, innocent persons who have learned from their mistakes and rigidly follow the Catholic religious canon. They try to create a contrast to others in behaviour. Non-believers are not as bad as the rest, unfortunately, they can't hold meetings on Sunday to have a talk." Another one made the following comment: "At first I wanted to indicate no, but yes, there is one thing. Believers can leave their cell for a while and change the surroundings (the chapel). I don't have that additional possibility." Another prisoner noted that "a large number of newspapers and books in the library explore Catholic religious themes."

These comments suggest that, in general, **there is no reasonable alternative to religious rituals or other practices of a similar nature for non-believers** (with the exception of so-called civil weddings and secular funerals, which non-believers and those who do not observe any religious rituals can apply for). Participation in religious practices generates spiritual experiences, gives other positive feelings and values – additional meetings, leaving the premises of the institution, talks with persons important to a prisoner. These values become the privilege of believers only, as non-believers are not provided with meetings or events giving such positive values. Moreover, believers can quite easily misuse their entitlements, for example, attend Mass to socialize, go to biblical meetings out of boredom or curiosity. Non-believers, for self-development or out of boredom, cannot, for example, claim the right to attend a meeting with fellow prisoners to discuss a book by Richard Dawkins: *The God Delusion*.

Note should also be taken of a prisoner's view that offers a dose of optimism: "Year by year, attitudes towards belief are changing and non-believers are treated just like believers."

6.6.1.4. *Issue of providing information*

To conclude the analysis of the results of the surveys of all adult inmates, a few formal issues need to be addressed. To recall, responding to whether they were questioned about their confession or religion during incarceration, as many as 117 (21 %) respondents replied yes. Such answers were given practically in all the surveyed institutions. After all, religious freedom in the Polish legal order includes the right not to disclose one's religion. Questions of such a private nature, in an institution where one is completely subjected to authority (a total institution), entitle one to put forward an argument that **the right to religious freedom is not respected in this regard in Poland.**

Responding to whether during the so-called informational interview they were informed about the possibility of performing religious practices, only 194 (34.89 %) respondents replied positively. In turn, as many as 328 (59 %) respondents indicated that they were not informed about the possibilities of performing religious practices (25 respondents gave no reply, 2 others could not recall). Importantly, one prisoner indicated that none of the penitentiary institutions in which he was incarcerated (he enumerated 6 – detention centres and a penitentiary facility) informed him about that possibility. **The right not to be asked about one's confession does not imply a lack of entitlement to information.** Every new incarcerated individual should have a full set of information about the religious practices performed in the institution (of different denominations and religions) and should also be given information on where and who to turn to as regards other religious practices (or other denominations). It is a slogan to argue that the effectiveness of respecting human rights begins with the provision of information on the applicable rights. The problem of informing convicted persons about their rights and obligations has already been reported in the Polish literature. A study carried out by Maria Niełączna shows that although several positive ways of providing information can be observed, convicts are generally deprived of it.[704]

It may be assumed that the identified shortcomings result from a lack of proper training of prison officers in that regard. The rights and freedoms of prisoners should undoubtedly be a permanent, fundamental element of such training. The training may not consist of listing the rights and freedoms, with religious freedom being one of the items on the list. Also our study shows that

---

704 M. Niełaczna, *Zmiany za murami? Stosowanie standardów postępowania z więźniami w Polsce*, Warszawa 2011, pp. 152 et seq.

this area of personal life is important for many prisoners, and international and national regulations confirm the rank and importance of these rights.

6.6.2. Religion and how it is practiced: a point of view of educators in penitentiary facilities and detention centres

The picture drawn by educators of penitentiary facilities is somewhat different, one could say, more positive than it is seen by prisoners. The questionnaire was completed by 164 educators.

Educators confirmed, for the most part, that convicts and pre-trial detainees often identify with their religion, wear religious symbols or display them in their cell. One of the educators pointed out that religious issues are often treated merely as tools, e.g., in connection with a diet, leaving the cell on the occasion of meetings of religious groups. As indicated above, there are legal grounds to question the legitimacy of practicing a particular religion.

The comments made by some educators indicating the need to obtain consent to hang a holy picture or respecting the prohibition on displaying such pictures are shocking. It seems that such practice is totally unacceptable and contrary to Polish and international regulations. It may be the case that the prison staff do not always have adequate knowledge of the current legal situation. Art. 110a § 1 PEC explicitly prescribes that the prisoner shall have the right to keep religious articles in his or her cell. The director's consent applies only to the possession in the cell of electronic or electrical equipment or other items, including those that enhance the aesthetics of the room or that are an expression of the prisoner's cultural interests.

The educators were sure that religious practices were available before the pandemic (on conditions applicable to isolation units) – this was claimed by 151 (92 %) respondents. They did not record requests for other forms of practice or complaints about their absence (which stands in contrast to the fairly common opinion of prisoners about the absence of Christmas-time pastoral visits, meetings with a clergyman, etc.). However, one questionnaire paid attention to the inadequate availability of a chaplain who, with one Mass a week, is unable to meet all the needs of prisoners. Other questionnaires contained a rather sceptical assessment of the involvement of chaplains in the question on difficulties encountered by prisoners in practicing religion. The educators wrote that "The weekly mass cannot be attended by everyone (because of groups, associates [conflicts]); it would be advisable to increase the number Masses for prisoners" or "Priests rarely initiate meetings on ordinary Sundays. On feast days there is no such problem."

One of the surveyed educators already in that place correctly noted that "the predominance of Catholic practices marginalizes other religious movements". The educators named the followers of other religions (excluding Roman Catholics) they had dealt with in the penitentiary institutions. These included followers of Islam, Eastern Orthodoxy, Hinduism, Pentecostalism and Jehovah's Witnesses. On the question of limitations encountered by followers of other religions, only 18 (11 %) educators acknowledged this problem. They identified a lack of access to/contact with chaplains of specific religions (not Roman Catholic) as the most common reason. One educator pointed out that Muslims "need so many objects for religious rituals, which may be a nuisance to their cellmates". The latter approach is confounding given that Art. 106 PEC prescribes that the convicted person shall have the right to possess the books, writings and objects necessary for the performance of religious practices.

It is also hard to ignore a comment made by one educator that Muslim representatives verify the apparent affiliation of prisoners very quickly by asking a few simple questions about Islam, which means that prisoners' affiliation remains only in the declaratory realm. Polish law does not give grounds for verifying a declaration of faith and checking how properly a follower fulfils his or her religious obligations. This position has been confirmed by the ECHR jurisprudence.

The educators made other, in our belief, scandalous comments, such as: "It's not a hotel" or "Islam ban from CZSW [Central Board of the Prison Service]."

The educators almost unanimously claimed that non-believers did not have to participate in religious practices (143 educators – that is, 87.2 %). However, 14 (8.5 %) educators conceded that such compulsion existed, for example, in the case of the broadcasting of Mass over the radio, the introduction of fasting Fridays. In response to a question about restrictions on religious practices during the pandemic, many educators emphasized that the restrictions affected prisoners to a lesser degree precisely because of the Masses broadcast on the prison radio.

In the opinion of the educators, the pandemic restrictions entailed limitations on religious practices, but they were not too severe or intense, and the services broadcast on the prison radio "saved the situation". At times, religious meetings were held on Skype. One questionnaire drew attention to "negative dimension" for many prisoners of restrictions in the sphere of religious practice. Many surveyed educators additionally noted that prisoners did not complain about restrictions in this area, some of them showed full understanding.

As regards the quality of the provisions on the practice of religion and religious freedom, the educators did not raise any major objections and delivered a favourable opinion on the existing regulations. Again, some shortcomings on the part of the churches were identified, such as "More frequent opportunities to attend Mass" and "Priests should be more accessible to prisoners. One Mass per week is not enough." A comment "Cooperation, contact with other religions should be established" can be seen as an objection of an organizational nature. In turn, another educator believed that "religious life is connected with spirituality and may be practiced on an individual basis". This comment can be seen in the context of the question on the quality of provisions as a negation of the right to exercise religious practices, which is ensured by law and international agreements.

Ignorance of law may also be evidenced by the answers to the last question on consent for minors to participate in religious practices. As many as 42 (25.6 %) educators did not give an answer to the question and a vast majority of the remaining ones replied that their institution incarcerated only legal adults. A large proportion indicated that the prisoner (even a minor) decides independently on the practiced religion. In two questionnaires, the prison director was indicated as the decision-maker, in one – the cultural-educational officer, another one pointed to "the disposing organ", others to a priest, chaplain or a representative of another confession (sic!). Two questionnaires had the answer that the decision was up to the minor's legal guardian. One may be well surprised by the ignorance of law shown by such comment: "No minors – there are young adults."

The legal issues of religious freedom are discussed in detail earlier. It should be pointed out that a minor can also be a young adult offender and penitentiary facilities and detention centres also incarcerate persons under the age of 18. As at 31 December 2022, 175 individuals incarcerated in Polish prisons have not attained the age of 18 years (one has not even attained the age of 16 years).[705] Moreover, an amendment to the Criminal Code means that since October 2023 it has been possible to incarcerate children aged 14 and older in penitentiary facilities and detention centres. The participation of minors in religious practices cannot be decided by a representative or an officer of a penitentiary institution or any clergyman. The current legislation provides that this should be done by the parent or legal guardian of the minor, taking into account the growing maturity of the child and his or her opinion in this regard.

705 See: https://www.sw.gov.pl/strona/Statystyka (accessed 12.07.2023).

6.6.3. Religion and how it is practiced: a point of view of juveniles in youth educational centres and correctional facilities

The questionnaires on the religious practices of children placed in connection with the committed act in youth educational centres or correctional facilities were completed by 209 juvenile charges. Their religiosity looks different from that of adult prisoners. When asked to define their attitude to faith, the juveniles replied as follows:

- practicing believer: 62 respondents, which was 29.66 % of the study population;
- non-practicing believer: 79, which was 37.8 % of the study population;
- non-believer: 48, which was 22.96 % of the study population;
- searching for faith: 5, which was 2.39 % of the study population;
- other: 7, which was 3.35 % of the study population; the respondents indicated: belief in myself, atheist, belief in the universe, satanist, "I believe that there is nothing out there, and even if there is something, I don't care";
- no reply was given in 8 questionnaires.

In total, there were 141 believers, which is 67.5 % of the study population.

Traditionally, Catholics were the biggest group 105 (74.5 % of believing juveniles), there were individuals of different denominations. Moreover, 59 (41.8 %) believers pointed to other religion (indicating most frequently in general terms "Christianity", much less frequently – "none", "none of the above", exceptionally: Satanism, pastafarianism, belief in oneself), 37 juveniles gave no answer.

The changes (dynamics) in the religiosity of juveniles during their stay in isolation centres look different from that of adult prisoners. **The number of individuals for whom religion lost importance is greater than the number of individuals for whom it took on importance in an educational centre or correctional facility**. It does not result from the juveniles' place of stay or their moral attitude manifested in a violation of law. It is due to a nationwide trend towards secularization, particularly evident among the youngest members of Polish society. Although this study does not aim to make an in-depth analysis of the religiosity of Polish youths,[706] it should be pointed out that against the background of other European states, the dynamics of change in the religiosity

706 See more: J. Baniak, *Religijność i moralność młodzieży polskiej w latach 1956–2018 na tle przemian cywilizacyjnych i społecznych. Studium socjologiczne*, Poznań 2022; J. Baniak, "Między akceptacją a kontestacją. Kościół w krytycznym spojrzeniu młodzieży polskiej", in I. Borowik, A. Górny, W. Świątkiewicz (eds.), *Globalny i lokalny wymiar religii*, Kraków 2016, pp. 148 et seq.; K. Kaźmierska, *Młodzież Archidiecezji Łódzkiej. Szkic do portretu*, Łódź 2018.

of Polish youths is, as given above, particularly evident and high. The level of declared religiosity in persons aged 15–24 fell from 91.6 % in 2002 to 82.1 % in 2018. In 2021, in the 18–24 year old population, the percentage of believers was 71 % (a decline of 22 % compared to 1992), and the number of non-believers increased by 28.6 %. In the same group, the proportion of regular practitioners also fell at the fastest rate, from 69 % in 1992 to 23 % in 2021, while the proportion of non-practitioners increased from 7.9 % do 36 %.[707]

It is worthwhile to recall the feasts and rituals important for the juvenile charges. They were asked to name the feasts and religious rituals they deemed important. The most frequent answers included Christmas (or Christmas Eve) and Easter. Some added Corpus Christi, All Saints' Day; New Year's Eve was mentioned several times. Others indicated that no feasts were important, a few alleged that, on the contrary, all feasts were important. The rituals that juveniles found important were Mass, prayer, the Stations of the Cross, Confession, Confirmation, Holy Communion or, as they indicated in general, the sacraments and the blessing of food. Baptism and marriage were mentioned occasionally. Likewise, a large proportion of respondents said that no sacraments and rituals were important. One of them added: "None. I am forced to go to church. I live with the nuns." This comment suggests a problem that is further addressed below.

Given that the study population consisted of individuals in many cases still covered by compulsory schooling, we were interested in their participation in religious instruction, which in Poland is offered as part of general education. Although the figures do not come as a surprise, many comments made by the juveniles raise great concern.

As the juveniles declared, 149 of them take religious instruction, that is, more than the declared number of believers and they represent 71.3 % of all juvenile detainees surveyed. At liberty, only 54 % of schoolchildren take religious instruction and their numbers are constantly dwindling (to compare, in 2010, 93 % of respondents participated in religious instruction).[708] It follows from our questionnaires that only 91 (43.5 %) respondents taking religious instruction indicated that it was their own choice. In the case of further 27 (12.9 %) juveniles,

---

707 W. Szymczak, P. M. Mąkosa, T. Adamczyk, "Attitudes of Polish Young Adults towards the Roman Catholic Church: A Sociological and Pastoral Analysis of Empirical Research among Young Adults and Teachers", *Religions*, vol. 13, no. 7, 2022, pp. 1 et seq.

708 See: Public Opinion Research Centre, *Polish religious landscape – a view from the foreground, Research communication no. 91/022,* https://www.cbos.pl/SPISKOM.POL/2022/K_091_22.PDF (accessed: 20.08.2023).

the parents were responsible for the decision, and in 31 (14.8 %) cases, the juveniles gave another reason, saying: because I want to, I've always attended religious instruction, because I have to – the nuns, "such is the compulsion", "not going does harm", "you cannot opt out", "compulsory lesson", "because we have to", "we have no choice", "no way out".

The above data are shocking and alarming. Individuals placed in such facilities are adolescents (the questionnaires were completed by juveniles up to the age of 14 years: 17 persons, 15–16 years of age: 76 persons, 17–18 years of age: 80 persons, 19 years of age: 16 persons, 20 respondents gave no answer), and are therefore at such an age that their individual and personal right to self-determination and religious freedom should already be respected. It is true that Polish law, especially concerning juveniles, does not respect this constitutional principle and leaves the decision on the participation in religious instruction exclusively to the parents. This requires legislative amendments, which has been suggested above. However, there is no legal basis for the decision on taking religious instruction to be forced by an educational centre / a correctional facility or its representatives, teachers or catechists.

Another serious formal shortcoming is the issue of obtaining information on the juveniles' confession by facility officers. In the questionnaires, 85 (40.7 %) juveniles revealed that they were asked about it and 49 (23.4 %) others admitted that their parents were asked about it. At the same time, 44 (21.1 %) juveniles were not informed about their rights in relation to religious freedom! It may thus be concluded that the standards of juvenile rights are violated in this regard.

The next questions were addressed to Catholics, who were a 155-person group, their participation in sacraments and other practices. Attention should again be given to Mass attendance and taking Holy Communion. During their stay in an institution, 51 juveniles attended Mass once a week and 8 attended Mass once a month. It may be concluded that 38 % juveniles attended Mass relatively regularly. In turn, 32 individuals (6+26), or 20.6 % Catholics, take Holy Communion. The same juvenile Catholics declared regular Mass attendance – 44 persons (35+9, in total 28.4 %) and taking Holy Communion regularly – 25 persons (7+18, in total 16.1 %) at liberty. Thus, the changes in this respect were not very radical. Importantly, when asked why they participated in the liturgy, the juveniles pointed to the need to attend Mass, to pray, faith, tradition, a possibility to solve problems. However, they also stated it was because "everyone/colleagues do it", because "they have to" or "they tell you to", because "it pays off", "it won't hurt", "out of boredom". Consequently, it is hard to argue that the relatively high participation rate was entirely voluntary.

The coercive element seems to be lacking in other practices, and these data should be recalled. Responding to whether they wore a cross, medallion or any other faith symbol permanently during their stay in the institution, 51 juveniles (36.2 % of believers) responded positively. On the question of the possession of a cross, holy picture or any other faith symbol in the room, 68 respondents (45.6 % of believers) responded positively. Moreover, 53 persons (35.6 %) observe Catholic fasts. On the question of accepting a Christmas-time pastoral visit during their stay in the institution, 47 persons replied they (31.5 %) accept it because they want to, 17 persons do it because they have to (8.1 % of all the juveniles).

To give a full picture, CBOS research shows a slow decline in the level of religious belief and a faster decline in the level of practice in Polish society. The process studied here is the fastest among the youngest. Sociological studies refer to two so-called youngest generations (age cohorts): the generation born between 1980–1996, referred to as millennials, and the youngest generation born in 1997 or later, referred to as generation 'Z'. The process of abandonment of religious practice is pronounced in all age cohorts, and rapid in the two youngest. In the millennial generation, the number of regular practitioners has decreased by 42.8 percentage points, the number of non-practitioners has increased by 22.7 percentage points, and this has happened in less than 24 years. In the youngest cohort, the number of regular practitioners has decreased by 32.7 percentage points, the number of non-practitioners has increased by 18.4 percentage points, but it all occurred in less than 7 years. Importantly, insofar as the process of abandoning regular religious practices is taking place gradually in the three oldest age cohorts (at different paces, but gradually), it clearly accelerates in around 2016 in the 'Y' generation, in around 2018 in the millennial generation, and it is an uninterrupted, rapid 'downhill slide' in the youngest cohort. By contrast, the percentages of non-practitioners in all age cohorts have been increasing since around 2017, most steeply in the two youngest cohorts.[709]

As regards juveniles of other denominations and non-believers, they did not report major problems in their questionnaires. Out of 9 individuals of other denominations, 2 individuals believed they were in a worse situation than followers of other religions (without citing any additional information), 1

709 See: Public Opinion Research Centre, *Religiosity of the youth against the background of the entire society. Research Communication no. 144/2021*, https://www.cbos.pl/SPISKOM.POL/2021/K_144_21.PDF (accessed 20.08.2023).

individual thought otherwise (a better situation). On the question of the necessity to participate in religious practices of another religion, two individuals replied positively, without citing specifically any practices. 44 respondents declared themselves non-believers (21.1 % of the juvenile population surveyed). Among them, 26 (59.1 % of non-believers) did not feel compelled to participate in any religious practices or rituals during their stay in the centre, while 11 respondents thought otherwise. When asked about onerous regulations relating to these issues, 5 respondents pointed to the lack of possibility of opting out of religious instruction or the lack of ethics classes instead of religious instruction. Again, the problem of the lack of real religious freedom in youth centres has been recorded.

6.6.4. Religion and how it is practiced: a point of view of educators of juveniles in youth educational centres and correctional facilities

The juveniles' comments were complemented with their educators' opinions. In this case too, the picture drawn by educators of penitentiary facilities is somewhat different, one could say, more positive than it is seen by prisoners. The questionnaire was completed by 108 educators.

They pointed out in the questionnaires that some juveniles were willing to admit their religion and wanted to talk about it, others, on the contrary, talked about their negative attitude towards their faith. Some juveniles did not want to talk about their religion at all. It seems that the argument "Juveniles placed in an institution frequently declare themselves non-believers, thus, they do not acknowledge their religion" is some sort of misunderstanding or even abuse. The comment suggests that the declared lack of faith is insincere and is a form of manipulation (concealment). Such an approach to juveniles in isolation units certainly does not deserve approval. It must be added that the further part of the comment offers an explanation: "During their stay in the institution, the attitude of juveniles changes towards faith. This is evidenced by an upward trend in the practice of faith, that is, attending Mass, services, going to confession, prayers before religious instruction (at times, boys pray the rosary in the evening), going on a pilgrimage to St. Anne's Mountain, taking part in weekend spiritual retreats organized by the Young on the Threshold Foundation, preparatory meetings for the sacrament of Confirmation, biblical circle, trips to Licheń." If all these activities are based on genuine willingness, one can only praise such a wide religious offer, but it is worse when the coercive situations described by the juveniles occur during such activities.

Some educators saw juveniles wear religious symbols, but as one of them pointed out, it was not always possible to assess correctly whether a cross is an element of religion or a piece of jewellery.

The educators believed that the juveniles did not experience major problems practicing their religion, both Catholics and followers of other denominations. Some pointed out that even the pandemic restrictions did not affect the situation much. Some educators stated that activities outside the institution (Masses in churches, pilgrimages) were restricted. The educators claimed the attitude of the juveniles towards the restrictions varied. Some seemed unaffected by the restrictions, others showed full understanding and did not demand certain practices. The educators also believed that some juveniles greatly missed attending Mass.

Responding to whether non-believers were forced to participate for organizational reasons in specific religious practices, 18 (16.7 %) educators replied yes, 83 (76.9 %) replied no. Their comments indicated that Mass attendance was voluntary, as was the case with other sacraments, and participation in the Christmas Eve was treated as part of tradition rather than a religious practice. Some, however, saw other aspects: "The organization of the institution takes into account Catholic feasts, e.g., fasts. Because there is one kitchen, juveniles declaring themselves as non-believers had to eat fish", or "Participation in spiritual retreats as school classes". Another educator made the following comment: "The juveniles have to be looked after at all times, so they had to be together with everyone else at Mass or religious holidays." Finally, the following comments hint at the positive dimension of compulsory participation: "For non-believers – a lesson on how to behave in a place of worship" or "Attending (presence at) Mass as a behavioural skills training in an open environment." **Searching for the rationalization of forced religious practices by pointing to other benefits to be gained by a juvenile is an utterly reprehensible attitude. Forced religious practice is already a violation of religious freedom, searching for substitute objectives means hypocrisy and cynicism towards juveniles.**

Educators working with juveniles showed much greater awareness of the legal solutions for giving consent for juveniles to take part in religious practices and religious instruction than educators from penitentiary facilities.

6.7. Data on chaplains and religious organizations cooperating with the Prison Service

For a complete picture of the opportunities for adult prisoners to exercise their religious freedom we submitted a request (BDG.0143.166.2023.PA) to the

Central Board of the Prison Service to provide information on the number of full-time chaplains employed in the Prison Service broken down by region, the denominations they represent, and the number and names of organizations of a religious nature that cooperate with the Prison Service broken down by regions.

In response to the first question we received the following list:

Number of posts for chaplains employed in the Prison Service broken down by particular regions and denominations they represent

Regional Inspectorate of the Prison Service	As of 30/06/2023		
	Denomination	Number of posts for chaplains	Number of employed chaplains
Bydgoszcz	Roman Catholic	8	15
	Polish Autocephalous Orthodox Church	0.5	1
In total		**8.5**	**16**
Katowice	Roman Catholic	4.8 + voluntary service	16
	Eastern Orthodox Church	0.6 + voluntary service	6
	Pentecostal Church	voluntary service	6
	Evangelical Church of the Augsburg Confession	1	1
	Seventh-Day Adventist Church	voluntary service	2
	Free Christians Church	voluntary service	2
	Baptist Christian Church	voluntary service	1
	Church of God	voluntary service	1
In total		**6.4**	**35**
Koszalin	Roman Catholic	6.7	14
	Eastern Orthodox	0.2	1
In total		**6.9**	**15**
Kraków	Roman Catholic	5.5	10
	Eastern Orthodox	1.3	2
In total		**6.8**	**12**

Lublin	Roman Catholic	6.95	12
	Polish Autocephalous Orthodox Church	3	8
	Greek Catholic Church	0.25	1
In total		**10.2**	**21**
Łódź	Roman Catholic	5.45	10
In total		**5.45**	**10**
Olsztyn	Roman Catholic	11.9	17 (+1 voluntary service)
	Eastern Orthodox	4.25	7 (+1 voluntary service)
	Evangelical Church of the Augsburg Confession	0.5	1
	Pentecostal Church	0.25	1
In total		**16.9**	**26 (+2 voluntary service)**
Opole	Roman Catholic	7.15	14
	Evangelical Church of the Augsburg Confession	0.65	1
	Eastern Orthodox	0.25	1
In total		**8.05**	**16**
Poznań	Roman Catholic	5	11
	Eastern Orthodoxy	0.4	2
	Pentecostal Church	0.5	1
In total		**5.9**	**14**
Rzeszów	Roman Catholic	3.25	10
	Eastern Orthodox	0.65	2
In total		**3.9**	**12**
Warsaw	Roman Catholic	8.7	13
	Eastern Orthodox	3	4
	Roman Catholic – nun	0.5	1
In total		**12.2**	**18**
SUM		**91.2**	**169**

Source: information from the Central Board of the Prison Service of 28 July 2023, letter BDG.0143.166.2023.PA

The above information allows the conclusion that the religious picture in Polish penitentiary facilities and detention centres is slightly richer that our study shows. This is because the chaplains represent religions whose followers were not recorded in our survey. It is an understandable phenomenon if one looks at the data (presented above) on the number of followers of religions other than Roman Catholicism in the entire Polish population.

The received information shows an uneven number of posts and number of chaplains in different regions. For example, the Regional Inspectorate of the Prison Service (Polish: Okręgowy Inspektorat Służby Więziennej; hereinafter: OISW) in Rzeszów has only 3.9 chaplain posts, although ministry is provided by 12 chaplains of two denominations, Łódź OISW has 5.45 chaplain posts and ministry is provided by 10 chaplains, all Roman Catholic. Olsztyn OISW has 16.9 chaplain posts, ministry is provided by 26 chaplains (+ 2 volunteers), representing 4 denominations. In turn, in Katowice OISW, 35 chaplains represent 8 denominations. These differences may in part be due to the number of penitentiary institutions within a given region and the number of prisoners incarcerated in them. However, it is more difficult to find a rational explanation for the differences in the number of denominations in the particular regions. It may in part be due to the greater or lesser interest and involvement of representatives of specific denominations, which in turn may be due (although not always) to the popularity of a denomination in a particular area.

Moreover, the general number of chaplains in Poland – 169 (with 91.2 chaplain posts) may give rise to doubts as to the real access of prisoners to a chaplain not only of minority denominations but also of the religion prevailing in Poland – Roman Catholicism. Assuming that, on 28 July 2023, 68,092 convicts and 8,319 pre-trial detainees were incarcerated (in total 76,411 incarcerated individuals),[710] on average, there are over 452 prisoners per chaplain. It is true that not all prisoners are religious, need contact with a chaplain or want to benefit from religious practices. Yet the suggested need for Christmas-time pastoral visits, complaints about too few opportunities to attend Mass, comments made by educators in penitentiary institutions about too little availability of chaplains, support the argument that there are too few chaplains in penitentiary institutions.

The response to the question about the religious organizations cooperating with the Prison Service took the form of a list:

Number and name of organizations of a religious nature cooperating with the Prison Service broken down by regions

710 See: Prison Service, *Information on the population of penitentiary institutions on 28 July 2023*, https://www.sw.gov.pl/strona/Statystyka (accessed 20.08.2023).

Regional Inspectorate of the Prison Service	As of 30/06/2023	
	Name of an organization of a religious nature cooperating with the Prison Service	Number of organizations
Bydgoszcz	Samaritania Prison Brotherhood	4
	Chapel of Jehovah's Witnesses	7
	Seventh-Day Adventist Church	2
	Baptist Christian Church	1
	Jewish Community of Gdańsk	1
	Pentecostal Church Chapel "Joy of Life"	1
In total		**16**
Katowice	Marian Legions	1
	Renewal in the Holy Spirit	1
	"Fileo" Christian Association of Rehabilitation Assistance in Cieszyn	3
	"Alpha – Poland" Kraków	2
	Do What You Love Agency of Speakers and Musicians Grzegorz Czerwicki	1
	Jehovah's Witnesses Association	10
	Muslim Religious Union in the Republic of Poland Supreme Muslim College	1
	Christian Evangelical Community	1
In total		**20**
Koszalin	Evangelical Brotherhood Association	1
	Jehovah's Witnesses Confessional Association	7
	Pentecostal Church	6
	Church of Free Christians	1
	Seventh-Day Adventist Church	3
	Evangelical Church of the Augsburg Confession	1
	Christian Community in Koszalin – stop	1
	Christian Charity Association	1
	Evangelical Church of Christian	1
In total		**22**
Kraków	Congregation of Albertine Sisters	1
	Alpha Association	1
	Jehovah's Witnesses	1
	Pentecostal Church	1
	Gideons International	1

In total		**5**
Lublin	Christian Chapel of Jehovah's Witnesses	6
	Evangelical Faith Christians' Church in Poland	2
	Prison Mission of the Pentecostal Church in the Republic of Poland	2
	Evangelical Christian Church Chapel Piątków	1
	Seventh-Day Adventist Church in the Republic of Poland	2
	St. Brother Albert's Society in Kodeń	1
	Church of God in Christ	1
	Baptist Christian Church	1
	Order of the Franciscan Sisters of Mary	2
	Church of Christ	1
	Evangelical Church of the Augsburg Confession	1
	Community of Canon John the Baptist	1
	Apostolic Community Legion of Mary	1
In total		**22**
Łódź	Renewal in the Holy Spirit	2
	Strong in the Spirit	1
	Caritas of the Diocese of Kalisz	1
	Alpha Association Poland	1
	Ahmadiyya Muslim Association	1
In total		**6**
Olsztyn	Pentecostal Church	6
	Prison Brotherhood "Elijah"	2
	Treaty Bible Society – Registered Association of Jehovah's Witnesses	7
	Chapel of the Baptist Christian Church	1
	Alpha Association Poland	1
	Caritas of the Diocese of Łomża	1
	Supreme Muslim College of the Religious Union of Poland	1
In total		**19**
Opole	Community of Canon John the Baptist	1
	The Awakened Association (Buddhists)	1
	Jehovah's Witnesses in Poland	10
	Pentecostal Church in Poland	9
	Roman Catholic Church	12
	Evangelical Augsburg Church	2
	Canonical Mission of the Orthodox Church	2

	Secular Missionary Movement Epiphany	1
	Baptist Christian Church Chapel I in Wrocław	1
	Seventh-Day Adventist Church	2
	Chapel of Christians in Grabów nad Prosną	1
	Prison Brotherhood	1
	International Association of Gideons	1
	Greek Catholic Church Wrocław	1
	Association of Jewish Communes	1
	Chapel of the Baptist Christian Church in Wrocław	1
	"Fileo" Christian Association of Rehabilitation Assistance	1
	Caritas of the Diocese of Opole Region Nysa	1
In total		**49**
Poznań	Jehovah's Witnesses	7
	Prison Brotherhood	4
	Evangelical Brotherhood Association	1
	Christian Pentecostal Community	5
	Church of God in Christ	2
	Seventh-Day Adventist Church	1
	Meek Workers of the Cross	1
	Secular Missionary Movement Epiphany	1
	Gideons	1
	Greek Catholic Church	1
In total		**24**
Rzeszów	Pentecostal Church	1
	Chapel of Jehovah's Witnesses	1
	Roman Catholic Church	1
	Roman Catholic Church	1
	"Watchtower" Jehovah's Witnesses	1
	Greek Catholic Church	1
	Fylake Mission – Evangelical Faith Church	1
	Seventh-Day Adventists	1
	Renewal in the Holy Spirit – Catholic Church	1
	Christian Chapel of Jehovah's Witnesses	1
	Prison Brotherhood	1
	Meetings with the Seminarians of the Seminary	1
	Seventh-Day Adventist Church	1

	Evangelical Faith Christians' Church in Poland	1
	Eastern Orthodox Church	1
In total		**15**
Warsaw	Treaty Bible Society – Registered Association of Jehovah's Witnesses Watchtower	6
	Pentecostal Church	5
	Muslim Religious Union	3
	Eastern Orthodox Church	3
	Roman Catholic Church	3
	Caritas of the Diocese of Siedlce	1
	Seventh-Day Adventist Church	2
	Church of Christ	2
	Evangelical Faith Christians' Church in Poland	1
	Alpha Course	1
	Shepherdess Sisters	1
In total		**28**
SUM		**226**

Source: information from the Central Board of the Prison Service of 28 July 2023, letter BDG.0143.166.2023.PA

Putting aside the inconsistencies in the nomenclature of the different organizations (different names for the same entities, repetitions), the above overview provides interesting information about the abundance of religious organizations involved in the work with convicts and pre-trail detainees. It is also important that organizations of religious denominations being in a marginal minority on the religious map of Poland appear relatively frequently. Moreover, the diverse forms of religious work in Polish penitentiary institutions also include the latest religious activities, e.g., Alpha courses.[711]

These data clearly show the differing accessibility of religious organizations of a given denomination among the particular regions. For example, Kraków OISW indicates only 5 religious organizations cooperating with the Prison Service while Opole OISW Opole has 18 different organizations, some of which were represented more often in a given region, which gave in total 49 organizations.

711 See: https://www.sw.gov.pl/aktualnosc/zaklad-karny-w-uhercach-mineralnych-alpha-w-wiezieniu and https://www.gosc.pl/doc/8193214.Kursy-Alpha-za-kratami-Wchodzisz-do-wiezienia-o-zaostrzonym (accessed 20.08.2023).

In this case too, the number of organizations largely depends on the activity and involvement of representatives of every denomination.

Recalling the comments by prisoners and educators from penitentiary institutions on the under involvement of some chaplains, reference should be made to the findings of a study carried out by W. Romanowicz and D. Tomczyszyn. In order to determine in practice the work and role of prison pastoral services in Polish prisons, the authors asked the prisoners serving a penalty of imprisonment in the External Division in Zabłocie (Biała Podlaska Penitentiary) to make an assessment. Over half of the respondents assessed the ministry services well or very well (respectively, 46.5 % and 4.9 %). An opposite view was expressed by 6.8 % of the respondents (very bad – 0.9 % and bad – 5.9 %). A very large percentage of the respondents had an ambivalent attitude to ministry – 18.8 % or had no opinion on the subject – 23.0 %. The researchers pointed out that due to the fact that the persons surveyed had already been in many other prisons, the question was not only about a specific chaplain or ministry, but it provided a general opinion.[712] The findings do not give cause for optimism.

One cannot ignore a study carried out by Jerzy Nikołajew among prison chaplains in 2006–2007.[713] In view of the expectations reported by prisoners, it is significant that 69 % of chaplains are over 40 years of age, 79 % of chaplains have chaplaincy experience of more than 10 years. Most importantly, 87 % of chaplains perform other duties in the parish (most often parson, vicar, catechist) in addition to their work in prison. Given the above, it is not surprising that prisoners and educators express opinions that chaplains are not always fully involved in prison ministry. J. Nikołajew also established that 50 % of the respondents come to receive pastoral service every day and 49 % once a week. It is concerning that 77 % of the respondents have no specialist training in working with prisoners, while the others justified their qualifications by having attended a course for therapists or having obtained a doctorate. One in five respondents is not familiar with the provisions of the Penal Enforcement Code, but 77 % of them read materials of the Supreme Prison Chaplain. It also follows from the study that chaplains look forward to amendments to enforcement law – 52 % believe that a provision on moral impacting on convicts is needed, 32 % support a regulation including religious impacting in the list foreseen by the Code. All the respondents (100 %) are sure that rehabilitation through faith is possible;

712 W. Romanowicz, D. Tomczyszyn, "Stosunek do religii…, pp. 96 et seq.

713 J. Nikołajew, *Duszpasterstwo więzienne…*, *passim* and J. Nikołajew, "Specyfika duszpasterstwa więziennego..., pp. 157 et seq.

attention was paid to God's love and mercy, the aspect of conversion, spiritual healing, obtaining forgiveness, regaining self-respect and seeking a right path in life. The conclusions drawn by J. Nikołajew seem fairly obvious – it is necessary to distinguish a group of prison chaplains, who would perform their duties in the penitentiary space (with no additional duties), increase the number of available chaplain posts, ensure specialist training. However, we are not convinced that it is necessary to amend the Penal Enforcement Code and introduce a provision on moral or religious impacting on prisoners in view of the need to bring about lasting changes in their attitudes. In the same way that we do not share the call for increased chaplain involvement in the development of rehabilitation programmes. This may put non-believers at a disadvantage or, more likely, put prisoners who abandon their faith while serving a sentence in an unfavourable position.

Conclusions

The research we have carried out, both dogmatically and through questionnaires, makes it possible to draw the most important conclusions regarding compliance with the religious freedom of persons deprived of their liberty. We are sure that although some shortcomings relate to the Polish regulations and Polish practice of the enforcement of sentences and educational and corrective measures that are isolationist in nature, the conclusions and postulates stemming from them are universal. The ECHR case-law provides evidence that violations of religious freedom are a problem encountered by more than one European state.

The most important findings include:

1. Irrespective of the presumably beneficial effect of religion on the modelling of the figure of a prisoner, religion, or more precisely, the right to profess and practice it, is "simply" the right of every human being and compliance with it does not require any justification or confirmation.
2. The approach presented in the German literature, under which the protection of belief does not depend on statistical criteria, sociological significance or the number of followers, should be considered appropriate. There is no sufficient constitutional basis to argue that the beliefs of dissidents are less protected than the collective beliefs shared by a religious community.[714]
3. The practice of making reservations and interpretative declarations when signing and ratifying international treaties is understandable – it enhances the commitment of states and a legal solution to a specific problem takes on a more universal character. However, reservations compromising the essence of an ensured right mean that a signed and ratified international agreement becomes fiction.
4. An analysis of the legal state at the international level showed an unacceptable lack of adequate regulations on religious freedom of juveniles in post-criminal isolation units. Children deprived of their liberty are one of the most vulnerable social groups, whose rights must be meticulously written down and then subjected to a scrutiny.
5. The downside is that the manner in which the standards of international law are applied to national penitentiary law is most frequently reduced to formulating vague statements to the effect that prisoners are entitled to

714 M. Germann, "Art. 4 GG…, margin no. 17.

exercise their right to manifest their religion or belief to the fullest extent possible that is consistent with the particular nature of the restrictions to which they are subject, and that national authorities are obliged to provide all prisoners, including pre-trail detainees, with the possibility to attend services and have contact with representatives of their confession.

6. The introduction of detailed provisions on the exercise of religious freedom into prison internal rules regulates the details that are missing in the generally applicable law, but it also gives rise to the risk that directors of particular prisons will make arbitrary decisions in the area of religious freedom of the prisoners incarcerated in a given institution. In turn, the fragmentation of the matter does not make it easy to verify whether it is actually being complied with. In such a case, the monitoring must be particularly careful. The German regulation may serve as an example of a more adequate approach.
7. An objection must be raised to the fact that most often disciplinary and security reasons inherent in the criminal enforcement regime justify the introduction of restrictions, which will result in the impossibility to manifest one's religion adequately.
8. It is unacceptable to impose disciplinary penalties in the form of restricting the right to religious practices.
9. The standard for the exercise of religious freedom by pre-trial detainees must be assessed as particularly bad.
10. Organizational and financial issues may not be an easy excuse to violate the rights of convicts; the state must make adequate efforts to fulfil the freedom of religious practices.
11. We call for the introduction of a ban on asking incarcerated persons about their professed religion, but we accept the obligation to provide full information on religious freedom rights during a so-called 'informational interview' together with information on where and how to obtain details on specific services and other practices of different confessions.
12. It can be concluded that even the regulations that refer directly to the performance of religious practices of the predominant religion (Roman Catholic Church) are not satisfactory from the perspective of the doctrine of that Church – for example, the obligation to attend Mass every Sunday.
13. The study confirmed the validity of the argument that "the rationale of many restrictions can be hidden under the cloak of 'prison discipline'. However, it must be recognized that not every administrative burden, inconvenience or nuisance has the force of a public order argument. Taking religious rights

seriously means accommodating diversity. This only works if it is understood and accepted that even the shackles of prison life can be loosened if and when human rights are at stake."[715]

14. It is no surprise that religious practices are presented most intensely in the group of Roman Catholics. The widespread presence of this denomination in Polish history and in present-day life means that its rituals are widely known and traditionally observed, and many organizational solutions (e.g. calendar of feasts and holidays, cuisine in communal feeding, availability of various artefacts and objects for worship) make it immensely easier to practise in everyday life. This is also the case in post-criminal isolation units.
15. Human rights in the form of freedom to practice religion exercised by believers in post-criminal isolation units is seen by non-believing prisoners as 'a privilege for the chosen ones,' often an unjust one. That perception is all the stronger, the harsher the isolation regime is – eg, non-believers have no alternative to attending the service, which would also give them an additional chance to leave the cell, not only when going for a walk. The same mechanism can be seen when comparing the situation of Roman Catholics and followers of other denominations, in particular non-Christian. The exercise of the right thus becomes a form of discrimination against other subjects when there are no alternative forms or when organizational reasons do not allow for the exercise of such forms. Remarkably, the German provisions on prison ministry apply to worldview communities involved in providing spiritual assistance to prisoners Poland lacks such regulations.
16. The lack of coercion (by order or blackmail) to actively participate in a particular practice does not mean that such practices are not imposed – the necessity to listen to Holy Mass on the prison radio, joint celebration of specific religious holidays, etc., are also a form of coercion to take part – in the passive form. Temperman argued that: "The Nelson Mandela Rules state that 'if any prisoner should object to a visit of any religious representative, his attitude shall be fully respected.' The European Prison Rules contain a more comprehensive prohibition of coercion: 'Prisoners may not be compelled to practise a religion or belief, to attend religious services or meetings, to take part in religious practices or to accept a visit from a representative of any religion or belief' (a rule that clearly is relevant to both the previous heading of prison church visits and to religious practises discussed under

715 J. Temperman, "Freedom of Religion…, p. 47.

the headings below). These are important additions since prisoners are, obviously, quite literally a 'captured audience' and hence relatively more vulnerable to religious coercion."[716]

17. The problem of violating the religious freedom of religious minorities and non-believers is exacerbated in extraordinary situations – for example, during a pandemic. Then the rights of the followers of the dominant religion are more easily satisfied, sometimes even at the expense of those of other confessions or non-believers.
18. The fact that some of the practices characteristic of (specific to) a given religion are performed does not automatically mean that religious freedom is exercised. Attending services is only one of the practices of a given denomination and it may not be a substitute for the remaining religious practices that are not available.
19. The study has also shown that the staff members of post-criminal isolation units are not always familiar with the current provisions on religious freedom.
20. Juveniles placed in youth educational centres and correctional facilities are undoubtedly a group most vulnerable to violations of religious freedom or are even forced to participate in them. It is desirable to determine the age from which juveniles have the right to decide independently on the right to participate in religious services and practices, for example, along the lines of the German regulations discussed above.
21. Educational impacting on the youth who ran afoul of law with a concomitant lack of respect for their right to religious freedom may not foster a self-reflective and restorative attitude in juveniles. Forcing the youth to participate in religious practices will not strengthen their religiosity and piety and it will exacerbate a culture of violence, disrespect towards others, and lying for a short-term gain. Such practices must be deemed to violate the international and constitutional standards and to be counterproductive to the process of impacting the juvenile.

Ultimately, it is legitimate to argue Poland is constantly striving to implement fully the coding standard of religious freedom in post-criminal isolation units, but the process can be considered to be neither advanced nor completed. The German standards, although scattered, appear to be more accurate and they better fulfil the proper standard of religious freedom of persons deprived of their

716 J. Temperman, "Freedom of Religion…, p. 58.

liberty. They ensure the right of non-believers better, but the presence of Muslim communities within it the German penitentiary system is still unresolved (due to the lack of a full regulation of the legal situation of various religious associations declaring a connection to Islam).

References

Abdi A., Soufinia A., Borji M., Tarjoman A., "The Effect of Religion Intervention on Life Satisfaction and Depression in Elderly with Heart Failure", *Journal of Religion and Health*, vol. 58, no. 3, 2019.

Abo-Zena M. M., Midgett A., "Developmental Implications of Children's Early Religious and Spiritual Experiences in Context: A Sociocultural Perspective", *Religions*, vol. 10, no. 11, 2019.

Abramowicz M. A., "Przedmiotowy zakres wolności religijnej", *Studia z Prawa Wyznaniowego*, vol. 10, 2007.

Alles G. D., "Rudolf Otto (1869–1937)", in A. Michaels (ed.), *Klassiker der Religionswissenschaft: Von Friedrich Schleiermacher bis Mircea Eliade*, München 2010.

Alston W. P., "Religion", in P. Edwards (ed.), *The Encyclopedia of Philosophy*, New York – London 1972.

Amir S. N., Juliana N., Azmani S., et al., "Impact of Religious Activities on Quality of Life and Cognitive Function Among Elderly", *Journal of Religion and Health*, vol. 61, no. 2, 2022.

Anderson J., "The catholic contribution to democratization's third wave: Altruism, hegemony, or self-interest?", *Cambridge Review of International Affairs*, vol. 20, no. 3, 2007.

Arloth F., "§ 21", in F. Arloth, H. Krä (eds.), *Strafvollzugsgesetze von Bund und Ländern*, München 2021.

Arloth F., "§ 53", in F. Arloth, H. Krä (eds.), *Strafvollzugsgesetze von Bund und Ländern*, München 2021.

Arloth F., "§ 157", in F. Arloth, H. Krä (eds.), *Strafvollzugsgesetze von Bund und Ländern*, München 2021.

Arloth F., "§ 182", in F. Arloth, H. Krä (eds.), *Strafvollzugsgesetze von Bund und Ländern*, München 2021.

Arloth F., Geiger T., "Der deutsche Strafvollzug nach der Föderalismusreform", in B. Mailcke, S. Schling (eds.), *Das Gefängnis auf dem Prüfstand. Zustand und Zukunft des Strafvollzugs*, Wiesbaden 2018.

Arshad M., "Schuld, Vergebung und Seelsorge im Islam", in B. Uçar, M. Blasberg-Kuhnke (eds.), *Islamische Seelsorge zwischen Herkunft und Zukunft. Von der theologischen Grundlegung zur Praxis in Deutschland*, Frankfurt am Main 2013.

Ausberg I., Ladeur K. H., *Toleranz – Religion – Recht. Die Herausforderung des »neutralen« Staates durch neue Formen der Religiosität in der postmodernen Gesellschaft*, Tübingen 2007.

Bäumer B., "Sakraler Raum und heilige Zeit", in J. Figl (ed.), *Handbuch Religionswissenschaft: Religionen und ihre zentralen Themen*, Göttingen 2003.

Badura P., "Art. 6 GG", in T. Maunz, G. Dürig (eds.), *Grundgesetz. Kommentar. Band II. Art. 6-16a*, München (100. EL Januar 2023).

Badura P., "Art. 7 GG", in T. Maunz, G. Dürig (eds.), *Grundgesetz. Kommentar. Band II. Art. 6-16a*, München (100. EL Januar 2023).

Bakan A. B., Arli S. K., Yıldız M., "Relationship Between Religious Orientation and Death Anxiety in Elderly Individuals", *Journal of Religion and Health*, vol. 58, no. 6, 2019.

Banaszak B., *Konstytucja Rzeczypospolitej Polskiej. Komentarz*, Warszawa 2012.

Banaszak B., *System konstytucyjny Niemiec*, Warszawa 2005.

Baniak J., "Między akceptacją a kontestacją. Kościół w krytycznym spojrzeniu młodzieży polskiej", in I. Borowik, A. Górny, W. Świątkiewicz (eds.), *Globalny i lokalny wymiar religii*, Kraków 2016.

Baniak J., *Religijność i moralność młodzieży polskiej w latach 1956–2018 na tle przemian cywilizacyjnych i społecznych. Studium socjologiczne*, Poznań 2022.

Barton G., Yilmaz I., Morieson N., "Religious and Pro-Violence Populism in Indonesia: The Rise and Fall of a Far-Right Islamist Civilisationist Movement", *Religions*, vol. 12, no. 6, 2021.

Bartosiewicz J., "Glosa do wyroku ETPC z dnia 17 grudnia 2013 r., 14150/08", Lex/el 2014.

Bartoszewicz J., "Wolność myśli, sumienia i wyznania w Polsce w świetle orzecznictwa strasburskiego", *Polski Rocznik Praw Człowieka i Prawa Humanitarnego*, vol. 3, 2012.

Bendix R., *Max Weber: An Intellectual Portrait*, Berkley 1977.

Berger P. L., *The Sacred Canopy: Elements of a Sociological Theory of Religion*, Garden City 1967.

Bielecki M., "Instytucje polskiego prawa penitencjarnego na tle nauczania Jana Pawła II. Wybrane problemy", in P. Marzec, J. Nikołajew (eds.), *Osoba i dzieło Ojca Świętego Jana Pawła II. Studium wybranych problemów*, Tomaszów Lubelski–Lublin 2009.

Black J. W., "Sex, Abortion, Domestic Violence and Other Unmentionables: Orthodox Christian Youth in Kenya and Windows into Their Attitudes about Sex", *Religions*, vol. 8, no. 5, 2017.

Bochenek K., "Zjawisko laicyzacji w społeczeństwie ponowoczesnym (konteksty filozoficzne)", *Wschodni Rocznik Humanistyczny*, vol. 16, no. 1, 2019.

Bogunia L., "Kilka uwag dotyczących obowiązków skazanego na karę pozbawienia wolności w jego statusie prawnym", in K. Indecki (ed.), *Aktualne problemy prawa karnego, kryminologii i penitencjarystyki. Księga ofiarowana Profesorowi Stefanowi Lelentalowi w 45. Roku pracy naukowej i dydaktycznej*, Łódź 2004.

Borecki P., "Państwo laickie w świetle dorobku współczesnego konstytucjonalizmu europejskiego", *Przegląd Prawniczy Uniwersytetu im. Adama Mickiewicza*, vol. 6, 2016.

Borecki P., "Status prawny osób bezwyznaniowych w Polsce", *Państwo i Prawo*, no. 4, 2007.

Borecki P., "Wolność sumienia i wyznania cudzoziemców w prawie polskim", *Studia z Prawa Wyznaniowego*, vol. 17, 2014.

Borowik I., "Doktryna religijna", in T. Gadacz, B. Milerski (eds.), *Religia. Encyklopedia PWN. Ciapinski – Fatima. Tom 3*, Warszawa, 2001.

Borowik I., "Religia i społeczeństwo. Tropami klasyków w teoriach współczesnych socjologów religii", in S. H. Zaręba (ed.), *Socjologia życia religijnego w Polsce*, Warszawa 2009.

Bowie F., *The Anthropology of Religion: An Introduction*, Malden 2006.

Bożek M., *System konstytucyjny Republiki Federalnej Niemiec*, Warszawa 2017.

Brady K. L., "Religious Sincerity and Imperfection: Can Lapsing Prisoners Recover Under RFRA and RLUIPA?", *The University of Chicago Law Review*, vol. 78, no. 4, 2011.

Bronk A., *Podstawy nauk o religii*, Lublin 2003.

Bronk A., "Religia", in T. Gadacz, B. Milerski (eds.), *Religia. Encyklopedia PWN. Parys – Rut. Tom 8*, Warszawa, 2003.

Brzozowski W., *Bezstronność światopoglądowa władz publicznych w Konstytucji RP*, Warszawa 2011.

Cebula S., *Prawa i wolności religijne we współczesnej Polsce. Ustawodawstwo a realia społeczno-kulturowe*, Kraków 2011.

Choczyński M., "Religijność senioralna w kontekście dobrostanu społecznego", in I. Borowik, S. Grotowska, P. Stawiński (eds.), *Religia wobec wyzwań współczesności z perspektywy nauk społecznych*, Warszawa 2018.

Cimşit M., "Islamische Seelsorge – Eine theologische Begriffsbestimmung", in B. Uçar, M. Blasberg-Kuhnke (eds.), *Islamische Seelsorge zwischen Herkunft und Zukunft. Von der theologischen Grundlegung zur Praxis in Deutschland*, Frankfurt am Main 2013.

Clear T. R., Hardyman P. L., Stout B., et al., "The Value of Religion in Prison: An Inmate Perspective", *Journal of Contemporary Criminal Justice*, vol. 16, no. 1, 2000.

Coester-Waltjen C., "Art. 6 GG", in I. Münch, P. Kunig (eds.), *Grundgesetz-Kommentar. Band 1. Art. 1 bis 69*, München 2012.

Cornel H., "Die Entwicklung des deutschen Strafvollzugs nach der Föderalismusreform des Jahres 2006 mit der Verlagerung der Gesetzgebungskompetenz auf die Bundesländer", *Neue Kriminalpolitik*, vol. 30, no. 1, 2018.

Crowley V., *Jung: A Journey of Transformation: Exploring His Life and Experiencing His Ideas*, Wheaton 2000.

Czakon W., "Rygor metodologiczny", in W. Czakon (ed.), *Podstawy metodologii badań w naukach o zarządzaniu*, Warszawa 2023.

Czarnecki R. S., "Meandry współczesnej laicyzacji", *Res Humana*, vol. 18, no. 3, 2009.

Davie G., Vincent J., "Religion and old age", *Aging & Society*, vol. 18, no. 1, 1998.

Davis R, E., Couper M. P., Janz N. K., Caldwell C. H., Resnicow K., "Interviewer effects in public health surveys", *Health Education Research*, vol. 25, no. 1, 2010.

Demmrich S., Wolfradt U., *William James: The Varieties of Religious Experience (1902)*, in Ch. Gärtner, G. Pickel (eds.), *Schlüsselwerke der Religionssoziologie*, Wiesbaden 2019.

Di Fabio U., "Art. 4 GG", in T. Maunz, G. Dürig (eds.), *Grundgesetz. Kommentar. Band I. Art. 1–5*, München 2022 (98. EL März 2022).

Dobieszewski J., *Filozofia religii. Wykład*, Warszawa 2022.

Drewniowska K., "Realizacja konstytucyjnej zasady rozdziału Kościoła od państwa – wybrane aspekty", in M. Stanulewicz, E. Plewa, C. Linowski (eds.), *Państwo wobec religii. Teraźniejszość i przeszłość*, Łódź 2021.

Durkheim E., *Les Formes élémentaires de la vie religieuse. Le système totémique en Australie*, Paris 2003.

Durón-Reyes D. E., Mondragón-Cervantes M. I., Jiménez-Acosta Y. C., et al., "Religion, spirituality, and old age: A review of the literature", *The Journal of Latin America Geriatric Medicine*, vol. 5, no. 2, 2019.

Dünkel F., "Die Europäischen Strafvollzugsgrundsätze von 2006 und die deutsche Strafvollzugsgesetzgebung", *Forum Strafvollzug*, vol. 3, 2012.

Dünkel F., Morgenstern C., "Germany", in F. Dünkel, S. Harrendorf, D. Zyl Smit (eds.), *The impact of COVID-19 on prison conditions and penal policy*, London – New York 2022.

Dünkel F., Schüler-Springorum H., "Strafvollzug als Ländersache? Der *Wettbewerb der Schäbigkeit* ist schon im Gange!", *Zeitschrift für Strafvollzug und Straffälligenhilfe*, vol. 5, 2006.

Dwyer J. G., "Parents' Religion and Children's Welfare: Debunking the Doctrine of Parents' Rights", *California Law Review*, vol. 82, no. 6, 1994.

Dźwigoł H., "Założenia do budowy metodyki badawczej", *Zeszyty Naukowe Politechniki Śląskiej. Seria: Organizacja i Zarządzanie*, vol. 78, 2015.

Ekardt F., Buscher D., "Föderalismusreform II: Reform der Finanzbeziehungen von Bund, Ländern und Kommunen", *Die öffentliche Verwaltung*, vol. 3, 2007.

Ellison C. G., "Religious involvement and subjective well-being", *Journal of Health and Social Behaviour*, vol. 32, no. 1, 1991.

Ellison C. G., Bartkowski J. P., Anderson K. L., "Are There Religious Variations in Domestic Violence?", *Journal of Family Issue*, vol. 20, no. 1, 1999.

Engels F., "Herrn Eugen Dührings Umwälzung der Wissenschaften (Anti-Dühring)", in: *Marks-Engels Werke. Band 20*, Berlin 1962.

Er S., *Der Strafvollzug als Zwischenstation der Radikalisierung. Eine Studie zu Strafgefangenen und Haftentlassenen muslimischen Glaubens anhand biographisch-narrativer Gesprächsführung*, Wiesbaden, 2021.

Evans-Pritchard E. E., *Theorien über primitive Religion*, Frankfurt am Main 1981.

Falski J., "Dyskryminacja ze względu na religię w miejscu pracy w kontekście orzecznictwa Trybunału Sprawiedliwości Unii Europejskiej", *Przegląd Sejmowy*, vol. 151, no. 2, 2019.

Farr T. F., "Diplomacy in an age of faith: Religious freedom and national security", *Foreign Affairs*, vol. 87, no. 2, 2008.

Figl J., "Gott – monotheistisch", in J. Figl (ed.), *Handbuch Religionswissenschaft: Religionen und ihre zentralen Themen*, Göttingen 2003.

Figl J., "Religionsbegriff – zum Gegenstandsbereich der Religionswissenschaft", in J. Figl (ed.), *Handbuch Religionswissenschaft: Religionen und ihre zentralen Themen*, Göttingen 2003.

Fitzgerald T., "Herbert Spencer's Agnosticism", *Religious Studies*, vol. 23, no. 4, 1987.

Florczak-Wątor M., "Art. 53", in P. Tuleja (ed.), *Konstytucja Rzeczypospolitej Polskiej. Komentarz*, Warszawa 2019.

Fox J., "What is religious freedom and who has it?", *Social Compass*, vol. 68, no. 3, 2021.

Frankenberg G., *Die Verfassung der Republik – Autorität und Solidarität in der Zivilgesellschaft*, Baden-Baden 1996.

Freud S., *Die Zukunft einer Illusion*, Wien – Zürich 1927.

Frick E., Lautenschlager B., *Auf Unendliches bezogen – Spirituelle Entdeckungen bei C. G. Jung*, München 2007.

Fröhmcke V., *Muslime im Strafvollzug. Die Rechtsstellung von Strafgefangenen muslimischer Religionszugehörigkeit in Deutschland*, Berlin 2006.

Fuller A. R., *Psychology and Religion. Eight Points of View*, Lanham – London 1994.

Gajdus D., Gronowska B., "O potrzebie działań na rzecz poprawy sytuacji więźniów. Uwagi na tle standardów międzynarodowych", *Toruński Rocznik Praw Człowieka i Pokoju*, vol. 4, 1996.

Garlicki L., "Art. 9", in L. Garlicki (ed.), *Konwencja o ochronie praw człowieka i podstawowych wolności, Tom 1, Komentarz do art. 1–18*, Warszawa 2010.

Garlicki L., *Polskie prawo konstytucyjne. Zarys wykładu*, Warszawa 2015.

Garlicki L., Derlatka M., "Art. 72", in L. Garlicki, M. Zubik (eds.), *Konstytucja Rzeczypospolitej Polskiej. Komentarz. II. Art. 30–86*, Warszawa 2016.

Geertz C., *The interpretation of cultures. Selected essays*, London 1993.

Germann M., "Art. 4 GG", in V. Epping, Ch. Hillgruber (eds.), *BeckOK Grundgesetz*, München 2022.

Ghosh P., "Die protestantische Ethik und der Geist des 87 Kapitalismus (1904–05; 1920)", in H. P. Müller, S. Sigmund (eds.), *Max Weber-Handbuch. Leben – Werk – Wirkung*, Berlin 2020.

Gill A., *The political origins of religious liberty*, New York 2008.

Glaser H., Makowicz B., "Die Grundrechte in der Verfassungsordnung Polens und Deutschlands – Ein Grundlagenvergleich. Prawa podstawowe w porządkach konstytucyjnych Polski i Niemiec – porównanie zasadniczych zagadnień", in H. Glaser, B. Makowicz, M. Wyrzykowski (eds.), *Die Grundwerte- und Grundrechtsordnung in Polen und Deutschland. System podstawowych wartości i praw w Niemczech i w Polsce*, Baden-Baden 2019.

Glendon M., "Making the case for religious freedom in secular societies", *Journal of Law and Religion*, vol. 33, no. 3, 2018.

Gliszczyńska-Grabias A., "Prawo do poszanowania wyznania i światopoglądu osadzonego", in *X Seminarium Warszawskie. Pozytywne i negatywne obowiązki państwa wobec osób pozbawionych wolności – aktualne wyzwania polskiego systemu penitencjarnego*, Warszawa 2017.

Głód F., "Życie religijne jako pryncypialna wartość człowieka", *Perspectiva. Legnickie Studia Teologiczno-Historyczne*, vol. 10, no. 1, 2011.

Gunn T. J., "The Complexity of Religion and the Definition of *Religion* in International Law", *Harvard Human Rights Journal*, vol. 16, 2003.

Gülker S., "Bronisław Malinowski: Magic, Science and Religion (1925)", in Ch. Gärtner, G. Pickel (eds.), *Schlüsselwerke der Religionssoziologie*, Wiesbaden 2019.

Günther F., "Wer beeinflusst hier wen? Die westdeutsche Staatsrechtslehre und das Bundesverfassungsgericht während der 1950er und 1960er Jahre", in R. Chr. van Ooyen, M. H. W. Möllers (eds.), *Handbuch Bundesverfassungsgericht im politischen System*, Wiesbaden 2015.

Golemboski D., "Religious Sincerity and the Reasons for Religious Freedom", *Political Research Quarterly*, vol. 73, no. 4, 2020.

Gonnerman M., "Tillich Paul", in D. A. Lemming (ed.), *Encyclopedia of Psychology and Religion*, New York 2010.

Góralski W., "Problem wystąpienia z Kościoła katolickiego w Republice Federalnej Niemiec", *Prawo Kanoniczne*, vol. 1, 2015.

Granat M., "Granice wolności religijnej w społeczeństwie pluralistycznym", in J. Krukowski, O. Theisen (eds.), *Kultura i prawo. Materiały II Międzynarodowej Konferencji na temat „Religia i wolność religijna w Unii Europejskiej"*, Lublin 2003.

Greengrass M., "The Edict of Nantes (1598)", in I. Dingel, M. Rohrschneider, I. Schmidt-Voges, S. Westphal, J. Whaley (eds.), *Handbuch Frieden im Europa der Frühen Neuzeit/ Handbook of Peace in Early Modern Europe*, Berlin – Boston 2021.

Hanc J., "*My chickens would love this!*. Nutraloaf jako przykład naruszenia prawa skazanego do otrzymania przyzwoitego posiłku", *Archiwum Kryminologii*, vol. 44, no. 2, 2022.

Heller B., "Gender und Religion", in J. Figl (ed.), *Handbuch Religionswissenschaft: Religionen und ihre zentralen Themen*, Göttingen 2003.

Hodge D. R., "Advocating for the forgotten human right: Article 18 of the Universal Declaration of Human Rights – religious freedom", *International Social Work* vol. 49, no. 4, 2006.

Hollerbach A, "§ 140", in J. Isensee, P. Kirchhof (eds.), *Handbuch des Staatsrechts der Bundesrepublik Deutschland. Band VI. Bundesstaat*, Heidelberg 2009.

Hołda Z., "Wstęp", in Z. Hołda, K. Postulski, *Kodeks karny wykonawczy. Komentarz*, Gdańsk 2006.

Hordecki B., "Struktura semantyczna pojęć *wolność sumienia i religii, wolność sumienia i wyznania* (część I)", *Środkowoeuropejskie Studia Polityczne*, no. 2, 2014.

Hordecki B., "Struktura semantyczna pojęć *wolność sumienia i religii, wolność sumienia i wyznania* (część II)", *Środkowoeuropejskie Studia Polityczne*, no. 2, 2015.

Hödl H. G., "Ritual (Kult, Opfer, Ritus, Zeremonie)", in J. Figl (ed.), *Handbuch Religionswissenschaft: Religionen und ihre zentralen Themen*, Göttingen 2003.

Hömig D., "Menschenwürdeschutz in der Rechtsprechung des Bundesverfassungsgerichts", in W. Lembcke (ed.), *Das Dogma der Unantastbarkeit. Eine Auseinandersetzung mit dem Absolutheitsanspruch der Würde*, Tübingen 2009.

Hörnle T., Huster S., "Wie weit reicht das Erziehungsrecht der Eltern? Am Beispiel der Beschneidung von Jungen", *Juristen Zeitung*, vol. 7, 2013.

Huber P., "Vor § 1 RelKErzG", in D. Schwab (ed.), *Münchener Kommentar zum Bürgerlichen Gesetzbuch. Band 10. Familienrecht II. §§ 1589–1921*, München 2020.

Huber P., "§ 5 RelKErzG", in D. Schwab (ed.), *Münchener Kommentar zum Bürgerlichen Gesetzbuch. Band 10. Familienrecht II. §§ 1589–1921*, München 2020.

Huber P., "§ 1631d", in D. Schwab (ed.), *Münchener Kommentar zum Bürgerlichen Gesetzbuch. Band 10. Familienrecht II. §§ 1589– 1921*, München 2020.

Hucał M., "Wolność sumienia i wyznania osób pozbawienia wolności w orzecznictwie ETPCz", in J. Nikołajew, K. Walczuk (eds.), *Wolność sumienia i religii osób pozbawionych wolności. Aspekty prawne i praktyczne*, Warszawa 2016.

Idler E. L., Kasl S. V., "Religion, Disability, Depression, and the Timing of Death", *American Journal of Sociology*, vol. 97, no. 4, 1992.

Jahn S. J., "Being Private in Public Space? The 'Administration' of 'Religion' in German Prisons", *Journal of Religion in Europe*, vol. 9, no. 4, 2016.

Jahn S. J., "Germany: Inequality in Legal Practice – Managing Religion in Prisons", in J. Martínez-Ariño, A. L. Zwilling (eds.), *Religion and Prison: An Overview of Contemporary Europe*, Cham 2020.

Jahn S. J., "Institutional Logic and Legal Practice: Modes of Regulation of Religious Organizations in German Prisons", in I, Becci, O. Roy (eds.), *Religious Diversity in European Prisons. Challenges and Implications for Rehabilitation*, Cham 2015.

Jakuszewicz A., "The doctrine of the margin of appreciation as a tool of relativisation of freedom of religion. Some reflections on the jurisprudence of the European Court of Human Rights", *Studia Prawnoustrojowe*, vol. 54, 2021.

James W., *The varieties of religious experience: A study of human nature being the Gifford lectures on natural religion delivered at Edinburgh in 1901–1902*, New York 1958.

Janyga W., *Przestępstwo obrazy uczuć religijnych w polskim prawie karnym w świetle współczesnego pojmowania wolności sumienia i wyznania*, Warszawa 2010.

Joseph, S., Castan M., "The International Covenant on Civil and Political Rights. Cases, Materials, and Commentary", Oxford 2013.

Josephson-Storm J., *The Myth of Disenchantment: Magic, Modernity, and the Birth of Human Sciences*, Chicago 2017.

Jung C. G., *Zur Psychologie westlicher und östlicher Religion*, Solothurn – Düsseldorf 1995.

Kaczamrek K., *Herbert Spencer a problemy socjologii religii*, Poznań 2007.

Kalisz T., "Zasady prawa karnego wykonawczego", *Nowa kodyfikacja prawa karnego*, vol. 17, 2005.

Kalisz T., "Osadzeni niebezpieczni. Procedura kwalifikacji, jej weryfikacja oraz zakres ograniczeń", *Nowa kodyfikacja prawa karnego*, vol. 43, 2017.

Kavros P. M., "Religion", in D. A. Lemming (ed.), *Encyclopedia of Psychology and Religion*, New York 2010.

Kavros P. M., "Religious", in D. A. Lemming (ed.), *Encyclopedia of Psychology and Religion*, New York 2010.

Kaźmierska K., *Młodzież Archidiecezji Łódzkiej. Szkic do portretu*, Łódź 2018.

Keher G., *Einführung in die Religionssoziologie*, Darmstadt 1988.

Kehrer G, "Max Weber (1864–1920)", in A. Michaels (ed.), *Klassiker der Religionswissenschaft: Von Friedrich Schleiermacher bis Mircea Eliade*, München 2010.

Kellerwessel W., "Das Recht der Kinder auf Religionsfreiheit – im Kontext der Rechte von Erziehungsberechtigten und staatlichen Pflichten", *Zeitschrift für Menschenrechte*, vol. 1, 2022.

Keppler K., Nestler N., "§ 21", in H. D. Schwind, A. Böhm, J. M. Jehle, K. Laubenthal (eds.), *Strafvollzugsgesetz – Bund und Länder. Kommentar*, Berlin–Boston 2013.

Kippenberg H. G., "Emile Durkheim (1858–1917)", in A. Michaels (ed.), *Klassiker der Religionswissenschaft: Von Friedrich Schleiermacher bis Mircea Eliade*, München 2010.

Kippenberg H. G., "(Welt-)Religionen", in H. P. Müller, S. Sigmund (eds.), *Max Weber-Handbuch. Leben – Werk – Wirkung*, Berlin 2020.

Kirkpatrick L., "An attachment theory approach to the psychology of religion", *International Journal for the Psychology of Religion*, vol. 2, no. 1, 1992.

Klinkhammer G., "Rudolf Otto: Das Heilige. Über das Irrationale und die Idee des Göttlichen und sein Verhältnis zum Rationalen (1917)", in Ch. Gärtner, G. Pickel (eds.), *Schlüsselwerke der Religionssoziologie*, Wiesbaden 2019.

Kohl K. H., "Edward Burnett Tylor (1832–1917)", in A. Michaels (ed.), *Klassiker der Religionswissenschaft: Von Friedrich Schleiermacher bis Mircea Eliade*, München 2010.

Konferencja Episkopatu USA, "Praktyki pobożności ludowej: podstawowe pytania i odpowiedzi", *Salvatoris Mater*, vol. 5, no. 4, 2003.

Knauer F., "§ 53 LandesR", in J. Fest, W. Lesting, M. Lindemann (eds.) *Strafvollzugsgesetze Bundes- und Landesrecht. Kommentar*, Hürth 2022.

Kohnle A., "Augsburger Religionsfrieden 1555", in I. Dingel, M. Rohrschneider, I. Schmidt-Voges, S. Westphal, J. Whaley (eds.), *Handbuch Frieden im Europa der Frühen Neuzeit/ Handbook of Peace in Early Modern Europe*, Berlin – Boston 2021.

Korzeniewska-Lasota A., "Zakres wolności sumienia i wyznania", *Studia Warmińskie*, vol. 48, 2011.

Korioth S., "Art. 137 WRV", in T. Maunz, G. Dürig (eds.), *Grundgesetz. Kommentar. Band VII. Art. 107–146*, München 2022 (98. EL März 2022).

Korioth S., "Art. 141 WRV", in T. Maunz, G. Dürig (eds.), *Grundgesetz. Kommentar. Band VII. Art. 107–146*, München 2022 (98. EL März 2022).

Kosek M., "Czy możliwa jest recepcja niemieckiego modelu podatku kościelnego w Polsce?", *Forum Teologiczne*, vol. 7, 2006.

Kosek M., *Podatek kościelny w niemieckim systemie prawnym*, Płock 2004.

Kościelniak W., Walczak K., *Kronika miasta Kalisza*, Kalisz 2002.

Kotowska M., Romańczuk-Grącka M., "Wolność religijna w warunkach izolacji penitencjarnej" in A. Nawój-Śleszyńska, J. Łuczak (eds.), *Wybrane problemy indywidualizacji wykonywania kary pozbawienia wolności i środków probacyjnych*, Łódź 2017.

Krukowski J., "Ochrona wolności religijnej w umowach międzynarodowych", *Roczniki Nauk Prawnych KUL*, vol. 3, 1993.

Krukowski J., *Wstęp do nauki o państwie i prawie*, Lublin 2004.

Krzywkowska J., "Prawo osadzonych do korzystania z posług religijnych w dobie pandemii COVID-19", *Studia Prawnoustrojowe*, vol. 55, 2022.

Kříž J., "Judicial search for a legal definition of religion", *Studia z Prawa Wyznaniowego*, vol. 26, 2023.

Kulesz Z., "Religijność w perspektywie psychologicznej", *Studia Elbląskie*, vol. 14, 2013.

Kuntze J., "Rechtsfragen zur religiösen Knabenbeschneidung", *Zeitschrift für evangelisches Kirchenrecht*, vol. 16, no. 1, 2013.

Kuriata A., "Źródła prawa muzułmańskiego wobec stroju kobiety muzułmanki", *Acta Erasmiana*, vol. 7, 2014.

Kübler F., "Lüth: eine sanfte Revolution (BVerfGE 7, 198 ff.)", *Kritische Vierteljahresschrift für Gesetzgebung und Rechtswissenschaft*, vol. 83, nos. 3-4, 2000.

Kühl J., *Die gesetzliche Reform des Jugendstrafvollzugs in Deutschland im Licht der European Rules for Juvenile Offenders Subject to Sanctions or Measures (ERJOSSM)*, Mönchengladbach 2012.

Kwieciński A., "Podstawy prawne realizacji prawa do wolności religijnej w warunkach izolacji penitencjarnej. Rozważania na marginesie dyskusji o zjawisku multikulturowości populacji więziennej", in M. Jabłoński (ed.), *Księga jubileuszowa na siedemdziesięciolecie Wydziału Prawa, Administracji i Ekonomii Uniwersytetu Wrocławskiego. Część 2*, Wrocław 2015.

Laubenthal K., *Strafvollzug*, Berlin 2019.

Lasocik Z., "Funkcjonowanie oddziałów dla tzw. „więźniów niebezpiecznych", *Archiwum Kryminologii*, vol. 31, 2009.

Lasocik Z., *Praktyki religijne więźniów*, Warszawa 1993.

Lawson E. T., "Defining Religion… Going the Theoretical Way", in T. A. Idinopulos, B. C. Wilson (eds.), *What is Religion? Origins, Definitions, and Explanations*, Leiden 1998.

Leblanc L. J., "Reservations to the Convention on the Rights of the Child: A macroscopic view of state practice", *The International Journal of Children's Rights*, vol. 4, no. 4, 1996.

Lelental S., *Kodeks karny wykonawczy. Komentarz*, Warszawa 2001.

Lelental S., *Kodeks karny wykonawczy. Komentarz*, Warszawa 2014.

Lepherd L., Rogers C., Egan R., Towler H., Graham C., Nagle A., Hampton I., "Exploring spirituality with older people: (1) rich experiences", *Journal of Religion, Spirituality & Aging*, vol. 32, no. 4, 2020.

Lepherd L., Rogers C., Egan R., Towler H., Graham C., Nagle A., Hampton I., "Exploring Spirituality With Older People: (2) A rigorous process", *Journal of Religion, Spirituality & Aging*, vol. 32, no. 3, 2020.

Lepsius O., "Die maßstabsetzende Gewalt", in *Das entgrenzte Gericht. Eine kritische Bilanz nach sechzig Jahren Bundesverfassungsgericht*, Berlin 2011.

Lindkvist L., "The Politics of Article 18: Religious Liberty in the Universal Declaration of Human Rights", *An International Journal of Human Rights, Humanitarianism, and Development*, vol. 4, no. 3, 2013.

Lindkvist L., *Religious Freedom and the Universal Declaration of Human Rights*, Cambridge 2017.

Locatelli A., "Emotions and/in Religion. Reading Sigmund Freud, Rudolph Otto, and William James", in I. Jandl, S. Knaller, S. Schönfellner, G. Tockner (eds.),

Writing Emotions. Theoretical Concepts and Selected Case Studies in Literature, Bielefeld 2017.

Luhmann N., *Funktion der Religion*, Frankfurt am Main 1982.

Ławniczak A., "Zasada poszanowania wolności i jej ograniczenia", in M. Jabłoński (ed.), *Wolności i prawa jednostki w Konstytucji RP. Idee i zasady przewodnie konstytucyjnej regulacji wolności i praw jednostki w RP. Tom I*, Warszawa 2010.

Łopatka A., "Konwencja Praw Dziecka w Polsce", in J. Bińczycka (ed.), *Prawa dziecka. Deklaracje i rzeczywistość*, Kraków 1999.

Machel H., *Więzienie jako instytucja karna i resocjalizacyjna*, Gdańsk 2003.

Maelicke B., "Konsequenzen der Förderalismusreform für den Deutschen Strafvollzug. Auszug aus einem Vortrag auf dem 14. Bundeskongress der Psychologinnen und Psychologen im Strafvollzugam 19. September 2006, Rostock", *Neue Kriminalpolitik*, vol. 118, no. 3, 2006.

Maelicke B., "Sinn und Unsinn der Föderalismusreform", *Neue Kriminalpolitik*, vol. 27, no. 3, 2015.

Malinowski B., "E. Durkheim, Les formes élementaires de la vie religiuse", *Folklore*, vol. 24, no. 4, 1913.

Malinowski B., *Magic, Science and Religion and Other Essays. Selected and with an Introduction by Robert Redfield*, Boston – Glencoe 1948.

Malinowski B., *Wierzenia pierwotne i formy ustroju społecznego. Pogląd na genezę religii ze szczególnem uwzględnieniem totemizmu*, Kraków 1915.

Malone J., Dadswell A., "The Role of Religion, Spirituality and/or Belief in Positive Ageing for Older Adults", *Geriatrics (Basel)*, vol. 8, no. 3, 2018.

Maroń G., "O pojmowaniu religii w polskim porządku prawnym", *Forum Prawnicze*, vol. 65, no. 3, 2021.

Martin D. A., *A general theory of secularization*, Oxford 1978.

Meyer-Ladewig J., Schuster S., "Art. 9", in J. Meyer-Ladewig, M. Nettesheim, S. v. Raumer (eds.), *EMRK. Europäische Menschenrechtskonvention. Handkommentar*, Baden-Baden 2017.

Mezglewski A., "Pojęcie *duchownego* w przepisach prawa polskiego o zawieraniu małżeństwa", *Studia z Prawa Wyznaniowego*, vol. 2, 2001.

McDaniel C., Davis D., Neff S., "Charitable Choice and Prison Ministries: Constitutional and Institutional Challenges to Rehabilitating the American Penal System", *Criminal Justice Policy Review*, vol. 16, no. 2, 2005.

McGuire M. B., *Religion. The Social Context*, Long Grove 2002.

Meler S., "Prawo więźniów do wolności religijnej", *Przegląd Więziennictwa Polskiego*, vols. 38–39, 2003.

Michalak A., "Wolności i prawa jednostki", in D. Górecki (ed.), *Polskie prawo konstytucyjne*, Warszawa 2015.

Mikołejko Z., *Między zbawieniem a Smoleńskiem*, Warszawa 2017.

Milczarek E., "Symbole i stroje religijne w przestrzeni publicznej – uwagi na tle orzecznictwa Europejskiego Trybunału Praw Człowieka", *Kościół i Prawo*, vol. 11, no. 1, 2022

Moberg D. O., "Research in Spirituality, Religion, and Aging", *Journal of Gerontological Social Work*, vol. 45, no. 2, 2005.

Morawska E. H., "Ochrona praw dziecka w świetle art. 72 Konstytucji RP. Uwagi na tle orzecznictwa Trybunału Konstytucyjnego", *Kwartalnik Prawa Publicznego*, vol. 7, no. 4, 2007.

Morgenthaler C., "Carl Gustav Jung (1875–1961)", in A. Michaels (ed.), *Klassiker der Religionswissenschaft: Von Friedrich Schleiermacher bis Mircea Eliade*, München 2010.

Müller H. P., "Vorbemerkung (1920)", in H. P. Müller, S. Sigmund (eds.), *Max Weber-Handbuch. Leben – Werk – Wirkung*, Berlin 2020.

Müller-Monning T., "Vor § 69 LandesR", in J. Fest, W. Lesting, M. Lindemann (eds.) *Strafvollzugsgesetze Bundes- und Landesrecht. Kommentar*, Hürth 2022.

Müller-Monning T., "§ 69 LandesR", in J. Fest, W. Lesting, M. Lindemann (eds.) *Strafvollzugsgesetze Bundes- und Landesrecht. Kommentar*, Hürth 2022.

Müller-Monning T., "§ 70 LandesR" in J. Fest, W. Lesting, M. Lindemann (eds.) *Strafvollzugsgesetze Bundes- und Landesrecht. Kommentar*, Hürth 2022.

Müller-Monning T., "§ 71 LandesR", in J. Fest, W. Lesting, M. Lindemann (eds.) *Strafvollzugsgesetze Bundes- und Landesrecht. Kommentar*, Hürth 2022.

Müller-Monning T., "§ 97 LandesR", in J. Fest, W. Lesting, M. Lindemann (eds.) *Strafvollzugsgesetze Bundes- und Landesrecht. Kommentar*, Hürth 2022.

Mrozek K., "Reguły Nelsona Mandeli", *Nowa kodyfikacja prawa karnego*, vol. 48, 2018.

Neugebauer G., "Max Weber: Die protestantische Ethik und der *Geist* des Kapitalismus (1904/1905)", in Ch. Gärtner, G. Pickel (eds.), *Schlüsselwerke der Religionssoziologie*, Wiesbaden 2019.

Neureither G., "Grundfälle zu Art. 4 I, II GG", *Juristische Schulung*, vol. 46, no. 12, 2006.

Niełaczna M., *Zmiany za murami? Stosowanie standardów postępowania z więźniami w Polsce*, Warszawa 2011.

Niewiadomska I., "Polski model resocjalizacji więziennej", *Teka Komisji Prawniczej PAN Oddział w Lublinie*, vol. 9, 2016.

Niemczyk J., "Metodologia nauk o zarządzaniu", in W. Czakon (ed.), *Podstawy metodologii badań w naukach o zarządzaniu*, Warszawa 2023.

Nikołajew J., *Duszpasterstwo więzienne. Tradycje, teraźniejszość, perspektywy*, Lublin 2009.

Nikołajew J., "Prawo do wolności religijnej więźniów według Jana Pawła II", in P. Marzec, J. Nikołajew (eds.), *Osoba i dzieło Ojca Świętego Jana Pawła II. Studium wybranych problemów*, Tomaszów Lubelski–Lublin 2009.

Nikołajew J., "Prawo osób pozbawionych wolności do wyżywienia przygotowywanego według wymogów religijnych. Regulacje normatywne a trudności praktyczne", *Kościół i Prawo*, vol. 4, no. 2, 2015.

Nikołajew J., "Reguły Minimalne i Europejskie Reguły Więzienne a prawo więźniów do wolności sumienia i religii w Polsce", *Studia z Prawa Wyznaniowego*, vol. 16, 2013.

Nikołajew J., "Specyfika duszpasterstwa więziennego w Polsce. Prezentacja badań własnych", *Teologia w Polsce*, vol. 3, no. 1, 2009.

Nikołajew J., *Wolność sumienia i religii skazanych i tymczasowo aresztowanych*, Lublin 2012.

Nongbri B., *Before Religion: A History of a Modern Concept*, New Haven – London 2013.

Nowe kodeksy karne z uzasadnieniami, I. Fredrich-Michalska, B. Stachurska-Marcińczak (eds.), Warszawa 1997.

Nowicki M. A., *Europejski Trybunał Praw Człowieka, Wybór orzeczeń 2008*, Warszawa 2009.

Nowicki M. A., *Wokół Konwencji Europejskiej. Komentarz do Europejskiej Konwencji Praw Człowieka*, Warszawa 2017.

Nörenberg H., "The Numinous, the Ethical, and the Body. Rudolf Otto's "The Idea of the Holy" Revisited", *Open Theology*, vol. 3, no. 1, 2017.

Noronha K. J., "Impact of Religion and Spirituality on Older Adulthood", *Journal of Religion, Spirituality & Aging*, vol. 27, no. 1, 2015.

Olszewska-Dyoniziak B., *Człowiek – kultura – osobowość. Wstęp do klasycznej antropologii kulturowej*, Wrocław 2001.

Olszówka M., "Art. 53" in M. Safjan, L. Bosek (eds.), *Konstytucja RP. Tom I. Komentarz do art. 1–86*, Warszawa 2016.

Ostendorf H., "Vorbemerkungen", in H. Ostendorf (ed.), *Jugendstrafvollzugsrecht*, Baden-Baden 2022.

Ostendorf H., "§ 1 Grundlagen", in H. Ostendorf (ed.), *Jugendstrafvollzugsrecht*, Baden-Baden 2022.

Ostendorf H., "§ 3 Unterbringung und Versorgung", in H. Ostendorf (ed.), *Jugendstrafvollzugsrecht*, Baden-Baden 2022.

Ostendorf H., "§ 6 Religionsausübung", in H. Ostendorf (ed.), *Jugendstrafvollzugsrecht*, Baden-Baden 2022.

Otto R., *Das Heilige. Über das Irrationale in der Idee des Göttlichen und sein Verhältnis zum Rationalen*, Gotha 1926.

Otto R., *The Idea of the Holy*, London – Oxford – New York 1958.

Ożóg M., "Noszenie chusty islamskiej w miejscu pracy a prawa i wolności innych podmiotów prawa", *Studia z Prawa Wyznaniowego*, vol. 17, 2017.

Pahl B., *Majątek kościołów i innych związków wyznaniowych. Zasady opodatkowania*, Olsztyn 2008.

Pałaszewski P., "Status tymczasowo aresztowanego, wobec którego wykonywana jest kara pozbawienia wolności (art. 223a k.k.w.)", in A. Kwieciński (ed.), *Postępowanie z wybranymi grupami skazanych w polskim systemie penitencjarnym. Aspekty prawne*, Warszawa 2013.

Paprzycki R., *Prawna ochrona wolności sumienia i wyznania*, Warszawa 2015.

Parker M. T., "The Freedom to Manifest Religious Belief: An Analysis of the Necessity Clauses of the ICCPR and the ECHR", *Duke Journal of Comparative & International Law*, vol. 17, no. 1, 2006.

Pasek Z., "Czy miesięcznice smoleńskie były uroczystościami religijnymi? Prawo a polska kultura religijna", *Studia z Prawa Wyznaniowego*, vol. 24, 2021.

Paszkowski M., Krzywkowska J., "Prawo osadzonych do opieki duszpasterskiej i wykonywania praktyk religijnych na przykładzie zakładu karnego w Barczewie", in J. Nikołajew, K. Walczuk (eds.), *Wolność sumienia i religii osób pozbawionych wolności. Aspekty prawne i praktyczne*, Warszawa 2016.

Pawela S., *Prawo karne wykonawcze. Zarys wykładu*, Warszawa 2007.

Pearce L. D., "The Influence of Early Life Course Religious Exposure on Young Adults' Dispositions Toward Childbearing", *Journal for the Scientific Study of Religion*, vol. 41, no. 2, 2002.

Pepper M., Powell R., "Domestic and Family Violence: Responses and Approaches across the Australian Churches", *Religions*, vol. 13, no. 3, 2022.

Pepper M., Powell R., McEwan T., "The Impact of Marriage Norms and Gender on Anglican Clergy Actions in Response to Domestic Violence", *Religions*, vol. 14, no. 6, 2023.

Petersen J., *Kirchensteuer kompakt. Strukturierte Darstellung mit Berechnungsbeispielen*, Wiesbaden 2020.

Pietrzak M., "Konstytucyjne podstawy prawa wyznaniowego", in M. Wyrzykowski (ed.), *Konstytucyjne podstawy systemu prawa*, Warszawa 2001.

Pietrzak M., *Prawo wyznaniowe*, Warszawa 2003.

Pierzchała K., *Destygmatyzacja przestępców w świetle Magisterium Kościoła oraz poglądów na resocjalizację*, Kraków 2016.

Płatek M., "Wybrane zasady kodeksu karnego wykonawczego z 1997 r. w świetle Europejskich Reguł Więziennych z 11 stycznia 2006 r.", in S. Lelental, G. B. Szczygieł (eds.), *X lat obowiązywania kodeksu karnego wykonawczego*, Białystok 2009.

Płatek M., "Zadania polskiej polityki penitencjarnej w świetle Europejskich Reguł Więziennych", *Czasopismo Prawa Karnego i Nauk Penalnych*, vol. 11, no. 1, 2007.

Pol, J. D., *Więzienna szansa*, Warszawa 2008.

Polak-Krusznik A., "Doniesienia z badań nad wykonywaniem długoterminowych kar pozbawienia wolności", in K. Mrozek (ed.), *Z problematyki badań empirycznych w prawie karnym wykonawczym. Część 2*, Wrocław 2021.

Pollack D., "Niklas Luhmann: Funktion der Religion (1977)", in Ch. Gärtner, G. Pickel (eds.), *Schlüsselwerke der Religionssoziologie*, Wiesbaden 2019.

Popper K. R., *The Logic of Scientific Discovery*, London – New York 2005.

Postulski K., *Kodeks karny wykonawczy. Komentarz*, Warszawa 2012.

Prantl H., "Der Winnetou des Strafrechts – Der Forscher und Lehrer Claus Roxin wird 75", *Süddeutsche Zeitung* of 15.05.2006.

Prantl H., "Scharf, schärfer, am schärfsten", *Süddeutsche Zeitung* of 12.08.2016.

Puga-Gonzalez I., Voas D., Kiszkiel Ł., et al., "Modeling Fuzzy Fidelity: Using Microsimulation to Explore Age, Period, and Cohort Effects in Secularization", *Journal of Religion and Demography*, vol. 9, nos. 1-2, 2022.

Puleng Motlalekgosi H., "Religious Freedom and the Law: A Reality or Pipe Dream for Prisoners in South Africa?", *Journal for the Study of Religion*, vol. 32, no. 1, 2019.

Przesławski T., "Pozycja i funkcje polityki penitencjarnej w naukach o polityce publicznej", in J. Kwaśniewski (ed.), *Nauki o polityce publicznej. Monografia dyscypliny*, Warszawa 2018.

Raday F., "Freedom from religion in international human rights law", in B. G. Scharffs, A. Maoz, A. Isaacson Wolley (eds.), *Religious freedom and the law. Emerging contexts for freedom for and from religion*, London – New York 2019.

Raza F., "Limitations to the Right to Religious Freedom: Rethinking Key Approaches", *Oxford Journal of Law and Religion*, vol. 9, no. 3, 2020.

Roffee J. A., "No Consensus on Incest? Criminalisation and Compatibility with the European Convention on Human Rights", *Human Rights Law Review*, vol. 14, no. 3, 2014.

Rogowska A., "Wolność sumienia i wyznania w świetle przepisów polskiego Kodeksu karnego wykonawczego", *Acta Erasmiana*, vol. 1, 2011.

Romanko A., "System państw świeckich na przykładzie wybranych państwa europejskich", *Biuletyn Stowarzyszenia Absolwentów i Przyjaciół Wydziału Prawa Katolickiego Uniwersytetu Lubelskiego*, vol. 15, no. 1, 2018.

Romanowicz W., Tomczyszyn D., "Stosunek do religii osób odbywających karę pozbawienia wolności a miejsce religii we współczesnym świecie", *Rozprawy Społeczne*, vol. 9, no. 3, 2015.

Rozner M., "Prawo do wolności religijnej w Europejskiej Konwencji Praw Człowieka z 1950 r.", *Studia z Prawa Wyznaniowego*, vol. 5, 2002.

Quinodoz J. M., *Sigmund Freud. An Introduction*, London – New York 2018.

Saiya N., *Weapons of peace: How religious liberty combats terrorism*, New York 2019.

Salgo L., "Gesetz über die religiöse Kindererziehung", in H. Engler (ed.), *J. von Staudingers Kommentar zum Bürgerlichen Gesetzbuch mit Einführungsgesetz und Nebengesetzen. Band 4. Familienrecht. §§ 1626–1631. Anhang zu § 1631: RKEG. §§ 1631a-1633*, Berlin 2002.

Sarnecki P., "Art. 53", in L. Garlicki, M. Zubik (eds.), *Konstytucja Rzeczypospolitej Polskiej. Komentarz. Tom II. Art. 30–86*, Warszawa 2016.

Schabas W. A., *The European Convention on Human Rights. A Commentary*. Oxford–New York 2015.

Schabas W. A., "Reservations to the Convention on the Rights of the Child", *Human Rights Quarterly*, vol. 18, no. 2, 1996.

Scharffs B. G., Maoz A., Isaacson Wolley A., "Introduction. Freedom of/form/ within religion: conceptually inseparable rights", in B. G. Scharffs, A. Maoz, A. Isaacson Wolley (eds.), *Religious freedom and the law. Emerging contexts for freedom for and from religion*, London – New York 2019.

Schäfter K. H., "§ 53", in H. D. Schwind, A. Böhm, J. M. Jehle, K. Laubenthal (eds.), *Strafvollzugsgesetz – Bund und Länder. Kommentar*, Berlin–Boston 2013.

Schäfter K. H., "§ 54", H. D. Schwind, A. Böhm, J. M. Jehle, K. Laubenthal (eds.), *Strafvollzugsgesetz – Bund und Länder. Kommentar*, Berlin–Boston 2013.

Schäfter K. H., "§ 157", in H. D. Schwind, A. Böhm, J. M. Jehle, K. Laubenthal (eds.), *Strafvollzugsgesetz – Bund und Länder. Kommentar*, Berlin–Boston 2013.

Schnepel B., "Edward Evan Evans-Pritchard (1902–1973)", in A. Michaels (ed.), *Klassiker der Religionswissenschaft: Von Friedrich Schleiermacher bis Mircea Eliade*, München 2010.

Schüler-Springorum H., "Strafvollzug und Föderalismus", in H. Schöch, R. Helgerth, D. Dölling, P. König (eds.), *Recht gestalten – dem Recht dienen. Festschrift für Reinhard Böttcher zum 70. Geburtstag am 29. Juli 2007*, Berlin 2007.

Schulz A. N., "O Konwencji o prawach dziecka i jej wpływie na prawo polskie", in M. Andrzejewski (ed.), *Prawa dziecka. Konteksty prawne i pedagogiczne*, Poznań 2012.

Schwarz K. A., "Kopftuchverbote für Minderjährige unter 14 Jahren in schulischen und vorschulischen Einrichtungen", *Neue Zeitschrift für Verwaltungsrecht*, vol. 5, 2020.

Schwierskott-Matheson E., *Wolność sumienia i wyznania w wybranych państwach demokratycznych*, Regensburg 2012.

Schweitzer F., "Children's Right to Religion and Spirituality: Legal, Educational and Practical Perspectives", *British Journal of Religious Education*, vol. 27, no. 2, 2005.

Segal R. A., "Animism for Tylor", in G. Harvey (ed.), *The Handbook fo Contemporary Animism*, London – New York 2013.

Selmer P., "Die Föderalismusreform – Eine Modernisierung der bundesstaatlichen Ordnung?", *Juristische Schulung*, vol. 12, 2006.

Sendyka P., "Narodziny *mitu smoleńskiego*", *Zeszyty Naukowe Uniwersytetu Jagiellońskiego. Prace Etnograficzne*, vol. 41, no. 1, 2013.

Seyyar A., "Die theoretischen Konzepte der Seelsorge aus islamischer Sicht", in B. Uçar, M. Blasberg-Kuhnke (eds.), *Islamische Seelsorge zwischen Herkunft und Zukunft. Von der theologischen Grundlegung zur Praxis in Deutschland*, Frankfurt am Main 2013.

Sharma A., *Problematizing Religious Freedom*, Dordrecht – Heidelberg – London – New York 2011.

Sieniatycki M., *Apologetyka, czyli dogmatyka fundamentalna*, Kraków 1932.

Sikorski J., "Duszpasterstwo więzienne", in M. Chmielewski (ed.), *Kościół w Polsce wobec potrzebujących*, Lublin 1994.

Sikorski J., "Duszpasterstwo więzienne", in T. Szymanowski, J. Cegielska, J. Czołgoszewski, S. Lelental, J. Pomiankiewicz (eds.), *Księga jubileuszowa więziennictwa polskiego 1989–2009*, Warszawa 2009.

Sitarz O., Jaworska-Wieloch A., "Prawo do praktyk religijnych osób osadzonych w areszcie śledczym i odbywających karę pozbawienia wolności w teorii i praktyce penitencjarnej", *Archiwum Kryminologii*, vol. 39, 2017.

Sitarz O., Jaworska-Wieloch A., "Legitimacy of the limitation of freedom of religion during imprisonment (in the light of polish and internation regulations)", *Law Journal of New Bulgarian University*, vol. 17, no. 1, 2021.

Sitarz O., Jaworska-Wieloch A., Hanc J., "A reconstruction of the international standards of religious education of juveniles in correctional institutions", *British Journal of Religious Eductaion*, vol. 45, no. 4, 2023.

Sitarz O., Jaworska-Wieloch A., Hanc J., "Prisoners' opinions about religious practices in Polish penitentiary facilities. An analysis of the results of a study", [Article submitted for review].

Sitarz O., Jaworska-Wieloch A., Hanc J., "Nowelizacja art. 106 § 1 k.k.w. i art. 110a § 1 Kodeksu karnego wykonawczego", *Prawo w Działaniu*, vol. 45, 2021.

Sitarz O., Jaworska-Wieloch A., Hanc J., "Obowiązek zgolenia brody? (Nie) uzasadnione naruszenie wolności uzewnętrzniania religii przez osoby pozbawione wolności (rozważania na tle wyroku Sądu Apelacyjnego w Krakowie z dnia 24 kwietnia 2018 r., I ACa 1217/17)", *Forum Prawnicze*, vol. 69, no. 1, 2022.

Sitarz O., Jaworska-Wieloch A., Hanc J., "Public opinion on freedom of religion (and its limitations) in penitentiary establishments in the light of international regulations A Polish perspective", *Approaching Religion*, vol. 12, no. 1, 2022.

Sitarz O., Jaworska-Wieloch A., Hanc J., "Religious freedom in the educational process conducted in isolation centers for juvenile perpetrators of criminal acts", in T. Huzarek, J. Wółkowski (eds.), *Educational Challenges of Religious Freedom*, Pelplin 2021.

Sitarz O., Jaworska-Wieloch A., Hanc J., "Wolność religijna w ośrodkach izolacji nieletnich w świetle polskich regulacji", *Prawo w Działaniu*, vol. 57, 2024.

Sobczak W., "Art. 18", in R. Wieruszewski (ed.), *Międzynarodowy pakt praw obywatelskich (osobistych) i politycznych. Komentarz*, Warszawa 2012.

Sowiński S., "Modele stosunków państwo – Kościół w Unii Europejskiej", *Studia Europejskie. Centrum Europejskie Uniwersytetu Warszawskiego*, no. 3, 2008.

Stackhouse M. L., *Globalization and Grace*, New York 2007.

Stańdo – Kawecka B., "Execution of Prison Sentences in Poland – 20 Years of Application of the 1997 Code of the Execution of Penalties", in K. Drenkhahn, B. Geng, J. Grzywa-Holten, S. Harrendorf, C. Morgenstern, I. Puren (eds.), *Kriminologie und Kriminalpolitik im Dienste der Menschenwürde. Festschrift für Frieder Dünkel zum 70. Geburtstag*, Mönchengladbach 2020.

Stańdo – Kawecka B., "Poland", in F. Dünkel, S. Harrendorf, D. Zyl Smit (eds.), *The impact of COVID-19 on prison conditions and penal policy*, London – New York 2022.

Stein M., *Jung on Christianity*, Princeton 1999.

Stern K., *Das Staatsrecht der Bundesrepublik Deutschland. Band I: Grundlagen und Grundbegriffe des Staatsrechts, Strukturprinzipien der Verfassung*, München 1984.

Stern K., "Idee der Menschenrechte und Positivität der Grundrechte", in J. Isensee, P. Kirchhof (eds.), *Handbuch des Staatsrechts der Bundesrepublik Deutschland. Band IX. Allgemeine Grundrechtslehren*, Heidelberg 2011.

Stolz F., "Bronislaw Kaspar Malinowski (1884–1942)", in A. Michaels (ed.), *Klassiker der Religionswissenschaft: Von Friedrich Schleiermacher bis Mircea Eliade*, München 2010.

Strenski I., *Thinking About Religion: A Reader*, Oxford 2006.

Strenski I., *Thinking About Religion: An Historical Introduction to Theories of Religion*, Oxford 2006.

Stringer M. D., "Building on belief: defining animism in Taylor and contemporary society" in G. Harvey (ed.), *The Handbook of Contemporary Animism*, London - New York 2013.

Swienko H., "Źródła i funkcje religii", *Euhemer*, nos. 3–4, 1986.

Szczygieł G. B., *Społeczna readaptacja skazanych w polskim systemie penitencjarnym*, Białystok 2002.

Szymanek J., "Wolność sumienia i wyznania w Konstytucji RP", *Przegląd Sejmowy*, vol. 73, no. 2, 2006.

Szymaniec P., *Koncepcje wolności religijnej. Rozwój historyczny i współczesny stan debaty w zachodniej myśli polityczno-prawnej*, Wrocław 2017.

Szymanowski T., Migdał J., *Prawo karne wykonawcze i polityka penitencjarna*, Warszawa 2014.

Szymczak W., Mąkosa P. M., Adamczyk T., "Attitudes of Polish Young Adults towards the Roman Catholic Church: A Sociological and Pastoral Analysis of Empirical Research among Young Adults and Teachers", *Religions*, vol. 13, no. 7, 2022.

Tanner N. P. (ed.), *Decrees of the Ecumenical Councils, Volume 1. Nicaea I to Lateran V*, London - Washington 2016.

Taylor E., *Primitive Culture: Research into the Development of Mythology, Philosophy, Religion, Art, and Custum*, New York 1871.

Temperman J., "Freedom of Religion or Belief in Prison. A Critical Analysis of the European Court of Human Rights' Jurisprudence", *Oxford Journal of Law and Religion*, vol. 6, no. 1, 2017.

Trociuk S., *Prawa i wolności w stanie epidemii*, Warszawa 2021.

Terrier J., "Emile Durkheim: *Les Formes élémentaires de la vie religieuse* [Die elementaren Formen des religiösen Lebens] (1912)", in Ch. Gärtner, G. Pickel (eds.), *Schlüsselwerke der Religionssoziologie*, Wiesbaden 2019.

Tillich P., "Christianity and the Encounter of the World Religions", in R. P. Scharlemann (ed.), *Religious Writings. Hauptwerke. Volume 5/Band 5. Writings on Religion/Religiöse Schriften*, Berlin–Boston 1988 [reprint 2020].

Truong M., Sharif M., Olsen A., Pasalich D., Calabria B., Priest N., "Attitudes and beliefs about family and domestic violence in faith-based communities: An exploratory qualitative study", *Australian Journal of Social Issues*, vol. 54, no. 4, 2022.

Tworuschka U., Klöcker M., "Ethik der Religion", in J. Figl (ed.), *Handbuch Religionswissenschaft: Religionen und ihre zentralen Themen*, Göttingen 2003.

Tyrakowski M., *Opodatkowanie dochodów Kościoła katolickiego w Polsce*, Warszawa 2005.

UNICEF, *Implementation Handbook for the Convention on the Rights of the Child*, Geneva 2007.

Veit B., "§ 1631d", in W. Hau, R. Poseck (eds.), *BeckOK. Bürgerliches Gesetzbuch*, München 2023.

Vergote A., *Religion, Belief and Unbelief. A Psychological Study*, Amsterdam – Atlanta 1997.

Voas D., "The Rise and Fall of Fuzzy Fidelity in Europe", *European Sociological Review*, vol. 25, no. 2, 2009.

Voigt-Goy C., "Warschauer Konföderation 1573", in I. Dingel, M. Rohrschneider, I. Schmidt-Voges, S. Westphal, J. Whaley (eds.), *Handbuch Frieden im Europa der Frühen Neuzeit/ Handbook of Peace in Early Modern Europe*, Berlin – Boston 2021.

Waardenburg J., *Classical Approaches to the Study of Religion. Aims, Methods, and Theories of Research. Introduction and Anthology*, Berlin – Boston 2017.

Walesa C., "Religijności rozwój", in T. Gadacz, B. Milerski (eds.), *Religia. Encyklopedia PWN. Parys – Rut. Tom 8*, Warszawa, 2003.

Walesa C., *Rozwój religijności człowieka. Tom I. Dziecko*, Lublin 2005.

Walesa C., "Psychologiczna problematyka człowieka dorosłego: struktura życia, droga życia i religijność", in C. Walesa, M. Tatala, E. Rydz, *Rozwój religijności człowieka. Tom III. Osoba dorosła*, Lublin 2023.

Walesa C., Tatala M., *Rozwój religijności człowieka. Tom II. Młodzież*, Lublin 2020.

Warchałowski K., *Prawo do wolności myśli, sumienia i religii w Europejskiej Konwencji Praw Człowieka i Podstawowych Wolności*, Lublin 2004.

Weber M., *Gesammelte Aufsätze zur Religionssoziologie I*, Tübingen 1963.

Westphal S., "Der Westfälische Frieden 1648", in I. Dingel, M. Rohrschneider, I. Schmidt-Voges, S. Westphal, J. Whaley (eds.), *Handbuch Frieden im Europa der Frühen Neuzeit/ Handbook of Peace in Early Modern Europe*, Berlin – Boston 2021.

Wiczanowska H., "Oddziaływanie doktryny marginesu uznania na rozstrzyganie konfliktu pomiędzy wolnością wypowiedzi a wolnością sumienia i wyznania w praktyce orzeczniczej Europejskiego Trybunału Praw Człowieka", *Przegląd Europejski*, no. 2, 2020.

Wienbracke W., "Der Verhältnismäßigkeitsgrundsatz", *Zeitschrift für das Juristische Studium*, no. 2, 2013.

Wienhold H., "Clifford Geertz: Religion as a Cultural System (1966)", in Ch. Gärtner, G. Pickel (eds.), *Schlüsselwerke der Religionssoziologie*, Wiesbaden 2019.

Winczorek P., *Komentarz do Konstytucji Rzeczypospolitej Polskiej z 2 kwietnia 1997 r.*, Warszawa 2000.

Wiśniewski L., "Prawo a wolność człowieka – pojęcie i konstrukcja prawna", in L. Wiśniewski (ed.), *Podstawowe prawa jednostki i ich sądowa ochrona*, Warszawa 1997.

Wiśniewski L., "Zakres ochrony prawnej wolności człowieka i warunki jej dopuszczalnych ograniczeń w praktyce", in L. Wiśniewski (ed.), *Wolności i prawa jednostki oraz ich gwarancje w praktyce*, Warszawa 2006.

Wnuk W., Marcinkowski J. T., "Psychologiczne funkcje religii", *Problemy Higieny i Epidemiologii*, vol. 93, no. 1, 2012.

Woleński J., "Sfera publiczna, sfera prywatna i wolność religijna", *Acta Universitatis Wratislaviensis. Przegląd Prawa i Administracji*, no. 110, 2017.

Woodbury R. D., Shaw T. S., "Christianity and democracy: The pioneering protestants", in D. R. Hoover, D. M. Johnston (eds.), *Religion and foreign affairs: Essential readings*, Waco TX 2012.

Woźniak W., "Duszpasterstwo więzienne a resocjalizacja", *Studia Teologiczne*, vol. 20, 2002.

Wróbel A., "Art. 10", in D. Miąsik, N. Półtorak, A. Wróbel (eds.), *Traktat o funkcjonowaniu Unii Europejskiej. Komentarz, T. 1. (art. 1–89)*, Warszawa 2012.

Yandell K. E., *Philosophy of religion. A contemporary introduction*, New York – London 2016.

Yinger M. J., *Religion, Society and the Individual*, New York, 1957.

Zawiślak M., "The limitations of religious practices in polish prisons", *Review of European and Comparative Law*, vol. 30, no. 3, 2017.

Zarzecki M., "Klasyczne i nieklasyczne definicje religii i religijności", in S. H. Zaręba (ed.), *Socjologia życia religijnego w Polsce*, Warszawa 2009.

Zdybicka Z. J., *Człowiek i religia. Zarys filozofii religii*, Lublin 1993.

Zdybicka Z. J., "Czym jest religia i dlaczego istnieje religia", in H. Zimoń (ed.), *Religia w świecie współczesnym. Zarys problematyki religiologicznej*, Lublin 2003.

Zdybicka Z. J., *Religia i religioznawstwo*, Lublin 1992.

Zieliński P., "Izolacja penitencjarna w dobie COVID-19 w aksjologicznym wymiarze praw człowieka", in J. Jaskiernia, K. Spryszak (eds.), *Powszechny system ochrony praw człowieka w czasie wyzwań pandemicznych. Tom I*, Toruń 2022.

Zinser H., "Sigmund Freud (1856–1939)", in A. Michaels (ed.), *Klassiker der Religionswissenschaft: Von Friedrich Schleiermacher bis Mircea Eliade*, München 2010.

Other sources:

Public Opinion Research Centre, *Religiosity of the youth against the background of the entire society. Research Communication no. 144/2021*, https://www.cbos.pl/SPISKOM.POL/2021/K_144_21.PDF (accessed 20.08.2023).

Public Opinion Research Centre, *Religiosity of Poles in the last 20 years. Research communication no. 63/2020*, https://cbos.pl/SPISKOM.POL/2020/K_063_20.PDF (accessed 20.08.2023).

Public Opinion Research Centre, *Polish religious landscape – a view from the foreground, Research communication no. 91/022*, https://www.cbos.pl/SPISKOM.POL/2022/K_091_22.PDF (accessed: 20.08.2023).

Gajos-Kaniewska D., "Trybunał: Zakaz zapuszczenia brody w więzieniu naruszył Konwencję Praw Człowieka", 17.06.2016, https://www.rp.pl/Dobra-osobiste/306179950-Trybunal-Zakaz-zapuszczenia-brody-w-wiezieniu-naruszyl--Konwencje-Praw-Czlowieka.html (accessed 18.07.2023).

Gemeinsam für Deutschland – mit Mut und Menschlichkeit) – https://archiv.cdu.de/system/tdf/media/dokumente/05_11_11_Koalitionsvertrag_Langfassung_navigierbar_0.pdf?file=1&type=field_collection_item&id=543 (accessed 22.09.2023).

Statistics Poland, *Religious confessions in Poland in 2019–2021*, Warszawa 2022 (https://stat.gov.pl/obszary-tematyczne/inne-opracowania/wyznania-religijne/wyznania-religijne-w-polsce-2019-2021,5,3.html (accessed 20.08.2023).

Statistics Poland, *Tables with final data on national-ethnic affiliation, language spoken at home and religious affiliation*, https://stat.gov.pl/spisy-powszechne/nsp-2021/nsp-2021-wyniki-ostateczne/tablice-z-ostatecznymi-danymi-w-zakresie-przynaleznosci-narodowo-etnicznej-jezyka-uzywanego-w-domu-oraz-przynaleznosci-do-wyznania-religijnego,10,1.html?fbclid=IwAR3nB6bh6bQij8apHTrNJ_wkWLpVR-eVnyl7zdL_hxInYPkb5jeHVJxe-OU (accessed 1.10.2023).

John Paul II, "Jubilee in Prisons. Homily of His Holiness John Paul II, Sunday, 9 July 2000", http://www.opoka.org.pl/biblioteka/W/WP/jan_pawel_ii/przemowienia/wiezienia_09072000.html (accessed 30.06.2016).

Lipka M., "7 key changes in the global religious landscape", 02.04.2015, https://www.pewresearch.org/short-reads/2015/04/02/7-key-changes-in-the-global-religious-landscape/ (accessed 29.08.2023).

Musterentwurf zum Landesstrafvollzugsgesetz vom 23. August 2011 – https://www.justiz.bremen.de/sixcms/media.php/13/Musterentwurf%20LStVollzG%2006%2009%2011.pdf (accessed 14.11.2022).

Pol J. D., "Czy religia jest w więzieniu koniecznie potrzebna?", https://jandezyderiuszpol.pl/publication/view/czy-religia-jest-w-wiezieniu-potrzebna/ (accessed 21.08.2023).

Statistical Portal, *Catholic Church – how many Poles attend Sunday Mass?*, 24.03.2023, https://portalstatystyczny.pl/kosciol-katolicki-ilu-polakow-bierze-udzial-niedzielnych-w-mszach/ (accessed 20.08.2023)

Sitarz O., Jaworska-Wieloch A., "Prawa osób tymczasowo aresztowanych na tle uprawnień przysługujących osobom odbywającym karę pozbawienia wolności", https://www.gov.pl/attachment/c57fff7b-2b4b-4b81-a75b-e7f7075b4a4c (accessed 22.09.2023).

Prison Service, *Information on the population of penitentiary institutions on 28 July 2023,* https://www.sw.gov.pl/strona/Statystyka (accessed 20.08.2023).

Spencer H., *First Principles*, London 1867 – https://oll.libertyfund.org/title/spencer-first-principles-1867?html=true#Spencer_0624_97 [accessed 29.08.2023].

Sweet W., "Herbert Spencer (1820–1903)", in J. Fieser, B. Dowden (eds.), *The Internet Encyclopedia of Philosophy*, https://iep.utm.edu/spencer/#H4 (accessed 29.08.2023)

https://alpha.org/ (accessed 20.09.2023).

https://bip.brpo.gov.pl/pl/content/reguly-nelsona-mandeli (accsessed 15.07.2023).

https://www.coe.int/en/web/commissioner/-/covid-19-pandemic-urgentsteps-are-needed-to-protect-the-rights-of-prisoners-in-europe (accessed 15.07.2023).

https://www.designalive.pl/strachy-o-bezreligijnym-chrzescijanstwe/ (accessed 20.09.2023).

https://www.ebos.pl/artykul/1741_niebezpiecznych_wiezniow_coraz_mniej.html (accessed 15.07.2023).

https://www.echr.coe.int/european-convention-on-human-rights (accessed 2.08.2023).

https://www.europarl.europa.eu/charter/pdf/text_en.pdf (accessed 2.08.2023).

https://www.globaldetentionproject.org/wp-content/uploads/2016/06/UN-Resolution-45-113.pdf (acceseed 16.09.2023).

https://www.gosc.pl/doc/8193214.Kursy-Alpha-za-kratami-Wchodzisz-do-wiezienia-o-zaostrzonym (accessed 20.08.20203).

https://www.ohchr.org/fr/instruments-mechanisms/instruments/united-nations-standard-minimum-rules-administration-juvenile (accessed 15.07.2023).

https://www.ohchr.org/en/instruments-mechanisms/instruments/international-covenant-civil-and-political-rights (accessed 2.08.2023).

https://www.ohchr.org/en/instruments-mechanisms/instruments/declaration-elimination-all-forms-intolerance-and-discrimination (accessed 2.08.2023).

https://www.ohchr.org/en/instruments-mechanisms/instruments/convention-rights-child (accessed 2.08.2023).

http://orka.sejm.gov.pl/Rejestrd.nsf/wgdruku/1214/$file/1214.pdf, (accessed 23.05.2022).

https://www.pewresearch.org/religion/2012/12/18/global-religious-landscape-exec/ (accessed 29.08.2023)

https://www.pewresearch.org/religion/2012/10/09/nones-on-the-rise/ (accessed 29.08.2023).

http://rycharski.artmuseum.pl/en/wprowadzenie (accessed 20.09.2023).

https://search.coe.int/cm/Pages/result_details.aspx?ObjectID=09000016805d8d25 (accessed 15.07.2023).

https://stat.gov.pl/spisy-powszechne/nsp-2021/harmonogram-publikacji-wynikow-nsp-2021/ (accessed 20.08.2023).

https://www.sw.gov.pl/aktualnosc/zaklad-karny-w-uhercach-mineralnych-alpha-w-wiezieniu (accessed 20.08.2023).

http://sw.gov.pl/Data/Files/001c169lidz/rok-2015.pdf (accessed 29.08.2023).

https://www.sw.gov.pl/strona/Statystyka (accessed 12.07.2023).

https://www.sw.gov.pl/aktualnosc/centralny-zarzad-sluzby-wieziennej-ograniczenie-odwiedzin-we-wszystkich-zakladach-karnych (accessed 19.07.2023).

https://www.theatlantic.com/magazine/archive/2003/05/let-it-be/302726/ (accessed 29.08.2023).

http://www.un-documents.net/a3r217.htm (accessed 2.08.2023).

https://wiadomosci.onet.pl/tylko-w-onecie/koronawirus-w-polsce-sluzba-wiezienna-przygotowuje-sie-na-radykalne-dzialania/qe8sb8t (accessed 17.07.2023)

https://archiv.cdu.de/system/tdf/media/dokumente/05_11_11_Koalitionsvertrag_Langfassung_navigierbar_0.pdf?file=1&type=field_collection_item&id=543 (accessed 14.11.2022).

https://www.justiz.bremen.de/sixcms/media.php/13/Musterentwurf%20LStVollzG%2006%2009%2011.pdf (accessed 14.11.2022)

Bulletin of the Commissioner for Human Rights. Materials. Status and nodal issues of the Polish prison system, part I, Warszawa 1995.

Zalecenie Nr R (87) 20 Komitetu Ministrów dla państw członkowskich w sprawie reakcji społecznych na przestępczość nieletnich (przyjęte przez Komitet Ministrów w dniu 17 września 1987 r. na 410. zebraniu Zastępców Ministrów), in P. J. Jaros (ed.), *Prawa dziecka. Dokumenty Rady Europy*, Warszawa 2012.

Zalecenie CM/Rec (2008)11 Komitetu Ministrów dla państw członkowskich w sprawie zasad europejskich dotyczących kar i środków alternatywnych stosowanych wobec sprawców nieletnich (przyjęte przez Komitet Ministrów w dniu 5 listopada 2008 r. na 1040. zebraniu Zastępców Ministrów), in P. J. Jaros (ed.), *Prawa dziecka. Dokumenty Rady Europy*, Warszawa 2012, pp. 555 et seq.

Case-law

Judgement of the Supreme Administrative Court of 23 January 1998 r., I SA 1065/97, LEX no. 34411.

Judgement of the Voivodship Administrative Court in Łódź of 11 September 2012 r., I SA/Łd 781/1, LEX no. 1266487.

BAG, Beschluß vom 22.03.1995, 5 AZB 21/94 (Hamburg), *Neue Juristische Wochenschrift*, no. 2, 1996.

BVerfG, Beschluß vom 8.11.1960, 1 BvR 59/56, *Neue Juristische Wochenschrift*, vol. 5, 1961.

BVerfG, Beschluß vom 24.02.1971, 1 BvR 435/68, *Neue Juristische Wochenschrift*, vol. 37, 1971.

BVerfG, Beschluß vom 19.10.1971, 1 BvR 387/65, *Neue Juristische Wochenschrift*, vol. 8, 1972.

BVerfG, Beschluß vom 14.03.1972, 2 BvR 41/71, *Neue Juristische Wochenschrift*, vol. 18, 1972.

BVerfG, Beschluß vom 17.12.1975, 1 BvR 63/68, *Neue Juristische Wochenschrift*, vol. 21–22, 1976.

BVerfG, Beschluß vom 16.05.1995, 1 BvR 1087/91, *Neue Juristische Wochenschrift*, vol. 38, 1995.

BVerfG, Beschluss vom 14.01.2020, 2 BvR 1333/17, *Neue Juristische Wochenschrift*, vol. 15, 2020.

BVerfG, Beschluß vom 8.11.2016, 1 BvR 3237/13, *Neue Juristische Wochenschrift*, vol. 4, 2017.

BVerfG, Urteil vom 15.01.1958, 1 BvR 400/57, *Neue Juristische Wochenschrift*, vol. 7, 1958.

BVerfG, Urteil vom 14.12.1965, 1 BvR 413/60, *Neue Juristische Wochenschrift*, vol. 4, 1966.

BVerfG, Urteil vom 19.12.2000, 2 BvR 1500/97, *Juristische Schulung*, vol. 5, 2001.

BVerwG, Urteil vom 15.12.2005, BVerwG 7 C 20/04, *Neue Juristische Wochenschrift*, vol. 18, 2006.

BVerfG, Urteil vom 31.05.2006, 2 BvR 1673/04, 2 BvR 2402/04, *Neue Juristische Wochenschrift*, vol. 29, 2006.

BVerwG, Urteil vom 26.09.2012, BVerwG 6 C 7/12, *Neue Zeitschrift fur Verwaltungsrecht*, vol. 1–2, 2013.

BVerwG, Urteil vom 11.09.2013, 6 C 25/12 (VGH Kassel), *Neue Zeitschrift fur Verwaltungsrecht*, vol. 1, 2014.

ECHR, Judgment of 12 July 1978, case of X v. United Kinghdom, application no. 7992/77.

ECHR, Judgment of 24 March 1988, case of Olsson v. Sweden, application no. 10465/83.

ECHR, Judgment of 22 June 1989, case of Eriksson v. Sweden, application no. 11373/85.

ECHR, Judgment of 25 May 1993, case of Kokkinakis v. Greece, application no. 14307/88.

ECHR, Judgment of 11 January 2005, case of Phull v. France, application no. 35753/03.

ECHR, Judgment of 21 February 2008, case of Alexandridis v. Greece, application no. 19516/06.

ECHR, Judgment of 4 March 2008, case of El Morsli v. France, application no. 15585/06.

ECHR, Judgment of 27 November 2008, case of Mann Singh v. France, application no. 24479/07.

ECHR, Judgment of 10 January 2010, case of Jaremowicz v. Poland, application no. 24023/03.

ECHR, Judgment of 17 February 2011, case of Wasmuth v. Germany, application no. 12884/03.

ECHR, Judgment of 7 March 2011, case of Jakóbski v. Poland, application no. 18429/06.

ECHR, Judgment of 23 October 2012, case of Kawiecki v. Poland, application no. 15593/07.

ECHR, Judgment of 26 April 2016, case of Izzettin Doğan and Others v. Turkey, application no. 62649/10.

ECHR, Judgment of 21 July 2016, case of Ivanova v. Bulgaria, application no. 46577/15.

ECHR, Judgment of 14 September 2016, case of Biržietis v. Lithuania, application no. 49304/09.

Judgment of the Constitutional Tribunal of 16 February 1999, SK 11/98, LEX no. 36175.

Kendall v. Kendall, 426 Mass. 238, 687 N.E.2d 1228 (Mass. 1997)

KG, Beschluß vom 9.12.1965, 3 VAs 34/65, *Neue Juristische Wochenschrift*, vol. 23, 1966.

Levitsky v. Levitsky, 231 Md. 388, 190 A.2d 621 (Md. 1963)

OGL Koblenz, 30.03.1987, 2 Vollz (Ws) 17/87, *Neue Zeitschrift für Strafrecht*, vol. 11, 1987.

OGL Koblenz, 8.12.1993, 3 Ws 591/93, *Neue Zeitschrift für Strafrecht*, vol. 4, 1994.

U.S. Supreme Court, *Davis v. Beason*, 133 U.S. 342 (1890).

U.S. Supreme Court, *United States v. Seeger*, 380 U.S. 163 (1965).

Notes on contributors

Olga Sitarz is an associate professor at the University of Silesia in Katowice (Poland), and a specialist in criminal law, criminology and penal enforcement law. She is a former judge of the District Court in Katowice, an active mediator at the Silesian Centre for Arbitration and Mediation and the head of the research project: 'The standards of respect the religious rights of persons detained in prisons, detention centres, educational and correctional centres for juveniles', financed by the National Science Centre (Poland). Her areas of interest include ageing, violence prevention, human rights in the perspective of criminal law, restorative justice, feminist analyses of law and gender.

Anna Jaworska-Wieloch, PhD, is an assistant professor at the University of Silesia in Katowice (Poland), and a specialist in criminal law, criminology and penal enforcement law. She was a social probation officer in criminal cases and currently she is a judge of the District Court in Gliwice (Poland). Her doctoral dissertation is a dogmatic and empirical study of the reasons for the revocation of conditional release in Poland (2016).

Jakub Hanc is a PhD student at the Doctoral School University of Silesia in Katowice (Poland). The focus of his research is criminal law and its history as well as penal enforcement law and medical law.

Ius, Lex et Res Publica
Studies in Law, Philosophy and Political Cultures

Edited by
Barbara Janusz-Pohl
Anna Jaron

Vol. 1 Anna Jaron: Socio-Economic Constitutional Rights in Democratisation Processes. An Account of the Constitutional Dialogue Theory. 2012.

Vol. 2 Stanisław Filipowicz: Democracy – The Power of Illusion. 2013.

Vol. 3 Teresa Dukiet-Nagórska (ed.): The Postulates of Restorative Justice and the Continental Model of Criminal Law. As Illustrated by Polish Criminal Law 2014.

Vol. 4 Agnieszka Kupzok: Enforcement of Patents on Geographically Divisible Inventions. An Inquiry into the Standard of Substantive Patent Law Infringement in Cross-Border Constellations. 2015.

Vol. 5 Alicja Jagielska-Burduk / Wojciech Szafrański: Legal Issues in Cultural Heritage Management. A Polish Perspective. 2016.

Vol. 6 Maciej Mataczyński (ed.): The Takeover of Public Companies as a Mode of Exercising EU Treaty Freedoms. 2017.

Vol. 7 Maciej Barczewski (ed.): Value of Information. Intellectual Property, Privacy and Big Data. 2018.

Vol. 8 Pawel Smoleń, Marcin Burzec: Introduction to Polish Tax Law. 2018.

Vol. 9 Łukasz Pohl, Konrad Burdziak: Judicial Interpretation of the 1997 Criminal Code Provisions on Self-Defence. 2019.

Vol. 10 Adam Szot: Judicial Review of Administrative Discretion. The Influence of Court Decisions on Administrative Actions. 2019.

Vol. 11 Michał Peno / Konrad Burdziak (eds.): The Concept of Modern Law. Polish and Central European Tradition. 2019.

Vol. 12 Leszek Leszczyński / Bartosz Liżewski / Adam Szot (eds.): Potential of Precedent in the Statutory Legal Order. 2019.

Vol. 13 Łukasz Bolesta: In Search of a Model for the Legal Protection of a Whistleblower in the Workplace in Poland. A legal and comparative study. 2020.

Vol. 14 Paweł Chmielnicki / Adam Sulikowski (eds.): New Perspectives on Legislation. A Comparative Approach. 2020.

Vol. 15 Marcin Burzec / Beata Kucia-Guściora / Paweł Smoleń: Agricultural Activity in Poland: A Fiscal and Legal Study. 2020.

Vol. 16 Magdalena Półtorak / Ilona Topa (eds.): Women, Children and (Other) Vulnerable Groups. Standards of Protection and Challenges for International Law. 2021.

Vol. 17 Josef Albert Fox: Die polnische Verfassung vom 3. Mai 1791. Hintergründe der Entstehung und der Außerkraftsetzung. Stellung Polens im Zeitalter der Aufklärung. 2021.

Vol. 18 Barbara Janusz-Pohl (ed.): Juvenile Justice Systems: Poland-Brazil-Portugal. 2021.

Vol. 19 Leszek Leszczyński: General Reference Clauses in the Judicial Process. Context of Legislative Intentions Interpretative Discretion. 2021.

Vol. 20 Francisco J. Campos Zamora: Das Problem der Begründung richterlicher Entschei- dungen. Eine Analyse auf der Grundlage der Theorie der juristischen Argumentation. 2021.

Vol. 21 Aneta Skorupa-Wulczyńska: Language Rights of the Citizen of the European Union. 2022.

Vol. 22 Mateusz Osiecki: International Legal Aspects of Aerial Terrorism. Methods of Law Enforcement in Avia-tion. 2022.

Vol. 23 Vladimír Sharp / Gabriela Blahoudková / Jakub Handrlica (eds.): Law, Pandemics and Ownership Restrictions. 2022.

Vol. 24 Piotr Kasprzyk / Anna Konert: Drones – Future of Aviation Law? Interference of Public Law in Private Law. 2023.

Vol. 25 Szymon Pawelec (ed.): Consensual Procedures in Criminal Law – Comparative Perspective. 2023.

Vol. 26 Dorota Pudzianowska: The Statelessness in Public Law. 2023.

Vol. 27 Bogusław Przywora / Aleksander Wróbel: Formalised Access to Pre-jurisdictional Free Legal Aid. Analysis based on Example of Ukraine, Poland, Great Britain and Sweden. 2023.

Vol. 28 Ewa Dawidziuk / Patricia Panero / Anna Tarwacka (eds.): Family, Law, and Society: from Roman Law to the Present Day. 2023.

Vol. 29 Marian Grzybowski / Bogusław Przywora / Aleksandra Syryt (eds.): Free Legal Aid, Theory, Legal Basis and Practice. European Standards. 2023.

Vol. 30 Karolina Gmerek: Trial as a Social Communication Occurrence. Interactions Between Professional and Non-professional Participants of a Trial. 2023.

Vol. 31 Paweł Wiliński (ed.): Effective Legal Remedies in Criminal Justice System. European Perspective. 2024.

Vol. 32 Olga Sitarz / Anna Jaworska-Wieloch / Jakub Hanc : On the (Non)existence of the Right to Religious Freedom of Persons Deprived of Liberty. A Reconstruction of the Normative Standard Based on Polish and German Regulations in Comparison With Empirical Studies. 2024.

www.peterlang.com